A HANDBOOK FOR FACULTY DEVELOPMENT

By William H. Bergquist and Steven R. Phillips

General Editor: Gary H. Quehl
Associate Editor: Jean B. Bernard

VOLUME 3

Copyright © 1981 by the Council of Independent Colleges, One Dupont Circle, Suite 320, Washington, D.C. 20036

Library of Congress Catalogue Card Number 80-69254
ISBN 0-937012-11-4

To our mentors and colleagues,
John Noonan
Walter Sikes
William Barber

Table of Contents

SECTION IV   PRESENT AND FUTURE

vi

Preface

For both of us, faculty development became a reality in four liberal arts colleges in upstate New York during the early 1970s. We had both been doing "faculty development" for some time, but had never labeled it as such or been committed to this work as a major way of having an impact on a college or university. Our mentors and colleagues during this period—Jack Noonan, Bill Barber, and Wally Sikes—taught us a great deal about how to work in a sensitive and effective manner with faculty with diverse backgrounds and needs. We have dedicated this third and final volume on faculty development to these three men in recognition of their impact on our personal and professional lives.

During our days in upper New York state, we were optimistic about the potential value of faculty development and hopeful about its use in contemporary colleges and universities. Our first volume on faculty development reflects this optimism as well as the rather primitive state of the art at the time of its publication (1975). We wince at some of our naive statements in this first volume, but continue to believe and find confirmation from many sources for our emphasis on personal and organizational as well as instructional development in attempting to improve the professional performance of college faculty.

By the time the second volume was published (1977), faculty development already had gained considerable momentum in American higher education and was becoming an accepted, funded, and professional activity on many campuses. The increased sophistication of faculty development concepts and procedures is reflected in the content of Volume 2. In this handbook we gave more attention to broad institutional issues than we did in Volume 1, as well as the needs and motivations of individual faculty members. Our optimism in Volume 1 was tempered by our recognition—and the recognition of most of our colleagues—that faculty development is inevitably embedded in a host of other institutional issues and priorities. At times, faculty development is driven by curricular reform or faculty evaluation. At other times, faculty development provokes change in these other areas. Faculty development had come of age, and with this maturation came a broader institutional perspective.

The third volume reflects yet another step in the brief life history of the faculty development movement. College and university faculty now seem to accept faculty development as a concept and a set of practices that are here to stay—though not significantly funded or supported under tight financial conditions. In this third volume, we couch our optimism in a deeper appreciation of the linkage between faculty development and the career development of individual faculty and the long-term planning and institutional research initiatives of colleges and universities.

Our own faculty development work has turned increasingly toward organization development and away from work with faculty in the classroom. Yet, in this third volume, we continue to emphasize instructional development and offer some of our own ideas about the ways in which a variety of instructional methods can be responsive to the increasing diversity of student needs, interests, and learning styles in the 1980s.

We also have used this third volume as an opportunity to reflect further on our own experiences in this field during the past ten years. We continue to be convinced that faculty development is an essential component in any systematic institutional development effort and we encourage our colleagues in the field to continue their efforts in advancing the theory and practice of faculty development while serving the critical needs of faculty in their own collegiate institutions.

The three volumes of *A Handbook for Faculty Development* could not have been written—let alone published—without the continuing encouragement and support of Gary Quehl, president of the Council of Independent Colleges, and general editor of this series of handbooks on higher education. We have worked closely with Gary since he first brought us together in New York state, when he served as executive director of the College Center of the Finger Lakes. Many of our ideas and most of our dedication to the field of faculty development can be directly traced to his sponsorship.

We also wish to acknowledge the superb assistance provided by other members of the CIC staff and, in particular, Jean Bernard, the associate editor for Volume 3.

Finally, we wish to express our appreciation to the Shell Companies Foundation Incorporated, who provided financial support for the production of this volume.

Section I

Introduction

Chapter One

The Tacit Dimensions of Faculty Development

The field of faculty development reached maturity in the late 1970s. Colleges and universities now teach courses about and conduct research on faculty development activities—a sure sign of respectability, even of middle age. There is a national association, the Professional and Organizational Development Network in Higher Education, which devotes much of its collective attention to faculty development matters. This organization publishes a quarterly journal and holds well-attended annual national conventions. Specific schools of thought and even statements of dogma now are found on the field, giving it the appearance of stability and discipline.

The maturation of faculty development as a resource for continuing professional and institutional improvement is welcomed and certainly needed. Though the field still lacks a firm theoretical base and, like most widespread initiatives in American higher education, has not received sufficient evaluation, faculty development practitioners can speak now with some confidence about their ability to help faculty members improve their performance both within and outside the classroom.

With maturation of either an individual or a movement comes an accumulation of assumptions, however, that often restrict or at least bias our perceptions and judgments about the world in which we operate. Though these assumptions may be issues of major concern in our youth, they rarely tend to be given central attention in our later life, remaining essentially unknown to us on a daily, working basis. Thomas Kuhn[1] identifies the paradigm that informs the problem-solving behavior of researchers in the mature sciences but cautions against the unwarranted extension of this analysis to the immature "preparadigmatic" social sciences and humanities. Michael Polanyi, a noted chemist and philosopher, however, suggests that perception and judgment in all forms are influenced profoundly by the "tacit knowledge" that we hold about ourselves and our world and that we attend from when acting in this world.[2] The distinction which Polanyi draws between "tacit knowledge" and "focal awareness" seems relevant to our understanding of the assumptions that underlie, inform, and influence the field of faculty development.

Polanyi notes that each of us is constantly *attending from* a large body of past experiences (memories), current sensations (bodily functions, incoming stimuli, feelings), and future expectations (hopes, anxieties, plans) when we are *attending to* something else (the object of "focal awareness"). That from which we are attending can never be focal, for to make it focal is to cease attending to something else and begin attending to that which previously was tacit. Thus, when I look out of a window at a tree, I am attending to the tree and from (or through) the window. If I attend to the window (noticing that it is dirty or tinted), then I cease to look at or attend to the tree. I must constantly shift my attention from the tree to the window and back to the tree if I wish to attend to both the tree and window. I cannot attend to both at the same time. Polanyi contends that we are constantly shifting our attention in this way, and that things which at one moment are tacit (e.g., the many adjustments made by one's body while walking) become focal at another moment (e.g., when beginning to climb a mountain). Since we must always attend *from* that which is tacit when attending *to* something else, the tacit domain is always influential but always inaccessible to our immediate awareness, as long as we choose to attend to something else.

In the field of faculty development, there are several dimensions of tacit knowledge that rarely come to focal awareness but which continually influence and even determine the nature of problems being addressed, the solutions developed, and the criteria used for evaluation. Three of these domains will be subject to focal attention in this chapter and will provide an organizing framework for the remaining chapters of this volume.

The first domain concerns collegiate instruction. We believe that faculty development practitioners, as well as college and university faculty, hold several basic assumptions concerning the teaching-learning process that often are untested and poorly understood. These assumptions influence the way in which faculty and faculty development practitioners conceive, solve, and evaluate instructional problems. Because these assumptions are tacitly held, they often limit our perspectives and bias our responses to these problems without our knowing it. For instance, one of the major mistakes made by many faculty development practitioners who began working in the field during the late 1960s and early 1970s concerned their often unrecognized bias in favor of "experience-based" or "student-oriented" instructional methods. As a result of frequent failure to acknowledge these biases, the field of faculty development has been viewed by some faculty as a thinly veiled attempt to promote specific, "innovative" teaching practices rather than as a resource that any faculty member might employ in the improved use of any instructional method.

The second domain of tacit knowledge that we shall explore concerns strategies for institutional development. Practitioners in the field of faculty development usually hold very strong assumptions about how development can be implemented most effectively and about who should be the immediate beneficiaries of this development. Different and conflicting models of faculty development have grown up largely around several assumptions that reside in this usually tacit domain.

The third domain concerns the history of faculty development itself. What is the nature and scope of the field? How did it begin? What can be learned from practices of the past? What will or could be the future role of faculty development in higher education? Once again, implicit and often untested answers to these questions inform and influence our work but rarely receive focal attention.

The remainder of this chapter is devoted to a description of these three domains and to a consideration of the impact that each has on current faculty development practice. Our discussion of each domain will conclude with a brief statement about the way this domain receives further attention in other chapters of this handbook.

A. The Instructional Domain

Any teaching event involves the interrelationship between at least two entities: (1) the student-learner and (2) a body of content or an experience that the student-learner is to acquire in some sense. The faculty member, as teacher, is expected to mediate and assist in the student's acquisition of this content or experience. In this role, the faculty member usually will choose to attend either to the content of the course or to the student. A faculty member who attends to the content indicates greatest concern with the subject matter being taught. She views the teaching enterprise primarily as an opportunity for students to learn something in an effective and efficient manner from someone who knows more about the area in question than the student. A good content-based teacher will specify clearly the instructional objectives to which she is teaching, will provide an equitable means of evaluating student achievement of these, will use a teaching method that maximizes student interest in the content of the course, and may even individualize the course of study for students so that differing learning styles, lifestyles, ages, skills, and backgrounds can be accommodated. The content-based teacher thus attends to the content that she is teaching while attending from a set of assumptions about what students need and want. The content-based teacher usually can provide an articulate statement about reasons for organizing content in a certain way. Furthermore, she tends to be quite knowledgeable about the subject area in which she is teaching. Of these issues, the content-based teacher is focally aware. She is usually much less articulate about or even aware of her assumptions about why or how students can best learn a particular content.

On the other hand, some faculty are inclined to attend to and be focally aware of students, and in doing so, attend from and be only tacitly aware of the content being taught. These faculty address themselves as being primarily in the business of helping students learn what the students want and need to learn. A good student-based teacher will help a student identify current needs, resources, and outcomes for a particular course of study or experience. He also will help the student identify and obtain institutional or community resources needed to achieve these outcomes, evaluate the extent to which these outcomes have been achieved, and learn something about the processes of learning itself (in the words of Donald Michael, "learning to plan and planning to learn."[3]).

Given the enormous demand on student-based teachers for exclusive attention to the needs and concerns of students, it is not surprising to find that these teachers will attend from a set of tacit assumptions about the content of the teaching enterprise. The student-based teacher's own biases, values, and concerns are not unimportant, since they significantly influence the ways in which this teacher interacts with students, but often in ways in which the student-based teacher is unaware. A classic example of the influence which tacitly held values have had on student-based teachers is to be found in the humanistic psychology movement of the later 1960s and early 1970s. Faculty who espoused humanistic psychology often have done meaningful work with students and are to be commended for the extraordinary attention they gave to many confused young men and women of this era. Yet the ultimate failure of many lay in a lack of focal awareness concerning the white middle-class values that underlie much of their work, and, as a result, the extent to which their consciousness-raising activities ("the greening of America") ignored important social, economic, and political realities.

In many ways the content-based and student-based teachers operate in the same manner. Both are concerned primarily with clear specification of desired learning outcomes. In the case of the content-based teacher, these outcomes are to be specified by him, as one who knows more about the content than do the students. The student-based teacher advocates specification of desired outcomes by the student who supposedly knows more about personal learning needs than does the teacher. Thus, the primary difference between the content- and student-based teacher is a matter of control: who specifies outcomes. The great debates concerning traditional versus non-traditional and behavioristic versus humanistic education have centered on this very issue.

A third type of teacher disagrees with both the content-based and student-based teacher. She takes issue with both concerning the ability to specify desired learning outcomes by either the teacher or student. This third teacher believes that learning takes place primarily through interaction between teacher and student, student and student, teacher and teacher, or student and experience—vicarious, simulated, or real. The learning that results from these interactions can never be fully specified ahead of time, because two or more independent entities (students, teachers, experiences) are meeting to interact from two or more different perspectives. Even if desired learning outcomes could be specified ahead of time, these outcomes would begin to interplay and modify one another once the faculty member, student, and/or experience began to interact.

An interaction-based faculty member is interested primarily in the creation of instructional settings in which a maximum amount of fruitful interaction will take place. She also is concerned with the analysis and synthesis of learnings that have emerged from the interaction. A good interaction-based teacher will be a creative educational architect. She will design educational programs that are exciting, diverse, and challenging for herself as well as her students. She will be supportive of students as they confront the ambiguity of this type of education and will attempt to clarify when appropriate. She will prepare students for these experiences and provide sufficient time for discussion and application after the experience.

The interaction-based teacher is attending to the interaction between the student and the content. She is attending from her own role as teacher. For both the content-based and student-based faculty members, their teaching role is relatively clear to themselves and others. The content-based teacher is the primary conveyer of content to the students. She is actively and visibly involved in assisting students to learn a basic body of information. Similarly, the student-based teacher is actively and visibly involved in assisting students to obtain their self-defined learning goals. Once the issue of control is worked out, the content and student-based teachers can settle into rather clearly defined roles.

The interaction-based teacher does not find this comfort readily. Her role is rarely defined with clarity, for she often works behind the scenes, being more the director than the actor, more the architect than the builder. The interaction-based teacher attends from a whole set of assumptions about her own role as a teacher, and, because these assumptions are rarely made explicit and rarely tested, they often are in conflict.

An interactive teacher, for instance, often operates from the assumption that she must be initially quite active and even charismatic to spark interaction among students. This strategy may be appropriate and can be employed successfully, as long as the teacher is not tacitly assuming that the instructor should *always* be active or entertaining. The interaction-based teacher, more than either the content-based or student-based teacher, is often accused of being manipulative or inconsistent—in large part because of a poorly-defined role and lack of personal insight about her own personal motives and goals.[4]

What are the implications to be drawn from this tripartite taxonomy of teaching modes? First, we suggest that the content-based teacher often can improve her classroom performance by gaining greater insight into the needs, styles, motivations, skills, and interests of students. Some reading about student development and some more extensive and informal contact with students can help the content-based teacher, as can some structured interviews she might conduct with students about their needs and interests.

The student-based teacher, conversely, should redirect his attention, at least temporarily, to a re-examination of his own discipline and the values associated with this discipline that he has retained. He also should reexamine his own personal goals for the course he is teaching. Many "innovative" faculty from interdisciplinary and experimental colleges throughout the United States that have closed down or become more traditional have admitted grudgingly that they have benefited personally from returning to their discipline and teaching traditional subject matter. They have discovered their own untested and often unrecognized disciplinary "roots" and feel that they will be better prepared to resume student-based teaching if and when they can return to an experimental setting. Experimental colleges that continue to survive and thrive often have been ones in which faculty enter the college for a short period of time (one to three years), then return to home departments and disciplines.

The interaction-based teacher must re-examine roles and functions and reflect on personal motivations and goals frequently. Involved in an ambiguous teaching-learning process, the interaction-based teacher must frequently be introspective to ensure that students are not being manipulated or subtly victimized by "social engineering."

A second implication concerns competing philosophies of education and psychologies of human behavior. Frequently, when one speaks of a philosophy of education in higher education, one is referring only to a generalized statement about overall goals for a specific academic program or curriculum. A philosophy of education should speak to the issue of epistemology: what are our assumptions about how people know and learn? Each of these three modes of teaching incorporates often tacitly a specific epistemology and an accompanying set of psychological assumptions about the nature of human behavior. These assumptions not only should be acknowledged, they also should become the basis for long-ignored discussions about epistemology and learning theory in the higher education community.

Both the content-based and student-based modes of teaching build on the assumption that one can clearly specify the knowledge, skills, or attitudes to be acquired and can specify the most effective means whereby this learning will take place. The interactive mode of teaching begins with the assumption that one cannot specify clearly or consistently how learning takes place. Thus, in discussions of content-based and student-based teaching modes one is likely to hear such words and phrases as "facts," "information," and "body of knowledge," which reflect an underlying epistemological stand that there is an objective reality that can be known. In discussions about the interactive mode one is more likely to hear about such things as "perspective," "framework," or "socially-constructed reality," which reflect a more relativistic epistemology. Interactive teachers tend to be skeptical about the value of teaching "facts" and conveying "information," because they believe that "facts" and "information" can be understood only in a particular social, political, cultural, or disciplinary context.

These three teaching modes also are informed by differing psychological perspectives. The content-based mode is most compatible with the behavioristic school of psychology. Content-based teachers are vitally concerned with issues of reward and reinforcement, for they wish to motivate students to learn subject matter that they, the teachers, deem important. Thus, the learning theories of the behaviorists are sometimes welcomed because they speak directly to the content-based question: "How do I motivate my students to learn what they are supposed to learn?" Reinforcement schedules, reward contingencies, and related strategies can provide answers to this question.

For the student-based teacher, motivation is not generally a problem, for the educational program is being tailored specifically to the existing needs and interests of the student. This approach to teaching was popular during the late 1960s and early 1970s precisely because it helped faculty deal with the motivational problems of students who did not want a traditional college setting. The psychological humanists have provided the student-based teacher with valuable guidance. The emphasis on personal, interpersonal, and ethical development which pervades humanistic psychology has been helpful to student-based teachers who assist students in clarifying current and future strengths, problems, and goals. The humanistic emphasis on autonomy and client-centered relationships also have strongly influenced the student-based mode of teaching.

For the interactive teacher, the most appropriate psychological theories come from gestalt psychology. The gestalt principle of a whole being greater than the sum of its parts can be applied to the interaction-based teaching assumption that the learning which emerges from interaction inevitably will be something other than and something more than the learning goals which each party brings to the interaction. The indeterminate nature of any complex open system (social, biological, or physical) speaks to the indeterminate nature of any "learning system." The gestalt school of psychology provides the interactive teacher with ideas about how to design learning environments and with some justification for accepting ambiguity.

The third and most important implication of this tripartite classification of college teaching concerns the methods of instruction that are being used by a faculty member. Certain instructional methods are particularly appropriate for content-based teaching, for they can be used effectively and efficiently to transmit information from the teacher (or other information source) to the student in a sensitive and exciting manner. Other instructional methods are not appropriate to content-based teaching for they do not provide the faculty member with sufficient control and predictability. Similarly, some methods are clearly more appropriate than others for use with student-based and interaction-based teaching. Some of the most serious problems confronted by faculty today are associated with a mismatch between the instructional method being used and the mode of teaching (and learning) that is desired by the faculty member. Chapters Three, Four, and Five survey a wide range of instructional methods that are appropriate to each of the three orientations to the teaching-learning process. Chapter Six then presents an integrated model for instructional development.

B. The Institutional Domain

The second domain of tacit knowledge we would like to explore concerns the unarticulated assumptions currently held about institutional development. Historically, those who have planned and implemented any institutional development program have tended to focus either on the personal development of individual members of the institution or on the formal and informal organizational structures existing within the institution. The theory and practice of institutional change (beginning with the work

8

of Kurt Lewin in the 1930s) began initially with an emphasis on personal development and change. If the heart and mind of individuals could be changed, institutions, the assumption was, would also be changed. The extensive use of sensitivity training and similar methods in the 1950s and 1960s reflect this orientation, as does the contemporary resurgence of interest in religious commitment as a solution to contemporary problems. During the later 1960s and 1970s, however, a growing disillusionment with such training as a means of achieving institutional change emerged, and the growing field of organization development gained increasing credibility as it abandoned sensitivity training and personal growth programs as the primary vehicle for institutional change. Organization development consultants became increasingly interested in organizational structures, reward and evaluation systems, management practices, problem-solving, decision making, and task-oriented team-building. An assumption was made that individuals behave as they do primarily because they reside in certain social systems that influence, constrain, and even determine their motivation and behavior.

As we enter the early 1980s, there appears to be renewed interest in the personal domain, in part resulting from increasing attention being given to stages and phases of adult development. Practitioners have become increasingly convinced that people residing in the same system will respond quite differently to comparable conditions if their own interests, needs, and concerns differ. Furthermore, even the same individual, residing in the same system from year to year, will change in the way she works and lives in this system, for her own interests, needs, and concerns change over time. The attention of many people who are trying to facilitate institutional development has focused on the careers of people within the institution, for the career represents a juncture between the individual and the organization. Career development represents a significant interplay between personal and organization development.

Underlying each of these three perspectives on institutional development (personal, organization, and career) are a set of assumptions, attitudes, beliefs, and values from which a practitioner attends while he is designing and implementing a program to address a specific institutional issue. An institutional development practitioner with a personal development perspective is attending from a set of humanistic values concerning the inherent worth of the individual and from an assumption that an organization is essentially nothing other than individuals in interaction. As in the case of the content-based instructor, who attends from a set of ill-formed assumptions about students, the personal development practitioner usually attends from a set of assumptions about organizational life that are untested and unrealistic. The personal development practitioner often will work actively to change attitudes, enhance skills, and increase the knowledge base of individual clients without giving adequate consideration to the profound and often destructive consequences of this development for the individual when she returns to an organization that may not value these attitudes, skills, and knowledge.

The institutional development practitioner holding an organization development perspective is equally as likely to be naive and uninformed about her tacitly-held assumptions regarding personal development. She often will attend from a belief that people are motivated primarily by monetary reward or formal recognition, from a belief that sensitive interpersonal relationships can be ensured through the design of appropriate structures and processes, and from an assumption that organizations are something more than the sum of the people in the organization. She believes (tacitly) that organizational procedures and processes have a life and validity that is somehow independent of the people who work with and respond to these processes and procedures. When an organization development practitioner does not re-examine and review frequently her knowledge about personal development, she runs the risk of designing and implementing programs that are inherently dehumanizing and ultimately detrimental to the institution.

A career development practitioner, like the interaction-based instructor, is attending to two things at the same time—attending to both personal and organization development initiatives as they interact in the arena of one's career. A career development practitioner is attending from a set of assumptions about how he can best facilitate this interaction and retain a balance between personal and organizational needs. Frequently, the career development practitioner unknowingly will come down on the side of either the people with whom he is working or the organization for which he is working. What should such a practitioner say to the employee who wants to find a job at another institution? Whose interests should be respected, the dissatisfied employee's or the institution's? One can assume (tacitly) that the dissatisfied employee is no longer of benefit to the institution, and, hence, that the institution is best served by the departure of the employee. Yet, it is usually not that simple. Employee training costs, disruption of service, reduced employee morale, and other factors contribute to a difficult decision. The career development practitioner, like the personal and organization development practitioner, frequently must review candidly and critically his own tacitly-held assumptions and values.

The personal, organizational, and career development perspectives are all prominent in the field of faculty development, although their relationship to the domain of instructional development will perhaps always remain inherently ambiguous. Chapter Eight provides a discussion of personal development and Chapter Nine a discussion of organization development. Chapter Ten then presents a somewhat more detailed discussion of the emerging interest in career development.

C. The Faculty Development Domain

Though for many faculty development practitioners the field seems to be less than a decade old, for others it is much older, an inherent part of any faculty member's professional obligations. The "new" faculty development practitioners attend from a host of assumptions about how faculty development should be conducted when attending to such "antiquated" practices as the faculty sabbatical and intellectually-inclined national conferences and institutes. Similarly "old-time" faculty members and deans attend from a variety of assumptions about the functions to be served and responsibilities to be met by faculty and deans when critically attending to contemporary faculty development practices.

The untested biases and values of contemporary faculty development practitioners are evident in many writings in the field over the past decade. Our own handbooks certainly reflect a neglect of most of the faculty development practices of the past. In describing a variety of faculty development practices and strategies in Volume 1, we failed to give any attention to sabbatical leave plans and policies, attendance at disciplinary conventions, or participation in national interdisciplinary institutes (such as those conducted for many years by the Danforth Foundation), even though these approaches to faculty development often have been found to be worthwhile for both personal and organization development. We began with the assumption that faculty often have been unable or unwilling to plan effectively for their own development and generally have not taken advantage of excellent professional development opportunities. We still believe this assumption is, unfortunately, often valid but we acknowledge the need for a more careful review of faculty development practices that were prevalent prior to 1970 and remain valuable today. Chapter Thirteen provides a rather extensive review of research literature and program descriptions concerning sabbatical leaves and interdisciplinary residential institutes for college and university faculty.

For faculty and administrators who continue to dismiss faculty development as an unnecessary or duplicative activity, we suggest a critical analysis of their own untested assumptions and values. The critics of faculty development are correct in stating that what faculty development practitioners now do used to be done by an effective academic dean or department chairperson. Unfortunately, many of these people no longer have the time for faculty development facilitation, for they are swamped with paper work, budgetary issues, and personnel matters. Furthermore, many do not have the skills or even the interest in faculty development activities, precisely because they were selected for their financial and administrative skills and inclinations. We look with some interest on the recent attempts by some colleges and universities to move faculty development practitioners into administrative positions. Will these new administrators redefine their jobs, learn new skills and attitudes, or somehow blend administrative, financial, and faculty development concerns?

Certainly one area in which these concerns can be brought together is the collection and use of information about faculty for planning faculty and institutional development. Faculty development, like all other forms of institutional development, must be built on a solid base of institutional research. Only in this way can the considerable resources of faculty development be fully employed in promoting the development of not only individual faculty members but also the institution as a whole. In Chapter Twelve we have suggested some ways in which institutional research might be applied specifically in a faculty development context.

In yet another way, administration and faculty development must be brought together. The skills needed to obtain funds for faculty development programs must not be left exclusively in the hands of those academic administrators who must be concerned, understandably, with a variety of other institutional priorities. Faculty development practitioners and faculty who wish to promote faculty development activities must master the skills of grantsmanship and see that these skills are used to advance both the faculty and institutional development goals of the college or university. Chapter Eleven is devoted to a discussion of grantsmanship for the funding of faculty development programs.

Those faculty members and administrators who tend to look at faculty development from the perspective of pre-1970 collegiate life need to become more fully aware of the changing institutional conditions to which faculty development programs seek to respond. Faculty development initiative must be examined from the perspective of recent literature on adult development and processes of institutional change and stabilization. Critics of contemporary faculty development practices also should become more fully aware of recent research on the outcomes of faculty development programs, especially since many of these critics have spoken against faculty development because it has not been evaluated sufficiently. It was disappointing to hear recently of an eminent member of the higher education community who dismissed the Teaching Improvement Program at the University of Massachusetts as "ineffective." In doing so, he totally ignored an excellent and convincing body of evaluative research on the effectiveness of this program. In Chapter Fourteen we have given some consideration to the issue of whether contemporary faculty development programs have been successful. We also point the way to future directions for faculty development programming, based on what we have already learned from the successes and failures of this difficult but valuable enterprise.

NOTES:

[1]Thomas S. Kuhn, *The Structure of Scientific Revolutions* (Chicago: University of Chicago Press, 1962).

[2]Our discussion concerning Michael Polanyi's concept of "tacit knowledge" is based on three of his works: *The Tacit Dimension* (New York: Doubleday, 1966), *Personal Knowledge* (Chicago: University of Chicago Press, 1958), and *Knowing and Being* (Chicago: University of Chicago Press, 1969), as well as a presentation on Polanyi's work and its implications for higher education made by Spencer Ludlow, assistant professor of philosophy at St. Andrews Presbyterian College, Laurinburg, North Carolina, during a faculty development seminar conducted at the college in August 1979. A videotaped copy of Ludlow's presentation is available from the Academy for Professional Development, P.O. Box 7328, Tacoma, Washington 98407.

[3]Donald Michael, *On Learning to Plan and Planning to Learn* (San Francisco: Jossey-Bass, 1973).

[4]Variations on these three different types of teachers have been described elsewhere in the literature on higher education. In Volume 1 of *A Handbook for Faculty Development,* a variety of teaching styles are described. Joseph Adelson's "priest" is a content-based teacher, and his "mystic healer" is student-based. Similarly, the teachers who are identified by Richard Mann as expert, formal authority, and socializing agent are content-based, and those who are "facilitators" tend to be student-based. Two of the three categories we identified ("content-centered teaching and learning" and "student-centered teaching and learning") correspond directly with the content- and student-based teaching modes in this chapter.

A difficulty arises in equating the interaction-based teaching mode with any of the existing teaching style taxonomies. Adelson's "shaman," Mann's "ego ideal," and our "instructor-centered" categories seem to describe interaction-based teaching in which a faculty member is not explicitly aware of his or her own needs for attention, recognition, or even subtle control. Joseph Axelrod's taxonomy may be of most value in describing the interaction-based teacher. He differentiates between two modes of teaching— didactic and evocative. The didactic mode involves acquisition of specific skills and knowledge, whereas the evocative mode involves unspecifiable inquiry and discovery. Axelrod goes on to differentiate among the emphasis, in evocative teaching, on the subject matter, the teacher, and the student. We would suggest that truly evocative teaching involves an interaction between the subject matter (content) and the student, and that effective evocative teaching also involves a clear recognition by the teacher of his or her own role (just as effective content-based teaching requires explicit knowledge about the student as well as the content, and effective student-based teaching requires explicit knowledge about the content as well as the student). We propose that the emphasis of an evocative (interaction-based) teacher on either subject matter (content) or the student moves the faculty member to one or the other two modes.

EXERCISE NUMBER ONE

TITLE: "Simulatum-of-the Swamp": A Simulation/Role Play Concerning Collegiate Education

SOURCE: William H. Bergquist and Steven R. Phillips

GENERAL DESCRIPTION: In the previous two volumes of *A Handbook for Faculty Development* we have suggested a variety of interactive exercises, such as card exchange, interviews, and group discussions, that help people surface their own tacitly-held assumptions about faculty development, teaching and learning, and institutional change. In this third volume, we offer a simulation that similarly will help participants articulate personally-held assumptions in these areas. Unlike the other exercises described in previous volumes, the "Simulatum-of-the-Swamp" simulation encourages participants to examine these assumptions as they are translated into action in a hypothetical college.

INSTRUCTIONS FOR USE: Typically, "Simulatum-of-the-Swamp" is run during a three- to five-day residential workshop. It also can be offered as an isolated event of three to four hours duration. It is particularly important that sufficient time (one to one and a half hours) be provided for post-simulation discussion. "Simulatum-of-the-Swamp" yields rich insights for many participants, as well as precipitating vivid experiences and strong emotions. The post-simulation discussion provides participants with an opportunity not only to share insights but also to diffuse these emotions. This discussion should focus on the outcomes (products, ideas, feelings) of specific attitudes, processes, and structures, rather than on personalities or interpersonal skills.

The director of the simulation should first find a set of four to five rooms or one large room that can be subdivided into four or five units. Materials for the simulation should also be assembled: (1) "Instructions," "Brief Overview of Simulatum-of-the-Swamp," "Organization Chart," and "Schedule" (one copy of each document per participant); (2) the role descriptions (one role description per participant); (3) name tags; and (4) paper, pencils, and other related supplies. In addition, at least five copies of "The Saint James Great Book Curriculum" and "A Competency-Based Curriculum" should be provided.

The simulation itself, as presented in the Schedule, lasts for two and one-half hours. An additional hour should be set aside for debriefing the simulation. This schedule can be made longer by adding time to each existing period, by extending the break time between periods, or by adding additional periods (for example, a sixth period devoted to another college-wide assembly, or a sixth or seventh period when committees meet again). Be sure to change the schedule sheet to reflect these modifications and change the role descriptions to reflect any additions or modifications in the assignment of formal responsibilities.

When the participants in the simulation are assembled, they should be given the "Instructions," "Brief Overview," "Organization Chart," "Schedule," and one of the role descriptions. Role Player Number Two also should be given the five copies of "A Competency-Based Curriculum" and Role Player Number Four the five copies of "The Saint James Great Books Curriculum." The role descriptions can be distributed randomly or by predesign. The participants usually should not be allowed to pick their own roles, nor should they be assigned to their current role at their real institution. If roles are to be assigned, care should be taken not to give a participant a role that "fits with his personality." This type-casting makes subsequent discussion about the simulation very difficult and often blocks significant learning. Personalities are more likely to be discussed, and participants are more likely to take negative comments as personal statements rather than as information about the role being played.

After the participants have had ample time to review the materials (approximately 30 minutes), the simulation director should answer questions and clarify as needed. The director also should be available during the simulation to answer further questions. The director should announce changes in periods during the simulation, each preceded by a five-minute warning.

The simulation director, or an associate, also might wish to add more fuel to the simulation by intervening at some point in the simulation as the President of Simulatum. The role to be played by the president should be formulated on the spot, in response to the continuing dynamics of the simulation. If the simulation is moving too slowly, the president might wish to make a unilateral announcement about some major policy change (like abolishing tenure), new program initiative (a movement toward competency-based instruction, for example), or a major new funded proposal (perhaps a $200,000 grant to do faculty development over the next three years). If the simulation is moving too fast (too much stress, conflict, or interpersonal tension), the president might wish to make a decision that ends certain discussions or focuses anger in his or her direction. Alternatively, the president can extend the duration of each period, offer an extended break between two periods, or add a new "peacemaker" role (external consultant, another assistant dean, and so forth). The role of an external consultant might be particularly valuable if one of the director's associates wishes to obtain some experience doing consultation or if participants in the simulation could benefit from further experience in working with an external consultant.

Upon completion of the simulation, the participants should be asked to spend a few minutes by themselves, reflecting on the following questions (or others of similar scope and content):
1. At what points during this simulation did you feel most effective? What were the conditions that enabled you to act effectively in the simulation?
2. At what points during this simulation did you feel least effective? What were the conditions that blocked you from effective action?
3. What if anything did you learn in this simulation about faculty development, curriculum design, personnel review procedures, and/or institutional leadership? What are the implications of what you have learned for your work on the "real-life" college campus?

When this period of reflection is concluded, the director may wish to bring all of the participants together to discuss their answers to these questions or may wish to ask participants to discuss their answers in several small groups before convening the entire group. At some point during the post-simulation discussion, participants may wish to share role descriptions with each other, though this should not occur immediately. At some point, the director also may wish to have participants meet with members of their own "department" or with committee "colleagues" to compare observations and role descriptions.

"Simulatum-of-the-Swamp" has been conducted in a variety of forms and settings over the past eight years. The responses of participants to the simulation are never the same and are always quite interesting—the simulation is rich and provocative. Before conducting the simulation in a workshop setting, one might wish to try it out among friendly colleagues or with a group of students who understand that this is a learning experience for both themselves and the instructor. Furthermore, one should conduct a complex simulation like "Simulatum" with the assistance of one or more colleagues who can help observe various continuing activities, share perceptions during the simulation, and lead the post-simulation discussion. If there are a sufficient number of potential participants in the simulation, several people might be assigned an observer rather than a participant role. They can sit in on various meetings while the simulation is taking place and contribute to the post-simulation discussion.

The complexity and ultimate unpredictability of a simulation in any new setting requires not only pilot-testing and careful debriefing, but also an openness to significant modification of the basic design of the simulation if it does not make sense in a particular setting. We encourage you to change, delete, and add elements to "Simulatum-of-the Swamp." It has been designed for and used primarily with small liberal arts colleges. The simulation can be changed readily to reflect the structures and dynamics of a larger university (name change, revised history, more roles, more complex administrative structures, and so forth). It can be revised in a similar manner to reflect the distinctive features of a vocational-technical, graduate, or professional school. It is only important that the simulation contain a set of relatively complex and realistic roles, played by people who must grapple with some of the central problems of a collegiate institution, which is what Simulatum-of-the-Swamp is all about.

SIMULATUM-OF-THE-SWAMP:
A SIMULATION/ROLE PLAY CONCERNING COLLEGIATE EDUCATION

Instructions:

You are invited to participate in an instructional simulation and role-play which can yield insights for you and your colleagues regarding the dynamics of change and stabilization in a collegiate institution—particularly regarding faculty development, curriculum development, and personnel review. In order to gain these insights we ask that you assume a role as a member of the academic community at a college called "Simulatum-of-the-Swamp"—a hypothetical institution that is faced with many of the problems and potentials of real-world colleges and universities.

In playing this role, you will be interacting with other people who also have been assigned roles and asked to engage in a variety of activities: planning and attending meetings, conducting or participating in workshops, talking informally with colleagues, and planning for new programs. A set of 15- to 40-minute periods have been set aside for these activities (see "Schedule"). This is not a competitive game with winners and losers, but rather a game in which the interests of each "player" are relatively compatible or incompatible with the interests of each other player. You are to do as good a job as possible in meeting the needs and concerns of the person whose role you are playing, as well as the needs and interests of Simulatum College.

The simulation begins with the assignment of roles. You will be given a role description sheet and are to sign your name at the top of this sheet. You probably will also be given a name tag or asked to make up a name tag indicating your name and the role you are playing (role player number and title). Read the information contained on this role description sheet carefully and try to imagine that you are this person. Not all of the information you will need to play this role is contained on this sheet. Some roles are described more fully than others. You will need to flesh out the role with your own experiences and your own sense of the person you are playing.

You also should read the "Brief Overview of Simulatum-of-the-Swamp" and review the "Organization Chart" for the college. It is important that you are familiar with the basic facts of the college as you begin the simulation so that you don't have to keep referring back to them after the simulation has begun (though you will be able to keep all of the documents with you throughout the simulation).

After you have read these basic materials, the simulation is ready to begin. Specific rooms (or sections of a room) have been set aside for each formal activity (meetings, assembly, workshop); several role players also may have been assigned an office or table in one part of the room. The director of this simulation will inform you of the locations. At the beginning of each period you are to go to the activity for which you have been assigned in the role description or, if no activity has been assigned, you can use this period to plan for future activities, meet with other players, and so forth. Depending on the role you are playing, you may even decide to do something other than what is expected of you. In some instances, you may be formally scheduled to do more than one thing. In these cases, you must choose which to do or must try to do both activities. In other cases, you may decide that some activity is more important than the formally-assigned one and hence will change your schedule. These decisions are totally in your hands and are based on your own personal priorities (given the role you are playing).

At the end of the simulation, time will be available for a discussion of your experiences as a member of the academic community at Simulatum-of-the-Swamp. The objective of this discussion is not to decide who did a good or bad job, nor would it be of much value to spend a great deal of time talking about the difference between simulations and the real world (obviously there are many—including more time to think in the real world—usually). Rather, you should reflect on and discuss insights you might have gained about how institutions run, how roles influence and even constrain behavior in academic settings, and how you are able or unable to influence specific institutional decisions given the roles being played. You also might wish to discuss the implications of these insights for curricular planning, faculty development, and/or personnel review processes on your own campus. Sometimes it is easier to observe and talk about processes that are occuring and have had an impact on us in a simulated setting than it is to talk about comparable "real-life" processes as they affect our daily work and life.

Simulatum-of-the-Swamp is a safe place to try out new roles and behavior. It is also a safe place in which to gain insights and in which to test out and discuss these insights. Enjoy the experience!

A BRIEF OVERVIEW OF SIMULATUM-OF-THE-SWAMP

The hypothetical college called "Simulatum-of-the-Swamp—better known as "Simulatum," "SOS," or (affectionately) "Old Swampee"—is a small, independent (private) college located in a midwestern community of 65,000. The college's enrollment has fluctuated recently, reaching a high of 1,245 students in 1969 and a low of 420 students in 1975. Current enrollment at Simulatum is 640. This enrollment figure is expected to increase to 700 within the next two years, but will tail off thereafter unless SOS can attract more "nontraditional" (older, less academically qualified) students.

There are currently 42 full-time faculty at SOS, with another 25 serving on a part-time basis. More than one-half of the full-time and most of the part-time faculty teach in one of three professional departments: business, nursing, and occupational therapy. Nine of the remaining faculty teach in the physical and behavioral science departments: physics and chemistry (two faculty); mathematics (two faculty); biology (two faculty); and psychology, sociology, and anthropology (three faculty). The humanities departments are: English and comparative literature (four full-time faculty), history and philosophy (two full-time faculty), visual and performing arts (three full-time faculty), and foreign language (one full-time faculty and several part-time). This simulation will concentrate on faculty in the humanities departments; the academic dean; assistant dean of the college; the director of the Learning Resource Center (also a member of the visual and performing arts department); the Curriculum, Faculty Development, and Promotion and Review Committees; the Dean's Council; and the College-Wide Assembly.

The president at SOS is a tough-minded, market-oriented ex-academician who has been at the college for five years, having previously served as the dean of liberal arts at a large midwestern university. The president is very supportive of instructional and curricular innovations—particularly as they attract new students and more external funds. The academic dean was appointed by the president three years ago, having previously served as chairman of the humanities department (now split into English and comparative literature, and history and philosophy). Beginning this year, the college has supplied the dean with an assistant, who is to represent the dean on some college committees and perform other functions as assigned by the dean.

With regard to curriculum development at "Old Swampee," there has been a long and often exasperating tradition of changing the core curriculum radically about every five years. Throughout most of the 1950s (a time of comparative curricular calm at SOS), the college offered a two-year, four-course Survey of Western Civilization sequence. This curriculum was replaced from 1960 to 1966 by three survey courses, each of which addressed central themes in western thought ("Freedom and Determinism," "Mind and Body") from a particular perspective: science, humanities, or the arts.

With the impact of Sputnik, the Watts riots, and early concern about Vietnam, SOS decided to turn to a more problem-oriented approach to the core curriculum. The core was reduced to two courses on "Contemporary Problems." One course focused on "Technology and Society," the second dealt with "Conflict in Contemporary American Culture." The faculty and administration at SOS were never very happy with this core curriculum. Old-timers spoke against the diminished size of the core (from four to three to two courses), while newer faculty and more traditional faculty decried the "ahistorical" nature of the new core and the absence of a disciplinary perspective. Thus, in 1970, the "contemporary problems" core was thrown out and replaced for four years by distribution requirements: selection of one survey course each from the physical or biological sciences, the social sciences, the humanities, and the arts.

In 1974, the faculty at the college adopted a new core curriculum and did away with distribution requirements. This core curriculum is still in operation at Simulatum—making it one of the longer-standing core curricula in the college's recent history. The current core curriculum consists of three courses. One course, titled "Shaping of Western Civilization," touches on 10 major figures and 10 major events in Western Civilization. The second course, "Modes of Critical Thinking," is taught by a variety of faculty. Each faculty member picks a particular problem or theme each year such as "Alienation and Technology" or "The American Depression" and shows how his discipline addressed this problem or theme. The third course, a "Senior Seminar," is meant to serve as an integrating experience. Groups of 10 to 15 students from two disciplines (differing combinations each year) meet with two professors from these two disciplines to identify and discuss contemporary world problems using the newspaper and a "textbook." Students are encouraged to think about their future roles as citizens in a complex and changing world.

In recent years, faculty have expressed some discontent about this curriculum, noting that (1) too much western civilization is being squeezed into one course, (2) there is too great an emphasis on western civilization and too little attention to third world cultures, (3) the courses are too individualized (especially "Critical Modes of Thought"), and (4) the courses too strongly emphasize the disciplines. The college's curriculum committee is now considering a major change in the core curriculum.

For many years, Simulatum College also has required its students to either take an English composition course or pass a writing proficiency test. Only about 10 percent of the students now are able to pass this test (50–60 percent of the students were able to pass the test during the early 1960s). The other 90 percent take the composition course. Five years ago, a foreign language requirement was eliminated. There is now some interest in adding a computer requirement—though inadequate staffing and limited computer facilities make this request impractical at the present time.

A second area of contemporary concern at SOS is faculty development. There has been very little consistent faculty or administrative interest in this area until the last two years. At this time, the president expressed concern about the lack of faculty development resources at SOS. A faculty development task force was set up for one year, which led in the past year to the formation of a standing Faculty Development Committee that reports to the faculty senate. Up to the present time, very little progress is evident with regard to faculty development. Some faculty stress instructional improvement, others stress competency in one's discipline or resources for the improvement of research and scholarship at SOS. The president relates faculty development directly to current and anticipated financial problems at SOS and to the need for a vital and innovative faculty. One year ago, the academic dean established a Learning Resource Center at SOS, which is directed (half-time) by a professor of art history (Role Player Number 12). Over the next few years, the dean would like this center to provide media and course design consultation services to faculty.

A third area of continuing concern for faculty and administration at Old Swampee is faculty, promotion, and tenure procedures. Over 70 percent of the faculty at SOS are tenured. Hence, there is deep concern that very few additional faculty should be tenured, yet recognition of the fact that the college wants to attract and retain younger faculty to keep "fresh blood" pumping through its academic arteries. The Promotion and Tenure Committee has given some consideration to early retirement plans, alternatives to the tenure track, and ways of keeping several faculty positions open for one year (a rotating "visiting professorship"). The committee also has been very concerned with the establishment of clear and equitable standards for the evaluation of untenured faculty now at Simulatum. Some tenured faculty express concern that the standards may be set so high that very few of the current tenured faculty would be granted tenure if they are reviewed again by these standards.

A final pervasive concern at SOS is finances. The college is barely able to stay in the black—a major accomplishment for a small liberal arts college. It does so, however, by paying low faculty salaries (at the 25th percentile by national AAUP standards), and by charging relatively high tuition for a small unknown liberal arts college. Student enrollment cannot continue to grow unless tuition is made more competitive. The tuition should remain at its current level for at least three more years, while tuition at other competitive colleges in the region goes up. Faculty salaries, however, must be increased if faculty morale is to remain at a moderately positive level. If faculty morale drops off, the quality of instruction (a selling point for SOS) will drop off and students will cease enrolling at Simulatum.

Finally, a few observations about the Old Swampee student body. Most SOS students are from upper middle-class families: white, conservative, and career-oriented. An increasing proportion of the student body, however, comes to SOS with substantial state or federal scholarships. These students come from a working-class background, are first-generation college students, and often lack communication and computational skills. This latter group of students may drop off with decreases in public support for student aid programs.

In the words of a famous Old Swampee graduate (recent commencement speaker): "There are times that demand but do not allow for leadership." How should this college address its numerous problems and challenges? How can your own leadership skills positively affect the life of this hypothetical college?

SCHEDULE

The Setting: This is the beginning of the school year at Simulatum. The students have not yet arrived. All faculty are required to be on campus for meetings of major faculty committees, for meetings of all academic departments, for a college-wide assembly (attended by students, staff and administrators after the school year begins), and for a faculty development workshop. Following is the schedule:

Period One (40 minutes)
    Curriculum Committee Meeting
    Faculty Development Committee Meeting
    Promotion and Tenure Committee Meeting
Break (5 minutes)
Period Two (15 minutes)
    Department Meetings
Break (5 minutes)
Period Three (30 minutes)
    College-Wide Assembly
Break (10 minutes)
Period Four (15 minutes)
    Curriculum Committee Meeting
    Faculty Development Committee Meeting
    Promotion and Tenure Committee Meeting
Break (5 minutes)
Period Five (25 minutes)
    Faculty Development Workshop
    Dean's Council
Post Simulation Discussion (One to one and a half hours)

ORGANIZATION CHART

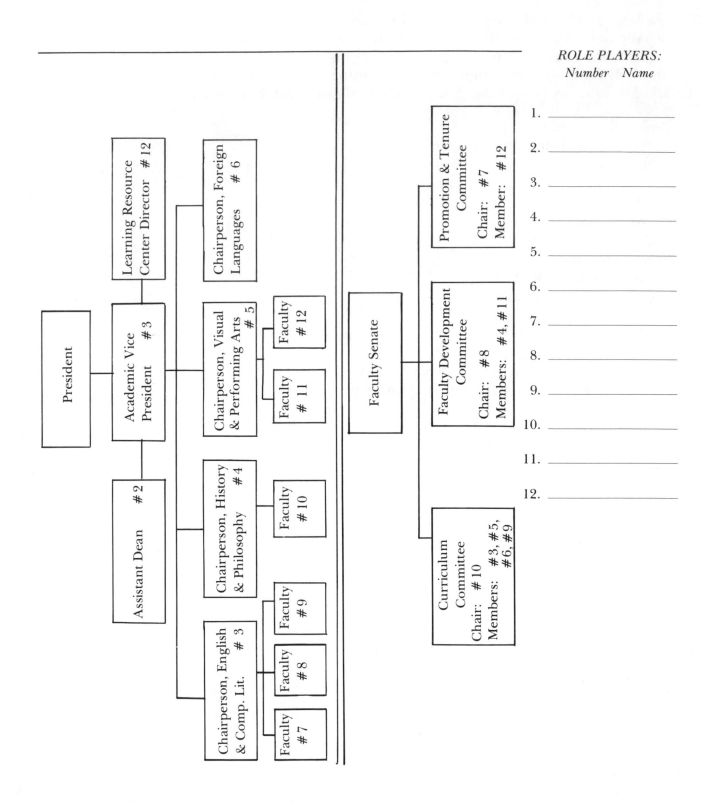

ROLE PLAYERS:
Number   Name

1. _____
2. _____
3. _____
4. _____
5. _____
6. _____
7. _____
8. _____
9. _____
10. _____
11. _____
12. _____

President

Academic Vice President   #3

Assistant Dean   #2

Learning Resource Center Director   #12

Chairperson, Foreign Languages   #6

Chairperson, Visual & Performing Arts   #5

Faculty #12

Faculty #11

Chairperson, History & Philosophy   #4

Faculty #10

Chairperson, English & Comp. Lit.   #3

Faculty #9

Faculty #8

Faculty #7

Faculty Senate

Promotion & Tenure Committee
Chair: #7
Member: #12

Faculty Development Committee
Chair: #8
Members: #4, #11

Curriculum Committee
Chair: #10
Members: #3, #5, #6, #9

THE SAINT JAMES GREAT BOOK CURRICULUM

The primary mission of the liberal arts education should be the search for freedom and rationality. Knowledge resides at the heart of this freedom and rationality, especially knowledge that is unified, that builds on the common heritage of all men and women, and that centers in essential values and a moral commitment. Men and women with a liberal arts education that reflects these concerns will be equipped to confront any life challenge and to become citizens in a free and sustainable world.

Saint James University is committed to a liberal education and believes that the path to that education can be plotted through the books written by the great scholars and teachers of our civilization. These books are eternally relevant, for they illuminate persistent and essential questions regarding the human experience. The words of these great men and women span the ages and speak to us about contemporary problems and potentials.

The Great Books are not read in isolation by the students at Saint James. The students meet in twice-weekly seminars of three hours duration to discuss these books with their colleagues and a faculty tutor. These seminars are held throughout the four years of a student's residence at Saint James. They serve as the unifying ingredient of the Saint James curriculum. Students at Saint James also participate all four years in a series of scholarly study programs. During the first year, each student apprentices with a senior student and faculty member on a scholarly project. During the sophomore year, a group of five students work together on a project, under a faculty member's supervision. At the junior level, each student embarks on his or her own independent research project, with only minimal faculty supervision. Finally, each senior level student directs a research project that involves one faculty member and a freshman student. Thus, during the four years of residence at Saint James, each student receives extensive experience doing scholarly work in a variety of settings (alone, with a group, and as an apprentice). Most of the scholarly efforts each year focus on a specific theme (such as the rise of science in western civilization), thereby allowing for extensive interchange of ideas and perspectives among students and faculty.

Individual courses also are taught at Saint James, so that each student might receive academic preparation in a particular field of study, as well as gain some acquaintance with contemporary disciplines and topics of debate. Approximately one-fourth of a student's academic preparation is taken in a major field, with another one-fourth being dedicated to courses on contemporary problems.

Saint James' List of Great Books

Over many years, the faculty at Saint James has sought to identify the seminal works of world civilization and to identify the most appropriate time in a student's academic career when these works should first be presented. The list changes each year, and some places are left open for books of particular interest to faculty who are conducting the seminars. Following is a list of the books now on the Saint James list:

Freshman Year
    Homer, *Iliad*
    Sophocles, *Oedipus Rex*
    Aristophanes, *Birds*
    Plato, *Republic*
    Aristotle, *Politics, Physics* (excerpts)
    Old Testament, *The Book of Job*
    New Testament, *The Gospel According to Matthew*
    New Testament, *Paul's Letter to the Corinthians*
    Moses Maimonides, *Epistle to Yemen* (excerpts)
    Augustine, *City of God* (excerpts)
    Aquinas, *Summa Theologica* (excerpts)
    Dante, *Divine Comedy*

Sophomore Year
    Chaucer, *Canterbury Tales* (excerpts)
    Machiavelli, *The Prince*
    Luther, *The Freedom of a Christian, Secular Authority*
    Calvin, *Institutes* (excerpts)
    Bacon, *Novum Organum*
    Shakespeare, *Richard II, Henry IV, Part One, Henry V, The Tempest, As You Like It, Hamlet, Othello, Macbeth, King Lear*

Junior Year
    Kepler, *Astronomy*
    Descartes, *Discourse on Method*
    Newton, *Principia Mathematica* (excerpts)
    Cervantes, *Don Quixote*
    Milton, *Paradise Lost*
    Pascal, *Pensées*
    Spinoza, *Theologico-Political Treatise*
    Locke, *Essay Concerning Human Understanding*
    Swift, *Gulliver's Travels*
    Berkeley, *Principles of Human Knowledge*
    Fielding, *Tom Jones*
    Hume, *Treatise of Human Nature*
    Smith, *Wealth of Nations*
    Kant, *Critique of Pure Reason*
    Goethe, *Faust*
    Hegel, *Introduction to the History of Philosophy*

Senior Year
    de Tocqueville, *Democracy in America*
    Lincoln, *Speeches*
    Thoreau, *Walden*
    Marx, *Das Capital*
    Darwin, *Origins of the Species*
    Freud, *Interpretation of Dreams, Civilization and Its Discontents*

Kierkegaard, *Fear and Trembling*
Dostoevski, *Crime and Punishment*
Tolstoy, *War and Peace*
Twain, *The Adventures of Huckleberry Finn*
Mann, *Death in Venice*
Kafka, *The Trial*

A COMPETENCY-BASED CURRICULUM*

A number of colleges have recently explored the nature of a liberal arts education and have concluded that a "liberally educated" person should exhibit certain competencies. The list of resulting competencies varies from college to college, but at least seven have been identified most often:

1. Competency in verbal and written communication
2. Competency in the identification, analysis, and solution of various problems
3. Competency in the identification of and commitment to a value system and the identification of implications for behavior emanating from these values
4. Competency in the understanding and appreciation of the artistic and aesthetic aspects of life and culture
5. Competency in the use of one's body for recreational and health-maintenance purposes
6. Competency in the understanding of the relationship among individuals, societies, and the physical environment
7. Competency in the analysis and formulation of action concerning contemporary problems through disciplinary and interdisciplinary perspectives

Each of these competencies can be defined and measured at several different levels and can serve as the basis for a student's selection of courses at a college or even for the creation of a curriculum that is not course-driven. This latter type of curriculum might involve the initial assessment of each student's level of competency in each of the seven areas upon arriving at the college, the determination of an educational plan for each student based on this assessment of competency, and the preparation of a portfolio by each student prior to graduation from college that documents accomplishment of each competency through a variety of methods (tests, essays, independent projects, completed courses, and so forth). The acquisition of competencies by students can occur through course work (all of which is optional), field experiences, apprenticeships, independent studies, or learning contracts (work with off-campus resources).

A competency-based curriculum enables a college to retain control over standards, while providing students with maximum freedom in determining the means by which they can best reach these standards given their preferred learning styles, unique career and life needs, and levels of initial competency and motivation.

*Taken from Susan Sterling-Alverno, "A General Model for Competency-Based Curricula," *Journal of Experimental Higher Education*, 8 (1979), 130–145.

ROLE DESCRIPTION NUMBER 1

NAME: _____

ROLE: Academic Dean

BACKGROUND INFORMATION: You have been at Simulatum for 10 years, having come to the college as chairman of the department of humanities (now split into two departments: English and comparative literature, and history and philosophy). You were appointed academic dean by the current president three years ago. You have just appointed a new assistant dean who can help you in any way you wish. Initially, that person has been assigned the role of liaison with the faculty. The assistant dean will represent you at Curriculum, Promotion and Tenure, and/or Faculty Development Committee meetings if you wish.

You established a Learning Resource Center a year ago, which is staffed one-half time by a professor of art history in the department of visual and performing arts (Role Player Number 12). The Learning Resource Center is currently no more than an agency for the collection and distribution of audio-visual equipment and materials (slides, movies, videotapes, etc.). You would like the Learning Resource Center eventually to take over the faculty development functions now being provided by an associate professor in the English literature department (Role Player Number 8). The art professor is not qualified to provide these services, but will retire in two years.

The faculty development program was established a year ago over your mild objections by the president. You thought that it would take resources and attention away from the newly-formed Learning Resource Center, which it has. Furthermore, you are not convinced that faculty will want to improve their teaching, unless provided with new instructional technologies and resources, or rewarded for their teaching (salary, promotion, tenure). Rewards cannot be used as an inducement, however, for SOS cannot afford major salary increases or many promotions. Furthermore, more than 70 percent of the faculty are tenured, hence few new faculty can be rewarded with tenure for excellence in teaching.

Currently, a major core curricular change is being considered by the Curriculum Committee of the college. This committee is appointed by the faculty senate, and you serve in an *ex officio* capacity on it. The committee is chaired by a member of the history and philosophy department (Role Player Number 10) who has been teaching European and American history for many years. He is effective and equitable in his dealings with colleagues—but not terribly energizing. The core curriculum change has been initiated by the faculty. While you are not opposed to a major change in the curriculum, you are uncertain whether such a change is necessary and are concerned about potential increases in instructional costs that a new curriculum might require. Any new curricular change will have to be approved not only by the Curriculum Committee, but also by a majority of the entire faculty. The proposal then goes to you for final approval. While you have the option of turning down any curricular change, this option cannot be used too frequently, for you will lose support of the faculty. The rejection of a major curricular proposal from the faculty probably would have to be based on unacceptable increases in instructional costs associated with the proposed change. If a curricular change is to occur, you hope that it will place increased emphasis on practical, career-related skills for students—though you do not want to push this idea, since the faculty have taken the initiative on this proposal.

You view yourself as a good manager—someone who can get the job done in a reasonable and practical manner. You do not think that open conflict contributes to sound decision making and would prefer to make decisions in a small group rather than in a large meeting. You feel close to the president, but are a bit uncomfortable with his occasional unilateral actions (for example, setting up the faculty development program).

When you became the dean three years ago, you separated English and comparative literature from history and philosophy, and made one of your best full professors (Role Player Number 3) chairman of the English and comparative literature department. A man who retired last year was made chairman of the history and philosophy department. You have just brought in a bright young analytic philosopher and interdisciplinary scholar to head this department.

Your relationship with the chairman of visual and performing arts (Role Player Number 5) is strained—especially since you became dean. This person was one of two other candidates for the dean's position, the third candidate coming from outside the college. The art professor who heads the Learning Resource Center is pleasant but no longer particularly effective. You have assigned him temporarily to head the Learning Resource Center to get him out of the classroom, at least half-time, for he is no longer an effective teacher. The art professor will be able to assemble and categorize a vast collection of art and history slides which could be of continuing value to the college after he retires.

The foreign language department at Simulatum College has been on the decline since the language requirement was removed five years ago. You supported the removal of this requirement but are now concerned that the college may have to abandon foreign language entirely. Currently, there is only one full-time faculty member in the department (Role Player Number 6). Other instructors are brought in on a contract basis to teach specific courses.

You have a Ph.D. in European history from the University of Wisconsin. You taught for six years at a small college in Ohio before coming to "Old Swampee" as chairman of the humanities department. Your area of academic specialization is 19th century German and French history, though you also have a secondary interest in 19th century American history.

You will preside over the Dean's Council (period five), which is composed of the department chairmen, your assistant dean, and yourself. You also will be responsible for organizing and conducting a college-wide assembly which will be held during the third period. You should identify the topic of the assembly by the end of period one, and announce or post it during the break between periods one and two.

Formal Responsibilities

Period One:
Preparation for College-Wide Assembly (period three) over which you preside and which you must design. You may wish to use this assembly for the

28

Curriculum and Promotion and Review Committees to report out their deliberations during the first period (but will have to inform these committees during the first period that they are to make a report during the assembly). You might also wish to make your own feelings known with regard to a new core curriculum, faculty development activities at Simulatum, and/or promotion and tenure procedures. The Faculty Development Committee might also want to report on its plans for the faculty development workshop that is to be held for all faculty during the fifth period. You might not be able to do all of this in the 25 minutes assigned to the College-Wide Assembly, hence you must set priorities.

Attendance at faculty committee meetings. Do you wish to attend and/or influence the proceedings of any of the committees? Do you want your assistant dean to attend any of the meetings— which ones?

Preparation for Dean's Council (period five). You will be meeting with all of your department chairmen and have an opportunity to discuss any issues on your mind (e.g., the core curriculum, faculty development, promotion and review procedures).

Period Two:

Preparation for College-Wide Assembly (period three)

Preparation for Dean's Council (period five)

Attendance at department meetings—do you want to attend? Have you been invited to attend?

Meeting with your assistant dean—do you want to define further his/her role? Do you want him/her to report on the faculty meetings he/she attended?

Period Three:

College-Wide Assembly

Period Four:

Consideration of results from the College-Wide Assembly—any actions to be taken, further contacts to be made?

Preparation for Dean's Council (period five)

Attendance at Faculty Committee meetings

Period Five:

Dean's Council

Faculty Development Workshop—should you, your assistant dean, and/or your department chairmen attend all or part of the faculty development workshop?

29

ROLE DESCRIPTION NUMBER 2

NAME: _____

ROLE: Assistant Dean

BACKGROUND INFORMATION: You have just arrived at Simulatum College and are only familiar with the information contained in "A Brief Overview of Simulatum-of-the-Swamp" and the Organization Chart. You have been appointed by the dean to assist primarily in a liaison role with the faculty. One of your initial responsibilities is to sit in, as a representative of the dean, on the Curriculum, Promotion, and Tenure, and Faculty Development Committees. You should check with the dean to be sure of these assignments. In addition, you might want to become acquainted with the faculty at SOS and find out about their needs and educational attitudes. You also might assist the dean in setting up the College-Wide Assembly for which the dean is responsible (during the third period).

   You have an Ed.D. degree from UCLA in educational administration. You taught in the English department of a California community college for four years before entering the doctoral program at UCLA. You are very interested in competency-based education and are concerned with the measurement of educational outcomes. You believe that higher education must do a better job of defining its goals and objectives and of assessing the extent to which these goals and objectives have been met. At an appropriate time during the meeting of the Curriculum Committee you might wish to introduce the accompanying document titled "A Competency-Based Curriculum"—though you probably should obtain the approval of the dean.

   At Stimulatum you have a faculty appointment (as an untenured assistant professor) and will be expected to teach two sections of English next term—after you have settled into the job.

Formal Responsibilities

   Period One
      Attendance at faculty committee meeting(s)—with dean's approval
      Meeting with dean to plan for College-Wide Assembly (period three) and/or
         Dean's Council (period five)
   Period Two
      Meeting with dean to plan for College-Wide Assembly and/or Dean's Council
      Reporting back to dean on proceedings of faculty committee meetings (period
         one)
      Attendance at department meetings—with approval of the dean and the
         departments
   Period Three
      College-Wide Assembly
   Period Four
      Attendance at faculty committee meeting(s)—with dean's approval
      Meeting with dean to plan for Dean's Council

Period Five
    Dean's Council
    Attendance at Faculty Development Workshop—with dean's approval

ROLE DESCRIPTION NUMBER 3

NAME: _____

ROLE: Chairman of the English and Comparative Literature Department

BACKGROUND INFORMATION: You have been a member of the Simulatum College faculty for seven years. You initially came as a member of the humanities department, teaching general survey courses for freshmen and sophomores in world literature and advanced-level courses in American literature. The current academic dean was chairman of the humanities department when you came as an associate professor. He was instrumental in getting your original appointment and the two of you have become good friends since that time.

Three years ago, the academic dean was appointed to his current position. The dean called for an immediate reorganization of the humanities department, breaking it into two departments (English and comparative literature, and history and philosophy). You were appointed by the dean to head the new English and comparative literature department. You now teach either one or two courses per term and serve one-half time as department chairman. You are a full professor and serve as a member of the Curriculum Committee and Dean's Council.

You have cordial working relationships with all three of the other members of your department. One member of your department (Role Player Number 7) is an associate professor, with a specialization in 17th and 18th century English literature. This professor serves as chairman of the Promotion and Tenure Committee, has been at SOS for five years, and is a rather traditional teacher and scholar. A second member of your department (Role Player Number 8) is also an associate professor, specializing in contemporary English literature, who has been at the college for six years. This professor is a bright and highly innovative teacher who serves as chairman of the Faculty Development Committee at Simulatum.

You have spent the last five years gently urging the dean to start a faculty development program—with little success. The dean wanted a Learning Resource Center which focused on audio-visual devices.

Two years ago, the president of SOS attended a national conference during which faculty development was discussed. He came away from this meeting convinced that faculty development would help the college (and particularly its public image). He knew of your interest in faculty development, asked the dean to appoint you as chairman of a one-year task force on faculty development. At the end of this one-year period, the associate professor of English literature (Role Player Number 8) in your department was appointed by the president as chairman of a new faculty development committee at Old Swampee and given responsibility for promoting instructional innovation and the professional growth of faculty. You believe that this member of your department will become an excellent leader and you are grooming the professor for your job.

You eventually would like to become an academic dean at a small college and believe that with the support of the current dean you can achieve this goal in the next two to three years.

Another member of your department (Role Player Number 9) is an assistant professor who has been at the college for four years and is now up for tenure. This faculty member specializes in Asian literature and philosophy and is something of a rebel who loves to teach students (in a rather traditional manner) about Zen philosophy and the writings of Herman Hesse and Carl Jung. You think that this professor, though a bit innovative and unpredictable, adds a valuable alternative perspective in the department. You are worried about the Promotion and Tenure Committee's evaluation of this individual.

You have a somewhat strained relationship with the chairman of the visual and performing arts, who views you as a crony of the dean and as a person who panders to the interests of students. As a candidate for the current dean's job, you believe that individual is suffering from sour grapes and is not to be trusted.

As a member of the Curriculum Committee, you would like to see some major changes in the curriculum, though you believe that other faculty must take the primary initiative because of your close relationship with the dean. You would like to see a curriculum that is relevant to current student interest—for example, a curriculum that emphasizes current American culture or problems of human ecology. You also would like to see a curriculum that is attractive to adults, because you believe that Old Swampee will have to begin attracting adults (through weekend courses and vocational courses) if enrollment is to remain at its current level.

Formal Responsibilities

Period One

Attendance at Curriculum Committee meeting: discussion of proposed change in core curriculum

Period Two

Preside over meeting of the English and comparative literature department: you may wish to use this time to determine the stance of your department with reference to core curricular changes, promotion and review procedures and/or faculty development at Simulatum. Alternatively, you may wish to discuss a departmental curricular change or faculty development initiative that could be a model for college-wide efforts.

Period Three

College-Wide Assembly

Period Four

Attendance at Curriculum Committee Meeting

Period Five

Attendance at Dean's Council

or

Attendance at Faculty Development Workshop

ROLE DESCRIPTION NUMBER 4

NAME: _____

ROLE: Chairman of the History and Philosophy Department

BACKGROUND INFORMATION: You have just joined the faculty at Simulatum College, having taught for seven years in the philosophy department at Saint James University, a prestigious midwestern institution. You are primarily interested in the history of ideas, though you have an analytic philosophy background that has led you also to be very concerned with the use and misuse of language. At Saint James you were involved in a great books program (see "The Saint James Great Book Curriculum") and were hired by the dean at SOS to bring this perspective to bear on SOS's history and philosophy department.

Since you have just arrived at Simulatum, you do not know the faculty very well. You will want to review "A Brief Overview of Simulatum-of-the-Swamp" and the Organization Chart to familiarize yourself with the institution. The curriculum committee at SOS is currently considering a major curricular reform. Although as a new member of the faculty you have not been appointed to this committee, you might want to provide them with a copy of "The Saint James Great Books Curriculum" and discuss this document with the committee—for any major curricular change inevitably is going to influence your own efforts to introduce a great books program into the history and philosophy department curriculum.

Because of your experience at a unique institution like Saint James, you have been asked by the dean to serve as a member of the faculty development committee. You would like to see the faculty at Old Swampee become more supportive of interdisciplinary education and would like to elevate the intellectual life of the college to make it more like Saint James.

You are an associate professor without tenure. Tenure review will occur in three years. You obtained your Ph.D. in philosophy from the University of Chicago, then joined the faculty at Saint James University. There is one other full-time member of your department (Role Player Number 10), who has taught American and European history (general survey courses) at SOS for many years, whose specialty is Colonial American history. The dean also is a member of your department, teaching one course in either American or European history each year. You are not responsible for teaching all of the philosophy courses at Simulatum College. In keeping with the Saint James tradition, you prefer to teach in small seminars and enjoy an aggressive, exciting, intellectual discussion with and among bright students. You are somewhat concerned that the students at SOS might not be intelligent enough for the pedagogical approaches you employ.

Formal Responsibilities

Period One

Attendance at Faculty Development Committee meeting: discussion of faculty development activities at Simulatum and preparation for Faculty Development Workshop (period five)

or

Attendance at Promotion and Tenure Committee meeting: determination of standards for promotion and granting of tenure to Simulatum faculty.

Period Two

Preside over meeting of the history and philosophy department: you may wish to use this time to determine the stance of your department with reference to core curricular change, promotion and review procedures, and/or faculty development at Simulatum. Alternatively, you may wish to discuss a departmental curricular change or faculty development initiative that could be a model for college-wide efforts.

Period Three

College-Wide Assembly

Period Four

Attendance at Faculty Development Committee meeting

Period Five

Attendance at Dean's Council

    or

Attendance at Faculty Development Workshop

ROLE DESCRIPTION NUMBER 5

NAME: _____

ROLE: Chairman of the Visual and Performing Arts Department

BACKGROUND INFORMATION: You have been a member of the Simulatum College faculty for 12 years and chairman of the visual and performing arts department for the past six years. You currently serve as a member of the Curriculum Committee and the Dean's Council. Three years ago you were one of three final candidates for the deanship. The current dean (then chairman of the now-defunct humanities department) was offered the job—you suspect—for several reasons. First, the president of SOS seems to be obsessed with public relations. The current dean promised to introduce a number of curricular innovations that supposedly would improve the image of the college. In fact, none of these innovations has taken place. Second, the current dean was the head of a large department, hence automatically had extensive faculty support. Third, there is more prestige associated with a Ph.D. in European history (the degree and discipline of the current dean) than with your Ed.D. in music.

You are responsible for the college band and orchestra, teach music history, and are released one-quarter time for administrative duties (though, in fact, you are teaching a full load when individual instruction for members of the band and orchestra is included). As a member of the Curriculum Committee, you are faced with an all-too-frequent problem—a new, untested curriculum will be proposed soon to replace an adequate, tested one. The current curriculum balances the different goals of the faculty and administration at Old Swampee and makes full use of the current knowledge and expertise of the faculty. The faculty would have to spend a great deal of time in planning and preparing for a new curriculum, thereby taking time away from students and teaching. The demands on faculty time are already unreasonable. A new curriculum would make these demands even worse.

A new curriculum also must be reviewed carefully to preserve academic standards and disciplinary integrity. If a new curriculum is designed to be attractive only to students (as the president and dean would like), the college will lose its credibility in the academic community. Similarly, the credibility of Simulatum College will be lost in the disciplinary associations if the college adopts an "innovative," free-form curriculum that does not respect disciplinary integrity.

You received your Ed.D. in music education at the University of Minnesota. For seven years prior to obtaining your doctorate, you taught music at a high school in Minneapolis. Your undergraduate degree is from Oberlin College.

Because of the extensive number of hours you spend in class and preparing for concerts, you do not have many close relations with other faculty at SOS. Your closest friend on the faculty is a professor who teaches art history in your department (Role Player Number 12). He is a hard-working and distinguished college teacher who knows much more about instruction than those younger faculty who are preaching faculty development and curricular innovations.

The other member of your department is a rather brash thespian, who runs the college's theater and teaches a course each year on speech and communication. This faculty member seems to want to be a "free spirit," and has been on the faculty for only two years, but already is talking about leaving. He is probably unable to get a job elsewhere because of his unwillingness or inability to work with other people. You need to keep checking on his work, because at times he is impractical, forgetting that he is at a college, rather than in a repertory theater in San Francisco (where he came from). His plays are often controversial and even risque. You are looking forward to this faculty member finding another job in the near future.

Formal Responsibilities

Period One
 Attendance at Curriculum Committee meeting: discussion of proposed change in core curriculum

Period Two
 Preside over meeting of the visual and performing arts department: you may wish to use this time to determine the stance of your department with reference to core curriculum changes, promotion and review procedures and/or faculty development at Simulatum. Alternatively, you may wish to discuss a departmental curriculum change or faculty development initiative that could be a model for college-wide efforts.

Period Three
 College-Wide Assembly

Period Four
 Attendance at Curriculum Committee meeting

Period Five
 Attendance at Dean's Council
  or
 Attendance at Faculty Development Workshop

ROLE DESCRIPTION NUMBER 6

NAME: _____

ROLE: Chairman of the Department of Foreign Languages

BACKGROUND INFORMATION: You have taught French and Spanish as a member of the faculty at Simulatum College for 12 years and have been chairman of the foreign language department for six years. During the past few years, your department has experienced a significant loss of students, largely as a result of the elimination, five years ago, of the requirement that all students take at least one year of a foreign language. Your department once had three full-time and two half-time faculty. You are now the only full-time faculty member; three other people are contracted on a part-time basis to teach specific courses. As a result, you have a heavy teaching load along with exclusive administrative responsibility for the department.

Your teaching load has become even heavier as a result of your own conviction that a foreign language department should be concerned not only with the acquisition of linguistic skills, but also with the study of the cultures that use these languages. Consequently, you are involved each term in team-teaching one or more interdisciplinary courses on a cross-cultural theme.

As a member of the Curriculum Committee you are concerned about any further decisions that would reduce demand on foreign languages. Five years ago, when you were not a member of this committee, the foreign language requirement was removed. You asked to become a member of the committee to ensure that this type of decision won't occur again.

Formal Responsibilities

Period One
   Attendance at Curriculum Committee: discussion of proposed change in core curriculum
Period Two
   This period is set aside for department meetings. Since you are a one-member department, you may wish to use this time to prepare a report for the Curriculum Committee (to meet again during period four), to meet with the dean to express your concerns, or in any other way you wish.
Period Three
   College-Wide Assembly
Period Four
   Attendance at Curriculum Committee meeting
Period Five
   Attendance at Dean's Council
      or
   Attendance at Faculty Development Workshop

ROLE DESCRIPTION NUMBER 7

NAME: _____

ROLE: Associate Professor in the English and Comparative Literature Department

BACKGROUND INFORMATION: You have been a member of the faculty at Simulatum College for five years, having previously taught for five years at the University of Nebraska. You came to SOS as an assistant professor but were promoted to the position of associate professor a year ago because of your extensive scholarship in 17th and 18th century English literature. You have published rather extensively in your field—six major publications—and, if given the option, probably would become a full-time scholar and researcher, abandoning the frustration of undergraduate teaching in a liberal arts college.

Because you are esteemed by your colleagues and have recently gone through the tenure review process yourself, the faculty has appointed you chairman of the Promotion and Tenure Committee. As head of this committee you hope to be able to encourage increased concern for scholarship among your colleagues. You appreciate the fact that SOS is an undergraduate liberal arts college but firmly believe that a faculty member must have something important to teach before becoming concerned about how to teach it. To quote a former colleague of yours at the University of Nebraska: "If it is not worth saying, it is not worth saying well!" Unless a faculty member is personally involved in original research or scholarship, that faculty member will lose intellectual vitality. You believe that all faculty being considered for tenure should have at least one publication in a respectable journal—or comparable evidence of scholarship. Faculty wishing to be promoted to the status of full professor should have at least four major publications and give evidence of a long-term commitment to their own continuing academic pursuits.

You respect the chairman of your department, under whom you have worked for the past three years—since the English and comparative literature department was split off from history and philosophy by the academic dean (former head of the combined humanities department). The current chairman is a good manager, though not a scholar, a bit too concerned about meeting the immediate needs and interests of students, and often uncritical of so-called "innovations" in teaching and curricular offerings. Nevertheless, the chairman has always supported your academic efforts.

Another member of your department (Role Player Number 8) is an associate professor who specializes in contemporary English literature. This person seems to be interested in scholarship, though devoting most attention to teaching and to faculty development matters. You disagree rather strongly with this emphasis on the instructional aspects of faculty development and with the new "innovative" movement in American higher education, which, you feel, does not embrace the traditional notion of faculty as respected and active intellectuals.

The third member of your department (Role Player Number 9) is a bit of a "nut" and intellectual lightweight, obsessed with popular literature and Eastern religions. Your department chair and colleagues in the department revealed their uncritical support for the whims of students when they hired this assistant professor four years ago (over your objections). You are now caught in a difficult situation, for this professor will be up for tenure review this year with no publications, but extensive (though probably superficial and suspect) student support. As chairman of the committee you are concerned that this student support might "win the day." You want to be sure that solid, intellectually-respectable criteria for tenure are established and maintained.

Formal Responsibilities

Period One

Preside over the Promotion and Tenure Committee meeting: the committee is to discuss new standards for determining promotion and tenure for faculty at Simulatum. Currently, there is only an informal set of standards (excellence in teaching, demonstration of scholarship, and record of service to the campus community). A department recommends promotion or tenure (based on a two-thirds vote of all tenured members of the department) for all faculty; the dean recommends promotion or tenure for department chairmen. The Promotion and Tenure Committee then reviews the application, and, upon a two-thirds vote, approves promotion or tenure. The recommendation then goes to the dean, who can veto the committee's decision, but must provide a rationale for any veto in writing to the committee within 30 days. The president and board of trustees at Simulatum then formally approve the promotion or tenure. This is a formality, though technically the president or board could overturn a promotion or tenure decision that has been approved by both the Promotion and Tenure Committee and the dean. Your committee, at this point, is to formulate a more precise and explicit set of standards (currently there is only a set of review steps, no explicit standards). You have no promotion or tenure decisions to make at this time. Other member of committee: Role Player 12.

Period Two

Attendance at meeting of the English and comparative literature department meeting

Period Three

College-Wide Assembly

Period Four

Preside over Promotion and Tenure Committee meeting

Period Five

Attendance at Faculty Development Workshop

40

ROLE DESCRIPTION NUMBER 8

NAME: _____

ROLE: Associate Professor in the English and Comparative Literature Department

BACKGROUND INFORMATION: You have been at Simulatum College for six years, having begun teaching there after receiving your Ph.D. in contemporary English literature from the University of California at Berkeley. While serving as a teaching assistant at the University of California you participated in several instructional effectiveness workshops and had one of your lectures videotaped and critiqued by a fellow T.A. You have been interested in teaching improvement ever since and were pleased to be asked by the president last spring to chair a new Faculty Development Committee. This committee emerged from a preliminary one-year task force (chaired by the head of your department), which had recommended that faculty development activities at SOS focus on instructional improvement.

You are on good terms with the academic dean of the college, though somewhat at odds about the future direction for faculty development at Old Swampee. The dean set up a learning resource center a year ago and released an old, incompetent art professor half-time to head up this center. The art professor has devoted his energy (the little he has) to accumulating a large number of art slides that will probably be of little use to anyone else. It is hard to believe that this is anyone's idea of what faculty development and instructional improvement should be.

Faculty development is in a rather challenging and difficult circumstance at the present time on the SOS campus. First, faculty evaluation and faculty development may be moving in different directions. The new head of the Promotion and Tenure Committee is a colleague of yours in the English and comparative literature department (Role Player Number 7). He is a good scholar—and the department needs some of this to remain intellectually vital and academically credible. However, this faculty member pushes those ideas and biases on everyone else and is currently arguing for a requirement that all tenured faculty have a certain number of publications. This could lead to problems in your department, for another faculty member (Role Player Number 9) in the department is up for tenure this year and has no publications.

While the chairman of the Promotion and Tenure Committee really believes what he is saying about publication requirements for tenure, he also has a personal war going with the faculty member in the department who is up for tenure. This young assistant professor introduces unorthodox subject matter into the classroom (e.g., the role of sexual mythology in contemporary drama) and teaches courses on Eastern philosophy and thought. Actually a rather traditional teacher, this person lectures a great deal and gives frequent examinations. The students like this professor, however, and especially appreciate the considerable attention given to their concerns (both inside and outside the classroom). This faculty member has little time for scholarship and shouldn't be penalized for giving students first priority.

Faculty development also is made more complex by a potential change in the core curriculum at Simulatum. If a new core curriculum should change the manner in which instruction occurs, there will be a great need for faculty development. You

41

are hoping that new instructional methods (e.g., simulations, role playing, contract grading) will be introduced to liven up a core curriculum that is now rather lifeless.

A third and final concern you have about faculty development at SOS centers on a possible tension between the academic dean and the president regarding future directions for faculty development at the college. The president seems to be supportive of your model of faculty development (focusing on instructional improvement), whereas the dean seems to be more oriented to the improvement of media services. You are anxious to get a clearer idea about how these two people stand on this issue and how you can help reconcile any major differences before these differences become disruptive.

Formal Responsibilities

Period One

Preside over the Faculty Development Committee meeting: the committee is to determine what the highest priorities are for faculty development at Simulatum and to design and implement a faculty development workshop during period five of the simulation. All faculty and some of the department chairmen will attend the workshop. The workshop will last 25 minutes. If you wish, you might collect information from Simulatum faculty about their faculty development interests before or as part of the workshop. You might wish to check with the dean about use of some time at the College-Wide Assembly. Other members of committee: Role Players 4, and 11.

Period Two

Attendance at meeting of the English and comparative literature department

Period Three

College-Wide Assembly

Period Four

Preside over Faculty Development Committee meeting

Period Five

Conduct the Faculty Development Workshop

ROLE DESCRIPTION NUMBER 9

NAME: _____

ROLE: Assistant Professor in the Department of English Literature and Comparative Literature

BACKGROUND INFORMATION: You have been a member of the faculty at Simulatum College for four years, having obtained your doctorate in Asian literature from the University of Chicago during your first year of teaching at Simulatum. You were hired by the English literature and comparative literature department for two reasons: (1) SOS had no one to teach comparative literature with any expertise outside of European culture, and (2) you had expressed an eagerness during the interview to work closely with students in a small liberal arts college. Since coming to SOS you have successfully met your obligations and the expectations of your colleagues. You teach courses in non-Western literature (primarily Asian) and work closely with students both inside and outside the classroom. You come to the college at an early hour each day (before any of your colleagues) and often stay into the evening. While you do not fault other faculty for going home at four or five in the afternoon (they have families and you are single), you hope that they fully acknowledge your extensive contribution to the students of SOS—especially now that you are up for tenure review and, you hope, promotion to associate professor.

Your concern about receiving tenure is justified, for a colleague of yours in the English and comparative literature department is the chairman of the Promotion and Tenure Committee (Role Player 7) and the two of you do not see eye to eye on many matters. This person is limited in many ways, insisting that all faculty grind out article after article, even if this takes time away from students. Concerned only with Western literature (specializing in obscure 17th and 18th century writers), this person seems to denounce all non-Western literature as "gobbledygook" or "pop-Zen." This faculty member could be a serious barrier to your receiving tenure, though you expect strong student support and the backing of many of your colleagues, including your department chairman and the other faculty member in your department (Role Player Number 8). You consider yourself a good teacher who uses solid academically respectable methods of instruction (lecturing, leading discussions) and evaluation (tests, essays, term papers). Though you have no publications to date—and are not going to until you have something really important to say—the attention you have given to students and the unique and much-needed non-Western perspective you bring to "Old Swampee" should win the day, and tenure, for you.

You serve as a member of Simulatum College's Curriculum Committee, and would like to see a stronger non-Western emphasis in the curriculum of the college. Too great an emphasis on Western cultures and languages has led to a parochial perspective among the students at SOS—as well as among many of your colleagues. You also would like to see a more individualized curriculum, which would allow students more choice in selecting courses and would minimize core requirements.

43

Formal Responsibilities

Period One
Attendance at Curriculum Committee meeting: discussion of proposed change in core curriculum

Period Two
Attendance at meeting of the English and comparative literature department

Period Three
College-Wide Assembly

Period Four
Attendance at Curriculum Committee meeting

Period Five
Attendance at Faculty Development Workshop

ROLE DESCRIPTION NUMBER 10

NAME: _____

ROLE: Full Professor in the History and Philosophy Department

BACKGROUND INFORMATION: You have been teaching at Simulatum College for 25 years, having received your master's degree in history from the University of Buffalo before coming to SOS. During most of your years at SOS, you have taught general survey courses on European and American history. You don't mind teaching these courses but look forward each year to teaching an upper division course on the American colonial experience. This course includes field trips, original research by the students on important, though often forgotten, figures in American colonial life. This course used to attract many students. Unfortunately, in recent years students have turned toward courses of more immediate "relevance"—such as business or nursing—or of immediate, short-term interest—such as Asian literature and philosophy. Students seem to be more interested in the roots of other cultures than in their own roots in American history.

You have been tenured for many years, and even served as head of the humanities department about 10 years ago (this department is now split into two departments: English and comparative literature, and history and philosophy). You could never be appointed to this position on a permanent basis because you don't have a Ph.D.

This year a bright young Ph.D. philosopher was hired to head up your history and philosophy department, replacing another philosopher who also headed the department. This new person seems well-intentioned, perhaps a bit impractical, but certainly interested in Western (if not American) history and culture, having been active in a great books curriculum at Saint James College.

Though you have never been department chair, the faculty senate recently asked you to serve as chairman of the college's Curriculum Committee. You appreciate this assignment, though you wish the faculty senate hadn't given you such troublemakers to work with. Other members of the committee include the chairman of the department of visual and performing arts, who is still sulking because of having been passed over for dean three years ago; an assistant professor from the English and comparative literature department, who is the one teaching Eastern literature and culture; and the chairman of the foreign language department (its only full-time member) who, understandably, is spending all available time and energy ensuring that foreign languages aren't dropped entirely from the curriculum (they were eliminated as a requirement several years ago).

Your task in chairing the Curriculum Committee is to review the current core curriculum (as described in "A Brief Overview of Simulatum-of-the-Swamp") to see if it is meeting the needs of current or prospective students at SOS, and to modify the curriculum if necessary. You feel that the committee should move cautiously in this area, for the core curriculum is central to the mission and vitality of a liberal arts college. You also want to be sure that the old core curriculum isn't overturned by a new one that would forget the roots of our contemporary American life in European and, especially, American history.

Formal Responsibilities

Period One

Preside over the Curriculum Committee meeting: the committee is to consider revision or significant change in the current core curriculum. You may wish to carefully review the history of core curricula at Simulatum as presented in the "Brief Overview" and to note in particular the list of objections to the current core curriculum. You may wish to begin with a consideration of the desired outcomes of a core curriculum at Simulatum. Other members of the committee: Role Players 3, 5, 6, and 9.

Period Two

Attendance at meeting of the history and philosophy department

Period Three

College-Wide Assembly

Period Four

Preside over the Curriculum Committee meeting

Period Five

Attendance at Faculty Development Workshop

ROLE DESCRIPTION NUMBER 11

NAME: _____

ROLE: Assistant Professor in the Visual and Performing Arts Department

BACKGROUND INFORMATION: You are the "theater" person at "Old Swampee" (you *love* this nickname), having arrived at this little college two years ago—straight from work in a small repertory theater in San Francisco. You enjoy running your own show at Old Swampee, though you feel a bit constrained by the parochial attitudes of many SOS faculty and most of the student body. You are able to put on two or three plays each year, usually one for public consumption (e.g., a musical or situation comedy), one a classic (Ibsen, *et al*), and one experimental (often a play written by one of your San Francisco colleagues). As you might imagine, reactions to the last of these are less overwhelmingly positive than reactions to the musical or comedy.

You expect to remain at Simulatum for only another year or two, when you hope to return to San Francisco or some other urban area. Consequently, tenure, promotion, and all that sort of thing aren't very important to you. You have been asked to serve on the Faculty Development Committee and look forward to this, since you feel that most faculty could do a much better job of "performing" in the classroom. They could at least learn how to avoid talking into the blackboard. Faculty could benefit as much as students from some of the training exercises you offer in the one speech and communication course you are required to teach each year.

The chairman of your department is not altogether pleasant. This person works hard as the one and only musician on the faculty, though wasting an enormous amount of time in keeping a mediocre band intact. The chairman also seems to be suffering from a bout with inferiority, having been passed over three years ago for the position of academic dean. You try to avoid any direct dealings with the chairman and maintain as much distance as possible.

The other member of your department (Role Player Number 12) is no great shakes either. An old, soon-to-retire professor of art history, this "colleague" mostly spends time collecting art slides. The collection is interesting and impressive— however, this professor never seems to be interested in much else. The academic dean recently appointed this person head of a new Learning Resource Center (probably to get this professor out of the classroom). Unfortunately, this person sits *ex officio* (whatever that means) on the Faculty Development Committee.

Formal Responsibilities

Period One
   Attendance at Faculty Development Committee meeting: discussion of faculty
      development activities at Simulatum and preparation for Faculty Development
      Workshop (period five)

Period Two
   Attendance at meeting of the visual and performing arts department

Period Three
  College-Wide Assembly
Period Four
  Attendance at Faculty Development Committee meeting
Period Five
  Helping to conduct the Faculty Development Workshop

ROLE DESCRIPTION NUMBER 12

NAME: _____

ROLE: Professor in the Visual and Performing Arts

BACKGROUND INFORMATION: You have been a member of the faculty at Simulatum College for 30 years, having previously taught at several art institutes and served as an assistant to several curators of museums in the midwest. You hold an M.A. in art history from Ohio State University and have taught general survey courses on Western civilization at SOS, as well as courses in the visual and performing arts department (formerly a part of the humanities department at SOS).

You are a distinguished and revered member of the faculty at Simulatum, having been a major architect of two core curricula at the college: a two-year Western civilization survey sequence that was in place at SOS from 1952 to 1960, and a one-year "Contemporary Problems" sequence that was in place from 1966 to 1970. Two years ago, the academic dean at Stimulatum asked you to head a major new initiative at SOS: a Learning Resource Center (LRC). While this center eventually will provide many different media services, you have decided to initially make use of your half-time position as head of the LRC to assemble a large collection of 35mm slides on the history and artifacts of various world cultures. These slides come from your own extensive collection of more than 3,000 slides, as well as from the collections of other faculty at SOS, alumni, museums, etc. You hope to be able to collect, classify, and store more than 10,000 slides within the next two years, giving SOS one of the largest collections of its kind in the world. This slide collection could be of significant value to faculty in many different disciplines as they seek to enrich and enliven their lectures and classroom discussions.

Some of the younger and more opportunistic faculty have ignored your efforts and have sought instead to establish a separate faculty development initiative. While you understand and even admire their independent and assertive ways (you were like this as a young, untenured faculty member), you wish they might learn from your experience and that of other mature faculty members at Simulatum. You have only the best interests of the college at heart: you have been tenured for many years, are only five years from retirement, and certainly are beyond the scramble for recognition and status at the college.

You are a close personal friend of the chairman of the visual and performing arts department, who has been at SOS for 12 years. This person runs the music program at SOS and is very supportive of your efforts and insights. Unfortunately, several years ago the chairman was an unsuccessful candidate for the position of academic dean at Simulatum, losing out to another chairman (department of humanities). The latter person is competent as the academic dean at SOS, though, not been particularly sensitive to the wounded pride of your department chairman.

A second member of your department (Role Player 11) is director of the SOS college theater. This person seems a bit brash and self-centered, though certainly qualified for the job. You try not to have too much direct contact with this faculty member, though at times have to mediate between him and your friend, the department chairman.

Formal Responsibilities

Period One

Attendance at Promotion and Tenure Committee meeting: determination of standards for promotion and granting of tenure to Simulatum faculty

or

Attendance at Faculty Development Committee meeting (you serve in *ex officio* capacity): discussion of faculty development activities at Simulatum and preparation for Faculty Development Workshop (period five)

Period Two

Attendance at meeting of the visual and performing arts department

Period Three

College-Wide Assembly

Period Four

Attendance at Faculty Development Committee meeting

or

Attendance at Promotion and Tenure Committee meeting

Period Five

Attendance at (or helping to conduct) the Faculty Development Workshop

At some time during the simulation you also will want to report to the dean on the Learning Resource Center. You also may wish to check with the dean to see if you should attend the Dean's Council (period two).

EXERCISE NUMBER TWO

TITLE: Case Studies on Faculty Development

SOURCE: Julie Hungar, Seattle Community College, William H. Bergquist, and Steven R. Phillips

GENERAL DESCRIPTION: In planning for faculty development, it is often possible to learn from other programs. This can be done by visiting other campuses or by reading descriptions of their programs. Or, members of a planning group can examine the outcomes of other faculty development programs and determine the desirability, appropriateness, and feasibility of efforts that would yield these outcomes (as suggested in Planning Document Number Two of Volume 1 in this series) or make use of case studies that present and illustrate some of the general issues associated with faculty development programming.

Six hypothetical case studies are presented here, each based on the actual faculty development plans and programs of one or more colleges or universities. The case studies are brief and provocative. Each one incorporates one or more central issues in faculty development programming: faculty ownership, communication, program priorities, budgetary reallocations, organizational home for faculty development, and so forth. Although the cases are taken from a diversity of institutional types, many of the specific problems addressed in each case are to be found in most institutional settings.

Several other case studies concerning faculty development currently are available. Chapters Six and Eight of Jack Lindquist's *Strategies for Change* (Washington, D.C.: Council for the Advancement of Small Colleges, 1978) are concerned in part with faculty development activities. Lindquist's case analyses are excellent, though the cases themselves are rather long and might have to be abridged if used by a planning group in a workshop or retreat setting. William Nelsen and Michael Siegel have edited a book titled *Effective Approaches to Faculty Development* (Washington, D. C.: Association of American Colleges, 1980) that contains 14 program descriptions which, in most instances, can be used as case studies. Information concerning cases in higher education also can be obtained from Charles Fisher, Director, Institute for College and University Administrators, American Council on Education, Washington, D.C., and from the Intercollegiate Case Clearinghouse, Harvard Business School.

INSTRUCTIONS FOR USE: A basic discussion concerning the use of case studies in higher education is offered in Chapter Five. While this discussion specifically describes the use of case methods in teaching students, the process is equally applicable in "teaching" faculty about faculty development.

When used to plan faculty development, these six case studies might best be presented in a five-step process. First, the stage is set for introduction of the cases: the case study method is described briefly and the overall purposes for considering a specific case are considered. In general, a specific case is chosen because it incorporates a particular problem or solution to a problem that the planning group is now confronting or soon will confront. A case study provides planners with an opportunity to detach themselves from their current constraints in order to look at a pressing problem from a new, external perspective. In other instances, a problem may be anticipated. The planning group prepares for the future problem by "trying out its wings" on a case study, thereby gaining new skills, insights, and experiences before having to confront the real problem.

Second, the planning group members read the case. Usually only 10 to 20 minutes are needed for this reading, given the brevity of these cases. The third step involves discussions about the case. This is obviously the most important step. The cases have been written in a purposely ambiguous manner so that discussion on any one of them can move in a variety of directions. Following are several questions that might be addressed in each of the six cases:

Case Study Number One: Carrier College
1. How should the president respond to the absence of the two professors?
2. Should the president be running the retreat? If not, who should be running it? How would you have designed this retreat? What themes, structures, activities would you suggest for the retreat?
3. In what other ways might the president respond to tensions existing between the two groups of faculty at Carrier?

Case Study Number Two: Newfound College
1. Do you think week-long workshops are an effective vehicle for faculty development? Why? Why not? How can they be made most effective?
2. How do you think the credibility of faculty can be built within the college? How do you give a "prophet" (faculty member) "honor in his own land (campus)?"
3. How might the academic dean at Newfound make most effective use of the release time positions and funds that are available for faculty development?

Case Study Number Three: The University of Great Plains
1. What could have been done earlier in this project to build a sense of faculty ownership?
2. How might the differences of opinion between the president and coordinator of faculty development have been avoided? How might they now be resolved?
3. What recommendations might you have made as a member of the evaluation team?

Case Study Number Four: Southwestern University
1. Should the faculty development committee address itself to the areas defined by the director of long-range planning?
2. Are some of the identified areas more appropriate to the committee than others?
3. What resources would the committee need if it were to take on the charge of the director of long-range planning?

Case Study Number Five: Wanger University
1. Which information is most important to look at in determining program priorities? What additional information do you need to make a satisfactory decision?
2. What values come into play when making this decision about faculty development at Wanger University?
3. How would you go about making a decision about budget cuts as academic vice president? Who would you consult? Why? What procedures would you follow? Why?

Case Study Number Six: Metropolis Community College District
1. How might you have prepared participants most effectively for the meeting?
2. How do you reconcile the differences among the various groups in terms of perceptions, goals, and expectations regarding staff development?
3. How do you think staff, faculty, and/or organization development should be conducted at MCCD in the future?

If the planning group is large (more than eight people), the initial discussion of a case might be conducted in sub-groups of four to six people. After these groups have discussed the case for 30 to 40 minutes, the total group might consider it for another half hour or so.

Step Four involves decision making. The planning group as a whole decides what action, if any, it would take at this point if it were confronted with the conditions described in the case in real life. This decision phase is important because it forces a group to confront real world problems. Many people feel uncomfortable about this step in a case study session, because they feel that they do not have a sufficient grasp of the "facts" to make a decision. Yet in the real world we often are asked to make decisions without complete information. Furthermore, the struggle over priorities (a central theme in many of these cases) often will be avoided by a case study group unless it is forced to make a decision.

The fifth and final step involves reflection on the case study experience. What has been learned from this case that can be applied in future planning for faculty development activities? Have we learned anything from the successes or mistakes inherent in this case or from our own successes or mistakes in discussing and making decisions concerning this case? This final period of reflection leads naturally into consideration of another case or into actual program planning by the group. When the latter course of action is finally taken, it is hoped that the group members will be able to approach their task with increased insight and a new sense of confidence: "If we can solve someone else's problem, we ought to be able to solve our own as well!"

CASE STUDY NUMBER ONE: CARRIER COLLEGE

TO: The Carrier College Faculty Community

FROM: Dr. John Martin, President

SUBJECT: Faculty Retreat Reservations

It has come to my attention that a few reservations for the upcoming faculty retreat have not yet been made with Sarah Grove. I encourage you to contact her no later than this Friday, January 16, as this is the deadline for meal counts at the Meditation Lodge.

I am sure all of you know how important it is that all members of the community join together in this event, not simply for the observance of our 20th year as a college, but more important, for the opportunity to forge even stronger bonds for moving into the future together as we reconsecrate ourselves to the exciting challenge of shaping young minds to be the leaders of tomorrow, and to carry their commitment as Christians with them as they assume that leadership.

* * * * * * * * * * * * * * * *

By the time the president has given the prayer that opens the first morning's convocation, everyone present is aware that two of the 60 members of the Carrier College faculty have not come to the retreat, which has been called by the president ostensibly to observe the college's anniversary, but actually to solve a problem in faculty unity.

The problem is of the president's own making: seeking to move this small, western Christian college up a few notches on the academic prestige ladder, he has brought in, over the past three years, a group of eight young faculty members from eastern colleges of some reputation. Unfortunately for their integration into the college community, the newcomers have brought a strong intellectual, discipline-based, and secular orientation, which places them in direct conflict with the institution's emphasis on Christian community and service and its lack of interest in and resources for research and scholarly activity.

Relations between the two groups have reached the point that one of the more outspoken of the old guard has labeled the newcomers the "Young Turks." The special connotation of the label in a Christian college has not been lost on the members of that small band; it carries additional overtones for one of them, an Iranian poet and Middle Eastern literature Ph.D.

While the president was enhancing the academic status of his college, he was also introducing a comprehensive faculty development program, generously funded by a private foundation, to which he has given a holistic cast by including spiritual and physical elements as well as an emphasis on instructional development. Finally aware of the rift in faculty unity, he has decided to use the annual faculty retreat (annual since receipt of the grant) to address the problem, not by confronting it directly, but by giving the faculty a charge to explore new directions for the college in a communal and interdisciplinary effort which they are to begin at the retreat.

However, the leader of the Young Turks is not present. He had led his friends in a boycott of the retreat, meanwhile managing to arrange an expense-paid invitation to deliver a paper at a psychology conference in the midwest on the retreat weekend. The second most influential member, an historian with two young children, has decided after the president's second memo that he cannot afford to stay away, and the rest of the group also has come—except for the Iranian poet, who became ill the day before the retreat. Among the established faculty there is universal skepticism about this illness and open anger at the psychologist.

Confident of his ability to lead his faculty by the power of benevolence and his skillful communication style, the president is leading the retreat himself. He has set the theme as "Carrier College: The Next 20 Years" and has planned small-group sessions where participants will brainstorm on this topic, then share ideas in the full group. By the end of the two days, he expects they will define a set of common goals for new projects which will unite members of the newcomers with their established colleagues in stimulating, positive efforts.

Because he has had training in group dynamics and some experience with groups in conflict, he understands the effect on the meeting of the two men's absence. He discovers, when the opening convocation breaks up and the groups form, that his plan for distributing the newcomers among the groups has either not worked or been subverted, for they have formed a group by themselves.

WHAT SHOULD THE PRESIDENT DO AT THIS POINT?

CASE STUDY NUMBER TWO: NEWFOUND COLLEGE

Setting

With the start of a new academic year, you, as the academic vice president at Newfound College, like to take stock of what has occurred at your small, liberal arts college over the past 12 months. Though at times you are not certain you can affect the course of history at Newfound profoundly, you continue to be at least curious about how things got where they are and what you might have done to improve the situation.

Background

Over the past three years you can point with pride to a faculty development program that was funded in part ($30,000 per year) from an outside agency and in part ($15,000 per year in release time and travel funds) by the college itself. Each summer over these three years, the college has provided five to ten week-long workshops for its faculty on a range of topics (from course and curriculum design to life and career planning). The workshop was offered both by faculty at Newfound and by external nationally known consultants. The $30,000 in external funds was used primarily to pay for external consultants ($15,000) and to provide small stipends ($250 per faculty member per workshop) for a total of 60 stipends ($15,000). The college provides one-third release time for one faculty member each spring to organize and coordinate planning for the summer workshops, as well as two quarter-time release positions per semester for faculty to follow up on professional development or course and curriculum development plans they formulated in workshops held during the previous summer.

Evaluation from the three years of workshops (24 workshops in all) generally has been quite positive. Some of the external consultants didn't seem to know about the level of instructional sophistication of most Newfound faculty and hence talked down to workshop participants; however, most of the external consultants did an excellent job. Newfound faculty appreciated their "fresh" and "cosmopolitan" perspectives. In many instances, the external consultants served primarily to reassure the Newfound faculty that they were doing excellent work both inside and outside the classroom.

The workshops conducted by Newfound faculty were rated quite positively (especially workshops on "Helping Students to Improve Their Writing" and "Student Advisement"). As the academic dean you had hoped that these workshops using internal resource people would serve as models for other efforts at colleague assistance. The results have been disappointing, for there is little evidence that faculty are turning to their colleagues more frequently for professional assistance. Most faculty either go it alone or look to such external assistance as books, external consultants, and national or regional conferences.

You are also disappointed about the lack of follow-up from the workshops. Faculty seem to be highly motivated by the end of most of the summer workshops and have many new ideas about how to improve their teaching, advising, and committee work. By the start of the fall term, however, and with the press of everyday business, there has been little evidence of substantial change that can be attributed directly to the workshops—with the exception of the faculty members who have been given release time to follow up on them. These faculty members have produced tangible changes and improvements in their work—though even they have indicated that they wish more support were available in terms of consultative assistance, secretarial time, and travel money during the term when they are working on the project. These release time faculty are particularly concerned about consultative assistance. They indicate that many of the good ideas their workshop leaders presented during the summer need to be clarified or amplified when the faculty member is actively engaged in planning for and implementing change.

Questions

As you sit at your desk reflecting on the program's successes and failures, several questions come to mind. What step should we take next? How do we improve follow-up? How do we more successfully encourage faculty members at Newfound College to make use of each other's expertise and experience? The external funding is no longer available. However, there is still release time available for faculty (one one-third release time position, for one term, and two quarter-time positions per semester) and $5,000 has been set aside in the college's budget for faculty development activities. The college also has a sabbatical program (two sabbaticals available per year, each for one semester at three-quarter salary).

HOW WILL YOU, AS ACADEMIC DEAN, RESPOND TO THESE QUESTIONS AND CONDITIONS?

CASE STUDY NUMBER THREE:
THE UNIVERSITY OF GREAT PLAINS

Background

The University of Great Plains (UGP) is a private, non-denominational institution with 4,200 students, located in a city of 150,000. Its largest academic unit is the College of Business Administration; other important components are the Schools of Education, Nursing, and Law; it also has a strong pre-law major in the liberal arts college.

Five years ago, the president of the university decided to inaugurate a faculty development program and was responsible for a successful grant application to a private foundation, which funded a three-year project. To the president, faculty development meant renewal within an individual's discipline, with a two-fold objective: increased publication and increased enthusiasm for teaching, which would be apparent to and motivating for students. In designing a program to support this view, he worked with the dean of the university but did not consult any faculty members. He also acted unilaterally in hiring a faculty development coordinator once the program was funded, selecting for the position a Ph.D. from an eastern liberal arts college who had moved from a teaching post in the humanities to faculty development work four years earlier.

While the coordinator's view of faculty development was quite different from that of the president, he sought the position because there was enough flexibility in the grant that he saw an opportunity to introduce some of his own ideas while carrying out those of the president, thus creating a fairly broad-based program.

The original proposal, developed by the president, had three major components: (1) departmental consultation to assist individual departments and schools on such matters as curriculum revision, teaching methodology, and departmental organization, with the individual departments free to design their own program and select appropriate consultants; (2) a series of voluntary workshops and seminars to deal with specific issues of teaching and learning; and (3) a program of teaching exchanges with faculty from other colleges and universities. The program was to be carried out by a full-time professional coordinator working with a faculty advisory board.

The coordinator proposed some changes in the original proposal, all but one of which were accepted. They included: more flexibility for departments in the use of departmental consultant funds, an increased off-campus workshop budget, and the administration of the Institutional Goals Inventory to all faculty and administrators and a representative sample of students to augment a two-year self-study just completed. This last change was rejected by the president as an unnecessary duplication of that study.

The Present

The three years of the grant period are nearly over, and UGP must assume full support of the faculty development program if it is to continue. During the second year of the grant, the coordinator had arranged for a formative evaluation by an

58

outside evaluator, and there had also been a report by the Faculty Development Evaluation Committee. During this final year, he has engaged two external evaluators to conduct a summative evaluation. This is now completed and will be presented to the faculty senate, which has been asked to make a recommendation to the administration concerning continuation of the program.

In general, UGP faculty have taken one of two distinct and opposing positions on the issue. The more traditional members, especially the liberal arts faculty, favor the departmental consultations and faculty exchanges, along with the already existing sabbatical leave program, as the worthwhile components of faculty development, directed as they are to the disciplinary concerns which they consider the real heart of their profession and not requiring the support of an outside program staff. Those faculty members who were interested in methods for improving instruction—chiefly from the Schools of Education and Nursing—found that the workshops, seminars, and classroom diagnosis had genuine impact on their teaching, and they supported continuation of the program in its current form, with the coordinator continuing to provide these services.

The report of the external evaluators identified these two points of view and pointed out that they demonstrated the success of the project staff in creating a comprehensive program which met the needs of both traditional, discipline-oriented members and those less conventional, more pedagogically-oriented. They also observed that a major source of resistance to the program had originated in the lack of faculty involvement in the initial program design, so that there was little understanding or sense of ownership in the project at the outset. As the various activities were introduced and adjusted to fit more closely the interests of the individual departments and faculty members, their usefulness became apparent, and the evaluators cited numerous cases of positive impact throughout the university from all facets of the program. They strongly recommended that UGP continue to support the program in its present form.

AS THE PRESIDENT OF THE UNIVERSITY OF GREAT PLAINS, WHAT DO YOU DO AFTER READING THIS REPORT?

CASE STUDY NUMBER FOUR: SOUTHWESTERN UNIVERSITY

Southwestern University is a multi-purpose public urban institution, which, for the last several years, has experienced unstable and declining enrollments and frequent turnover at senior administrative levels. A new president—the third in five years—has been hired recently, largely by the board of trustees, whose charge to him is to return the institution to a stable, if reduced, state. Immediately upon his arrival on campus, the new president noted that a major problem facing the university was that a number of distinctly separate groups with generally legitmate interests were planning, with varying degrees of intensity and continuity, different institutional futures. In his opening remarks to the faculty four months ago, he indicated that one of the university's greatest challenges, as well as one of its most pressing opportunities, is to bring these diverse groups together, reconciling their views as much as possible to lay the groundwork for a stable future.

One of the new president's first official acts was to bring in from his previous institution a woman as director of planning and development, a position new to Southwestern. Her task was, according to the president, to bring the institution's diverse groups together through the creation of a long-range plan for the university. As a first step in that process, the new director of planning has begun meeting with various campus groups to lay the foundation for the planning process. She has just asked to meet with the university's Faculty Development Committee.

In existence for three years, the Faculty Development Committee is an elected group largely concerned with reviewing proposals for sabbaticals, distributing a modest research and teaching improvement fund, and planning two short instructional improvement workshops each year. The new director of planning wants to explore the possibility of charging this committee with helping define the university's needs for faculty professional development, including the identification of areas for retrenchment and/or retraining, allocation of sabbaticals and research funds, and the provision of assistance for faculty wishing to explore non-academic careers.

HOW SHOULD THE DIRECTOR APPROACH THE FACULTY DEVELOPMENT COMMITTEE?

CASE STUDY NUMBER FIVE: WANGER UNIVERSITY

Situation

You are the academic vice president at a prestigious private university (Wanger University) with an undergraduate enrollment of 15,000 and a graduate enrollment of 4,000 students. While Wanger University is not fighting for its life (it has a substantial endowment), it is facing a 12 percent cut in its total budget for the coming fiscal year, due to lower enrollment, higher costs, and reduced support from external grants and alumni giving. One of the areas in which you have considered a budget cut is the Center for Instructional Research and Development (CIRD), which currently receives $225,000 from the university (along with about $20,000-$40,000 per year in external foundation support). You must judge the relative worth of this center and determine whether budget cuts can and should be made in this area.

Background

In 1953, the Institute for the Study of Higher Education was established at Wanger University with minimal fanfare but considerable hope on the part of the president of Wanger, who wanted to see the study of higher education elevated to disciplinary status (or to at least come out from under the shadow of elementary and secondary education). The Institute continued as a small operation, with two Ph.D. research psychologists and a secretary, until the late 1960s when the pressures of student unrest provided impetus for more careful examination of educational issues in higher education.

The Center for Instructional Research and Development was established in 1969 as a unit of the Institute and was given the chance to conduct research on alternative instructional methods and designs and on ways of helping Wanger University faculty to improve their classroom instructional performance. An Ed.D. instructional development specialist was hired to head this new center and initially was given a budget of $150,000. Within three years CIRD expanded to a staff of three professionals, an audio-visual production technician, a secretary, and a budget of $200,000. The director of CIRD also obtained a three-year grant in 1973 for $150,000 ($50,000 per year) to support several new program initiatives and research projects. Additional small grants have been obtained occasionally, usually amounting to about $20,000 to $40,000 per year.

Currently, CIRD is viewed positively by the faculty at Wanger. The director and two other professional staff all have doctorates, publish frequently, and hold faculty positions. Staff members work closely with the academic departments and department chairs at Wanger and have demonstrated the effectiveness of their work with Wanger faculty with sophisticated pre- and post-studies of student performance and learning in courses being taught by faculty who have received CIRD consultation and those who have not.

The consultation being provided by CIRD consists primarily of assistance to faculty in the design of their courses. CIRD staff members help faculty clarify their goals and objectives for the course, identify the educational needs of their students, identify and use the instructional resources of the university (audio-visual, library, laboratories), and gain mastery in the use of various instructional methods (such as simulations, case studies, and learning contracts). Usually the CIRD staff work with teams of faculty, rather than individual faculty members, to ensure continuity of effort and continuing departmental support for CIRD activities. CIRD has also concentrated on work with large, multi-section courses at the lower division, undergraduate level to maximize impact on students (greatest number of students at the earliest possible stage in their intellectual development).

On the negative side, CIRD absorbs a rather large chunk of the budget and generates very few student credit hours. The three professional staff at CIRD currently teach only four upper division or graduate courses, all with low enrollment (understandable given the specialized topics being addressed, such as "Instructional Design," "Sociology of the Classroom," "Organizational Change: Theory and Research"). The number of faculty who are making use of CIRD services also has dropped off. Whereas 30 to 40 faculty made use of CIRD consultation in the mid-1970s, currently only 20 to 30 faculty are being served each year. The success of CIRD consultation continues to be very impressive—however, at the present time faculty do not seem to be particularly interested in the impact of their teaching. They seem to be more concerned about keeping up with their discipline (and need hard money and sabbaticals to do this) and conducting significant research (and need secretarial support, computer time, and sabbaticals to do this).

Current Status

Following are the major budget items for CIRD in the current fiscal year:

A. Expenditures

Item	*Amount*	
1. Salaries and Benefits		
a. Director	$ 38,000	
b. Associate Director	28,000	
c. Instructional Development Consultant	26,000	
d. Secretary	14,000	
Total		$106,000
2. Faculty Release Time (to work on course design)		
a. Summer Stipends	60,000	
b. Single Course Release (During Fall and Spring Terms)	40,000	
Total		$100,000
3. Audio-Visual Equipment and Supplies		
a. Television Equipment (purchase and repair)	$ 10,000	
b. 35mm Slide Production	8,000	
c. 16mm Movie Production	7,000	
d. Miscellaneous	5,000	
Total		$ 30,000

Item	Amount	
4. Staff Travel	$ 8,000	$ 8,000
5. General Supplies (including printing)	$ 13,000	$ 13,000
Total Expenditures		$257,000
B. Income		
1. Institutional Funds	$225,000	
2. External (Grant) Funds	32,000	
Total Income		$257,000

Records for the past academic year indicate that the following consultative services were provided:

Project	Number of Faculty Involved	Days of Consultation Provided by CIRD
I. School of Liberal Studies		
A. Department of Psychology		
1. Introduction to Psychology (Psych 101)	4	30
2. Abnormal Psychology (Psych 325)	2	6
B. Department of History		
1. Survey of American History (Hist 104)	2	10
2. The American West (Hist. 440)	1	18
C. Department of Religion		
1. Survey of World Religions (Relg 120)	2	18
D. Department of Biology		
1. Environmental Studies (Biol 256)	1	12
II. School of Business and Management		
A. Department of Management		
1. Organizational Behavior (Mgmt. 525)	2	10
B. Department of Finance		
1. Basic Accounting (Fnce 104)	3	25
III. School of Allied Health		
A. Department of Nursing		
1. Introduction to Nursing Practices (Nurs 312)	6	40
Total	23 faculty	169 days

63

CIRD staff members also have completed the following research projects or reports during the past 12 months:
1. Improving Student Rentention of Psychological Principles in an Introduction to Psychology course: a three-year follow-up study.
2. Comparison of Student Learning Styles in Liberal Arts and Professional School Settings
3. Humanizing the Behavioral Objective: Toward a New Theory of Collegiate Instruction

---

In the area of instructional support you, as academic vice president, must cut between $50,000 and $100,000. These budget cuts must come from CIRD and/or from one of the following:
1. Library (specifically, book purchases)
   —Maximum possible cut: $30,000
2. Audio-Visual Equipment (specifically, maintenance of current equipment)
   —Maximum possible cut: $10,000
3. Test Scoring Services (specifically, staff and computer time for processing of machine-scored examinations from undergraduate courses)
   —Maximum possible cut: $5,000
4. Faculty Development Funds (specifically, travel funds, sabbatical funds, secretarial support for preparation of manuscripts)
   —Maximum possible cut: $50,000

Alternatively, some or all of the budget cuts could come from:

1. Release of Untenured Faculty
   —Maximum possible cut: $60,000
2. Freeze on New Hires
   —Maximum possible cut: $80,000
3. Reduction in Number of Part-Time Faculty
   —Maximum possible cut: $35,000

Any of these latter three actions would increase the teaching load of some faculty (currently set at nine hours per term).

WHAT ACTION ARE YOU TO TAKE AS THE ACADEMIC VICE PRESIDENT?

CASE STUDY NUMBER SIX: METROPOLIS COMMUNITY COLLEGE DISTRICT

The Situation

The vice president in charge of educational administration at a large, multi-campus, urban community college (Metropolis Community College District, MCCD) has called a meeting of the steering committees for the faculty, administrator, and support staff development programs, each of which operates as a separate entity, and of a newly formed organizational development resource group made up of college administrators and faculty. The purpose of the meeting is to present to these groups the idea of creating a unified staff development program, coordinated by one administrator who would work with all of the committees to develop and carry out the program. The committees would participate in preparing a job description for the new position and in screening candidates for selection by the district president.

Each of the groups brings a specific agenda to the meeting, and while the vice president is aware of these agendas, he does not realize the strong feelings associated with them, mainly among the staff and faculty groups. Of all those invited to the meeting, only the support staff committee has been officially informed by the vice president of his intention to create the new position.

AGENDAS:

Support Staff. This group has the longest history in development, having begun its program five years earlier as an *esprit* generating, bootstrap operation led by several effective and institution-wise members of their employees' association. They promoted the concept of development so successfully through involvement in a federal grant to one of the MCCD campuses that they were eventually given district support for a full-time coordinator and a budget which they used to put on workshops and provide tuition grants for outside training. During the last two years, since the original coordinator moved on to an administrative job, the program has run into problems with the district administration, which is perceived by some staff members as unsupportive of the program. At the same time, some members themselves have become dissatisfied with the work of their coordinator. This past spring, giving a state-ordered budget cut as the reason, the administration eliminated the coordinator position, and the person holding the job left the institution.

Despite their own dissatisfaction with the work of the coordinator, the support staff is almost universally upset by the way the change was carried out, and skeptical of the vice president's assurance that their program would fare as well under the leadership of a new super-coordinator. And, although the staff program has worked cooperatively with the faculty, they are as distrustful of faculty as of administration because of some old struggles; they anticipate that faculty would take control of any combined program.

Faculty. Because of political problems with an earlier administration and with many of their own members, the MCCD faculty did not develop a program as early as the support staff did. However, prior to the creation of the support staff program, faculty had won, through union negotiations, a full release-time position for a coordinator of faculty evaluation. The year after the district funded the support staff program, an equal amount was set aside for faculty development, and the task of carrying it out was added to the duties of the evaluation coordinator. Faculty support for the program was sought with the assurance that it would not be dominated by administration nor used as a tool to force the use of evaluation, which has been entirely voluntary for tenured faculty. In the year and a half of its existence, the development program has gained participants steadily, and the number of faculty using evaluation has increased, although the only direct connection of the two activities is through their coordination by the same person.

The faculty development steering committee's first concern is hence to maintain faculty confidence in the program. The role of the faculty release coordinator is fundamental to this effort; therefore, the committee will oppose any action that appears to erode the coordinator's position. At the same time, handling both evaluation and development is a taxing job, and the coordinator spends a good deal of time in administrative and support tasks that could well be handled by someone else without damaging the faculty's trust. In addition, the faculty program has a relatively good relationship with administration, due in part to the program's close ties to the executive committee of the MCCD faculty union, which give it a firm basis for support and enable it to benefit from the solid negotiating and problem-solving relationship between union and management.

Administrators. The MCCD development program for administrators began during the year just past, formed less to meet a demand than out of an interest in appearing fair to all employee groups. A steering committee was called together by the vice president; they have been making grants for individual and group development projects and seeking their colleagues' ideas concerning other activities. Thus far, the committee's work has been done in addition to their regular jobs; while the number of administrators is fairly small, so that a full-time coordinator is unnecessary, some support staffing would be required if the program is to grow beyond its present rather minimal scope. The administrative development committee has been very willing to cooperate with the two longer-established committees and has demonstrated no concern for increasing its own territory. At the same time, they would have no problem with the creation of an administrative position to provide coordination among the programs, since it would make their committee work easier and they have no fear that the other two groups might encroach on their territory.

The District Administration. Both the MCCD vice president for educational administration (who has been in this newly created position for a little over a year) and the district president are committed to the idea of employee development as a means of improving the way the institution functions, although neither has had experience with development programs as such. They have expressed awareness of the need for employee involvement in decisions affecting their work life, and a willingness to work with the employee associations to bring this about. The associations are a relatively strong faculty union, whose contract gives faculty a considerable voice in instructional matters as well as in areas of pay and working conditions, and a support staff association which is less forceful and increasingly dissatisfied. No group represents administrators.

At the same time, both administrators point out the need for increased economy and productivity as financial support for the college decreases and costs increase. With 85 percent of the budget devoted to personnel costs, and a large share of that in faculty salaries, they are especially concerned that the most effective use be made of faculty time, and this stimulates their interest in instructional improvement programs and evaluation. They are also concerned, however, with the cost of development efforts, and would like to ensure that the money spent in this area is in fact achieving demonstrable improvement in the effectiveness of the college's service to its public. They believe a unified, centrally-administered program will provide this assurance.

AS THE MCCD ADMINISTRATIVE VICE PRESIDENT, HOW DO YOU CONDUCT THIS MEETING?

Section II

Instructional Development

Chapter Two

Instructional Development: An Overview

Collegiate teaching is a complex and subtle process. Some say it is a science or technology, others say it is an art. For virtually all college faculty members, it is always a bit elusive. What seems to work in one setting, with one group of students, is not inevitably going to be successful in another setting or with another group of students. Many faculty members have acknowledged that it is precisely when they are confident that they have mastered a particular procedure or body of material that they are most likely to appear stale and uninspiring to their students.

There are no simple or direct rules to govern the selection of a specific teaching method or to indicate to a faculty member when a particular method is inappropriate. Knowledgeable educational researchers widely accept the position that no one method is better than another. Given the increasing diversity of student learning needs, skills, and styles, and an increasing diversity of settings in which teaching takes place, it would seem obvious that a faculty member should not master one specific method and use it on all occasions but rather should become pedagogically eclectic, with sufficient knowledge in the use of a variety of teaching methods to be able to match up appropriate methods with specific student learning and environmental characteristics.

Unless a faculty member is able to exert significant control over the type of students he will teach and the type of educational environments in which he will work, he is advised to become broadly acquainted with a variety of teaching methods. To assist faculty in acquiring preliminary knowledge of a range of methods, we have provided a survey of 22 teaching methods in the next three chapters of this handbook and have classified these methods according to their primary affiliation with one of the three different modes of teaching that were identified in Chapter One: (1) content-based, (2) student-based, and (3) interaction-based.

A classification system is presented in Table One.

The placement of any one specific method in a single teaching mode should not be considered absolute or unalterable. Obviously, the same instructional method can be used in a variety of ways and for a variety of purposes. As we describe each of these methods, we occasionally will make reference to its use in conjunction with one or both of the other teaching modes. Also, we will discuss some of the problems associated with inappropriate use of this method in other teaching modes. Those instructional methods that are most appropriate to the content-based mode of teaching will be described and discussed in Chapter Three. Those methods that are most appropriate to the student-based mode will be discussed in Chapter Four, and those that are appropriate to the interaction-based modes will be discussed in Chapter Five.

Chapter Six describes the major features of an instructional consultation process that is sensitive to both the implementation of specific instructional methods and to the overall design of a course or curriculum. Acquaintance with an instructional method does not ensure its effective or appropriate use. Faculty development practitioners need

TABLE ONE

CLASSIFICATION OF INSTRUCTIONAL METHODS

Content-Based Instructional Methods

> Lecture
> Question-and-Answer/Recitation
> Reading
> Programmed Instruction/Computer-Assisted Instruction
> Audio-Visual Technologies
> Audiotutorial Laboratory
> Personalized System of Instruction
> Fantasy/Suggestopedia

Student-Based Instructional Methods

> Tutorial
> Independent Study
> Learning Contract
> Field Placement: Sheltered/Real
> Student-Generated Course: Faculty Led/Student Led/Jointly Led

Interaction-Based Instructional Methods

> Seminar/Discussion Group
> Laboratory/Studio
> Symposium/Debate
> Team-Teaching
> Case Study/Socratic Method
> In-Class Discussions: Learning Cells, Buzz Groups
> Simulations: In-Basket/Hands-On/Computerized
> Role Playing: Faculty/Student

to be knowledgeable not only about alternative methods and designs but also about the most effective ways in which to assist faculty in the consideration and use of these methods and designs.

Chapter Three

Content-Based Instructional Methods

A. Lecture

The three instructional methods used most frequently during the past century—lectures, seminars, and tutorials—each effectively serves one of the three modes of teaching. Lecturing is an effective vehicle for conveying content, seminars effectively stimulate interaction, and tutorials serve the individual needs of students. Each of the other methods to be described in the next three chapters is to a remarkable degree merely an extension of these three basic methods. Thus, one should avoid labeling any of the three modes as "traditional" or "innovative," for all three have been in existence for many years.

Lecturing is undoubtedly the most common method of instruction now being used by collegiate faculty. At least 70 percent of the faculty on a typical college campus make extensive use of lecturing to convey information to students. Given the universality and popularity of lecturing, we certainly need not describe what occurs during a typical lecture. Some information concerning the improvement of lecturing skills might be of value, however, for most faculty rarely have access to this type of information. One of the most valuable resources for increasing lecturing skills is the Teaching Improvement Process first developed at the University of Massachusetts. This technique is described in some detail in Volume 2 of *A Handbook for Faculty Development*. In addition, useful suggestions regarding the organization and delivery of lectures may be found in Wilbert McKeachie's *Teaching Tips*, Michigan State University's pamphlet on "The Lecture Method," and a series of programmed instructional materials on lecturing that have been prepared by the Instructional Resources Center at San Jose State University. These instructional materials are most effectively used when coupled with the diagnostic and teaching activities of the University of Massachusetts Teaching Improvement Program.

We emphasize the importance of improving lecturing, because for many faculty this improvement is the key to using other instructional methods. As we observed in Volume 1 of this series, a faculty member often will be resistant to the consideration of so-called "nontraditional" instructional methods until he feels comfortable in the use of more acceptable methods: lecturing, tutoring, advising, and conducting seminars.

Lecturing is recommended in a variety of instances when a body of content is to be conveyed to students. First, when information is not contained in a book, set of slides, movie, or videotape, it may have to be communicated by lecture. Second, in a lecture, a faculty member can convey not only a body of content but also his enthusiasm for or unique perspective on this content. Third, the lecture enables a student to see "a mind working" first-hand, for an effective lecturer frequently will demonstrate the process of exploration, analysis, and synthesis.

On the negative side, lecturing is, first, not a particularly efficient mode for transfering knowledge. Other methods (particularly reading) are more efficient for the transfer of information. Second, a lecture often is a process of one-way communication, for there usually is very little feedback to the lecturer on his performance. Third, and even more important, students rarely receive immediate feedback on their own acquisition of the lecture content. Other content-based methods, especially the personalized systems of instruction discussed later in this chapter, provide better feedback mechanisms. Fourth, as a number of educational researchers and practitioners have recently shown, some students seem to learn primarily through visual or kinesthetic rather than auditory modes, which, because of the lecture's primarily oral nature, further limits the effectiveness of this method.[1]

Although some of these problems can be reduced by using shorter lectures followed by some other kind of instructional method either to provide students with some feedback on their mastery of the lecture content or to present the same information in a visual or kinesthetic manner, the lecture method will always carry with it a number of limitations. Faculty who are genuinely interested in improving their teaching effectiveness, therefore, would be well advised to develop command of at least a few other teaching methods. Even though these methods may not or even should not replace the lecture method entirely, they can serve to vary the instructional pattern, increase student motivation and, perhaps, make lectures, when they are used, all the more effective.

B. Question and Answer Recitation

Most collegiate teachers attempt to overcome the one-way communication problems of lecturing by interspersing their lectures with question-and-answer or recitation sessions. Typically, a faculty member will encourage students to ask questions at any time during a lecture or will pause periodically to entertain or ask questions. The questions that a faculty member asks can either be open-ended or close-ended. Close-ended questions are those with a specific right-or-wrong answer (as in "When did Columbus 'discover' America?"), whereas open-ended questions have no answers (as in "What might have happened if Columbus had not 'discovered' America?"). Open-ended questions tend to move toward an interactive mode of teaching, whereas close-ended questions lead to recitation.

"Recitation" is a rather antiquated word that evokes images of willow-stick discipline and an emphasis on the three Rs. Yet recitation is used frequently in the contemporary college classroom (especially in foreign language courses) and may be used with even greater frequency in the future as many experts in the field of literacy advocate more oral recitation and reading in the college classroom to improve reading and writing. Recitation usually involves a request by the faculty member for specific information from the students or for demonstration of a specific skill. The faculty member often will call on students as a means of ensuring that the students have done their homework or as a means of gathering informal information about the current level of student performance. When carefully prepared and equitably conducted, recitation can be an effective and even enjoyable teaching device. A trusting and supportive environment, however, is essential for recitation to be constructive to students. Usually, this implies that recitation is used by the faculty member to encourage learning and to insure that all students have been given adequate attention, not as a means of student evaluation, which should take place in other settings, using other devices.

C. Reading

Along with lecturing and question-and-answer sessions, assigned reading is the most common method of instruction. It is surprising, in fact, that reading has not become even more dominant. With the wide availability of inexpensive printed material, lecturing should be superceded by reading more frequently than is the case. Many faculty members, complaining about the inability of their students to read, find themselves lecturing even more than in the past, while assigning even less reading.

Reading holds several distinct advantages over virtually any other instructional method. First, it is highly efficient as a vehicle for transmitting information. Second, it involves minimum involvement on the part of the faculty member, in terms of interaction with the student. Third, reading is the most portable of instructional methods. It can take place at any time and in many different settings. Fourth, it is a very inexpensive method of instruction, at least for the institution, since the students usually purchase their own books. Finally, reading enables a student to receive highly diverse, up-to-date, expert information from more than one source. No faculty member, in isolation, can hope to compete with several carefully selected books in terms of providing insightful and provocative information. Certainly, one of the most important roles to be played by faculty is the review and selection of books for assignment in courses they are teaching.

Several disadvantages also should be noted. First, a book does not provide students with direct human contact. Second, the book rarely is able to offer students very useful feedback on their own level of comprehension or performance. Third, students are rarely motivated to read unless they are stimulated by some other source of ideas, such as their teacher, fellow students, or experience.

Some of the more recent innovations regarding college textbooks include the opportunity for faculty to compose their own book of readings, which is printed and bound by a publisher, and the availability of some textbooks in not only a single bound edition, but also in separately-bound sections for faculty who wish their students to read only a portion of a book. There have also been major breakthroughs in the use of graphics to supplement the printed word; these graphics not only contribute aesthetically to the book, they also prove valuable to the nonverbally-oriented student. With tighter student and institutional budgets, however, one wonders how long these new graphics will be provided.

D. Programmed Instruction/Computer-Assisted Instruction

Programmed instruction is the first of the so-called "nontraditional" content-based methods that we have identified. Like many of the other "nontraditional" methods that we will describe, programmed instruction was offered by many of its early, ardent advocates as a panacea for the instructional ills of the academic world. Like the other methods, programmed instruction was not embraced enthusiastically by many faculty, but rather took its place as one of a variety of instructional tools that are available to serve a diversity of learning needs.[2]

Initially, programmed instruction was proposed as a means of overcoming feedback problems associated with both lecturing and assigned reading. A basic tenet of behavioristic learning theory is that immediate reinforcement for successful performance of a specific task is essential to learning. Programmed instruction provides this reinforcement by insuring that a student masters one set of instructional material before proceeding to the next and periodically reviews past material before moving on to new material.

In the past, programmed instruction was accomplished primarily through the printed word. Students were given a programmed instructional text that first introduced them to some information (e.g., "William Shakespeare was a major playwright during the Elizabethan era of English history"). Then, on a second page (usually interspersed with other new information), the student is asked a close-ended question about this new information (e.g., "During what era in English history did William Shakespeare write plays?"). The question often not only tests for retention of some part of the initial informational statement (e.g., "During what era . . . ?") but also repeats (reinforces) other parts of this statement (William Shakespeare wrote plays). At a later point in the programmed text, a different question might be asked which tests for retention of and reinforces other parts of the statement (e.g., "For what type of artistic endeavor was William Shakespeare noted during the Elizabethan era in English history?").

Typically, the acquisition is answered by selection of one or more responses in a multiple choice format. After the student has answered the question, he determines the correct answer (usually by turning to the next page of the programmed text). If his response matches the correct response, the student proceeds to the next page or to new statements or questions located on the same page. If the student's response does not correspond with the correct answer, then he is asked to note the correct answer or, if the correct answer requires some explanation, he may be referred back to the initial statement.

The student proceeds through the programmed text in this manner, being exposed intermittently to new information, tested for retention of old information, and referred back to previous information if unable to give the correct response. When observing a group of students working through a programmed text, one is usually impressed with the sound of rustling pages as students turn back to previous statements, check out answers on succeeding pages, or turn to new information on a new page.

Programmed instruction has never been very popular other than in courses taught by ardent behavioral psychologists and some biological scientists. The major criticisms voiced concerning programmed instruction include: (1) a programmed text interrupts the flow of information, so that it is hard to build a concept step-by-step, (2) a programmed text is often frustrating and not very exciting for students (at least after their initial interest in the "gaming" quality of the text), (3) very few programmed texts are available outside the behavioral sciences, (4) the composition of one's own text is very time-consuming, and (5) programmed texts cannot very easily test for appreciation, synthesis, or other higher-order learning.

In several settings and for several purposes, however, programmed instruction is useful and appropriate. First, in learning and retaining a set of definitions, numbers, locations, or related "fact," a short programmed text can be quite helpful, for this type of text dramatically increases the probability that students really will know the "facts" once they have completed the text. Second, programmed instruction is appropriate when an instructor is not available. Programmed ("self-instructional") texts have been used very successfully to serve students in remote locations, hospitals, and prisons. If the feedback and encouragement of an instructor is not available, programmed instruction is a viable alternative.

Third, programmed instruction can be employed very successfully when conveyed and monitored by a computer rather than a printed textbook. Computer-assisted instruction (CAI) has kept programmed instruction alive during the past five to ten years and holds the promise of becoming a widely-used instructional tool by 1990. In making use of CAI, a student sits at a computer keyboard and interacts with the computer much as a student would interact with the programmed textbook—with several important differences.

Generally, while signing in, the student is asked his name by the computer, as well as information about the material he wishes to cover during the session. The computer begins by providing the student with some printed information. For example:

Computer: Hi Jim. Today you've said you want to work on some ideas about William Shakespeare, a famous English playwright. First of all, do you know what a playwright is? Which of the following definitions of a playwright seems most accurate:
(1) someone who writes short stories about sports
(2) someone who writes dramatic presentations for the theatre
(3) someone who writes novels

Jim: (Types in . . .) 2

Computer: Good, Jim, you're right. OK. Let's talk a bit about where and when William Shakespeare wrote plays . . .

The interaction between Jim and the computer would continue with the computer providing new information when Jim makes the wrong response (e.g., "Sorry, Jim, you gave the wrong answer. Let's go back and review some things we talked about earlier.") This branching and recycling process is not difficult to program, though much more complex and sophisticated routines have been written. The most widely-known and used CAI program is "PLATO," which was developed at the University of Illinois.

Computer-assisted instruction holds several major advantages over programmed instructional textbooks and many other instructional methods as well. One advantage concerns logistics. A CAI student does not have to fumble back and forth through the pages of a book. The computer rapidly returns to a previous statement, asks a question, provides an answer, and so forth. Second, while programmed instruction textbooks often seem remedial and are offensive to some students who prefer to read "straight" books, the computer is a new and widely respected tool. As a result, students in a remedial program usually are not ashamed to inform peers that they are "going over to work on the computer for a while." While this aspect of computers will soon diminish, CAI is now blessed with the aura and mystery of high technology. Furthermore, in working with computers, the CAI student is becoming acquainted with a tool that may be of significant value in future vocational activities.

Another advantage of the computer as an instructional tool is its capacity to forget. Though computers are usually touted for their memories, the ability of the computer to forget past failures is extremely important. One student in a Boston-area college recently commented that she liked CAI because she could return to the computer after having done miserably, and the computer would treat her as a student who had never made an error. Very few faculty members are as willing to forget past failures. The computer is infinitely patient. It will keep working with a student until the student wishes to stop and never conveys any signs of boredom or contempt (unless programmed to do so).

E. Audio-Visual Instruction

As in the case of programmed instruction, some prophets and advocates in the higher education community were convinced during the 1950s and early 1960s that various audio-visual technologies were going to reform teaching and learning at the college level. During the golden years of the 1960s, when there were significantly more dollars for collegiate instruction than now, a great deal of money was spent for movie projectors, TV monitors, 35mm slide projectors and so forth, as well as for A-V facilities and staff to maintain and monitor this equipment. Much of this money was wasted, unfortunately, for very few dollars were spent in teaching faculty how to use audio-visual technologies in their classroom, or even in trying to convince faculty of the usefulness of A-V facilities.

Audio-visual technologies have not revolutionized higher education. However, they are clearly here to stay, and in an attempt to reach the nontraditional learner more successfully, many educators are now turning to educational television, motion pictures, and other mass media. An important lesson that is just now being learned by most faculty members who use A-V, however, is that they cannot compete with the mass media for the student's attention. Faculty who produce their own videotapes often end up with inactive "talking heads" that pale by comparison to the programs produced by educational and commercial television. Faculty must learn to use these technologies in ways that are not yet possible for the mass media. A faculty member, for example, can use a videotape as a basis for classroom discussion, interrupting the tape on frequent occasions for reaction and clarification. Students usually will feel freer to criticize and argue with a speaker on videotape than with a speaker in person.

Faculty have found audio-visual technologies to be of value in several respects. First, A-V provides variation. Students who grow tired of listening to the instructor's voice and viewpoints, may pay closer attention to another person or to information that is being presented visually. Second, A-V technologies provide yet another means whereby a faculty member can teach students who prefer visual or kinesthetic instructional methods. Third, professionally-prepared A-V presentations often are more interesting and transmit more information in a shorter period of time than a lecture. Fourth, a teacher often does not have to be present for the showing of a movie, slide show, or video-tape replay. Although this makes some conscientious faculty a bit uncomfortable, they might better spend class time working on some aspect of the course. Finally, A-V materials can be made available to students on an individual basis. We now turn to an instructional method that makes full use of this individualization.

F. Audiotutorial Instruction

If a faculty member does not have to be present during an A-V presentation, then it also is apparent that students need not all be assembled at the same place at the same time to receive instruction. One can set up A-V equipment at a specific location and ask students to come to this location at a time of their own choosing (within limits) to view, listen to, or work with these materials. This allows for maximum individualization for each student in terms of time and duration of instruction and gives students immediate access to A-V equipment and other instructional materials that are not available in the usual classroom.

There are at least two sources of inspiration for the audiotutorial method.[3] One source is the language laboratory that has been used for the teaching of foreign languages for many years. The second and more direct source is Samuel N. Postlethwait, a biologist at Purdue University, who first made use of tape-recorded study guides, related texts, and films placed at study areas in a laboratory setting. Postlethwait's audiotutorial method has been used in numerous disciplines and has been modified for a variety of purposes.[4]

Typically, an audiotutorial room is set aside for at least part of a term. Usually this is accomplished more easily in the natural or behavioral sciences, where laboratories have been set aside for specific courses, than in a humanities course for which a specific room is rarely assigned. If a classroom cannot be found, an audiotutorial lab can be set up in a reserve book room, at a series of carrels in the library, at a dormitory, or even in a student union. An audiotutorial lab usually consists of five to 20 booths in which are placed some combination of books, slide projectors, video recorders, audio recorders, TV monitors, record players, pictures, artifacts, research equipment, models, or tape loop projectors. Each booth contains instructional material on a specific topic. Typically, a student will move from booth to booth over a period of several weeks or an entire term; work at each booth usually takes about one hour.

A lounge area is sometimes provided in the audiotutorial lab where students can converse informally with one another, the instructor, or a teaching assistant. Coffee and soft drinks often are provided. The instructor or teaching assistant often is available in the audiotutorial lab not only to monitor student progress and the A-V equipment, but also to become acquainted with the students, answer questions that might arise from materials presented in the lab, and engage in discussions concerning particularly interesting ideas that have emerged from the instructional materials. Many faculty who use the audiotutorial method find they have more time to talk with students than when making extensive use of lecturing or other non-laboratory methods.

A faculty member also may place a log book in the laboratory or in each booth. Students make comments and ask questions in this book. The instructor periodically checks the book, making comments and answering questions.

An audiotutorial laboratory can be limited or extensive in scope. At one extreme, the laboratory might be set up for one week near the start of a course. Four or five short modules might be offered that introduce several of the major themes of the course as well as some terminology. At the other extreme, an entire course can be structured around the audiotutorial laboratory, with 10 to 15 modules of one- to two-hour duration offered to students. As is the case with any instructional method, the audiotutorial laboratory can be over-used. When first using an audiotutorial lab, a faculty member should limit its scope. The lab usually is most successful when used to convey an impression or image of a particular time or place or to convey something about the context within which a particular event has occured. The audiotutorial lab also is well used to "spice up" dull material (terms, definitions) that must be learned.

Some faculty members shy away from audiotutorial labs because of the work involved in setting them up. This problem can be overcome by assigning the task of designing each module to students in an advanced course, or to students taking the course one term prior to the use of the audiotutorial lab. Students in an upper-division course on Shakespeare, for instance, might be given the task of selecting printed works, dramatic recordings, and historical material, and constructing a booth in which these materials could be placed. This booth then becomes one module in an introductory level "Survey of World Literature" course. Students in the Shakespeare course should find this task interesting and challenging. They will learn more about Shakespeare and probably construct a better instructional module for their fellow students than could the instructor working alone.

Similarly, students in a "Survey of World Literature" course could learn about several famous authors by creating audiotutorial modules for each author. Each student in the course would be a member of a small task group that is assigned a particular author; this group would be responsible for construction of this author's module. Members of the group would also review, critique, and help to improve the other modules. A completed audiotutorial lab could thus be available the next time this survey course is taught. Students in the subsequent course might be given the task of improving the existing modules further, or of creating new modules that focus on other major authors. The audiotutorial lab can be an engaging learning device in both its construction and use.

G. Personalized System of Instruction

Just as the audiotutorial laboratory is a logical extension of the use of audio-visual equipment in the classroom, so is the so-called "Personalized System of Instruction" (PSI) a logical extension beyond programmed instruction. PSI was developed by Fred Keller, a Skinnerian psychologist, who was given the challenging task of designing a psychology program from scratch for a new Brazilian university. Two major concepts underlie PSI and its various derivations: mastery and self-paced learning.[5]

Mastery learning begins with the assumption that if certain instructional units of a course are prequisite to other units, then a student should have "mastered" this prerequisite material before moving on to the next unit. In an "Introduction to Psychology" course, for instance, the instructor may believe that students should learn about perception, learning, and motivation before tackling personality theory or social psychology. Advocates of mastery learning argue that if perception, learning, and motivation are prerequisites, then a student who exhibits inadequate knowledge of this material should not move on to personality theory or social psychology until a more acceptable level is attained and exhibited. Mastery is typically set at a rather high level (90–95 percent), and students are given ample time and assistance when studying for the tests. Mastery learning requires that multiple versions of a test be available, so that a student can be retested if he is unable to reach mastery during the first testing period.

The second concept, self-pacing, builds on the assumption that people learn in different ways and at different rates. An advocate of self-pacing would propose that it is unfair to test all students in the same room at the same time. Some students learn best when covering a rather large body of material in a relatively short period of time (blocked learning), while other students learn best when new material is acquired in small chunks over a relatively long period of time (spaced learning). Students who prefer blocked learning will want to take tests on the acquired material at different times and at different intervals than students who prefer spaced learning. Standards need not differ for these two types of learners. Only the ways in which new materials are presented and the ways in which tests are given on these materials need to differ.

Mastery learning and self-pacing are brought together in PSI (though they are not always coupled together in variations on the PSI method).[6] Students are confronted, typically, with a series of instructional units or modules. If PSI is the only mode of instruction being used, usually there are seven to 15 modules per course, each of which an average student will complete in one to two weeks. Using "Introductory Psychology" as an example, PSI modules might be: (1) Introduction, (2) History of Psychology, (3) Physiological Psychology, (4) Perception, (5) Thinking and Problem-Solving, (6) Learning, (7) Motivation, (8) Personality, (9) Developmental Psychology, (10) Abnormal Psychology, (11) Social Psychology, and (12) Psychology as a Career. If PSI is used for only part of a course, or in conjunction with other instructional methods, then the modules will be fewer in number or of shorter duration.

Each module usually begins with a pre-test that the student takes to determine his current level of knowledge and proficiency in this area of instruction. If the student already exhibits mastery level ability, he can move on to the next module. If he does not yet exhibit mastery (usually the case), then he participates in some instructional program through which the material of this module is presented. A variety of instructional methods can be used in this segment of the PSI procedure. Often, reading and programmed instruction are used. The audiotutorial laboratory is particularly compatible with PSI, for each booth can provide the instructional program for a specific PSI module.

When the student has completed the instructional materials in a specific module, he takes a post-test on this material. If mastery is exhibited on this post-test, the student proceeds to the next module. If the student has not attained mastery, he once again is exposed to the instructional materials associated with this module. For these students, a different instructional method might be used or new instructional materials presented so that the student has been given every opportunity to learn this material. A second post-test is then given, as are a third and a fourth if necessary. Usually, if the student has not passed the second or third post-test, the instructor will offer a different type of test, or will personally sit down with the student to find out what he knows and what the problem might be with the instructional materials. A tutor might be assigned to those students who are encountering problems with a specific module. The design of a typical PSI course has been portrayed graphically in Figure One.

The PSI method of instruction offers several advantages over other methods, as well as having several disadvantages. One advantage is a shift in the role of the instructor to enable him to operate more directly in behalf of the student. PSI enables the instructor to establish certain standards against which the student's performance is judged. When a student has met this standard (after having completed a particular instructional unit designed or selected by the instructor), his success reflects positively on both himself and the instructor. By contrast, under normal conditions, where curve grading is in effect, the faculty member's colleagues might object if all of his students receive high grades, because other faculty might believe that he is contributing to the deterioraton of academic standards. A faculty member who uses PSI should solicit agreement from his colleagues that the tests he is giving and the standards of mastery he has set are acceptable. Then, if all the students attain mastery, the instructor should be commended for excellence in teaching, rather than condemned for lowering stan-

81

FIGURE ONE

DESIGN OF A TYPICAL PSI COURSE

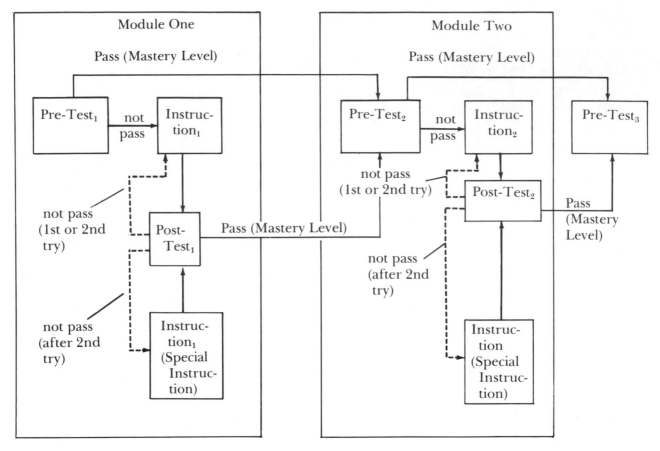

dards. Placed in this position, the PSI instructor is usually more amenable to helping students prepare for tests, overcome learning blocks, and reduce test anxiety. He is not caught in the ambiguous position of having to "find" the lower student quartile (Ds and Fs) to preserve a grading curve.

A second advantage of PSI concerns its flexibility and individualization. Within limits, each student can work at his own pace and take tests at a time when he wishes to do so. A student can work hard on a course and progress through several modules when the workload in other courses is relatively light. Optimally, students get to choose between several instructional methods and/or modes of testing—at least if they encounter problems the first time through the module. With the use of pre-tests, a student can avoid sitting through lectures or reading books that cover material already mastered. If students come into a course with widely divergent backgrounds and skills— as is increasingly the case—the pre-tests are particularly valuable. The opportunity for a student to test out of certain modules is particularly important if the course is either required or a major prerequisite to other popular courses.

A third advantage concerns the opportunity for a PSI instructor to focus his attention on students who find the course difficult. Often, students who are overwhelmed with a course will be quiet during classroom discussions or will cease attending class. They often are reticent to ask for the instructor's assistance. PSI provides a monitoring device whereby these students can be identified and served. If a student is not progressing at a normal rate through the modules, or is encountering difficulties with a specific module, the instructor will know fairly early in the term, and can set up special appointments or tutoring services, or both, for this student.

Faculty who use other content-based methods can monitor student progress, of course, through frequent use of short quizzes. Unfortunately, quiz results may reveal more about the poor timing of the test for an individual student than about any inherent problems that student is experiencing with the subject matter. Even if a faculty member identifies a student in trouble, other course obligations preclude extensive attention to the problem student. The PSI instructor usually is freed from many of these distracting obligations and hence can devote adequate time and attention to the problem student—provided the faculty member can overcome some of the logistical disadvantages to which we now turn.[7]

One major disadvantage of PSI concerns its incompatibility with the registration, crediting, and scheduling procedures of most collegiate institutions. Rarely is a student allowed to take an indefinite or unlimited amount of time to complete a course. Usually, if a student has not completed a course by the end of the term, he is given a low grade or an incomplete, which is changed to an "F" if the course is not finished within a specific period of time. At most institutions, therefore, a "pure" form of self-paced PSI is not feasible. A student must keep in mind that all the modules must be completed by the end of the term (or by some other deadline set by the instructor).

A second, related disadvantage concerns the assignment of grades in a PSI course. If a student has "mastered" all of the modules in a course, shouldn't he receive a grade of "A" for the course? If all students in a course have completed the modules, then shouldn't they all receive an "A"? At some colleges and universities this "grade inflation" is allowed. At others, it is not. PSI has been modified in several ways to accommodate this problem. Sometimes, a separate set of quizzes or a final examination is given for grading purposes. The pre- and post-tests associated with each module are not used for grading purposes, but rather to help a student monitor his own progress and to prepare for the graded quizzes or exams. Alternatively, time is used as a grading criterion. Students who finish the PSI modules first receive an "A." Those who finish the modules at a slower pace receive a "B," and so forth. Both of these grading procedures (especially the latter one) seem to defeat the purpose and spirit of PSI.

A somewhat more satisfactory grading procedure is responsive to another of the disadvantages of PSI—namely, the need for tutorial assistance in conducting an effective PSI course. In order to get an "A," a student not only must complete the PSI modules, but also must provide a certain number of hours of tutorial assistance for other students. Similarly, to get a "B," a certain fewer number of tutorial hours are required. The student is not being rewarded for working faster, *per se*. Rather he is being rewarded for teaching other people, having rapidly completed the modules himself. A justifiable assumption is made that the student will learn even more about the content of the module if he must teach it to someone else. Through use of this grading option, the instructor receives valuable tutorial assistance.

The grading problem also can be confronted and solved by including PSI as only one element in a course. A faculty member, for instance, might use several PSI modules near the start of a course to introduce the basic terminology, definitions, and concepts of the course. Students are told that they must complete the PSI modules by the fourth week of the course if they are to comprehend and use the concepts to be presented during the remainder of the term. Or the instructor might be a bit more persuasive by stating that these modules must be completed by the fourth week of the term if the student is to receive either an "A" or "B" for the course. Another, more rigorous option might be that the instructor requires completion of the modules by the fourth week if the student is to remain in the course.

PSI modules can be used along with other instructional methods. An instructor might give lectures, hold discussion sessions, and provide periodic simulations or case study sessions along with the PSI modules. A final grade would be determined on the basis of performance in each segment of the course. Thus, all students completing the PSI modules could receive grades of "A" for this segment of the course, yet not necessarily receive an "A" for the entire course.

The problem of tutorial assistance in a PSI course can be confronted in several ways other than making use of students taking the class. The problem is actually much broader than just tutorial assistance. A PSI instructor is faced with a number of clerical demands, including test administration and record keeping, as well as with high-level demands for the construction of tests and the production or selection of instructional materials. Most instructors in larger institutions, who are using PSI in introductory courses, are able to hire teaching assistants to administer the tests and keep records. In smaller institutions, the instructor may have to obtain work-study assistance or ask students taking the course (for an "A" or "B") or students enrolled in advanced courses to provide these services. The latter solution to the clerical problem is not very satisfactory, however, for student assistance with clerical tasks rarely can be justified as an "educational" experience, whereas tutorial assistance can be. Thus, clerical demands are a serious disadvantage for PSI, particularly in smaller institutions.

Problems associated with test construction and instructional materials preparation are more easily solved—at least for introductory-level courses—if the instructor is willing to use tests and materials that have been prepared by others. The Center for Personalized Instruction at Georgetown University has information about existing PSI courses in many fields. An instructor can borrow sample test items from the numerous textbooks he receives each year. Instructors at small colleges should consider setting up a consortial arrangement with faculty from nearby colleges who teach in the same discipline and wish to use PSI for the same introductory course. In this consortial arrangement, faculty colleagues can prepare or select instructional materials and construct test items cooperatively.

Students in advanced-level courses can assist in the preparation of instructional materials and construction of test items. As in the case of the audiotutorial booths, this assistance can be justified as an educational activity. In preparing materials and test items, the advanced students often will be more creative and sensitive to the needs and learning styles of the introductory-level students than is the instructor.

Another disadvantage of PSI is student reaction against this particular method. While some students appreciate the clarity of course structure and requirements in PSI, others react against what they perceive as the inhuman or mechanistic quality of the design. Many students cannot find sufficient self-discipline to manage a self-paced course. This disadvantage is most apparent when a course is designed exclusively around PSI.

The instructor is also likely to find a "pure" PSI course dissatisfying at times. A faculty member who uses PSI in a history course speaks of sitting around ("holding up the walls") with nothing to do while the students are learning the materials independently in each module. He was very busy when setting up the modules, but feels he is expendable now that the course has begun. This history instructor now makes use of PSI on a more limited basis. In their excellent discussion of PSI in Ohmer Milton's *On College Teaching,* Schiller and Markely emphasize this potential disadvantage of PSI:

> Perhaps the most difficult demand of the PSI system for most teachers to deal with is the role change it forces. They must become course designers and course managers rather than performers. They must forego the immediate gratification of lecturing for the delayed gratification of improved student performance at the end of the course.[8]

In summary, Keller's Personalized System of Instruction is a valuable instructional tool that effectively meets certain educational needs, such as ensuring student acquisition of basic concepts and facts. PSI is not universally applicable for all students in all courses, however, and often is best used in conjunction with other methods.[9]

H. Fantasy/Suggestopedia

When closely examining the ingredients of a particularly effective lecture, one often discovers the speaker's ability to convey or elicit vivid visual images. A widely respected lecturer on 20th century Irish literature, for instance, is able to bring the students into the Irish Rebellion through the use of carefully chosen stories, images, and illustrations, and through tone of voice, pauses, and gestures. The student's own fantasy work is central to this lecturer's goal of conveying something about the context within which Irish writers created works of art.

Fantasy can be conceived as slowed-down lecturing. Rather than speaking at 150 or 200 words per minute, an instructor might provide only 30 to 60 words per minute, relying on the student to produce a rich fantasy based on these words. This "directed" or "guided" fantasy technique has been used in a variety of disciplines. In an ecology course, an instructor may ask his students to imagine that they are asleep and about to wake up in the year 2020. The instructor then asks the students to imagine living through a typical day in that year, and in doing so presents several statements about what the world might be like at this time in the future. After having fantasized, either in their heads or on paper, the students are encouraged to describe and talk about their images and the implications of these images for current and future public policy. Discussions about future conditions often are much richer and more insightful when based on the student's fantasies about the future than when based solely on verbal discussions.

Fantasy can be used profitably in the sciences and mathematics. Three-dimensional models often can be conveyed more effectively through fantasy than by being drawn as two-dimensional figures on a blackboard. Students can imagine walking around to the back side of a cube that is floating in space. They also can imagine an animal that does not in fact exist, but could exist if adapting to a specific and unusual set of environmental conditions. In the humanities, fantasy can be used broadly and creatively, not only to help a student become immersed in a particular story, painting, or musical composition, but also (as in the case of the Irish literature lecture) to become immersed in the context within which the artist is working.

To employ fantasy successfully in the classroom, the instructor must establish a restful and reflective atmosphere. If possible, a comfortable room should be selected. The lights should not be bright, and outside noises and visual distractions should be kept to a minimum. If the instructor feels comfortable in doing so, the students should be instructed to lean back in their chairs or, if possible, lie down on the floor, close their eyes, and spend a few moments separating themselves from outside concerns and activities. This latter process of disengagement can be facilitated by asking the students to spend a few moments concentrating on their breathing—not speeding it up or slowing it down, but just paying attention to it. Students also might be instructed to attend to their body as it accommodates to and assists in the breathing process. An instructor familiar with progressive relaxation techniques also can use these in preparing students for a fantasy. Faculty who are not satisfied with the outcomes of a fantasy conducted in the classroom often have not given sufficient attention to these preliminaries.

In foreign language fields—and increasingly in other fields as well—fantasy has been used in a somewhat different manner. A technique called suggestopedia, or the "Lozanov method," which was first used in Bulgaria and has been used more recently by American educators in teaching German, French, and Spanish, relies heavily on fantasy.[10] Suggestopedia is probably the most controversial of the content-based instructional methods we shall consider. It also may be of greater potential benefit to students than any of the previously-described methods.

Suggestopedia is a subtle and complex process, for which instructors must be trained. Several of its intriguing goals and features are: (1) conveying a positive attitude about the ease with which seemingly difficult materials can be learned, (2) providing a warm environment that is conducive to receptive and relaxed learning, (3) aiding the memorization of terms or rules through the use of music and rhythm, and (4) aiding the acquisition of concepts through use of fantasy.

Faculty members who have made use of suggestopedia report impressive success in teaching the rudiments of a foreign language in a short period of time to students (and even faculty members) who previously experienced considerable difficulty in learning a second language. The techniques of suggestopedia are being modified now for broader use and have even been popularized under the banner of "super-learning." At least one faculty member from each collegiate institution should become familiar with this new instructional method before it becomes popularized and watered down, as an inappropriate "super-solution" to a wide range of instructional problems.

I. General Observations about Content-Based Methods

Each of the instructional methods we have just described can be used effectively by collegiate faculty to convey a specific body of information that has been deemed important by the faculty member (and, perhaps, his colleagues and others in the field). If a faculty member is uncertain about what he wishes the student to know or do as a function of taking the course, these methods may be inappropriate. If the faculty member is uncertain about the information to be conveyed because he believes that students should have a greater say in determining course content, he may wish to consider the use of student-based methods discussed in Chapter Four. If the instructor is uncertain because he is not convinced that much of what he wants a student to learn in his course can be specified prior to the course, the interaction-based methods described in Chapter Five may be more appropriate.

When choosing any content-based method to convey a specific body of information, a faculty member will want to consider the following questions:

1. *Receptivity:* How open are my colleagues, the students who probably will take this course, and other leaders at this institution about the use of "nontraditional" methods?

2. *Individualization:* To what extent will students taking this course need a program that is individualized in terms of location, time, instructional mode, testing mode, and student/instructor interaction?

3. *Learning Skills:* How prepared will most students be when entering this course? How diverse will the backgrounds and intellectual abilities be of students entering this course?

4. *Learning Styles:* What will the dominant learning styles be of students entering this course? Do I want to match the dominant learning styles with compatible instructional methods, materials, and teaching styles, or do I want to challenge the students with incompatible instructional methods, materials, and/or teaching styles?

5. *Continuity:* What instructional precedents have been established in previous courses that the students probably will have taken? Which of these precedents should be preserved? For what courses, programs, or careers is this course preparatory? What are the implications of this preparatory obligation for the methods used in this course?

6. *Resources:* What people, materials, time, and money are available for the development and implementation of this course? To what extent can these resources be counted on over the short and long run?

7. *Constraints:* What limitations are inevitably confronted in conducting this course with reference to people, materials, time, and money? How do these limitations influence the design of this course and the selection of instructional methods?

The lack of receptivity to new methods may argue for the use of lecturing, reading, question and answer sessions, and recitation, whereas the need for individualization may argue for the use of programmed instruction, computer-assisted instruction, audiotutorial laboratories, and PSI. The latter four methods also would be advisable if the background preparation and intellectual skills of students are inadequate or diverse.

A faculty member should consider the use of a variety of content-based instructional methods if he will encounter students with a variety of learning styles and should consider interaction-based or student-based methods if independent, competitive, divergent, accommodating, intuitive, or feeling styles are prevalent. If the faculty member must be sensitive to the educational achievements of students in courses, programs, or careers that precede or follow this course, he may wish to be more careful about the use of methods that are not being used elsewhere. On the other hand, if the continuity issue centers primarily around the accomplishment of specific goals, then several of the less conventional methods might be most appropriate: programmed and computer-assisted instruction, and, in particular, PSI.

With a fair amount of time, money, and assistance, a faculty member may wish to receive training in the use of suggestopedia, so that the learning of students potentially can be significantly accelerated and so that students with fear of a certain discipline or content area can lose this fear and be successful in this field. Adequate resources also speak in favor of audio-visual technology, audiotutorial laboratories, computer-assisted instruction, and PSI. If available resources are severely limited, the faculty member may wish to explore the use of fantasy in the classroom (which requires only the imagination of the faculty member and the students), as well as audiotutorial laboratories that have been built by students. Limited resources should not restrict faculty to traditional methods, but, instead, should challenge them to find low cost ways of using new methods that are responsive to the individualized and changing needs of students.

NOTES:

[1] J. E. Hill and D. N. Nunnery, *The Educational Sciences* (Bloomfield Hills, Michigan: Oakland Community College, 1973).

[2] The body of literature regarding the use of computer-assisted instruction in the college classroom continues to grow at a rapid rate. Several recent articles reflect the diverse use of CAI in a variety of disciplines: (1) *geography:* Allan Collins and others, "Effectiveness of an Interactive Map Display in Tutoring Geography," *Journal of Educational Psychology,* 70 (1980), 1–7; (2) *medicine:* Robert G. Votaw and Barbara B. Farquhar, "Current Trends in Computer-Based Education in Medicine," *Educational Technology,* 18 (1978), 54–56; (3) *logic:* I. Larson and others, "Performance Models of Undergraduate Students on Computer-Assisted Instruction in Elementary Logic," *Instructional Science,* 7 (1978), 15–35; (4) *music:* Fred T. Hofstetter, "Instructional Design and Curricular Impact of Computer-Based Music Education," *Educational Technology,* 18 (1978), 50–53; (5) *economics:* Mark Henry and David Ramsett, "The Effects of Computer-Aided Instruction on Learning and Attitudes in Economic Principles Courses," *Journal of Economic Education,* 10 (1978), 26–34; (6) *sociology:* Bebe F. Lavin, "Can Computer-Assisted Instruction Make a Difference?" *Teaching Sociology,* 7 (1980), 163–179. Excellent sources of additional information about CAI are the *Journal of Computer-Based Instruction, Educational Technology, Instructional Science,* and *Creative Computing.*

[3] The audiotutorial method is defined by William Schiller and Susan Markely in "Using the Personalized System of Instruction," in Ohmer Milton, *On College Teaching* (San Francisco: Jossey-Bass, 1978), p. 157, as follows:

> The audiotutorial system typically uses a multimedia approach often with study guides provided by audiotape rather than by written text. It uses a central study-laboratory where students can view films, inspect demonstration experiments, conduct simple experiments themselves, and work through other instructional materials at their own pace. Self-pacing and control over repetition are present; however, in early versions of the system, examinations were scheduled at common times and mastery was not enforced, with grades being given in the conventional manner. Later versions have instituted the mastery requirement and differ from PSI [Personalized System of Instruction—to be discussed later] primarily in the heavy investment in media which Keller [the founder of PSI] did not rule out, but which he perceived as luxuries.

[4] The audiotutorial technique continues to be used in a variety of disciplines—mostly the sciences. In recent years audiotutorial methods have been used (and described in the literature) in the field of chemistry (Hubert L. Youmans, "Students are Differing Folk: An Operational System of Placing Students in Chemistry," *Journal of College Science Teaching,* 6 [1976], 92–93) and in anatomy and physiology (John A. Kalmbach, "Success Characteristics of Students in an Audio-Tutorial College Course: A Descriptive Study," *NSPI Journal,* 19 [1980], 43–46). The journal of the National Society for Performance and Instruction *(NSPI Journal)* is an excellent source of articles about audiotutorial instruction—as well as programmed instruction and other "instructional technologies."

[5] Initially, Fred Keller identified five distinctive features of a "pure" PSI course design in "Goodbye Teacher ... ," *Journal of Applied Behavioral Analysis,* 1 (1968), 83:

1. The go-at-your-own-pace feature, which permits a student to move through the course at a speed commensurate with his ability and other demands upon his time.
2. The unit-perfection requirement for advance, which lets the student go ahead to new material only after demonstrating mastery of that which preceded.
3. The use of lectures and demonstrations as vehicles of motivation, rather than sources of critical information.
4. The related stress upon the written word in teacher-student communication.
5. The use of proctors, which permits repeated testing, immediate scoring, almost unavoidable tutoring, and marked enhancement of personal-social aspect of the educational process.

We have emphasized the first two of these features because the remaining three features are no longer common to all PSI courses, or seem to be secondary in importance to the first two.

[6] An alternative to Keller's PSI method exemplifies the use of mastery without self-pacing: the Mastery Learning system developed by Benjamin Bloom includes mastery (unit-perfection) but in many instances does not allow for self-pacing, because students may work together "under a teacher's direction until performance on a mastery test shows the need for remedial steps for some." William J. Schiller and Susan M. Markely, "Using the Personalized System of Instruction" in Ohmer Milton, *On College Teaching,* p. 156.

[7] Schiller and Markely (in Ohmer Milton, *On College Teaching*) note that

> A benefit that is an outgrowth of the gradual improvement of the course is the reduction in instructor preparation time that is required for successive offerings. Although the initial offering will require at least as much time as any well-prepared conventional course, and probably more, each successive offering typically requires less and less instruc-

tor effort until little is required beyond setting up the mechanics . . . We are assuming, of course, that the course content is not something that changes drastically in short periods of time . . . which would argue against such intensive development [pp. 168–169].

[8]*Ibid.*, p. 162.

[9]A growing body of literature concerning the use of PSI in a variety of fields is now available. Some of the fields in which articles have recently been written are: (1) *chemistry:* L. J. Hughes and others, "Origins of Life: An Interdisciplinary Course in Chemical Evolution for Undergraduates," *Journal of Chemical Education,* 55 (1978), 521–524; (2) *human physiology:* Maurine Giese and Michael Lawler, "Development and Implementation of a PSI Course in Human Physiology," *Journal of Allied Health,* 7 (1978), 268–273; (3) *mathematics:* Matthew J. Hassett and Richard B. Thompson, "PSI in College Mathematics," *American Mathematical Monthly,* 85 (1978), 760–763; (4) *geology:* Robert S. Andrews, "Customizing Geology in the Self-Instruction Mode," *Journal of Geological Education,* 25 (1977), 108–111.

[10]Several recent articles on suggestopedia provide an overview regarding the use of this method in foreign language instruction: (1) Louis B. Mignault, "Suggestopedia: Is There a Better Way to Learn?" *Canadian Modern Language Review,* 34 (1978), 695–701; (2) Gabriel L. Racle, "Can Suggestopedia Revolutionize Language Teaching?" *Foreign Language Annuals,* 12 (1979), 39–49; (3) Dragon Milivojevic, "New Directions in Foreign Language Teaching," *Journal of Thought,* 14 (1979), 273–279.

Chapter Four

Student-Based Instructional Methods

A. Tutorials/Independent Study

Most colleges and universities offer some form of individualized instruction that is responsive to the diverse needs, interests, and competencies of students. In the case of both tutorials and independent study programs,[1] the student is periodically given the full attention of a faculty member or graduate assistant. The faculty member tailors his role, expectations, and provision of resources to meet the needs of the individual student.

Both the tutorial and independent study method begin with an initial "contracting" phase, during which the interests and needs of the students are assessed and critiqued by the faculty member and plans for the program are formulated. While this initial "contracting" phase may be quite short (or even *pro forma* in the case of many tutorials), it differentiates these two methods from interaction-based methods. A faculty member cannot walk into either a tutorial or independent study program with a preplanned agenda or design. A student must be actively involved in decision-making processes if the tutorial or independent study program is to be successful and truly student-based.

Tutorials typically differ from independent study programs in four important ways. First, tutorials focus on the acquisition of a specific body of knowledge or skills, whereas independent studies usually involve the production of a written or oral report, term paper, essay, journal, or research project. Second, tutorials usually involve close monitoring of student progress, whereas independent study programs generally are supervised less intensively and even sporadically.

Third, tutorials generally require that faculty serve in the role of primary resource person to the student. This method is student-based in that the faculty member tailors his approach and presentation to the immediate and personal needs of the student he is tutoring. However, in the actual processes of the tutorial, the faculty member may resemble a content-based instructor—lecturing, questioning, answering questions, and testing for the acquisition of a specific content. By contrast, the independent study method more closely resembles interaction-based instruction. The faculty member helps the student grapple with a specific problem, and in doing so serves as a facilitator of the student's exploration. He may even join the student in exploring unknown or ambiguous domains or knowledge.

A fourth difference between tutorials and independent study programs concerns their use. Whereas tutorials have been used in recent years primarily to assist students who are having problems in completing their academic work, independent study is offered most frequently to students with excellent academic records who have exhibited self-discipline and motivation. Regardless of their differences, the tutorial and independent study methods have served as the primary means by which the individual differences of students have been addressed by American colleges and universities over the past two centuries.

B. Learning Contracts

Though the independent study and tutorial methods are responsive to the interests and immediate needs of students, they may not be of maximum educational benefit to students over the long run, for they often fail to take into account the current status and educational goals of the student. Independent study programs usually focus on the student's final report rather than on what the student learns in the process of producing this report. While the tutorial does focus on student learning, it tends to focus on short-term learning goals without reference to how these goals relate to longer-term educational objectives. A learning contract enables a faculty member and student to explore jointly the past learning and the long-term educational goals of the student, the extent to which the gap between current levels of learning or competencies and desired levels can and should be reduced or eliminated, the resources that are available to students for achieving the desired levels, and the means by which the student's progress toward the achievement of these levels has been achieved by means of this learning contract.

While there is a wide variety of learning contract procedures, most share a number of common steps.[2] Generally, they begin with some assessment of past learning on the part of the student. Typically, a set of learning categories are identified. These categories may encompass a set of skills, several areas of knowledge, or a set of roles or job functions. In each of these categories (usually six to 12 in number), the student's current level of learning is assessed. For example, if the categories are skill-based, the student's past experiences in learning how to write, perform mathematical computations, or apply critical thinking might be assessed. What has the student been exposed to in his past life, inside and outside of formal educational institutions, that has aided him in the acquisition of these skills?

Some learning contracts do not focus on the assessment of past experiences but rather on the assessment of current levels of competence. How competent is the student in the areas of writing, mathematical computation, or critical thinking? These competencies might be assessed by means of performance tests, demonstrations, documentation, or self-appraisals. Whether assessing past learning experiences or current competencies, the student and faculty member begin by examining the current learning status of the student.

The student and faculty member next turn to an identification of learning goals. Using the same categories as used for the assessment of current learning, the student and faculty member identify and clarify the student's learning goals. The student might ask himself: What must I learn in each of these areas to be successful in my chosen field? Given my future life or career plans, which categories are most important to me and which are least important? When I think of the problems and challenges that I will face at particular points in my future life, what skills knowledge, or attitudes are going to be most important for me? Given my unique strengths and weaknesses, which categories are in need of greatest learning and development? The assessment of past learning or current competencies and future learning goals is often conducted through the development of a learning profile, such as the one exhibited below in Figure Two. First, the current level regarding each skill is assessed. As can be noted, this hypothetical student has been found to be highly competent in the areas of oral communication and interpersonal relationships, moderately competent in the areas of computation and problem-solving, and relatively incompetent in writing and critical thinking. In the assessment of desired levels of competency, the student indicates a desire to arrive at a moderate level of competency regarding writing and computation, but high levels of competency regarding critical thinking, oral communication, and interpersonal relationships. He is particularly concerned about acquiring high levels of skill in the area of problem-solving.

The next step in the learning contract process concerns the identification of gaps between current and desired states of learning. The biggest gaps in the Figure Two profile exist between the current and desired levels of writing, critical thinking, and problem-solving. While in the case of problem-solving, the student already exhibits a moderate level of competency, he wishes to be at a very high level. In the case of both writing and critical thinking, the student currently exhibits low levels of competency and wants to advance to moderate and moderately high levels. The student seems to be satisfied with the current levels of computation, oral communication, and interpersonal relationships. The stage is now set for the formulation of a learning contract between the faculty member and student based on jointly identified gaps between current and desired states. The faculty member and student identify realistic goals for the narrowing or elimination of the gap between current and desired learning levels. No one learning contract (or course) will address—let alone eliminate—all gaps. An effective learning contract will reduce or eliminate some of the learning gaps based on the immediate interests and resources of both the student and teacher. Other learning contracts will help to fill other gaps.

Often a learning contract is offered to students at the end of their academic career. The learning contract is used, in this instance, to ensure that any deficiencies in the student's educational experiences at the college or university are addressed and, it is

FIGURE TWO

HYPOTHETICAL LEARNING PROFILE

Category (Skill)	Level of Competency		
	Low	Moderate	High
Writing	X_1. . . . . .X_2		
Computation		X_1 X_2	
Critical Thinking	X_1. . . . .X_2		
Oral Communication			X_1 X_2
Problem-Solving		X_1. . . . . .X_2	
Interpersonal Relationships			X_1 X_2
Key: X_1 = current level of competency			
X_2 = desired level of competency			
. . . . . = gap between current and desired levels of competency			

hoped, corrected. When used as a terminal educational resource for students, a learning contract should be responsive to all or most of the "learning gaps," for the student will have no other opportunity in this educational institution to respond to these gaps. Alternatively, the student will be given direct assistance with one or more of the gaps and additional assistance in planning for ways in which the other gaps might be narrowed or eliminated following graduation. This latter approach acknowledges that the student is (or should be) a "lifelong learner" who need not meet all desired competency levels while enrolled in college.

Having identified realistic goals for a learning contract, the student and faculty member turn to the identification of resources that are available to the student for the achievement of these goals. Educational resources that are identified may reside primarily in the faculty member, in which case the contract will resemble a carefully conceived tutorial. The resources might reside instead primarily in the student and be engaged primarily through the student's active engagement in a specific project. In this latter case, the learning contract may closely resemble a carefully conceived independent study program.

Often the resources will reside elsewhere in the academic community (other faculty, other students, books, ongoing campus activities, formal classroom events) or off-campus (particularly in the case of external degree institutions). The faculty member not only helps the student identify relevant resources, but also assists him in gaining access to these resources (telephone calls, letters of reference, funding, and so forth).

A faculty member not only helps students clarify educational goals and identify educational resources, he also assists in the evaluation of the overall educational experiences of the students under these learning contracts. The faculty member will help students assess levels of competency or learning levels at the end of the project and perhaps at several points during the learning contract period to determine the extent to which the "learning gap" has been filled. A faculty member often will also help the students assess what they have learned about their own learning processes and perhaps reassess learning goals or current levels of learning. The learning profile itself, in other words, may be modified as the student is exposed to new educational resources.

With the completion of the learning contract, the student should have successfully reduced or eliminated gaps between current and desired levels in certain of the learning categories. The contract represents an agreement between the faculty member and student that both are accountable for progress toward the identified educational goals of the student in reducing the gap between current and desired levels. Neither party to this contract is solely responsible for the achievement of these goals, and both parties must be held partially responsible for the failure to achieve these goals. A learning contract requires mature interpersonal relationships and educational commitments on the part of both the student and faculty member. Many students (and faculty members) are not prepared to enter into this type of relationship and commitment, hence the learning contract must be used selectively and with considerable discrimination.

When used effectively and sensitively, the learning contract can be responsive to a variety of student needs and interests. An individualized learning contract can take on many different forms and structures. It can encompass a variety of other instructional modes (including lectures and seminars) based on the student's and faculty member's assessment of the most appropriate educational resources that should be provided for the student in his achievement of desired educational goals.

C. Field Placements

Learning contracts provide students with access to resources throughout the educational community and even to off-campus resources. While the learning contract usually will provide students with diverse experiences that relate directly to a varied set of needs, students sometimes will benefit more from a single, intensive field experience that provides continuity and gives students a sense of accomplishment—much as in the case of a successfully completed independent study project.[3]

Some field experiences are "sheltered" in that they give students a taste for the "real world," yet restrict the number and type of problems being confronted by the student in this field experience. A sheltered field experience might take place through an internship that is set up on-campus. A business major, for instance, might serve as an administrative assistant to an academic department chairman, or an education major might serve in a staff capacity to a college-wide curriculum committee. A sheltered field experience might be set up off-campus with an employer/supervisor who is committed to (and perhaps even paid for) the learning of the student. Nursing students are typically placed in this type of sheltered environment when first working in a hospital or clinic.

A "nonsheltered" real-world field placement is advisable at the end of a student's academic career, during which the student can pull together a variety of skills, areas of knowledge, and attitudes. This type of placement also can serve as a "wilderness" experience in which the student is challenged to use his existing knowledge and skills and to gain a sense of self-reliance and self-confidence. If a student is plunged into a real-life field placement as an orienting experience, extensive discussion should follow this placement and the student should receive adequate peer and supervisory support while in this setting.

In aiding a student through field placement, a faculty member often will have to learn new skills, for he may be working with a student in a domain that is not of the faculty member's own making. Faculty members must be able to anticipate and tolerate unpredictable events and must be able to assist students in extracting new learnings from even the most complex and difficult situations. Just as the interaction-based instructor will use the case method to show students how to solve complex problems, so will the field placement instructor assist students in confronting complex situations by employing problem-solving and interpersonal skills. Faculty development often is required not only in terms of this facilitation of student learning in complex settings, but also in terms of the faculty member's knowledge of the problems being confronted by his students in the field placement. Some colleges even encourage a joint faculty-student field placement. This is particularly appropriate when the placement is the first in a certain type of social institution or specific organization.

D. Student-Centered Courses

While the tutorial, independent study, learning contract, and field placement methods usually take place outside the formal classroom, a fourth type of student-based method often makes extensive use of the classroom. This classroom, however, is more responsive to the individual and immediate needs of students than is usually the case. Student-generated courses may be one of three types: (1) the course initiated by students but led by a faculty member, (2) the course initiated by a faculty member but led by students, or (3) the course initiated and led by students.

During the late 1960s and early 1970s many colleges and universities provided opportunities for students to suggest and even design courses that were to be taught by faculty. The students often helped select faculty to teach these courses, though faculty usually had the right to refuse this offer. Although there may no longer be strong student interest in controlling the curriculum of a college or university in the early 1980s, there may still be a need for courses that respond directly and sensitively to the changing needs and concerns of students. If students are given the opportunity to identify the themes for specific courses, this curricular responsiveness might be increased. Faculty and administrators who are concerned about the academic integrity of such courses will be at least partially appeased by the presence of a faculty member in the classroom. Student-generated courses provide faculty with an excellent opportunity to teach in new areas that directly reflect student interest. A faculty member is given the enviable opportunity to teach a course that he knows will interest a significant portion of the student body.

Courses that are initiated by faculty, but taught by students, have been offered for many years. They provide exceptional students with an opportunity to accept a challenging teaching assignment, thereby increasing their interest in the knowledge they acquire from a college or university. The faculty-initiated/student-taught course also provides students in the course with often untapped resources (their peers) and helps a college or university expand its range of curricular offerings.

Typically, advanced or honors students are given the opportunity to teach part of a course or to work with one section of a large, introductory course. In other cases, a student might co-teach with a faculty member. In some instances, students may be given sole responsibility for teaching a course that has been initiated by faculty. This occurs most frequently in large research universities in which highly qualified advanced graduate students are paid to teach undergraduate courses. Even in undergraduate colleges, however, students have been given an opportunity to teach courses. Foreign students, for instance, are sometimes asked to teach language courses or courses concerned with the history or culture of their homeland. In other instances, students returning from an extensive field placement are asked to teach a course based on their experience. A special honors program can be established which identifies two or three exceptional students each year who are given an opportunity to teach a course involving an area of personal interest and competency.

The third type of student-generated course harks back to the late 1960s. At that time, a number of courses and even entire academic programs were initiated and conducted by students. The so-called "free universities" represented the extreme and culminating outcome of this movement toward increased student autonomy and curricular control. Throughout the United States free universities sprung up with or without formal institutional affiliation or sanction. Students (and other community people) established curricula and conducted courses on a variety of topics. In some instances, the free universities were only free in terms of the spirit of the program. Students had to pay tuition, just as they would if they enrolled in a private college. Concerns about finances, facilities, and faculty soon forced many of these free universities into a state of premature respectability— which led to their demise.

While the free university movement often yielded bizarre and counterproductive results, it is unfortunate that many significant learnings from this movement were lost in the counter movement back to more traditional educational models. The free university movement, for instance, provided its participating "faculty" with invaluable experiences in curricular planning, management, marketing, and teaching. Few colleges provide students with this type of practical (yet sheltered) experience. Temporary educational simulations (described in Chapter Five) closely resemble the free university in their encouragement of significant learning concerning the formation of a new institution, program, or course. We should not let the valuable lessons of the late 1960s pass us by, but should instead seek to identify those attributes of the free university movement that are appropriate to our current educational institution and those types of learnings that are particularly responsive to the unique educational needs of college students in the 1980s. Any student-based method of instruction might benefit from such an examination.

E. General Observations about Student-Based Methods

In responding to the increasingly diverse needs of students, a faculty member must be a competent juggler who can work simultaneously with individualized time, place, format, modes of instruction, modes of evaluation, and so forth. A student-based faculty member must have access to a large pool of information about community (on- and off-campus) educational resources, as well as become fully acquainted with the particular styles, skills, and motivations of each student being served. Not all faculty are prepared or willing to devote detailed attention to students through the use of tutorials, independent study programs, learning contracts, or field placements. Not many colleges or universities, furthermore, offer the organizational flexibility or latitude that will enable students to formulate and/or run their own courses and programs.

Faculty who are moving into student-based instruction may need to engage in professional development programs that not only introduce faculty to new student-based methods, but also help the faculty member to explore his own attitudes regarding loss of some control over the instructional process. Tom Clark offers some excellent suggestions regarding faculty development in student-based instructional settings in Chapter Six of Lindquist's *Designing Teaching Improvement Programs.*[4]

The movement toward student-generated or student-taught courses and, for that matter, toward increased use of field placements, requires attention to organization development issues. Just as many faculty will express some reservatons about losing some control over the instructional process in one-on-one relationships with students, so will they express reservations about losing control over an entire course. New organizational structures may have to be established which enable students to gain increased control over at least one or two courses without the faculty having to abandon control over a major portion of the curriculum. As American colleges and universities confront an increasingly older and more sophisticated student population, faculty in these institutions will need to become increasingly prepared to offer student-based instruction and give these students greater curricular control.

NOTES:

[1]Under a grant from the Carnegie Foundation for the Advancement of Teaching, the College of Wooster conducted a study of independent study programs in the United States during the late 1950s. The results of this research project are presented in

Robert Bonthius, James Davis, and J. Garber Drushal's *The Independent Study Program in the United States* (New York: Columbia College Press, 1957). Those conducting the research defined independent study programs as follows:

> An independent study program is one which provides a formal opportunity on an institution-wide basis for the pursuit of special topics or projects by individual students, under the guidance of faculty advisers from organized courses, for honors only or for credit toward graduation, available to students who meet certain requirements or required of all students [p. 9].

They found that independent study programs have a long history in American higher education and that as of the late 1950s, more than one-fourth of the four-year undergraduate colleges in the United States had an institution-wide required or voluntary program of independent study. This percentage has no doubt increased since that time. In most colleges and universities there are also special category courses (such as "Special Problems in Biology"), which also include, at least informally, independent study components.

[2]Thomas Clark, "Creating Contract Learning," in Ohmer Milton, *On College Teaching* (San Francisco: Jossey-Bass, 1978), p. 213, summarizes the contract learning process as follows:

> The contract process is one in which two individuals—a faculty member and a student—negotiate about teaching and learning. The process begins with a discussion of who the student is, what the student's goals and objectives are, why the student wants to study particular content and skill areas, how the learning will be accomplished, what resources will be employed, how the learning will be evaluated, and how much credit will be awarded. Similarly, the faculty member indicates what expertness he or she possesses, the alternative ways in which the learning can be accomplished, alternative resources that may be employed, and what level of student performance is expected. The process assumes that there are two active participants—not an active teacher and a passive student. This transaction between student and faculty member is the essential component of contracting.
>
> The outcome of this process is a written agreement, usually called the learning contract. Although institutional practices vary somewhat, most learning contracts have four parts. These are descriptions of: (1) the student's long-range purposes, goals, or objectives, (2) the student's specific objectives for the period of time in which the particular contract is in effect, (3) the learning activities in which the student will engage, including a description of the content and/or skills to be mastered and the mode of study to be employed, a designation of what learning resources will be used, and the amount of credit the institution will award upon satisfactory completion of the learning activities, and (4) the methods and criteria or standards that will be used to evaluate the student's performance.

[3]John Duley, in his "Editor's Notes" to *Implementing Field Experience Education* (San Francisco: Jossey-Bass, 1974), pp. vii–viii, identifies and briefly describes eight different types of field placement programs:

> *Cross-Cultural Experience.* A student involves himself in another culture or subculture of his own society in a deep and significant way, either as a temporary member of a family, a worker in that society, or as a volunteer in a social agency, with the intention, as a participant observer, of learning as much as he can about that culture and his own.
>
> *Professional Training.* A student serves in assigned responsibilties under the supervision of a professional in the field of education, medicine, law, social work, nursing, or ministry, putting the theory he has learned into practice, gaining skills in the profession, and being evaluated by his supervisor.
>
> *Institutional Analysis/Career Exploration.* "A student has a temporary period of supervised work that provides opportunities to develop skills, to test abilities and career interests, and to systematically examine institutional cultures in light of the central theoretical notions in a chosen academic field of study." (Zauderer, 1973, p. 1)
>
> *Work Experience (Cooperative Education).* "Cooperative Education is that education plan which integrates classroom experience and practical work experience in industrial, business, government, or service-type work situations in the community. The work experience constitutes a regular and essential element in the educative process and some minimum amount of work experience and minimum standard of successful performance on the job are included in the requirements of the institution for a degree." (The National Commission for Cooperative Education, 1971)
>
> *Service-Learning Internship.* "Service-learning has been defined as: the integration of the accomplishment of a task which meets human need with conscious educational growth. A service-learning internship is designed to provide students responsibility to meet a public need and a significant learning experience within a public or private institution for a specified period of time, usually 10 to 15 weeks." (Sigmon, 1972, p. 2)
>
> *Social/Political Action.* A student secures a placement, under faculty sponsorship, which gives him the opportunity to be directly engaged in working for social change either through community organizing, political activity, research/action projects, or work with organizations seeking to bring about changes in the social order. He also usually fulfills a learning contract made with his faculty sponsor.
>
> *Personal Growth and Development.* A student undertakes a program in an off-campus setting that is designed to further his personal growth and development, such as the wilderness survival programs of the Outward Bound Schools, or an apprenticeship to an artist or a craftsman, or residence in a monastery for the development of his spiritual life, or participation in an established group psychological or human relations program.
>
> *Field Research.* A student undertakes an independent or group research project in the field under the supervision of a faculty member, applying the concepts and methods of an academic discipline such as geology, archaeology, geography, or sociology.

[4]Jack Lindquist, ed. *Designing Teaching Improvement Programs* (Washington: Council for the Advancement of Small Colleges, 1978).

HANDOUT NUMBER ONE

TITLE: Learning Contracts

SOURCE: Adapted from Joan Creagar, *Alternatives in Science Teaching* (American Association for the Advancement of Science, 1973)

GENERAL DESCRIPTION: Many faculty are reluctant to experiment with learning contracts not because of lack of interest but rather because of limited information and examples. Once a department or even an individual faculty member tries out the process, successful examples and experiences will accumulate rapidly. The following handout is intended to supply the initial information needed to help move a faculty member from an interest in to the actual use of learning contracts.

INSTRUCTIONS FOR USE: Although "Learning Contracts" presents a self-contained discussion, it probably should not be used without comment. Instead, it should be distributed in a workshop or consultative setting in which faculty can have an opportunity to discuss and even try out learning contracts in terms of their particular disciplines and courses.

LEARNING CONTRACTS

Among various alternate approaches to teaching, the learning contract is perhaps one of the most potentially valuable. Since it can be used with a group of students as well as with individuals, and since it is not dependent on previously prepared learning "packages," modules, or technology, it generally proves more flexibility than other systems of individualized instruction. The following discussion will (1) describe the components of a learning contract, (2) describe the relationship between contractual learning and learning theory, (3) examine the preparation and use of learning contracts, (4) describe the role of the teacher in contractual learning, (5) discuss some problems of implementation, and (6) describe the components of an evaluation process.

The Learning Contract

A learning contract is an agreement between one or more students and a faculty member. A contract should include a learning goal and specific learning objectives. It can be written to meet the specialized needs of an individual student or a small group of students, or it can be written to describe the requirements of a course for a large number of students. If grading is a part of a learning system, the contract could specify what is required for each letter grade. Regardless of which of these circumstances apply, the students and the faculty member, by the terms of the contract, understand what is expected. Learning contracts provide an advantageous learning situation for students in that they are encouraged to have a say in the content of the contract in so far as their experience allows. The activity of stating a learning goal and determining how to accomplish it is a valid learning experience in and of itself. Beyond that, there is an important motivating factor involved in participating in defining one's own learning goals.

The learning goal is a statement of the overall purpose of the course or learning experience. The specific objectives to accomplish an overall goal should each include particular activities to be undertaken, resources to be used, and time limits to be met. Because this is a contract, the responsibilities of both the student and the faculty member should be specified for each objective. In addition, the criteria and procedures to be used in evaluating the level of performance on each objective should be specified at the time the contract is negotiated.

Finally, identifying information (name, address, and telephone number of the student and the faculty member, the title, mode of learning, credit hours, and beginning and ending dates for the course or learning experience) should be specified in the contract. Signatures agreeing to the contract and signatures certifying completion of the terms of the contract along with a grade, if appropriate, should be included. Appended to the contract should be a record of work accomplished and how it was evaluated.

Relationship of Contractual Learning to Learning Theory

While a learning contract can be negotiated for virtually any type of learning, the advantage of contractual learning is that students are actively involved in the learning process itself. Students can participate in defining learning goals and planning how to accomplish them. The process of negotiating a contract, along with the learning experiences involved in carrying it out, can lead to more insightful learning. Motivation also is strengthened by the student's participation in the planning of what is to be learned and how it is to be done.

How to Use Learning Contracts

A learning contract can be prepared for virtually any learning situation. In a traditional setting, the instructor could prepare a contract which contains a few options but largely reflects what the instructor expects the students to accomplish. While this does not allow the student the benefits of other modes discussed below, it does have the advantage of letting the students know what is expected. The act of signing a contract in which the responsibilities of both the student and the instructor are specified causes both parties to make a commitment to each other.

In the seminar situation more student participation is generally possible and student involvement in the planning of the seminar could be encouraged. The first sample contract presented at the end of this discussion illustrates that students can have a lot of latitude in determining how they will satisfy the course objectives even though the objectives may be defined by the instructor.

A contract for independent study could be prepared by the student and reviewed by a faculty member. In this case the planning process is largely the responsibility of the student, but the contract would not be signed unless the faculty member agreed to the terms of the contract. The fact that neither party signs a contract unless the terms are mutually agreeable prevents students from engaging in learning experiences that are not academically sound or that are not within the bounds of available resources and expertise.

An internship, which is a learning experience involving on-the-job training or some other form of practical experience, generally involves the approval of a faculty member and of an individual in the practical setting. The on-the-job supervisor would accept some responsibilities for the student's training and would agree to a contract only if the experiences described in the contract were actually available. The faculty member would give approval only if the contract specifies legitimate learning that is acceptable for academic credit.

These examples are probably not exhaustive of the kinds of experiences a student might propose. One of the advantages of contractual learning is that students have the freedom to prepare contracts for almost any variety of learning experience, but they must obtain faculty approval of the proposed experience before undertaking the activities.

An entire curriculum could be designed by a student and proposed in a series of learning contracts. This option allows maximum flexibility to the student. The provision that faculty approval must be obtained—that the goals of the experience must be mutually agreeable—prevents abuse of the contracting process.

The Role of the Teacher

In contractual learning the role of the teacher may be as traditional as in a formal class or as non-traditional as in the case of a student who proposes his own entire curriculum in a series of contracts. Traditionally, the teacher does all of the planning, provides all of the resources, and serves as the only evaluator. When this is the case, the role of the teacher remains quite traditional—and most of the advantages of the contract have been forfeited. In contractual learning where the student is involved in the planning process, the role of the teacher is to: (1) assist in the planning process by offering realistic counsel or finding someone with the expertise to counsel the student about what learning is necessary to meet his career or personal learning goals, (2) provide resources or help the student arrange for the use of resources, (3) serve as a human resource, (4) be a co-learner with the student in some instances, and (5) be one of the evaluators of the student's accomplishments. If students also engage in self-evaluation, as is often the case in contractual learning, the faculty member might assist the student in developing the ability to evaluate his own work. Whatever the responsibilities of the faculty member, they should be specified in the contract.

Problems of Implementation

One of the major problems in contractual learning is that when students are first given the opportunity to participate in the planning of their own learning experiences, they simply do not know how to say what they want or think they need. The solution to this problem is not for the faculty member to assume the responsibility for planning; rather, the student should be given the opportunity to learn to plan his own learning. Often a preliminary contract designed to offer the opportunity to explore many possibilities is what is needed for a student who seems not to know what he wants.

Another problem, which also reflects the student's lack of opportunities for experience, is the problem of the student who does not know how to evaluate his own work. Again, opportunities should be provided to engage in self-evaluation and to compare self-evaluations with the evaluations of several other people more experienced in a given subject area.

From the faculty member's point of view, there may be too many students doing too many different things at any one time. It takes experience in contractual learning (or any other mode that allows flexibility for the students) for a faculty member to learn to say no, not just because a proposed learning experience is not academically acceptable, but simply because the faculty member is overloaded. It is more considerate to a student to say, "Sorry, I don't have time to supervise that contract this term," than to agree to the contract and then not fulfill the agreed upon responsibilities.

Finally, procrastination is a problem that plagues both students and faculty members. If there are no meeting times or deadlines for certain activities specified in a contract, it is all too easy to let things ride. As long as there are courses with serious consequences for missing a deadline, the more flexible learning experiences will have second priority. To avoid procrastination contracts should have built-in deadlines for both the student and the faculty member. Problems with procrastination can be minimized by participants signing contracts only if they expect to find the activities inherently rewarding; people procrastinate less when they enjoy what they are doing.

Evaluation Procedures

The evaluation of contractual learning provides the opportunity and challenge of designing an evaluation procedure that applies to a learning situation involving a great variety of ways of learning. The student is involved in the evaluation process along with the faculty member. One of the failings of traditional education has been that it puts the faculty member in a position of being the only authority to pass judgment on a student's performance. While a faculty member's experience does give him a vantage point from which to evaluate a student's performance, if the student has no role in the evaluation process, he has no opportunity to learn to judge his performance. In this system each person involved in the contract (including on-the-job supervisors, where applicable) is involved in the evaluation process. Narrative evaluations are encouraged wherever possible. The following criteria are suggested as a checklist for the preparation of each evaluation.

Student Performance:

(1) Did the student complete the specific objectives? (Test results can be used here.)
(2) Did the experience contribute to the achievement of the stated learning goal?
(3) In which of the following cognitive and affective behaviors did the student demonstrate significant improvement and in which is improvement most needed?
   (a) careful judgments and critical thinking
   (b) interpretation of written materials, oral materials, non-verbal materials
   (c) oral and written communication
   (d) ability to analyze complex systems into their component parts and to perceive interactions
   (e) ability to synthesize information and ideas from various sources into coherent wholes
   (f) ability to evaluate information, project future possibilities, and make choices and commitments
   (g) ability to ask relevant questions
   (h) demonstration of creativity
   (i) demonstration of humaneness
(4) Is the student able to function as an independent learner?
(5) Did the student regularly prepare for and participate in group activities, if any?

Faculty member (and on-the-job supervisor, where applicable) performance:

(1) Did the person assist in planning?
(2) Did he facilitate student learning, including fostering of abilities listed in item (3) above?
(3) Was he accessible to the student when needed?
(4) Did he fulfill the responsibilities specified in the contract?
(5) Did he demonstrate:
   (a) ability to guide student to answers to relevant questions?
   (b) the quality of creativity?
   (c) the quality of humaneness?

Adequacy of the learning environment:
  (1) Was the environment conducive to learning?
  (2) Were the necessary resources provided? (including equipment, supplies, and facilities)

If a grade is to be given on the student's performance, each participant should indicate the grade he would recommend. Also, if there were any changes in the terms of the contract during its execution, the changes should be described and appended to the contract.

After each participant has prepared a narrative evaluation, the faculty member should determine whether there are discrepancies that should be resolved and, if so, should meet with the student (and supervisor, if applicable). In any case, students should be able to see the evaluations so that they can compare their self-evaluation with the other evaluation(s).

Sample Contracts

The following format is suggested to cover a variety of learning situations.

Learning Contract for _____
                         (course number and title or description of experience)

Credits_____   Mode of learning: Grading option:
                          ____formal course   ____objectives specify
Dates: ____seminar   letter grade
Beginning:_____ , 19 ___ ____independent study   ____pass-fail
Ending: _____ , 19 ___ ____internship   ____other: _____
                          ____other   Final grade: _____

Agreement between:

Student _____ phone_____ date_____ _____
                                                            (signature)

and

Faculty _____ phone_____ date_____ _____
                                                            (signature)

(Attach statement of learning goals and learning objectives.)
(Attach statement of evaluation.)

Completion signatures:

_____ date_____ and _____ date_____
      (student)   (faculty)

_____

Natural Science Contract

The following is a sample of the learning goal and objectives for a three-semester-hour seminar designed as an introduction to the natural sciences to be offered in three weeks on a "total immersion" basis.

Learning Goal: Develop a working knowledge of the scientific method and at least ten scientific principles by applying the method and principles to the design of an idealized human environment.

Learning Objectives:

A. Analyze the basic physical and biological needs of human beings by listing and describing at least six components of need that should be met by an ideal environment. This objective should be completed in writing by *day 3* of the seminar for discussion and evaluation by seminar participants.

B. Complete option 1 or 2:

1. Propose a consistent system of meeting the needs derived from objective A. Tasks necessary to accomplish this will include: (a) Read and interpret scientific literature pertinent to the problem and prepare a 3000-word annotated bibliography of readings, (b) apply problem-solving models (which will be demonstrated in seminar meetings) to the design of the system, (c) communicate orally to the seminar group and in writing (3000 words) the characteristics of your idealized environment, and (d) demonstrate the application of at least ten scientific principles in the operation of your environment (one-page summary appended to the paper from [c] should list and describe briefly the principles).

2. Select one factor of an idealized environment and complete items (a), (b), (c), and (d) above using a single factor. This objective should be completed by *day 10* of the seminar. The faculty member and students participating in the seminar will evaluate the degree to which each item is completed satisfactorily; they also will be concerned with the creativity, humaneness, and future projection demonstrated in the written and oral report.

C. (To be done concurrently with objective B.) Design and carry out an experiment using the scientific method to test the effects of one component of your ideal environment. Tasks to complete this objective: (a) background reading on scientific method, (b) consideration of principles of experimental design in designing your experiment, (c) careful observation during the carrying out of your experiment, and (d) thorough reporting of method, observations, and conclusions. This objective should be completed by *day 10*. The faculty member will evaluate the written report of your experiment according to the degree to which each of the above tasks was completed satisfactorily.

D. Present a 15-minute oral report on the results of your activities in this seminar sometime during *days 11–14* of the seminar. Reports will be evaluated by student peers according to the degree to which tasks described above were accomplished and according to the tasks described in objective E.

E. Apply the valuing theory (to be presented in the seminar) to the idealized environments described by each of the other participants in the seminar. This objective is to be accomplished during *days 11–14* of the seminar as the reports are given.

F. Complete an evaluation form about this learning experience on *day 15* and complete all procedures pertaining to the processing of the learning contract. *Syllabus to include:* Required and suggested readings on (a) scientific principles, (b) scientific method, (c) design of experiments, (d) problem solving, and (e) valuing.

Required Readings

Hypothesis, Prediction, and Implication in Biology (scientific method)
The Biosphere—A Scientific American Book (scientific principles)
*Science for Society—*A bibliography (a reference book)
Reprints on problem solving and valuing—to be distributed by faculty member, when needed.

Optional Readings

Design with Nature by McHarg
Concepts of Ecology by Kormondy
Ecology and Field Biology by Smith
Population, Resources and Environment by Ehrlich and Ehrlich
Environments in Profile by Kaill and Frey
The House We Live In by Blau and Rodenbeck
The Biological Time Bomb by Taylor
Man and the Environment by Jackson
The Environmental Handbook by DeBell
The Environment in Fortune (magazine)
Environmental Science Laboratory Manual by Strobe
Ecotactics by The Sierra Club
The Environmental Reader by Godfrey
The Year of the Whale by Scheffer
Under the Sea Wind by Carson
The Sea Around Us by Carson
The Edge of the Sea by Carson
No Deposit-No Return by Johnson
The Practice of Water Pollution Biology by U.S. Dept. of Interior
Nature Study for Conservation by Brainerd
Everyman's Guide to Ecological Living by Cailliet, Setzer and Love

---

The following is a sample of the learning goal and objectives for a traditional, graded survey of 18th century literature.

Learning Goal: Develop an understanding of the basic outlines of 18th century literature.

Learning Objectives:

A. Demonstrate understanding of the major works of Alexander Pope, Jonathan Swift, and Samuel Johnson.

B. Demonstrate a general familiarity with the more important works of three of the following minor writers: Matthew Prior, Bernard Mandeville, Richard Steele, Joseph Addison, John Gay, William Collins, Thomas Gray, Christopher Smart, Oliver Goldsmith, and William Cawper.

C. Demonstrate an understanding of the history of the 18th century as it relates to the literature of the period.

Evaluation:

Each student may contract for a desired grade. The following specific objectives are to be completed for a grade of C:

1. Attend class regularly and be prepared to discuss the works assigned on the enclosed day-to-day syllabus [not included in this sample contract].

2. Complete at a satisfactory level three 7- to 10-page papers, one each on the major works of Pope, Swift, and Johnson; dates for the completion of these papers are indicated on the syllabus. If, in the judgment of the instructor, any paper mentioned here or elsewhere is not executed at a satisfactory level, the paper will be returned for revision until that level is reached.

3. Complete at a satisfactory level two additional 8- to 10-page papers, one on your three chosen minor writers and one on the relationship of 18th century history to the literature of the period.

The following specific objectives are to be completed for a grade of B:

1. Complete at a satisfactory level all of the requirements for a C discussed above, with the exception of one of the major authors papers discussed in (2) below.

2. Complete at a satisfactory level an in-depth study of all of the major and a representative selection of minor works of either Pope, Swift, and Johnson; this study should culminate in a 20- to 25-page paper on that author (that paper to replace the shorter paper on that author under the requirements for a C discussed above).

The following specific objectives are to be completed for a grade of A:

1. Complete at a satisfactory level all of the requirements for a B discussed above, with the exception of the 20- to 25-page research paper.

2. Complete at a satisfactory level an in-depth comparison of two of the major authors of this period; this study will result in (a) a major (about 30-page) study of the two authors, and (b) a one-class period presentation and discussion of your findings to the class late in the semester.

HANDOUT NUMBER TWO

TITLE: Guidelines for Experience-Based Learning Journals

SOURCE: Adapted from a similar document developed by William Keeney, Bethel College, North Newton, Kansas

GENERAL DESCRIPTION: Although some students will have had experience with keeping a diary or journal, many will be unfamiliar and perhaps even uncomfortable with a formal journal, particularly one which is intended to demonstrate college-level learning. Yet for many students, a journal may be essential in providing an opportunity for the reflection and integration necessary to complete the experiential learning cycle. The following guidelines may be useful in suggesting areas for consideration as students set about the process of keeping a journal record of their learning.

INSTRUCTIONS FOR USE: These guidelines should be discussed in detail with students prior to the beginning of their learning experience and agreement should be reached concerning which specific aspects of a particular experience are to be emphasized or addressed. If the material is not too personal, copies of previous journals based on these guidelines should be provided as examples.

GUIDELINES FOR AN EXPERIENCE-BASED LEARNING JOURNAL

Experience is not learning. To learn from experience, you should engage in description, analysis, reflection, interpretation, and evaluation. A journal or periodic report can assist in that process. Journals need not cover every phase of your experience, but they should show the major learnings and elements that went into that experience. Normally, entries should be made in the journal at least weekly. The following guidelines are intended to suggest areas for consideration and reflection as you keep your experience-based learning journal.

1. You should enter an experience with goals and expectations. It would be helpful to articulate these as you consider an experience. They may be in terms of (a) work and living experiences, (b) personal satisfactions or growth, (c) learning possibilities, or (d) skills development.
2. If you worked in an organization, describe your position.
   A. Your title or the title of the job or assignment you had.
      Name of your immediate supervisor.
      Position of your job or assignment in relation to others in the organization.
      Describe the assignment.
      In what way will the assignment contribute to your long-range career plans?
      What are your ideas or plans for a career? Are they changing or being reinforced?
   B. The Work Environment
      Would you describe the work environment as pleasant, tough, neutral, threatening?
      Do others appear to be happy?
      Do people make suggestions to their supervisors or superiors?
      Do they feel that management hears their complaints?
      Can you give examples of listening or not listening?
      Do any of the people appear bored or restless? If so, how could that be eliminated?
      What do you do to counteract boredom?
   C. The Personnel
      How many people are working in the organization?
      Describe them: age, sex, background.
      Describe the organizational structure (perhaps you can get an organization chart). What are the number of levels between the top position and the lowest?
      Are the workers organized into a union or its equivalent? If so, briefly describe the union or organization.
3. Skills Development
   A. What new skills are you acquiring?
   B. What skills already acquired are you reinforcing? Consider the full range of human skills: manual, technical, communication (speaking, listening, reading, writing), artistic, interpersonal, social, or political.

4. Self-Understanding
   A. How does this experience affect your understanding of yourself?
       Your relationship with others? Your further education and experience?
   B. How does your experience affect your value commitments, a life philosophy,
       your religious life?
   C. What is your evaluation of your motivations, your competence?
   D. Have you learned of new strengths or weaknesses? Are there areas you have
       discovered to work on?
5. Cross-Cultural Experiences
   A. If you are working with people of other races, nationalities, religions, etc.,
       what problems have you met in trying to adjust to their values, their ways of
       doing things, their expectations of themselves and you?
   B. Where do you find their ideas, attitudes, morals, etc., better or more
       dysfunctional than your own?
   C. How do you react to what is different? Can you appreciate variety or do you
       prefer the familiar and routine?
6. Academic Experiences
   A. How does your experience connect with any of your past or present studies in
       providing realistic meaning or understanding of them? (Consider both general
       education studies and specialized studies in your major field.)
   B. What new knowledge are you acquiring: (a) of personal value, (b) about the
       world in general, (c) as additions to your field of study or career possibilities?
   C. Have you developed in new disciplines for learning, for managing your time,
       for self-motivation? Have you found any new problem areas you want to
       pursue further? Will the experience affect your choice of courses in the
       future? If so, how?
7. Evaluation
   A. You may want to revise your goals or expectations periodically. Some people
       suggest setting goals a year at a time and then reviewing objectives a month at
       a time to see how you are meeting goals and expectations. For those in an
       assignment longer than six months, perhaps some review should take place
       every six months or mid-way in your experience if it is less than a year.
   B. How could your experience be more beneficial? What are the major negative
       aspects of the experience? How much depends on you, on the situation, on
       others with whom you work and live, on your supervisors?
   C. What suggestions would you have for improving the program in which you are
       participating? What suggestions do you have to pass on to your employer or to
       the organization where you are working?
   D. What suggestions would you make to another student who might be
       considering this job or assignment in the future?
   E. Describe any specific problem situations arising during your work
       experience—not necessarily involving you, but within range of your
       operation—which were of educational import and how they were resolved.
   F. Indicate ideas, suggestions, questions you have in mind as you look forward to
       your next job or assignment.

Chapter Five

Interaction-Based Instructional Methods

A. Seminar/Discussion

With lectures and tutorials, seminars and discussion groups form the historical base for contemporary college teaching. Most of the other interaction-based instructional methods derive from the seminar and discussion group format[1]—at least for instruction in the humanities. Laboratories and studios provide comparable bases for faculty in the sciences and arts. An effective seminar provides an environment in which faculty and students can interact openly to discuss issues, problems, and perspectives that do not lend themselves to easy resolution or solution. A seminar is usually ineffective, first, when the faculty member wishes to use it as a forum for the dissemination of specific information or for the promotion of particular perspectives or solutions to particular problems (the content-based methods described in Chapter Three are more appropriate for these latter goals), or, second, when the faculty member uses this setting as a vehicle for encouraging student control of the instructional process (student control is more successfully incorporated in the individualized methods discussed in Chapter Four).

As designer and facilitator, as well as resource person, a faculty member can contribute a great deal to the interactive processes of a seminar or discussion group. As the designer of such a class, he can encourage a discussion process that is both thoughtful and interesting, creative and systematic, and that enhances everyone's sense of his own worth as a contributor to this process. Several designs have been found to be particularly successful in meeting these objectives.

Seminars can be designed so that each student has an equal opportunity to participate. This is usually done by asking each student to lead the discussion for one session or to present a brief paper or oral report. While this method can be quite successful, it tends to put a single student on the spot (with accompanying performance anxiety) and does nothing to address the problem of different rates of participation from class to class on the part of other members of the seminar. Equal rates of participation can be encouraged by periodically surveying the total seminar group to elicit each member's reactions to an idea, or by occasionally asking the seminar to break into two-person groups, so that each member of the seminar can convey his ideas to at least one other person.

The verbal contributions of group members also can be controlled. Each group member can be limited to a certain number of verbal presentations that last for more than one minute. At the end of each seminar (or at a mid-point in a seminar session) the most verbally active member can be asked to remain quiet for the next session (or remainder of the current session). Alternatively, after any one member of the seminar has spoken, he can select the next person to speak. The selected person then can either present his own ideas and then select another person, or pass to another person. While this type of constraint on the flow of conversation in a seminar may seem artificial and even arbitrary, it can be done with grace and humor as a way of encouraging the participation of less vocal members. No method, however, should be employed which *requires* a silent member to contribute on a regular basis. Such methods are threatening and rarely enhance anyone's learning.

Unfortunately, methods that merely encourage equal distribution of discussion in a seminar rarely elevate the quality of discussion. A tool called "synectics" (which is briefly described in Chapter Six of the second volume of this series) can enhance the quality as well as the equity of seminar discussions. Under synectics guidelines, a seminar participant is requested to paraphrase the central idea presented by the last speaker to talk and to indicate at least three positive features of this idea before stating his own idea or criticizing the idea of the previous speaker. Synectics guidelines encourage active listening, constructive reactions to ideas, and intellectual interaction. Since seminar participants who are verbally overactive often do not listen or build on the ideas of other participants, synectics also will discourage overactive participation. More extensive discussion of synectics can be found in William J. Gordon's *Synectics*.[2]

Whereas synectics encourages convergent thinking, several other group techniques enhance the quality and equity of discussion by encouraging divergent, creative thinking. Brainstorming is the most popular of these techniques and is briefly described and discussed in Chapter Six of Volume 2 of the faculty development handbook. Charles Clark's *Brainstorming* provides a rather popularized, yet detailed exposition of this type of technique. Another tool, called divergent delphi, also is described in Chapter Six of Volume 2. While synectics, brainstorming, and divergent delphi are described in the second volume in relationship to consultation on course design, they are equally appropriate in seminar settings.

Handout Number Three in the first volume of this series contains several other design suggestions for facilitating classroom discussion. We will expand on several of these suggestions. First, as Patricia Barnes-McConnell suggests, all students in a discussion group

> should have at least one, preferably multiple, common experiences or frames of reference from which to begin. Examples include a written common experience such as a case history, a story, a report, a news article, a book, and so on, the reading of which is required of all students. It might be a class handout or work assignment. A common verbal experience might be a lecture, a speech, a guest presentation, or a panel. Movies, slide shows, television programs, or media interviews are common audio-visual experiences. A common simulated experience might be a role-playing session or a simulation game, and a common real-life experience might be participation in a community research survey, individually assigned visits to community agencies, group field trips, or observation of some community activity.[3]

In a recent, striking example of this, the noted anthropologist and systems theorist, Gregory Bateson, has described a class in which he began by placing a crab shell on a table. The participants in this class were to determine how they would know this had once been a living thing if they had come from another planet. A discussion also can be designed, of course, around a debate or adversarial format.

We have suggested that a faculty member can serve as facilitator and resource person, as well as designer of a seminar session. As the facilitator, a seminar leader should make use of and model all the interpersonal skills and techniques that we have described and discussed in the previous two volumes: using paraphrase, giving constructive feedback, describing feelings, observing and analyzing decision-making processes, analyzing problems, and so forth. These skills and techniques—as well as several others—are considered in Sections III and IV of Volume 1 and Chapters Eight and Nine of Volume 2. Many seminar leaders seem to find paraphrasing and constructive feedback (Volume 1, Handouts Nine and Ten) to be particularly important. As the facilitator of a complex interpersonal process, a collegiate seminar leader also should give serious consideration to participation in the teaching improvement process that is described in Chapter Four of Volume 1 and Chapter 5 of Volume 2.

As a resource person, the faculty member who is leading a seminar should keep several things in mind. First, there is a fine line between a resource and a lecturer. A faculty member must keep in mind that resources (historical information, bibliographic references, quotations, alternative points of view, etc.) are only of value in a seminar if they enhance group discussion. The resources are used in a seminar as a means, not as an end in themselves. A faculty member should avoid providing resources to a seminar group if one or more student participants can provide them instead.

Second, a faculty member must avoid getting trapped into the expert role when conducting a seminar. Often it is advisable to ask another faculty member or student who is familiar with the topic at hand to attend the seminar as an expert guest. This frees the faculty member to serve as facilitator and mediate between the guest and seminar participants. The facilitator ensures that the guest's contributions are heard and used, yet do not dominate the group's discussion. Exercise Number Three can provide a useful way for considering the use of information and control in small groups.

Alternatively, the faculty member can begin the seminar with a brief lecture in which important background information is conveyed. He then changes roles to become a discussion facilitator. The background information might be inserted instead into a seminar after discussion has continued for 30 minutes to an hour. Background information often will distract a seminar group and hinder open and free discussion. A faculty member sometimes can tailor his presentation or background information more effectively and efficiently if his is first given an opportunity to listen to the seminar discussion for a few minutes.

Third, resources should be presented as neutrally as possible. A faculty member usually holds a distinct advantage over student seminar participants; simply put, he knows more about the topic than they do. If the background information is presented to bolster an argument being made by the faculty member rather than to enrich a discussion, the faculty member's intervention as a resource person is likely to evoke resentment or a sense of failure on the part of the students and result in less open and enthusiastic discussion. The faculty member should limit and balance informational interventions so that the background material that is presented cannot be used exclusively by students on one side of an argument. Since a seminar or discussion group should be addressing a topic or problem that does not have a single or obvious solution, a faculty member should not feel he is forfeiting academic integrity by being careful that he is equitably reinforcing all sides of an argument or a variety of alternative solutions to a problem.

B. Laboratory/Studio

As is the case with most interaction-based methods of instruction, there always is a lingering temptation for the scientist to make use of the laboratory and, to a lesser extent, for the artist to make use of the studio as a place in which to teach specific subject matter. When the laboratory or studio becomes a tool for content-based instruction, it loses its vitality and purpose. Even though the outcomes of almost any contemporary laboratory experiment are known to the instructor, and even though the student is being asked to learn specific laboratory skills, there is still room for ingenuity and individual diversity in the way in which the student conducts the investigation, analyzes the resulting data, and writes up his report. If the student is merely walking step by step through a laboratory "cookbook," the value of the laboratory should be questioned; much more efficient ways exist in which to learn about specific steps that have been taken in the past to solve certain problems or scientific puzzles. Science faculty can overcome the problem of "dry labs," however, by making the laboratory experiements interesting and a bit open-ended.

The biological, physicial, and behavioral scientists should not lay exclusive claim to the laboratory. This mode of instruction should be available to all faculty, in all disciplines. What would a philosophy laboratory look like? How might an historian or art professor make use of a laboratory experience in teaching American history or introduction to painting? One of the greatest services that a faculty development practitioner can provide is linkage between faculty in the arts and humanities, on the one hand, and the sciences on the other. So-called "traditional" faculty in physics, biology, or psychology, who have had years of experience in designing and running laboratory-based courses, can assist other faculty in the "innovative" use of laboratory procedures in other disciplines. This linkage not only aides the course design process, but also helps to break down the long-standing barrier between C. P. Snow's "two cultures." Such collaboration also may encourage the science faculty member to change his own self-definition as a "traditional" instructor, thereby opening him up to the consideration of other methodologies in his own classroom.

What might a laboratory look like in the humanities or arts? Several areas lend themselves readily to the laboratory. Logic can easily be taught in a laboratory setting as can historiography. An English literature course on the contemporary novel might include a "laboratory" in which students are given separate lines from a single poem with which they are not familiar and asked to reconstruct the poem as they think the author wrote it. A painting laboratory might require a student to examine systematically the visual and aesthetic effect of several different types of brushstrokes or the predominant use of dark colors at the top or bottom of a still life or landscape.

In a similar manner, the traditional barriers between the arts and other academic disciplines can be crossed by asking non-art faculty to consider the use of studio instruction in one or more of their courses. What does the art or music professor do in the studio that also can done with comparable impact in other disciplines? How, for instance, does the art professor encourage the student to work on technical skills at one moment, greater creativity the next? To do this, several art faculty might be videotaped in the studio, then asked to comment on what happened, with the commentary perhaps being dubbed in on the videotape. A faculty seminar on "the use of studio learning outside the arts" could then be conducted, with faculty from inside and outside the arts

113

watching and listening to the videotape and accompanying commentary. Discussion would ensue concerning the ways in which the art (and non-art) faculty encourage and balance off technical skills acquisition and creativity. The seminar might conclude with some consideration of specific ways in which a studio could be established in a non-art course.

Discussions concerning the use of laboratories and studios outside the sciences and arts reveal underlying scheduling and resource problems that confront any faculty member in the humanities (as well as in many of the behavioral sciences and arts) who attempt to use an interaction-based instructional method in their teaching. There is a long-standing precedent for science courses to include laboratories and creative/performing arts courses to include studios. Furthermore, there is a precedent for these laboratories and studios to be scheduled for two- to three-hour blocks of time and for other courses not to be scheduled during lab and studio hours (often Tuesday and Thursday afternoons). Often the laboratory or studio is reserved for one course. Each student in the lab or studio often has a desk, cabinet, or shelf space where he can keep work-in-progress. Perhaps most important, the lab or studio instructor often is given more hours to work with his students than are other instructors, because lab or studio work is considered equivalent to homework in other classes. Hence, a biology course might meet for seven hours per week (three hours of lecture and four hours of lab), yet generate the same amount of credit as a literature course that meets for only three or four hours per week. Even if the biology instructor is able to give one extra hour of academic credit for the lab, this hour of credit is being given for a disproportionately large number of contact hours.

If faculty in the humanities and behavioral sciences are to make use of interactive methods, then like their colleagues in the sciences and arts, they must be able to design their courses in three- to four-hour blocks of time that are not in conflict with a large number of other courses. Interaction-based courses also should be held in rooms that provide permanent work space (or at least storage space) for students, so that they might continue project work from day to day.

Humanities and behavioral science faculty must be able to compete for course credits on an equitable basis with science and arts faculty. There should be humanities and behavioral science "laboratories" or "studios" that count as homework equivalents. Alternatively, each course should include a laboratory or studio option that is assigned an extra unit of credit. Unless every faculty member is provided with flexible scheduling capabilities, appropriate work and storage space, and equitable credit arrangements, many of the interaction-based methods to be described in this chapter will be inaccessible to faculty in many disciplines.

C. Symposium/Debate

Deliberation and debate is a long-standing tradition in the history of collegiate education. In American higher education this tradition is evident in the debating societies that played a central role in the intellectual and social lives of many students during the 19th and early 20th centuries. It also is evident, though more subtly, in the contemporary emphasis in American higher education on the development of analytic and critical skills. There is less of a tradition in American higher education for the symposium, though this mode of instruction has a long history and is accepted as a valid and even laudable instructional method by most faculty members in American collegiate institutions.

Typically, a symposium involves three or more panelists and an audience. The panelists may make formal presentations of 30 minutes or more, may make only a few opening comments, or may begin with no formal statement. The essence of an exciting and provocative symposium usually is not the opening comments, but rather the discussion that takes place among panelists or between panelists and members of the audience. Those symposia that tend to emphasize the opening comments by the panelists often seem to neglect the primary characteristic of the symposium, namely, the presence of several experts or articulate spokesmen for a specific perspective in one place at one point in time. If the panelists are not given ample time to interact, one wonders why they were brought together in the first place.

Colleges frequently conduct symposia outside the formal academic course schedule. Many colleges and universities, for instance, offer one or more special thematic conferences each year during which several symposia are conducted. An assumption often is made in planning for and funding such symposia that they offer extraordinary educational opportunities for students, faculty, and other members of the academic community (as well as bringing some visibility and even increased credibility to the college or university). One might challenge the assumption, however, that institution-wide symposia hold much educational value. Students (and faculty) rarely are provided with any background information—let alone courses—to prepare for the symposium. Ideally, a series of "in-house" educational activities should precede an institution-wide symposium for participants to benefit fully from the viewpoints being presented. Furthermore, several educational events should be scheduled after the symposium, so that the rich offerings can be discussed and digested fully. Videotapes of the presentations and discussion, for instance, might be viewed and discussed by groups of students and faculty after the event. If the symposium is of a general nature it might even be discussed for one term in many of the courses being taught at the college or university. In this way the topics of the symposium can be viewed from a variety of disciplinary perspectives.

The symposium mode of instruction should not be restricted to institution-wide events, but instead should be brought into individual courses. There is no reason why a faculty member couldn't invite several of his colleagues, knowledgeable members of the local community, or knowledgeable students to serve as members of a symposium panel. Team-teaching (an instructional method to which we turn shortly) need not be restricted to the formal assignment of two or more faculty members to one course. A faculty member who is officially responsible for a course can ask colleagues to join him for one or more symposia. While most faculty are aware of this option, it is used suprisingly rarely.

Another way in which symposia can be employed centers on the relationship between courses that are taken by students to meet distribution requirements for graduation. If a cluster of courses all can fulfill distribution requirements in one area (such as foreign language proficiency, critical thinking, or math literacy), a "cross-course symposium might be held each term for students enrolled in each of these courses. This symposium itself might involve faculty from each course, other faculty at the institution, or outside experts. The symposium would address a theme that in some way integrates or at least temporarily draws together these separate courses. A symposium on the nature of language and culture, for instance, might involve all students who are taking a foreign language course (or computer science course) to meet a distribution requirment. Similarly, a symposium on "alienation and modern man" or some similar theme may be required of all students taking humanities courses to meet a distribution requirement in Western civilization.

This type of integrating symposium can be of value not only as a compromise between a standard required core curriculum and distribution requirements, but also as an annual or semi-annual faculty development activity, for it encourages interdisciplinary and integrative thinking and discussions and research among those faculty who must prepare for the symposium. With minimal additional time or money, most colleges and universities with distribution requirements in their general education program can improve the overall quality of this program (and faculty teaching in this program) through the use of cross-course symposia.

In recent years, debates, like symposia, have been conducted outside the confines of specific courses. Many colleges and universities support intercollegiate debate teams or sponsor intramural debates on contemporary issues. Debates also could be employed more frequently in many courses. In making use of debates in the classroom, the ultimate "neutrality" of the debate must be preserved. An effective debater should be able to argue on either side of an issue. He should be able to identify the strengths and weaknesses of any position and recognize the validity of multiple perspectives on an issue or problem. Two students in a course, for instance, might be given the assignment of researching both sides to a particular issue. When beginning the debate, a flip of the coin is used to assign sides. In this way, students grow to appreciate the complexity of intellectual issues and the inherent danger of simplistic thinking.

A debate should have one or more judges to assess the relative worth of each debater's argument. Often the role of judge can be as full of learning as the role of debater. A panel of student judges can be assigned the task of weighing both sets of arguments presented by the debaters. Critical faculties obviously must be brought to bear in making a decision. Just as students who are working on a case study must ultimately make a difficult decision when faced with a wealth of conflicting data, so must the debate judges make a difficult decision while faced with complexity. After making a decision, the judges also are faced with the task of communicating their reasons for the decision and of providing each debater with constructive feedback concerning his performance.

A classroom debate often can be enriched and enlivened by setting the debate in an historic context. A debate on fishing rights in the Atlantic ocean, for instance, can be enhanced by asking students in the class to imagine that this is an international hearing at the United Nations. Students might be asked to read recent United Nations reports. The specific topics of debate might be extracted directly from an actual hearing. Similarly, a theological debate might be set hypothetically in a Dayton, Tennessee courtroom, the papal chambers, or a Buddhist monastery. A debate need not be conducted as a sterile, intellectual exercise, for it can potentially involve issues of historical or contemporary importance.

D. Team Teaching

One might argue that team-teaching is not an instructional method but rather a description of the instructional resources available in a course. "Team-teaching" implies

116

that there are two or more faculty members formally assigned to teach a course. Yet, team-teaching is more than this—or at least should be more. Simply to put two or more faculty members in a classroom together is not enough to ensure that the learning of students or faculty will be enhanced. Most team teaching, in fact, either operates on a rotational basis or involves the domination of a seminar by two or more faculty. The first instance is in essence a traditional course taught by two faculty; while the second may be exciting for the faculty, very little real communication may be taking place between them and students.

Effective team-teaching always involves a complex and often tenuous balance among three parties: Faculty Member A, Faculty Member B, and the students. Central to such a complex balance is the relationship between the faculty members involved. Each should have an understanding of the other's educational philosophy, teaching style, and intellectual assumptions. Often, this information only emerges gradually over the semester or term. Instrument Number One, "Team Teaching Inventory" can be used profitably to accelerate this process before the course begins. Unneeded conflict between faculty can undermine a team-teaching effort seriously and, with a little investment of time at the outset, often can be avoided.

The relationship between each faculty member and the students is, however, perhaps just as important as the relationship among the faculty themselves. The three parties in a team-teaching situation can relate in a variety of ways. One faculty member can preside, with the second serving as a monitor, mediator, or discussion facilitator. The presiding faculty member may be the content expert—allowing the second faculty member to attend extensively to interpersonal aspects of the classroom. Who isn't being heard? How do we encourage the quiet students? What can be done to elevate the level of trust or increase risk-taking behavior in this classroom? Ideally, these roles will be reversed frequently, so that each faculty member can attend primarily to the content at times and at other times to the process.

Alternatively, one of the faculty members can serve as the "teacher" for one or more segments of the course, while the second faculty member serves as a "master learner." In the latter role, a faculty member is tackling a new area of study (not just "faking it"). The faculty member works alongside the students in learning new knowledge and skills. As a master learner, the faculty member models the skills of learning-how-to-learn, facilitates group discussion, asks "foolish" questions like any student, and becomes acquainted with students in a new way and from a new perspective. The "master learner" concept is valuable as an instructional technique and as a vehicle for continuing faculty development.

A third possible relationship between team-teaching faculty and students leads us into role-playing and back to debate. Each of the faculty members assumes a particular role as a specific historical figure or as a spokesman for a specific school of thought. Each role might be played consistently by one faculty member throughout a term, or faculty members may shift roles. In a team-taught course on "Psychology and Society," for instance, one professor might represent a Skinnerian perspective on society throughout the course, while a second professor might represent a perspective that Carl Rogers would take. Since both the faculty members and students might weary of each professor consistently playing one role, the two might switch roles periodically. The students also might assume certain roles which complement those being played by the faculty team.

From week to week, members of the faculty team might assume new roles that are appropriate to the different topics being addressed. In a philosophy course, for instance, two faculty members initially might assume the roles and philosophical positions of Socrates and Aristotle. At a later point, they might assume other complementary roles as famous philosophers or theologians or representatives of major schools of thought. As we shall note more fully later, these roles need not be played in a dramatic manner. Costumes, mannerisms, and other "theatrical" aspects of a role need not be used. The faculty member need only attempt to present the intellectual perspective and spirit of the person or school being represented. Team-teaching which incorporates role playing, the master learner concept, or the mediator/facilitator function can yield rich learning experiences for students that usually are inaccessible to the faculty member who teaches alone.

E. Case Study/Socratic Method

An unfortunate consequence of the typical isolation of professional schools from undergraduate education is the failure of most liberal arts faculty members to understand and appreciate the potential use of instructional methods being used in professional schools. The case study method, which is used extensively in business schools and in some law schools, and the "Socratic" method, which is used in many different forms in most law schools, are appropriate for instruction in any discipline. While the two methods are quite similar, the case study method usually involves more preparation by the student before the start of a class session.

The case study method is associated most closely with the Harvard University School of Business, though it is used in most graduate schools of business and management. Charles Fisher describes the case study method as follows:

> A case study may be defined as the factual account of human experience centered in a problem or issue faced by a person, a group of persons, or an organization. It describes real situations in real settings that require or suggest the need for discretionary action. The case study method, then, is the process of using this written case to effect learning by involving the participant in at least three interdependent stages of activity: reading and contemplating the case by oneself; analyzing and discussing the case with others in a group session or sessions; and subsequent reflection upon the case, the discussion, and his or her own attitudes and behavior.[4]

This case study method is clearly suitable for a variety of students and disciplines. Four features are usually critical in planning for and conducting a case study.

First, the case itself must be prepared carefully. Some say that effective case writing is an art. It certainly involves highly sophisticated skills of analysis, synthesis, and communication.

> Typically, the beginning of a case study presents a brief overview of the problem or situation, thus involving the reader. The setting and other descriptive information follows. The facts are presented, either chronologically or else in a manner relating to salient aspects of the problem, so as to lead up to major decisions that must be made or to significant circumstances that require analysis and discretionary evaluation. Therefore, the ends are often left untied, with the outcome not known, the actions unjudged, and the motives not presumed. The participants are required

118

to make their own analyses and judgments, assessing for themselves the consequences or implications of various decisions or actions.[5]

In some instances, a case may be broken into two or more parts. The reader is given the first part of the case and asked to determine how he would solve a specific problem. At some later point he is given the second part of the case which describes the decision that actually was made in response to this problem. The reader can in this way compare his own proposed action to that actually taken. He often is then presented with a new or modified problem emerging from the actual action taken and asked once again to respond to this problem. This routine may be repeated three or four times if the case is rich and rather detailed or if it involves actions that were taken over a rather long period of time.

A case usually should be presented in no more than 20 to 30 pages (including documents). Longer cases tend to offer too much detail. Furthermore, they are inclined to be didactic rather than provocative. They are written in a manner than conveys important "lessons" about the case, rather than in a manner that allows the reader to derive his own lessons. An effective case will encourage reflection, deliberation, and discussion. It will not provide answers or even offer analysis. If carefully selected, the case will defy simple solutions or uni-dimensional analysis. The reader of a case should be confronted with a problem that can be approached from a number of different perspectives, each of which is valid and useful. Most cases close with a set of questions that have been formulated by the case writer or by others who have used the case. These questions serve as catalysts for deliberation and discussion, rather than serving as definitive statements about how the case should be approached. These questions often are just as important as the case itself.

When the case study method is applied outside schools of business, law, and public policy, the case may take on somewhat different form. In a literature course, for instance, the "case" may be the first half of a short story or play. The reader is asked to determine at this point how he thinks the story or play will or should proceed. The reader may be asked to predict or suggest the future course for the development of a particular character, plot, or theme in the story or play. Comparisons then can be drawn between the reader's predicted or suggested scenario for the remainder of the story or play, and the scenario that was actually developed by the author.

In other fields such as police science, psychotherapy, or nursing, the "case" may be a videotape. A particular scene is enacted up to a certain point. The tape is then stopped and the viewer is asked to indicate what action he would take at this particular point in time. The videotape is then continued, portraying one course of action and its consequences. In the natural or behavioral sciences, a case may consist of the first two-thirds of a research report. The introduction, methods (procedures), and results sections are included. The reader is asked to indicate what he would say in, and how he would organize, the discussion and conclusion sections of the report.

A second central feature of the case method concerns student preparation for the class discussion of a case. Students are asked not only to read a case, but also to prepare their responses (decisions) concerning actions to be taken, based on an analysis of the central features of the case. A student must be able to justify his actions; given the fact that a case should not have one "right" answer, the analysis and justification may be more important than the student's specific choice of actions.

119

In many instances, students not only prepare for the case separately but also as a member of a case study group or team. Small groups of students meet, perhaps with a tutor or teaching assistant, to discuss the case and to arrive at a consensus concerning actions to be taken. Some case instructors ask one of the case study groups to make the classroom presentation or to lead a discussion on the case. Others are primarily interested in the responses of individual students and use the case study groups only to refine student responses before they enter class.

A third central feature of the case study method is the way classroom discussions concerning the case are managed. At this point the interactive quality of the case method is particularly apparent. Instructors who come from a content-based perspective are also likely to run into trouble with these discussions. A case study should not be used if the instructor wishes to make a specific point. A short lecture, with illustrative examples, is more appropriate. A case instructor should encourage discussion and debate among the students. By his verbal and nonverbal probes and reactions, the instructor should encourage risk-taking behavior and divergent thinking. If students feel that the instructor has a particular solution in mind for the case, they will expend energy trying to figure out the instructor's preferences rather than their own.

Several strategies often are used to elicit substantial and vigorous case discussions. First, an instructor might ask one student or case study group to present one or more of the central "facts" of the case, then ask the rest of the class to discuss not only the validity of these facts but also their bearing on the decision to be made in this case. The instructor could then ask another student or group to present another set of facts, followed by a similar critique and discussion. The instructor might then turn to one or more students' or groups' decisions concerning the problem being confronted in the case and other students' comments and critiques concerning these decisions.

A case study instructor might instead encourage a more open and free-wheeling discussion of the case, structuring the students' deliberations more subtly through the use of questioning strategies and blackboard or flip-chart space. Before the class begins, the instructor determines the major categories within which the students' comments about the case are likely to fall. He assesses the various tracks that students are likely to take in successfully confronting the case, and identifies those tracks that often are filled with pitfalls and deadends. He sets aside various areas of the blackboard for specific categories of student response and develops questioning strategies that are likely to encourage student movement along successful trains of thought.

The instructor opens discussion with some general question (e.g., "What seems to be going on in this case?"). The students' responses to this question are placed at a particular location on the blackboard. The responses of other students are placed in other locations. Various spaces on the blackboard need not be labeled. Students may not even be aware of the instructor's classification scheme. The students will be aware, however, of the relationship among various ideas that are being presented by their colleagues. Some ideas will be clustered together. Other ideas will be located at opposite ends of the blackboard. Students will learn something about the analysis of a problem, as well as the synthesis of wide-ranging and seemingly disparate information by observing their instructor in action.

A fourth central feature of case methodology is somewhat more elusive. An effective case study destroys the traditional dichotomy between head and heart. It is truly an interactive method in that a student cannot sit back and speculate abstractly about

120

alternative courses of action. He must instead make a choice, placing his own values, conceptual skills, and even intuition on the line. Many students are uneasy when first confronting this aspect of the case methodology, for they are used to viewing the classroom as a world of ideas, rather than as a place of decisions and actions. Case studies consequently may be particularly appropriate in courses that are being offered to undergraduate or graduate students toward the end of their academic careers, for case studies enable students to experience the "real world" of decision-making and problem-solving while the resources (and protective shield) of the academic institution are still available. On the other hand, if presented and used in a careful and supportive manner, case studies can be quite valuable in the early years of college to help students explore the practical application of ideas and theories often missing in introductory courses.

The Socratic method, like a case study, forces a student to make difficult choices. In doing so the student is examining his own values, learning new conceptual skills, and gaining experience in the acquisition and distillation of complex and often contradictory information. Though the Socratic method has been used primarily in legal education, it is potentially of value in virtually any discipline. The Socratic method, as it is used in most contemporary law (and even philosophy) courses, only vaguely resembles the educational methods used by Socrates. Whereas Socrates was the primary speaker (his educational method might be described as an "interrupted monologue"), the contemporary "Socratic" instructor primarily makes use of open-ended or leading questions to provoke discussion among his students. Typically, the instructor poses a particular problem at the start of a class session to which students are to respond. How would you solve this problem? Why would you solve it in this manner? The instructor then will comment on or (more likely) ask other students to comment on the solution, ask for the student's rationale, or add something to the problem to change its character slightly so that students must reexamine the appropriateness of their earlier responses.

In a law course, an instructor might begin by describing a particular auto accident in which one driver is clearly at fault. The students are asked to make a decision regarding fault or financial responsibility, or both, or to argue for one or the other party. Specific principles of law can be applied to this case. The instructor may then add a complication to the case (e.g., noting that the driver who was not at fault had been drinking before the accident). Students must now grapple with this somewhat more complex problem, to which simple and straightforward principles may not apply. Typically, the instructor continues in this way, adding various "complicating" conditions to the case, which challenge his students to become problem-analyzers and solvers, rather than just memorizers of legal rules.

In a philosophy course, an instructor similarly might challenge his students by asking them to examine their own simplistic solutions to specific philosophical problems. Philosophy professors often use the Socratic method in challenging a student's definition of "fact" or "truth." Beginning with a simple hypothetical situation in which a student is asked to determine whether or not something is "true" (e.g., "Is it true that Columbus discovered America?"), the instructor may then challenge the students concerning their response to this situation ("What about the 'Indians' who met Columbus?" "Was there an 'America' when Columbus landed on San Salvador Island?" "What then did Columbus discover?" "Columbus' name was actually 'Christophero Columbo.' What does this imply about truth?") A student is asked to grapple with these complex conditions and in doing so to confront and perhaps modify his own concepts about "truth."

The Socratic method also is appropriate in other less obvious disciplines. A political science or economics professor might wish to use this method to help a student develop critical appreciation or healthy skepticism of current public policy. A nursing instructor may wish to use a Socratic dialogue to expand nursing students' awareness of different approaches to patient care or the effect of certain public or hospital policies on patients.

Faculty use of both the case study and Socratic methods of instruction holds significant faculty development implications. Neither method can be employed readily without the instructor's exposure to and training in its use. A faculty member who would like to make use of the case study method should sit in on business school courses being taught by this method. Similarly, an instructor who wishes to make use of the Socratic method should observe a variety of law courses in which this method is being used. More than a single session should be observed, for both methods are only fully appreciated when observed in use with several different kinds of problems and several different modes of student discussions.

Both the case study and Socratic methods can be taught fairly easily to faculty. A three- to five-day training workshop before the start of a fall term or, perhaps better, at the end of the spring term, will enable a group of faculty to begin making use of one or the other of these methods. If several faculty are trying out one of these methods at the same time, they can benefit from each other's experience. To encourage this sharing of experiences, as well as to provide follow-up training, occasional sessions of two to three hours should be scheduled during the year following the full workshop. Faculty members who participated in the workshop should be encouraged to sit in on each other's classes and meet after class to discuss the instructor's use of the case study or Socratic method.

F. In-Class Discussion

A class that is large or structured primarily around lectures and question-and-answer sessions need not exclude interaction-based methods. Several in-class discussion methods are particularly appropriate for use in conjunction with these classes, foremost of which are the so-called "buzz group" and "learning cell" methods. Both have been described briefly in Handout Number One of the first volume of this series, and the buzz group method has received more detailed attention in Handout Number Four of that same volume. We would like to convey a few additional ideas, however, about each method and its use in the classroom.

The buzz group (named after the "buzzing" sound generated by many groups of people talking at the same time) enables members of a class (especially a class of more than 20 students) to converse with one another and be heard and understood by at least a small number of student colleagues. Usually, when a faculty member attempts to elicit discussion in a large class, or in a class that is accustomed to his lecturing, most of the students are hesitant to speak. No one wants to make a fool of himself in front of a large number of people. Most students either remain quiet or risk a statement only when quite confident of its validity. Hence discussions tend to be either nonexistent or mundane. Those discussions that do occur tend to be directed primarily to the instructor, especially if he has just finished lecturing. A few students may be quite active in classroom discussion, but their contributions are not always helpful, nor does their often indiscriminate participation tend to encourage the participation of other students.

If the class is periodically broken up into small groups of five to seven students, discussion can take place readily. Students are more likely to talk in a small group setting among their peers. Furthermore, unorthodox ideas can be expressed in the relatively safe confines of the buzz group. These ideas also may be expressed more readily before the whole class by a spokesman for the group, for this person is conveying the ideas of anonymous members of the group rather than necessarily his own ideas. In a buzz group setting, each student will have sufficient "air-time" to present his own opinions and, if his ideas win the day, will usually have an opportunity to share them with the whole group as well. The overall quality of discussion in the classroom also is improved through the use of buzz groups. Only the best or most interesting ideas as a rule get expressed when the groups are asked to share their discussion outcomes. Mundane or ill-formed ideas generally are ignored in brief reporting-out sessions.

Some faculty find that these buzz groups—or "caucus" groups, as they are sometimes called—are not successful in eliciting discussion. This lack of success often can be attributed to one of several errors. First, the instructor might not have made clear what is to be discussed in the buzz group. Students should be given a specific question to answer, problem to solve, or issue to discuss. One or more groups also should be expected to report on the outcome of their discussion once the total class has been reconvened. If a group knows that it might be chosen, the discussion is likely to remain more focused and directly related to the topic at hand.

Second, the buzz group might have lasted too long. In most instances, buzz groups should meet for no more than 10 or 15 minutes. If a specific topic is being addressed and the group is small in size, this should be sufficient time. If the topic is particularly complex, the total class might convene after 15 minutes, with each group (or several groups) reporting on the outcomes of its discussion up to that point. With the best ideas from several other groups in mind, members of the class might then reconvene in their groups for another 10 or 15 minutes of discussion. In any 50-minute class period, buzz groups might meet for two 10- to 15-minute periods each followed by five- to ten-minute reporting periods and concluding with a five-minute summary or new statement of the question, problem, or issue by the instructor.

Third, some faculty run into logistical and related time problems by assigning groups to adjacent classrooms or to other areas of the building. A great deal of time is lost in moving from place to place, continuity is disrupted, and confusion prevails. These difficulties can be eliminated by asking all of the buzz groups to meet in the same classroom. The room may be noisy and students may initially have a hard time hearing each other. However, they soon learn how to listen, perhaps even more closely than in a quiet room. Furthermore, the noise level often adds excitement to the discussion. Students overhear fragments of other discussions, which leads to broader perspectives and adds continuity to their discussion. The one prerequisite to using buzz groups in a single classroom is that chairs must be placed in small circles, then turned toward the front of the classroom for general discussion. Buzz groups are hard to conduct in a single classroom when the chairs are bolted to the floor or can't be moved due to administrative policy.

Fourth, a faculty member may not have tried the buzz group a sufficient number of times before abandoning it. Students are not accustomed to this mode of instruction and hence often are uncomfortable in talking with fellow students in small groups. After three or four buzz group sessions, however, new buzz groups usually can be formed and underway in less than two minutes. The efficiency of buzz groups can be increased further by keeping membership in each buzz group constant, at least for a period of several weeks. Each group of students either always sits together (highly efficient but a bit regimented) or has its own place in the room. In the latter case, members of a group move to chairs in their designated place in the room whenever buzz groups are convened.

Several variations on the buzz group have been employed quite successfully. Each group can be assigned a particular school of thought or particular person in history. Whenever the class breaks into buzz groups, each group must tackle the question, problem, or issue posed by the instructor from the perspective of this particular school of thought or person. This technique is particularly effective when used in conjunction with faculty role-playing discussed below. Two additional variations on buzz groups may be found in Handout Number Three.

A learning cell, like a buzz group, relies heavily on peer learning. It differs from a buzz group in that the method is not used to facilitate small group discussions but rather to share information between two people, or among two or more groups of people. The usual learning cell consists of two people, one of whom has been given responsibility for learning one set of information, the other person being given responsibility for learning a second set of information. During class (or during a special session) the two students meet together as a learning cell to share information and, at times, to test each other on acquisition of this information. This sharing of information among students, based on selective reading by each student, often is done informally outside the classroom when a group of students form their own study groups, with each member of the group taking primary responsibility for one section of the course material to be covered. The learning cell legitimizes this sharing of ideas and brings it into the classroom.

A learning cell can be justified on several grounds. First, many faculty members are confronted with the ambitious goal of asking students to gain some general knowledge in a large number of areas and extensive knowledge in one or two areas. The learning cell fits nicely with this model, for a student can become quite knowledgeable in one or more areas. By teaching another student what he has learned, this student will gain even greater mastery of an area. In other areas, the student will acquire more limited knowledge. What he has acquired from a student colleague will be screened through this second student's own value system, experiences, and so forth.

Learning cells also can be justified as a vehicle for interaction and exchange of ideas. Each student has a chance to discuss and clarify ideas with a colleague. In this way, the learning cell serves a comparable function to the buzz group.

Third, the learning cell allows for alternate modes of testing. The "teacher" in a learning cell can be asked to draft a set of questions which will be given to the "learner." The teacher will be graded on the basis of the question he asks and on the basis of the learner's success in answering these questions. This form of grading reinforces cooperation rather than competition and constantly focuses on the learning of both students.

Several variations on the regular learning cell may be noted. First, a learning cell can comprise more than two people. For example, a learning cell might be composed of the same number of members as there are chapters in the major textbook for a course. The learning cell thus becomes a "human textbook." Each student reads the entire textbook, but concentrates on a specific chapter, doing additional reading, meeting with members of other learning cells who have been assigned the same chapter, and meeting with the instructor for formal help sessions. When any member of the learning cell has problems with a particular chapter, he obtains assistance from the cell's "expert" on this chapter. At the end of the term, when the students are reviewing for the final exam, each learning cell member assumes responsibility for leading his colleagues through a review of his particular chapter. The final grade for each student might be based in part on the performance of other members of the learning cell on items related to his particular chapter.

Another learning cell model is similar to one noted above in relationship to buzz groups. Each member of the cell is assigned a different school of thought or historical person. Whenever the learning cell meets to study a particular topic, each member of the cell is assigned the task of determining how his specific school of thought or person would relate to this topic.

A third alternative blends the learning cell and case study methods. Each member of a learning cell is assigned the task of acquiring knowledge in a specific area related to the topic of the course, or is assigned the task of representing a specific discipline in addressing the interdisciplinary topic of the course. The learning cell meets as a case study group each week to discuss and analyze a specific case. Each member of the learning cell contributes not only in a general way to the group discussion, but also specifically in his area of expertise or perspective.

Both the buzz group and learning cell encourage extensive interaction in the classroom. While neither method demands the subtle skills of a case study or Socratic dialogue, they both can be deceptive, in terms of design and execution. Faculty members may wish to work with colleagues when they first make use of these methods. A joint sharing of problems and observations of each other's classroom can be of significant value when buzz groups and learning cells are employed.

G. Simulations

This particular method more than any other to be considered defies simple or summary description, for much needs to be said about the design and implementation of instructional simulations. Yet in some sense little need be said, for simulations are nothing more than the games we made up as children to entertain ourselves and to learn about our social and physical environments. As one noted designer of instructional simulations has pointed out, the best way to learn how to design and run a simulation is to play a lot of games and participate in many simulations. We will take an intermediate position concerning prerequisites for designing and conducting simulations. We will say a few things about what simulations are and are not, offer a few suggestions, and invite the reader to plunge into some games and try out a few simulations with friends, colleagues, and interested students.

First, what is a simulation? A simple four-cell table might help answer this question. Imagine that in any social system there are two entities: the social setting and the people who are to be found in the system. When the setting is real and the people in the setting are being themselves (real), the social system might be labaled "the real world." When the setting is real, but the people are not being themselves, then "role playing" is taking place. This instructional method will be described in the next section of this chapter. When both the setting is unreal and the people are not being themselves, there is "drama." Finally, when people are being themselves, but the setting is not real, we have a simulation or game. (See Table Two.)

The distinction between simulations and role playing is important, though often blurred in the actual design of simulations and role plays. Most instructional simulations teach people about what it is like to operate within a certain social structure or setting. The people are asked to be themselves and to do the best job possible—often under difficult conditions—in relating to other people, making decisions, or performing certain skills. In a role play, on the other hand, a participant is expected to relate to other people, make decisions, or perform skilled tasks not in the way he normally would, but as the person he is playing would.

The distinction is drawn most clearly in competitive sports. The setting at any sporting event is clearly artificial. Rules are arbitrary, yet players are expected to comply. A defensive player cannot steal the football, for instance, while the offense is in its huddle. The players, however, are expected to "be themselves" and do their best job possible while playing the game. Only in a few marginal sports (such as professional wrestling) do we allow "role playing."

A simulation, therefore, involves the design of an artificial situation in which "real people" are placed to act in a realistic manner. This artificial setting may be a simulated classroom, corporate board room, or 16th century courtroom. Often a simulation is designed so that one or two of the participants in the simulation are in the center of the action, with other participants playing supporting roles. In other simulations, each participant is given the same amount of information, the same goals, and the same opportunity to achieve these goals. This type of simulation tends to be more "gaming" than the first type. The real world rarely provides as equitable a chance for all people to succeed as this type of simulation does. The first type of simulation, however, is often more realistic and hence more frustrating and instructive.

A major decision regarding simulations for many faculty concerns the use of existing designs and materials or the production of new ones. Simulations exist in abundance in many fields and are well-documented in several publications: Robert Horn's *The*

TABLE TWO

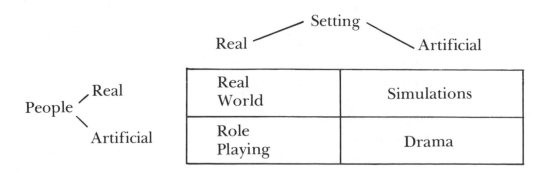

126

Guide to Simulations/Games for Education and Training and Ron Stadsklev's *Handbook of Simulation Gaming in Social Education.*[6] Packaged simulations vary widely in quality, however, and such simulations should be pilot-tested with colleagues or student volunteers before being used in the classroom.

If a faculty member decides to design his own simulation, a fair amount of time needs to be set aside for this process. If possible, the faculty member should have colleagues available with whom to share ideas and test elements of the simulation. A week-long simulation design workshop is an excellent setting in which faculty can work, collaboratively, on simulations and receive expert assistance. Other valuable faculty development assistance includes colleague critiques of the simulation after its first use in the classroom and periodic evening seminars for faculty (and students) that are devoted to testing out a variety of simulations.

In making use of simulations, some faculty focus on the design and implementation of the game, without giving adequate consideration to the discussion and reaction session that should follow the game. At least a third as much time should be spent "debriefing" a simulation as went into the playing of it. Thus, a three-hour simulation should be followed by at least a one-hour discussion. This session enables the faculty member to defuse any feelings that may have been generated by the simulation, as well as clarify student learnings from the event and consider the application of these learnings in other settings. Because a simulation often focuses on the impact of organizations and settings on the behavior of people, the emotions generated by a simulation are important. A simulation participant who experiences profound anger at the behavior of another participant should examine the structures of the simulation that precipitated this behavior, the existence of similar structures in "real" settings, and the ways in which resultant emotions can best be confronted in these settings. This type of learning can be significant and far-reaching.

H. Role-Playing

As in the case of simulations, role-playing involves artificiality—though, as noted above, the actor rather than the setting is, in some sense, artificial. Whether a student or faculty member, the role-player assumes a new persona, representing ideas, perspectives, and interests of a particular person in history. The role-player in some way tries to get into the heart and head of the person he is representing. Whereas one need only understand a particular point of view to be able to represent it effectively in a debate, the role-player must be able to empathize with, as well as understand, the point of view of the person being represented.

In some instances, a faculty member may wish to play a role himself to convey more vividly and accurately something about a particular person or point of view being studied by his students. A faculty member need not become overly dramatic in this endeavor. Costumes are not needed. The faculty member need not emulate the mannerism of the person being represented or the speaker's accent, favorite phrases, or typical mode of instruction. Only the spirit and perspective of this person need be captured by the role-playing faculty member.

Generally, a faculty member will begin by briefly describing a particular school of thought or historical context, then describing the person to be role-played and the reason for selecting this person. The faculty member indicates to his students that he is going to temporarily "become" this person, discussing the person's ideas in the first person ("I believe that . . .") and answering student's questions as this person probably would respond. Students should be reminded that this is a role-play and told that sufficient time will be set aside at the end of the period to discuss the merits of the case being made by the person being played. The primary objective of any role-play should not be to determine if the person being role-played is "right" or "wrong" but rather to acquire a deeper appreciation and understanding of this person's point of view.

The simple act of shifting from a lecture about a person or idea to a role-play in which this person or idea is being represented first-hand can greatly enhance a presentation and enliven the interaction between students and faculty. As a rule, students are more likely to interact actively and creatively with a faculty member if he is in role. As in the case of faculty-centered debates and team-teaching, students also are able to observe and model the faculty member in his attempts to appreciate fully a particular point of view before attempting to analyze this point of view critically (which occurs during the discussion session that should follow the role play).

As noted above, role-playing also can serve as an effective adjunct to team-teaching. Two or more faculty members can each adopt specific roles and engage in a debate or symposium. This approach is particularly valuable if the faculty members take several minutes after the debate or symposium to reflect on and discuss their individual roles and relationships with the other role-players. This follow-up discussion often is of greater value than the actual role-play. Students should be actively involved in this discussion, describing what they observed about the interaction between the faculty role-players. How did particular positions being espoused by each faculty role-player change as a function of specific interactions with other role-players? What does this indicate about the point of view being represented by each role-player?

Students also benefit from assuming specific roles and playing them out in the classroom. In a seminar on psychobiography, for instance, each student is asked to present a psychologically-based history of a famous person from a first person perspective. The presenter becomes that person. He conveys something about his personal history and the impact of this history on the decisions he made and actions he took during his life. The student role-player answers questions directed to him by other students and faculty members from the perspective of the person he is playing. During part of the discussion period each week, all students in the course take on the role of the particular people they are studying, and interact with one another in these roles. Time should be set aside at the end of the course for general discussion of the seminar. Students should drop their roles during this final session. This session is even more critical than in the case of faculty role-playing, for discussion time is needed to gain perspective on what occured during the seminar and to defuse any feelings that might have been aroused.

Role-playing on the part of either faculty or students holds several advantages over other instructional methods. First, role-plays are inherently interesting. One has only to witness the success of Steve Allen's "Meeting of the Minds" on PBS. This program probably would be rather dull for most listeners if it involved no more than a discussion of specific topics from the viewpoint of several historical figures. By "embodying" the people who represent different ideas, Steve Allen's colleagues infuse the program with unpredictability and insight. This involves more than "good theater" (though the Allen players do wear costumes and use some props). The players must know the ideas and perspectives of the people they are role-playing—which brings us to the second advantage of role-playing.

Role-playing is a highly motivating educational enterprise for students. When given the assignment of "getting inside" a particular historical figure, students often are inspired and enthusiastic. They are likely to do more background research if asked to play the role of a particular person than if asked to report just on this person's ideas. Furthermore, because the student may have to answer questions or confront situations or questions that were never posed for the person being role-played, he must study not only the content of the person's pronouncements but also his general perspectives and attitudes—a valuable exercise for any of us living in a complex and changing world.

Role-playing holds yet another advantage; it encourages interaction between students. Many students feel safer in the formal exchange of ideas in a classroom when playing a role than when being themselves. The shy or reticent student often can be encouraged to participate in classroom discussions by being given the role of a person who has a perspective that is rather uncomplicated yet relevant to many topics being addressed in the classroom.

When performed by the faculty member, a role-play provides variation in the usual classroom presentation and enables the faculty member to explore and speculate on the ideas of the person being role-played without always having to qualify the statements being made ("Freud might have said this, given these circumstances . . ."). Furthermore, the role-playing instructor can elicit the full-blown imagination of his students. With minimal costume or scenery, he can turn the classroom into a 16th century studio or a 19th century chemistry laboratory. In this setting, an instructor can explore many dimensions of another person's life and works in interaction with his students. This is possible with very few other instructional methods.[7]

I. General Observations Regarding Interaction-Based Methods

By their very nature, interaction-based methods defy precise description and categorization. Each time one of these methods is used it will yield somewhat different results and, it is hoped, both the students and faculty member will learn from this unpredictability. Because control resides outside either the student or instructor during an interaction-based classroom experience, everyone is likely to feel a bit uncomfortable at times. Therefore, interaction-based methods should be used with care by collegiate instructors. Students must have some confidence in their own capacities to gain knowledge or skills in relatively unstructured settings. Similarly, the instructor must feel comfortable with the content area in which interaction will take place. He also must feel confident that basic information will either be presented effectively in some other part of the course or will necessarily emerge as a consequence of a particular interaction.

An interaction-based method should not be used—as often seems to be the case—when a faculty member is unprepared for class, nor should it be used if a faculty member wants to make a specific point or present a certain perspective. Students will feel cheated in either case and—more important—may not know why they feel cheated. The strong reaction of many students against interaction-based methods is often based on this lack of faculty preparation or indirect presentation of a bias.

Many of the interaction-based methods, as noted throughout this chapter, require some preparation and practice before being used in a classroom. Interaction-based instruction is probably more of an "art" than a "science" (as opposed to PSI, for instance). Only with experience will most faculty become effective in the use of this type of instruction. Safe environments should be provided in which faculty can try out these methods, and support groups should be available so that faculty can share their successes and failures with colleagues who are also exploring the use of these challenging and vital modes of instruction.

NOTES:

[1]For the purpose of the present discussion, we are equating seminars and discussion groups. In general, academicians seem to use the term "seminar" when referring to the dominant use of a discussion format in a course and the term "discussion group" when referring to an occasional use of discussion.

[2]William J. Gordon, *Synectics* (New York: Harper and Row, 1961). Also see Gordon, *Synectics: The Development of Creative Capacity* (New York: Macmillan, 1968) and George M. Prince, *Practice of Creativity: A Manual for Dynamic Problem Solving* (New York: Harper and Row, 1970).

[3]Patricia Barnes-McConnell, "Leading Discussions," in Ohmer Milton's *On College Teaching* (San Francisco: Jossey-Bass, 1978), pp. 71–72.

[4]Charles Fisher, "Being There Vicariously by Case Studies," in Milton, *On College Teaching*, p. 262. As Fisher notes on p. 260, R. C. Bauer has defined several different types of case methods of instruction:

> the *case problem,* which briefly presents the facts and the problem itself; the *case report,* which provides the basic elements with little supporting information and gives the decision(s) and results; the *case study* (or *history*), which is a longer, more complete account, not necessarily with a readily identifiable problem, but containing the results and sometimes the implications and analysis of actions; and the *research case,* which is the most comprehensive, including more on observable events, factors and a complete diagnosis.

We are focusing on the third of these types.

[5]Fisher, in Milton, *On College Teaching*.

[6]Robert E. Horn, ed., *The Guide to Simulations/Games for Education and Training* (Cranford, New Jersey: Didactic Systems, 1976) and Ron Stadsklev, *Handbook of Simulation Gaming in Social Education,* parts one and two (University, Alabama: Institute of Higher Education Research and Services, 1974, 1975).

[7]While there is not a very large body of literature currently available on the use of role playing in the college classroom, that which is available indicates the diverse use of this technique, for example: (1) Noel C. Eggleston, "Role Playing: The Atomic Bomb and the End of World War II," *Teaching History: A Journal of Methods,* 3 (1978), 52–58; (2) Richard C. Jones, "Metamorphia: A National Development Game," *Journal of Geography,* 77 (1978), 126–136; (3) S. Scott Whitlow, "Role-Play Format Stimulates Interest in Ad Ethics Course," *Journalism Educator,* 32 (1978), 11–13. An excellent source of ideas about role playing scenarios (as well as case studies and simulations) is *Intercom,* a journal published by the Center for War/Peace Studies of the New York Friends Group.

EXERCISE NUMBER THREE

TITLE: Improving Class Discussion: A Murder Mystery

SOURCE: Adapted from an exercise and workshop design by Peter Frederick, Wabash College, in turn adapted from a design by Bette Erickson, University of Rhode Island

GENERAL DESCRIPTION: If a faculty member would like to improve the quality of discussion taking place in his class, it would seem appropriate to devote at least some in-class time to a consideration of the principles of effective discussion. Many faculty are reluctant to do this, however, perhaps less because they are unwilling to "waste" that class time than because they do not know how to go about addressing such an issue. The following exercise provides an engaging method for a faculty member without any special training in group dynamics to help his students look at ways of improving class discussion.

INSTRUCTIONS FOR USE: The class should be broken down into groups of 13. Each group should be assigned two or three observers. The instructor may wish to be a member of one of the groups, an observer, or the judge. If one of the first two roles is chosen by the instructor, a student should be selected to be the judge.

The exercise begins with the judge reading the following directions to the groups and observers:

"Each member of each group will receive two cards containing clues that will help solve a murder mystery. If you put all the facts together, you will be able to solve the mystery. You must find the *murderer*, the *weapon*, the *time* of the murder, the *place* of the murder, and the *motive*. When you think you know all the answers and the group agrees, write your answer on a piece of paper and give it to me. I will only tell you whether all five answers are right or wrong. If one or more parts of your answer is wrong, I will not tell you which part is not correct.

"You may organize yourselves in any way you like in order to solve the mystery. You may not pass your clues around and you may not leave your seats. All sharing of clues and ideas must be done verbally with the whole group.

"Are there any questions?"

Once any questions have been answered, the judge should give each group member two index cards on each of which a different clue to the mystery has been typed. Once the mystery has been solved, the group and its observers should engage in a discussion of the way in which the group worked together. Such questions might be addressed as "How did we work together— or did we?"; "Who performed what kinds of roles in the group?"; "What did we learn about participation in groups?"; and "How can the learnings in this problem-solving 'discussion' be translated into more typical discussion groups?" If time permits the group also might read and discuss "Effective Group

131

Process" (Volume 1, Handout Number Six), "Understanding and Being Understood" (Volume 1, Handout Number Eight), "Observation of Leadership Functions" (Volume 2, Instrument Number Thirteen), or "Understanding the Other Person" (Volume 2, Exercise Number Nine).

MURDER MYSTERY CLUES

When he was discovered dead, Mr. Kelley had a bullet hole in his thigh and a knife wound in his back.

Mr. Jones shot at an intruder in his apartment building at 12:00 midnight.

The elevator operator reported to police that he saw Mr. Kelley at 12:15 a.m.

The bullet taken from Mr. Kelley's thigh matched the gun owned by Mr. Jones.

Only one bullet had been fired from Mr. Jones' gun.

When the elevator man saw Mr. Kelley, Kelley was bleeding slightly, but he did not seem too badly hurt.

A knife with Mr. Kelley's blood on it was found in Miss Smith's yard.

The knife found in Miss Smith's yard had Mr. Scott's fingerprints on it.

The elevator man saw Mr. Kelley's wife go to Mr. Scott's apartment at 11:30 p.m.

The elevator operator said that Mr. Kelley's wife frequently left the building with Mr. Scott.

Mr. Kelley had destroyed Mr. Jones' business by stealing all his customers.

Mr. Kelley's body was found in the park at 1:30 a.m.

Mr. Kelley had been dead for one hour when his body was found, according to a medical expert working with police.

Just before going off duty at 12:30 a.m., the elevator man saw Mr. Kelley go to Mr. Scott's room at 12:25 a.m.

It was obvious from the condition of Mr. Kelley's body that it had been dragged a long distance.

Miss Smith saw Mr. Kelley go to Mr. Jones' apartment building at 11:55 p.m.

Mr. Kelley's wife disappeared after the murder.

Police were unable to locate Mr. Scott after the murder.

When police tried to locate Mr. Jones after the murder, they found him in a distant city.

The elevator man said that Miss Smith was in the lobby of the apartment building when he went off duty.

Miss Smith often followed Mr. Kelley.

Mr. Jones had told Mr. Kelley that he was going to kill him.

Miss Smith said that nobody left the apartment building between 12:25 a.m. and 12:45 a.m.

Mr. Kelley's bloodstains were found in Mr. Scott's car.

Mr. Kelley's bloodstains were found on the carpet in the hall outside of Mr. Jones' apartment.

Answer: After receiving a superficial gunshot wound from Mr. Jones, Mr. Kelley went to Mr. Scott's apartment *where he was killed by* Mr. Scott *with a* knife *at 12:30 a.m. because* Mr. Scott was in love with Mr. Kelley's wife.

INSTRUMENT NUMBER ONE

TITLE: Team Teaching Inventory

SOURCE: Adapted from the "Co-Facilitating Inventory" in John E. Jones and J. William Pfeiffer, eds., *The 1975 Annual Handbook for Group Facilitators* (La Jolla, California: University Associates, 1975), pp. 223–229.

GENERAL DESCRIPTION: Faculty sometimes find themselves in team teaching situations with very little actual information about the person with whom they are teaching. As the course progresses, each may become more and more familiar with the other's style and assumptions until, by the end of the course, they have become an effective team. On the other hand, unarticulated assumptions about teaching may cause increasing difficulties, until both faculty and students are relieved when the course is finally over. The "Team Teaching Inventory" is intended to raise issues of teaching style, philosophy, and assumptions before the course begins to help ensure as positive an experience as possible.

INSTRUCTIONS FOR USE: This inventory can be used as part of a workshop on team teaching or can be incorporated into the planning process of a specific course. In both cases, the inventory is intended to be used by faculty who will actually be teaching together. The inventory concludes with a series of questions team teachers may wish to consider at the conclusion of individual class sessions.

TEAM TEACHING INVENTORY*

Name: _____

Date: _____

Course or class session: _____

I. PREWORK
   A. Learning Theory
      In the space below write a statement of about 100 words to explain your concept of how people learn.

*Adapted from John E. Jones and J. William Pfeiffer (Eds.), *The 1975 Annual Handbook for Group Facilitators*. San Diego, CA: University Associates, 1975. Used with permission.

B. Personal Motivation
    Complete the following sentence:
    I am involved in team teaching because . . .

C. Expectations
    I expect the following things to happen in the class we will be team teaching:

      1.

      2.

      3.

      4.

      5.

6.

7.

8.

9.

10.

The *best* thing that could happen in this class/course would be . . .

The *worst* thing that could happen in this class/course would be . . .

E. Teaching Style
   The following are my typical actions or responses in the type of class/course we will be working with:

   1. When starting a class, I usually . . .

   2. When one or two students begin to dominate a class discussion, I usually . . .

   3. When the class is silent and not really participating in the discussion, I usually . . .

   4. When one or two students are silent during a class discussion, I usually . . .

   5. When I begin to get a number of questions from a class during a lecture, I usually . . .

   6. When a student comes late to class, I usually . . .

   7. When a class discussion seems to be getting off the point, I usually . . .

8. When a student directly challenges my position, point of view, analysis, or interpretation, I usually . . .

9. When two or more students begin to argue with each other, I usually . . .

10. When the class gangs up on one individual in the class, I usually . . .

11. When ending a lecture, I usually . . .

12. When ending a class discussion, I usually . . .

In a class discussion, I generally talk (a) about a quarter of the time, (b) about half the time or (c) about three-quarters of the time.

a _____   b _____   c _____

The thing that makes me most uncomfortable in a class like this is . . .

F. Team Teaching Experience

In the space below, identify those courses/classes that you have taught with someone else. Which were most successful and least successful? Why? What problems did you encounter as a team teacher?

II. INTERVIEW
  A. Background
    1. Share your answers to the pre-work. What are your responses to or concerns about your partner's information?
    2. Discuss further your experience in team teaching situations.
    3. Share your current efforts at professional or personal growth as they relate to this course.
    4. Describe some of your characteristic teaching behaviors, patterns, or strategies. Would any of these appear idiosyncratic to your partner?
    5. Identify any attempts you will be making in this course to expand or improve your teaching style.
    6. Come to a consensus about the expectations and experiences of the students in the class. Discuss your reactions to the makeup of the class, its size, and any other special considerations.

  B. Operating Norms
    1. Decide where each of you will sit in class sessions.
    2. Decide who will say the first/last words in each session.

3. Decide on your standards for class attendance for both yourselves and the students.
4. Where, when, and how will we deal with problems that might develop between us?
5. Can we agree to disagree in front of the class?
6. Is it possible to "use" each other's excitement and enthusiasm; that is, can I be "out" while you are "in"?
7. What kind of feedback would each of us like from the other about what happens in class?
8. What is nonnegotiable with each of us as team teachers?
9. How will we let the students in the class know about how we plan to work together?

C. After Class
   1. On a 10-point scale, how did the class go?
   2. What was happening during the class?
   3. Are any problems emerging in the behavior of either the class as a group or individual students? What, if anything, are we going to do about it?
   4. What did I do during class that was effective?
   5. What did I do during class that was not effective?
   6. How are we working together as team teachers?
   7. Have we made any agreements about how we are going to teach this class that might need renegotiation?
   8. What is each of us going to do in the next class session?

HANDOUT NUMBER THREE

TITLE: Buzz Groups: Two Variations

SOURCE: William H. Bergquist

GENERAL DESCRIPTION: Buzz groups are almost infinitely flexible, limited only by the imagination of the instructor and students. Two variants, candidates for even further elaboration, are presented in the following handout.

INSTRUCTIONS FOR USE: "Buzz Groups: Two Variations" is self-explanatory and can be distributed without comment or used to initiate discussion or a workshop session. This handout is best used in conjunction with "A Look at Buzz Groups" (Volume 1, Handout Number Four).

BUZZ GROUPS: TWO VARIATIONS

A. Fish Bowl

In a "fish bowl" buzz group one works on a question, problem, or issue while another group observes (without making comments). After a short period of time (10 to 15 minutes), the observing group members are asked to make comments on the observed group's discussion. These comments might focus on the content of the discussion; the way in which the group approached the question, problem, or issue; or the processes of the group (communication, decision making, leadership). The latter area of focus and feedback needs to be supervised closely and should be used for the specific purpose of improving the discussion process in the buzz group. Sometimes feedback is given to the total buzz group being observed. In other instances, the feedback is given by specific members of the observing group to specific members of the group being observed. Usually, the two groups will switch places and repeat the process during a second buzz group session.

B. Pyramid

This method involves the selection of different, though interrelated, topics of discussion for each buzz group and the structuring of relationships among groups. The total class is given the task of generating solutions to a specific problem described by the instructor. One set of buzz groups (approximately two-thirds of the class) works in one part of the classroom generating alternative solutions to the problem. At the same time, a single buzz group situated at the other end of the room defines a set of criteria by which solutions to the problem should be evaluated. A third set of buzz groups, placed in the middle of the classroom, is given the task of determining strategies whereby they can select the best solution generated by the first set of groups in order to sell those ideas to the single group.

Each buzz group first meets for 15 minutes. Then members of the first set of groups present their ideas to one or more of the middle groups. The approach to be taken is determined by members of both groups. While this is going on, the single group decides how it will conduct its review of proposals. With the start of a third 15-minute period, each middle group presents to this group (1) the best of the solutions it has received from the outer groups, (2) some combination of solutions recommended by several of the outer groups, or (3) its own solution. The single group then judges the worth of each solution, based on the criteria it has established. A general classroom discussion follows, focusing systematically on each stage of the problem-solving process.

HANDOUT NUMBER FOUR

TITLE: Eight Strategies for Role Playing in the College Classroom

SOURCE: Steven R. Phillips, based in part on R. C. Hawley, *Value Exploration through Role Playing* (New York: Hart, 1975), and G. Shaftel and F. R. Shaftel, *Role Playing the Problem Story* (National Conference of Christians and Jews, 1952).

GENERAL DESCRIPTION: Role playing can be a most engaging teaching method, for it allows students to act out, rather than just talk about, course material. It also can be a bit frightening to some faculty. The following handout provides eight simple strategies for role playing that can help all but the most reluctant to try out this approach.

INSTRUCTIONS FOR USE: This handout is best used either in conjunction with a training session on role playing or as a discussion piece which introduces faculty to the use of this technique.

EIGHT STRATEGIES FOR ROLE PLAYING IN THE COLLEGE CLASSROOM

Strategy Number One: The Blackboard Press Conference

The instructor draws a face on the blackboard, then introduces the "guest" as, for instance, George III, by saying something like, "Class, we've been studying the reign of George III and the relationship of that period of British history to the American Revolution. We now have the honor of His Majesty's presence in class today. Are there any questions you would like to ask him?" The class is asked to form buzz groups for a few minutes to generate questions, which the instructor then lists without comment. After several are up, the instructor then asks if there is anyone who would like to answer for the King.

This is both a very low threat introduction to role playing and an almost certain way of generating an active class discussion. The figure interviewed may be almost anyone, of course, from literary and historical figures to famous scientists, scholars, and researchers.

Strategy Number Two: The Open Chair Press Conference

This is similar to Strategy Number One, except the guest is presumed to be sitting in the open chair. As students begin to respond for the person being interviewed, they can be encouraged to actually move into the open chair.

A variant of this strategy is to have three or four students—who have perhaps done some research on the topic—sit or stand behind the open chair and speak for the guest.

Strategy Number Three: The Individual Press Conference

The next logical step from the previous two strategies is to have an individual student playing the role of the interviewee. This is an excellent way for a student who has done some special research on an actual figure to enrich and enliven a class session, but the press conference could also be a more spontaneous interview of a literary, historical, or scientific figure.

An interesting variant on many of these role plays is the introduction of an "alter ego" in the form of another student who stands behind the first role player and has the freedom to articulate the hidden messages or feelings that may lie behind the dialogue being conducted. If this technique is used, it is less important to be concerned with the "correctness" of what the alter ego offers than with his perceptions and contributions to the role play.

Strategy Number Four: Parts

Instead of asking students to role play individual characters, it is possible to have them play parts of a single character. Historical or literary characters, for instance, are often divided against themselves. To take perhaps the most famous example from literature, Hamlet is in many ways several characters: the college student, the

145

courtier, the suitor of Ophelia, the son of Gertrude, and the avenger of his father's murder. Each of these individual parts of Hamlet's character could be role played; the resulting interior dialogue is one way of illuminating the conflicts with which Hamlet is faced.

Strategy Number Five: What would happen if . . . ?

This is a slightly more complex approach to role playing than the interviews discussed above, in that it involves two or more characters. Essentially, this strategy brings together characters whose differences (or similarities) will spark interchange and discussion.

What would happen if . . .

Freud and Skinner were to get into a conversation about the nature of man?

Ophelia, Desdemona, and Lady Macbeth were members of a panel discussion on women's liberation?

Newton and Einstein were to discuss the nature of knowledge?

The possibilities of developing such significant relationships are almost endless, limited only by the course material and the imagination of the instructor.

Incidentally, in a two-person role play, it is sometimes useful to have the players reverse roles once or twice after the role play has begun. This often enlivens the dialogue and helps students see different possibilities and points of view.

Strategy Number Six: Identifications

One by one and in private students are assigned the roles of major characters in a literary, historical, or business situation; no one knows the role of any of the others. The task of the role players is to engage in a discussion with each other in such a way as to help themselves, the other role players, and the rest of the class identify the role each is playing. The discussion that follows this role play should focus on how and why the players articulated their roles and how close their expression was to the actual characters.

Strategy Number Seven: Six Characters in Search of a Novel

One way of getting students more actively involved in an issue or dispute is to develop a role play in which all of the major figures are present. A single student may play each role or several students may play each of the several roles. If the second approach is taken, the students playing each role should perhaps have time to meet together to discuss their character.

Strategy Number Eight: The Problem Story

The instructor reads the first part of a very short story, narrative poem, historical account, case study, or scientific investigation, stopping just at the crisis or turning point of the narrative. Students are assigned appropriate roles and they play out the story to whatever conclusion they invent. Following the active discussion this strategy almost always creates, the instructor finishes reading the account.

HANDOUT NUMBER FIVE

TITLE: A Compendium of Techniques and Sub-Techniques

SOURCE: Anthony Grasha, University of Cincinnati

GENERAL DESCRIPTION: This handout describes 12 different instructional methods and provides suggestions as to their use and purpose. The methods are all appropriate to a traditional classroom and will usually be of interest to most faculty members.

INSTRUCTIONS FOR USE: The handout can be distributed without comment, used as the basis for a discussion of alternative teaching methods, or reviewed prior to a workshop session intended to demonstrate one or more methods.

A COMPENDIUM OF TECHNIQUES
and
SUB-TECHNIQUES

TECHNIQUES

### THE SPEECH	X Speaker
Definition: A carefully prepared oral presentation of a subject by a qualified person. Often used with other techniques.	XXXXXXXXXXX
	XXXXXXXXXXX
Purpose for which used: (1) Prepare information, identify or clarify problems, and present analysis of controversial issues; (2) stimulate and inspire audience and encourage further inquiry.	XXXXXXXXXXX
	Audience

### THE FORUM	Resource Person(s) Moderator
Definition: A period of open discussion carried on by members of an entire audience (25 or more) and one or more resource people, directed by a moderator. It is generally used to follow other techniques (speech, panel, symposium, interview, demonstration, or role-play), giving audience opportunity to participate. The audience may comment (to be distinguished from Question-Answer period when audience is only to ask questions of the resource person), raise issues, offer information, as well as ask questions.	X X
	XXXXXXXXXXXX
	XXXXXXXXXXXX
	XXXXXXXXXXXX
	Audience
Purpose for which used: (1) Clarify and explore ideas; (2) attain verbal audience participation.	

### THE PANEL	Moderator X
Definition: A group of up to six people of special competence in the subject and ability to express themselves hold a purposeful conversation under the leadership of a moderator in front of an audience.	Resource X X Resource People X X People
Purpose for which used: (1) to identify, explore, and clarify issues and problems; (2) to bring several points of view and a wide range of informed opinion to an audience; (3) to gain understanding of component parts of a topic and identify advantages and disadvantages of a course of action.	XXXXXXXXXXX
	XXXXXXXXXXX
	XXXXXXXXXXX
	Audience

148

THE COLLOQUY

Definition: Involves two to four resource people (as in a panel), some people from the audience, and a moderator. The audience representatives discuss the topics with the resource people under the guidance of the moderator.

Purpose for which used: (1) Stimulate interest; (2) identify, explore, clarify, and solve issues and problems; (3) present to resource people the audience level of understanding.

```
              Moderator

Resource  X          Audience
People  X   X      Representa-
          X   X      tives
        XXXXXXXXXXXX
        XXXXXXXXXXXX
        XXXXXXXXXXXX

              Audience
```

THE SYMPOSIUM

Definition: A series of related speeches by two to five qualified people speaking with authority on different phases of the same or related topics. They do NOT speak with each other but, under the direction of the moderator, make presentations. A symposium is often used with a panel or forum.

Purpose for which used: (1) Present organized information, showing a wide range of authoritative opinion about a topic, and setting forth an analysis of several related aspects of a topic; (2) help people ts of a topic; (2) help people see relationships of various aspects of a topic to the topic as a whole; (3) stimulate thinking in people with similar backgrounds and interests.

```
              Moderator
                 X
Speakers  X          X  Speakers
          X              X

        XXXXXXXXXXXX
        XXXXXXXXXXXX
        XXXXXXXXXXXX

              Audience
```

THE EXPANDED PANEL

Definition: A combination presentation and discussion in which six to 12 people hold discussion surrounded on three sides by the audience, followed by an arrangement in which the entire group will discuss the topic. The moderator choses when to close the discussion, which then forms into a large group for general discussion.

Purpose for which used: (1) Secures active participation from whole audience; (2) Stimulates interest in topics of mutual interest.

```
          Exploratory
       Discussion Group

              X
        x   X   X   x
       x  X         X  x
       x               x
       x  X   X   x
       xxxxxxxxx
          Audience
       Expanded Panel
          x  X  X x
        x x       x
        x           x
        x xxxxxxxx x
```

GROUP DISCUSSION

Definition: When engaged in by trained people under trained leadership, group discussion is a purposeful conversation in which participants explore, teach, and learn about a topic of mutual interest. Groups usually number from six to 20.

Purpose for which used: (1) To identify, explore, learn about, and solve problems and topics of mutual interest in which each participant is both teacher and learner; (2) to achieve maximum participation and encourage growth of all participants.

```
        Leader
      x  x  x
    x          x      x  Observer
    x          x
    x          x      Recorder
    x          x
      x  x  x
                      Name
                      Cards
```

ROLE-PLAYING

Definition: A spontaneous acting out (without script) of a situation, condition, or circumstance by selected members of a learning group which emphasizes relationships between people and portrays typical attitudes. Following the role-play the group discusses, interprets, and analyzes the action which took place.

Purpose for which used: (1) Dramatically illustrate interpersonal problems; (2) gain insight into others' feelings and discover how they might react under certain conditions; (3) develop skill in problem solving and diagnosis; (4) help audience members gain insight into their own behavior and attitudes.

```
        Role-Players
         X        X
      X              X

   XXXXXXXXXXXXXXX
   XXXXXXXXXXXXXXX
   XXXXXXXXXXXXXXX

         Audience
```

THE INTERVIEW

Definition: A five- to 30-minute presentation in which an interviewer systematically questions and explores various aspects of a topic with one or two resource people before an audience. The resource people know in advance the nature of the questions to be asked.

Purpose for which used: (1) To present information informally, and provide, through the interviewers, a bridge between the audience and the resource people; (2) to explore and analyze problems, clarify issues, stimulate interest in topic; (3) to gain impressions from authorities on experience they and the audiences have in common.

```
   Resource
   People       Interviewer
     XX              X

   XXXXXXXXXXXXXXX
   XXXXXXXXXXXXXXX
   XXXXXXXXXXXXXXX

         Audience
```

A sub-technique is like a technique, but it is used for a shorter period of time and is used to modify or adapt a technique to the requirements of a particular learning situation. A sub-technique cannot stand alone.

BUZZ SESSION

Definition: An audience divided up into small groups (about six members per group) to discuss a topic or perform a task assigned them. They meet briefly, usually not more than 10 minutes.

Purpose for which used: (1) Gain audience involvement through discussion, identify needs and interests, and receive contributions from those who do not speak in larger group; (2) enable a large group to evaluate a learning experience.

```
      x
   x    x          With
   x    x          Moveable
      x            Chairs

   xxx    Front row turns
   xxx    around if chairs
          are not moveable
```

AUDIENCE REACTION TEAM

Definition: Three to five audience representatives who may interrupt the speaker at appropriate times for clarification of obscure points or to help the speaker treat the needs of those present.

Purpose for which used: (1) Ensure that an audience understands a subject which might be difficult to communicate or might be presented "over their heads."

```
Speaker  X

            X     Audience
             X    Reaction
            X     Team

   xxxxxxxxxxxxxxx
   xxxxxxxxxxxxxxx
   xxxxxxxxxxxxxxx

         Audience
```

IDEA INVENTORY

Definition: Often called "brainstorming," this is a spontaneous outpouring of ideas for five to 15 minutes on a topic of interest or need. As many ideas as possible are recorded but not discussed during this period. Quantity is preferred over quality.

Purpose for which used: (1) When several alternative ideas are wanted prior to a decision; (2) when many ideas are wanted.

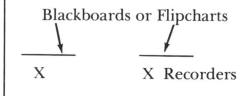

```
   Blackboards or Flipcharts
        ↓           ↓
   _____    _____
   X              X  Recorders
          X  Leader
        X   X
        X   X
        X     X   Audience
        X     X   Partici-
        XXXXXX    pants
```

151

SCREENING PANEL

Definition: Three to five people from the audience discuss the educational needs of the group in the presence of a speaker or resource person so that person can adjust his presentation to the needs, interests, and level of audience understanding.

Purpose for which used: (1) To help resource people or speakers gain insight into needs and interests of learning group; (2) to involve audience and encourage them to express their needs.

```
                Moderator
                    X
        Resource  X  X    Audience
        People  X      X  Representa-
                    X    tives


              xxxxxxxxxxxx
              xxxxxxxxxxxx
              xxxxxxxxxxxx
```

REACTION PANEL

Definition: Two to five people from the audience or special resource people listen to a presentation (speech, symposium, or panel), then hold a purposeful conversation in reaction to the presentation. This sometimes is followed by a forum.

Purpose for which used: (1) To stimulate audience interest; (2) to clarify, solve, evaluate from audience or authoritative point of view the presentation.

```
              X       Moderator

        X                 X  Speaker
        X   Reaction
        X   Panel

            xxxxxxxxxxx
            xxxxxxxxxxx
            xxxxxxxxxxx
```

HANDOUT NUMBER SIX

TITLE: Guidelines for Observing and Reporting on Experiential Learning Activities

SOURCE: J. T. Hansen, University of Puget Sound, Tacoma, Washington

GENERAL DESCRIPTION: Observing and reporting on individual and group behavior is an important aspect of an intensive, interactive learning experience. The following document describes ways in which observation and feedback can help participants better realize the potential for learning that lies within any experiential event. Sensitive use of these guidelines can help participants achieve greater self-awareness and increased congruence between their intentions and actions and can assist groups in developing open and supportive patterns of behavior.

INSTRUCTIONS FOR USE: Depending on the length and complexity of the contemplated learning experience, responsibility for observing and reporting on the event may be assigned to one or more people. These observers should have a thorough understanding of the activity that is about to take place, as well as considerable familiarity with the following guidelines. Because of this dual responsibility, observers perhaps should be selected well in advance of the event and briefed by one or more staff members on both the activity and the process of observation and feedback. These guidelines should be distributed and discussed during that briefing. In selecting observers, be aware that since reporting should follow the learning experience fairly quickly, considerable dexterity and speed will be required.

Variations:
   1. "Guidelines for Observing and Reporting on Experiential Learning Activities" might well be distributed in conjunction with "Characteristics of Constructive Feedback" found in the first volume of this series.

GUIDELINES FOR OBSERVING AND REPORTING ON EXPERIENTIAL LEARNING ACTIVITIES

I. Observation

   A. Be sure you understand the purpose and potential dynamics of the activity you are about to observe so that you can define both expected and unexpected results.

   B. Observe how the participants use space, especially if the activity involves formal or informal subgroups. What are the boundaries, where do communications occur, how is territory maintained and extended?

   C. Pay very close attention to language. Note precise terms, not your own equivalents. Note value words, how they change, and the assumptions within them.

   D. Note carefully the non-verbal behavior of individuals and subgroups. Record disparities between verbal and nonverbal communication, moments of tension and humor, the effects of decisions, conflicts, cooperation, and so forth.

   E. Notice the roles assigned to and assumed by individuals and subgroups. Note the functions of each, incuding changes in power, authority, respect, affection, and conflict.

   F. Note ways in which authority, division of labor, negotiation, decision making, and communication occur. Identify moments at which changes happen.

   G. Record and analyze evidences of the values and assumptions of participants.

II. Reporting

   A. The purpose of your report is to give participants an outside, objective perspective on their experience.

   B. Description is the essence of constructive, illuminating feedback. Remember that the most useful data is very specific and often overlooked. Remember that people often act from several motives simultaneously. Respect the multiplicity in both the data and possible analyses.

   C. Your report to the group should be succinct and expressed in common language. Explain the organization of your report very briefly. Be certain to pace your presentation so that your observations are comprehensible and illuminating to participants who have been intimately involved in an experience which may have affected them intensely. Give the group time to discuss your observations and be prepared to intervene politely when you think it is time to move on. Use humor where appropriate, and remember that some feedback is best given privately.

   D. Although exercising due restraint, descriptive analyses and generalizations are appropriate. These should include disparities between expected and unexpected results, differences among subgroups, verbal and nonverbal behavior, and other aspects of the experience identified above.

   E. Since most small group activities focus on decision making, report on the patterns and types of decision-making procedures used by individuals and subgroups. How do individuals affect the group, what coalitions are formed, what changes happen and how, and to what extent are decisions based on factual data or values?

154

Chapter Six

Instructional Consultation

In the previous two volumes of this series, we have addressed the issue of instructional consultation from two different perspectives. First, in both volumes we described procedures for assisting faculty in the improvement of their classroom teaching, relying primarily on the teaching improvement process first developed at the Clinic for the Improvement of Teaching at the University of Massachusetts. Second, in Volume 2 we described several different procedures for assisting faculty in the design or redesign of their courses, relying heavily on procedures developed by Robert Diamond and his colleagues at the Center for Instructional Development at Syracuse University. In the present chapter, we shall attempt to integrate these two approaches to instructional consultation into a general model of problem solving applicable to instructional issues.

More specifically, we will describe an integrated process of instructional consultation that is appropriate whether one is ultimately going to assist a faculty member with course or curricular design or with the day-to-day processes of classroom teaching. We will precede this description with a discussion of the domains in which the instructional consultation must work and the tools the faculty member will need while working in each of these domains. This discussion will set a context for our subsequent description of an integrated instructional problem solving process.

A. The Domains of Instructional Consultation

An experienced instructional consultant often will find himself involved in three different domains—the domain of information, the domain of values, and the domain of ideas. The way in which he will need to relate to a faculty member in each of these domains and the tools he will need to use differ significantly. As a consultant to a faculty member in the informational domain, one is attempting to serve the faculty member by providing him with valid and useful information that will enable him to perform his instructional functions more effectively. The faculty member is provided with information concerning his current modes of instructional performance, alternative modes of performance, and the context within which current performance and potential alternative performance might be assessed. The appropriate tools in this domain are primarily derived from research: questionnaires, observation forms, tests, audio and video recordings, and so forth.

In the informational domain, an instructional consultant will offer information to a faculty member about the students with whom the faculty member is working, about the environment in which the faculty member is teaching, and perhaps about the faculty member himself. Instructional consultation programs that concentrate on course and curricular design, such as those offered at Syracuse University and Michigan State University, often provide faculty with information about their students through use of questionnaires, institutional information, and demographics. Institutional research projects that are offered by and for faculty—such as those described in Chapter Twelve—

often provide faculty with information about such environmental characteristics as institutional goals (as perceived by various constituencies); levels of morale among students, faculty, and administrators; and instructional costs. The Teaching Improvement Process of the University of Massachusetts provides faculty with systematic information about themselves as they perform in the classroom.

Rather than provide faculty members with information about their current practices, an instructional consultant might provide information about alternative practices. Many consultants provide faculty members with reading materials about various teaching methods (such as are described in Chapters Three, Four, and Five) or alternative curricular models such as those described in *Developing the College Curriculum*.[1] Since faculty rarely have sufficient time to sift through a large volume of literature on higher education instruction, they might benefit greatly from specific suggestions about further reading made by an instructional consultant who is familiar not only with the literature but also with conditions being faced by the faculty member. Thus, instructional consultation should couple information about the faculty member's current situation (students, environment, and the faculty member) with information about alternative directions available to him.

This holds true even when the information about alternative approaches is being offered in a workshop. All too frequently, instructional workshops do not provide follow-up. Thus, a faculty member might gain new insights about and increased interest in a particular instructional method or design but be unable to act on this insight or interest in the classroom. A workshop should be used primarily to whet the appetite of a faculty member. More intensive one-on-one consultation usually is needed to effect significant change and improvement in instructional performance. If a workshop is being conducted on simulations, for instance, follow-up services might include assistance in the design of a simulation, in-class observation of the simulation when it is first used, periodic sharing of experiences among the faculty who participated in the workshop and tried out new simulations in their classes, or the establishment of an informal network on simulations within the college (or in conjunction with neighboring colleges).

In consulting with faculty on values, an effective instructional consultant will be supportive—yet often challenging. He will help a faculty member clarify his own attitudes regarding the teaching-learning enterprise and the implications of these attitudes for his instructional performance. Effective consultation regarding values will yield greater clarity and commitment regarding goals and objectives for a course or curriculum and an operational philosophy of education. Tools for working in the values domain include interviews, reflective exercises and journal writing, negotiation skills, and skill-building workshops.

In the domain of values, an instructional consultant can serve one of three functions: values-inculcation, values-clarification, or values-expansion. In the inculcation of values, a consultant might promote the value of a specific approach to instruction (such as student-led discussions) or a specific approach to the design of a course (such as objectives-based design). Values are inculcated through exposure to exemplary programs, endorsements by respected experts or colleagues, or first-hand experience in a sheltered setting (workshop, simulation, or pilot-test project). Values clarification is performed by the consultant who assists a faculty member in specifying desired outcomes for a course or instructional unit or in identifying the primary, implicit assumptions made by an academic department. An instructional consultant will use values expansion when introducing a faculty member to an entirely new area of instruction (for example, field experiences) or raising a faculty member's consciousness about the needs of a new student population.

The third domain, ideas, is addressed by an instructional consultant when he assists a faculty member in expanding the options available to his teaching. This is done by promoting both divergent and convergent thinking on the part of the faculty member, usually, or at least initially, in a group setting. Divergent thinking involves the use of such creative problem-solving techniques as brainstorming, divergent delphi, and morphological analysis ("dial-a-course")—techniques that are described in Chapter Six of Volume 2 in this handbook series. Convergent thinking is facilitated by use of synectics, delphi techniques, and other agreement-producing strategies. These techniques also are described briefly in Chapter Six of Volume 2 of this series and Appendix One of *Developing the College Curriculum*.

In generating new ideas and coming to agreement on ideas that have been generated, a faculty member will be working in the domains of information and values as well, for ideas must be responsive to both. While each domain is independent and requires separate consultative strategies, the three domains often interact, particularly when a consultant is helping a faculty member solve an instructional problem or resolve an instructional conflict. We turn now to an exploration of the interaction among the domains of information, values, and ideas as they relate to instructional problem-solving.

B. Interaction Among Domains in Solving Problems

Six steps often are initiated in solving any problem: (1) problem sensing, (2) problem analysis, (3) problem solving (generating an ideal solution), (4) problem solving (generating a realistic solution), (5) formative evaluation, and (6) summative evaluation. Each of these steps is appropriate in solving instructional problems and may involve the efforts of an instructional consultant as well as a faculty member. Each step requires interaction between two of the three domains (see Figure Three). Following is a brief description of each step and the way in which an instructional consultant might assist a faculty member in solving an instructional problem.

First, in the sensing of problems, an instructional consultant helps a faculty member determine whether there is a significant discrepancy between the current situation and a desired state. The current situation is determined through the generation of information, while the determination of a desired state requires values clarification, expansion, or inculcation. An instructional consultant might, for instance, help a faculty member determine if a particular course "is going well" by first helping him identify his own personal expectations for the course and the expectations of other members of his department regarding the course (values domain). The consultant then collects data from students (interviews, test performance, questionnaires) about the outcomes of the course as it is being conducted (information domain). To the extent that there is a discrepancy between the current and desired states, a "problem" exists. The consultation will stop at this point if a faculty member wishes to go his own way in selecting ways in which to correct his problem.

Alternatively, he might assist in the analysis of the problem that has just been sensed. Problem-analysis (step two) focuses on the causes of the problem: why is there

157

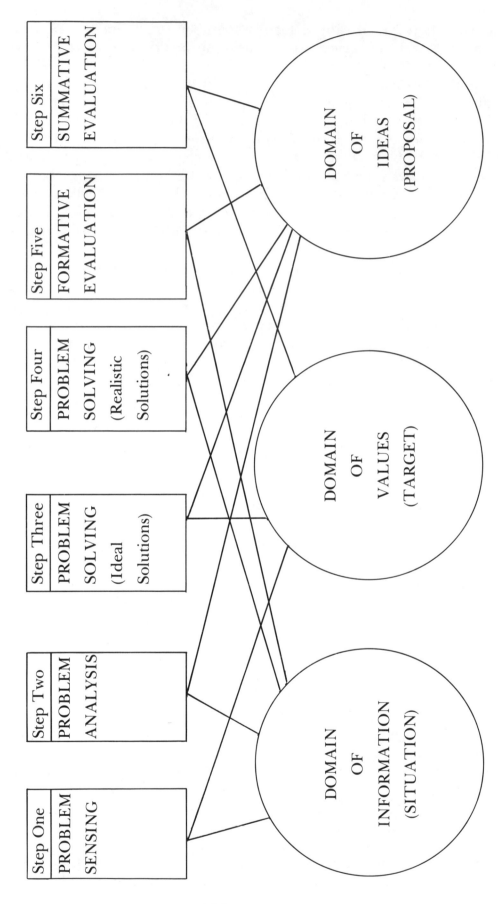

FIGURE THREE

A Six-Step Problem-Solving Sequence

158

a discrepancy between current and desired states? This inquiry requires the interaction between the domains of information and ideas. First, the consultant and faculty member should explore past (historical) conditions to determine the cause of the problem: what patterns of behavior typically elicit this unwanted student response? What has been done over the past year that blocks student progress in this area? What hasn't been done during the past year that should have been done to promote student progress in this area? The consultant and faculty member then explore the causes of a problem by testing out alternative ideas that can lead to its solution, since we often only find the sources of a problem by testing for its solution. This preliminary testing of solutions must be conducted in a safe environment in which the faculty member can learn from mistakes as well as successes.

A faculty member, for example, who is confronted with a problem concerning inadequate student writing skills in a management training program, may first want to identify the causes of this problem by collecting or looking at collected information about students who have already participated in the program. What were the student's writing skills when he entered the program? Were there any points during the program when the writing skills seemed to drop off (or significantly increase)? The faculty member and instructional consultant must become detectives in examining accumulated information about the past.

They must also become experimenters who test out new ideas to find the source of inadequate writing skills. If the faculty member hypothesizes that the students are unable to write because the topics they are addressing are of minimal interest, a pilot-test can be set up in which students are able to write about something of significant personal interest. Results from this "experiment" help the faculty member determine if student disinterest is a significant cause of the writing problem. Other pilot-tests or experiments can be devised and initiated by the faculty member and consultant.

Whereas problem sensing involves an interaction between information and values, and problem analysis an interaction between information and ideas, the third step (problem solving) involves an interaction between values and ideas. A faculty member and consultant generate alternative solutions (derived from the problem analysis) based on the goals, objectives, or expectations of the faculty member (determined during problem sensing). This initial generation of alternative solutions requires that the faculty member temporarily suspend "realistic" judgment (use of information) so that an "ideal" strategy might be formulated which will solve the identified problem. In other words, given extensive resources, time, skills, and money how might this problem be solved?

Frequently this "idea" step in a problem-solving sequence is ignored or avoided by many faculty. An instructional consultant should encourage his client's consideration of the ideal and discourage premature closure on ideas that initially may not seem "realistic." Creativity may be hampered when realism is introduced too early in a problem-solving process. As Robert Diamond has noted:

> Experience has shown that it is most efficient to start with the best possible program and then modify it according to the specific administrative, material and human constraints that exist. Limiting the original design to meet anticipated constraints tends to reduce both its flexibility and quality and thus generate an inferior program. Another reason for trying to

159

develop an optimum design is that many of the traditional restraints are unnecessary and, in some instances, are unreal.[2]

The fourth step in a problem-solving sequence requires an interaction between ideas and information. At this point the faculty member must examine each possible "ideal" strategy in light of information concerning constraints, resources, money, and so forth. Whereas the third step tends to encourage divergent thinking, the fourth encourages convergent thinking. An instructional consultant should assist a faculty member in identifying "researchable" questions that can be asked about the various "ideal" strategies that were formulated during step three. These questions should provide answers that will enable the faculty member to select or formulate a "realistic" instructional method, design, or strategy. An instructional consultant also can help a faculty member identify the information that must be collected to answer these questions. In addition, he can assist in the collection and analysis of this information.

The fifth step in a problem-solving sequence involves the ongoing assessment and evaluation of a strategy that has been selected for solution to an instructional problem. This step yields formative evaluation information to be used in the ongoing monitoring of the instructional process. An instructional consultant can aid a faculty member in the identification of criteria for evaluation and tools for the generation of formative evaluation information. This step recycles the faculty member back to problem sensing and problem analysis and engages him in an ongoing instructional planning process. This step usually eliminates the need for further consultative assistance in this instructional area.

The final step in a problem-solving sequence involves interaction once more between ideas and values. A summative evaluation is conducted to determine the extent to which the consultant's intervention and faculty member's work on the problem has helped the faculty member achieve desired outcomes, goals, and objectives as identified during the initial problem-sensing step. An instructional consultant often aids in the design and implementation of this summative evaluation, though preferably this step is conducted by the faculty member in conjunction with another person or group. An instructional consultant should not be placed in the uncomfortable and potentially conflicting situation of having to be the final judge of his own work. During a summative evaluation, information is collected and analyzed which enables the faculty member and others to answer the question: Have the desired outcomes, goals, or objectives been achieved? A more detailed, experimentally-based evaluation is required to answer the question: Has this specific intervention assisted in the accomplishment of the desired outcomes, goals, or objectives? Ideally, a summative evaluation should answer the second question.

C. Concluding Observations

The three consultative domains just described—information, values, and ideas— and the six-step problem-solving sequence just outlined are not as elaborately drawn out as were the more specific instructional improvement and course design consultation sequences described in the first two volumes of this series. Our intention has been to suggest that these specific consultative sequences hold much in common and can be incorporated under one general problem-solving rubric. These specific consultative sequences also closely related to a generic model of consultation that is described in some detail in *Consultation in Higher Education.*[3] Chapters Two and Three of this book are devoted to a 10-step model of collegiate consultation that closely parallels the specific models of instructional improvement and course design consultation. Following is a summary statement of this model:

1. *Entry:* the client contacts the consultant
2. *Initial Contracting:* the consultant and client reach a preliminary agreement concerning their working relationship
3. *Information Collection:* the consultant (often in collaboration with the client) collects additional information about the client system
4. *Information Analysis:* the consultant (often in collaboration with the client) assembles and synthesizes the information to arrive at a valid and useful description of the client system
5. *Information Feedback:* the consultant conveys the description of the client system to the client in a manner that promotes understanding and movement from reflection to action
6. *Recontracting:* the consultant and client reach a new agreement about their relationship, based on the information that already has been conveyed and their experience in working together
7. *Planning for Intervention:* the consultant and client determine the nature and design of activities that will be responsive to the problems and needs identified by the client and information gathered during previous stages
8. *Intervention:* the consultant provides specific services for the client that are responsive to the problems and needs of the client system
9. *Evaluation of the Intervention:* the client and consultant determine the extent to which the intervention successfully responded to the client's problems and needs, and was compatible with the contractual relationship between the client and consultant
10. *Recontracting/Exit:* the client and consultant determine whether further work is needed and to what stage the consultant should return if further work seems appropriate; if no further work is needed, the client and consultant plan for and initiate the consultant's exit in a manner that insures continuity of action taken as a result of the consultation[4]

In the formation and use of an instructional consultation service for faculty, one might benefit from review of the ten-step model and from reflection on the manner in which this model and/or the six-step problem solving sequence described in this chapter might be incorporated fully into a comprehensive consultative model. Such an integration is possible and perhaps necessary, given the complex and changing needs of faculty for assistance in the formulation of teaching strategies and designs for a heterogeneous student population.

NOTES:

[1]Arthur W. Chickering and others, *Developing the College Curriculum: A Handbook for Faculty and Administrators* (Washington, D.C.: Council for the Advancement of Small Colleges, 1977).

[2]Robert Diamond and others, *Instructional Development for Individualized Learning in Higher Education* (Englewood Cliffs, New Jersey: Educational Technology Publications, 1975), pp. 41–42.

[3]Daniel H. Pilon and William H. Bergquist, *Consultation in Higher Education: A Handbook for Practitioners and Clients* (Washington, D.C.: Council for the Advancement of Small Colleges, 1979).

[4]*Ibid.,* pp. 19–20.

Section III

Personal and Organizational Development

Chapter Seven

Personal and Organizational Development: An Overview

In the first two volumes of this handbook series we have offered a variety of discussions, instruments, and exercises in the areas of both personal and organizational development. We have called attention to the importance of team building, decision making, and conflict management for the successful operation of committees, departments, and divisions. We have attempted to outline at least some of the dimensions of effective academic leadership. And we have identified approaches to personal growth ranging from discussions of teaching to the development of interpersonal and helping skills. Yet in spite of these efforts, we have failed to articulate a comprehensive view of the role of personal and organizational development in higher education.

Perhaps the task has simply been too difficult. In many ways faculty development has been a first attempt to apply some of the insights of the applied behavioral sciences on a broad scale to American colleges and universities, and the sheer difficulty of that undertaking may have precluded clear thinking and writing. Perhaps we simply did not know enough. Certainly very few institutions even to this day have made a very significant attempt to incorporate personal and organizational dimensions into their planning and programming. Little actual experience was then available—and not a great deal more has been amassed in the last few years. And perhaps higher education is simply immune to the systematic promotion of personal and organizational growth. Divided and isolated into departments, divisions, and disciplines, the individuals and groups that make up our academic organizations may simply lack the interdependence needed for human relations and structures.

And yet the effort must be made once more, for if American higher education is going to survive the inevitable traumas of the 1980s with a sense of humaneness and dignity, it simply must give greater attention to the human and organizational dimensions of the enterprise. To assist in this undertaking we have provided in this volume three rather comprehensive although not necessarily lengthy chapters on personal, organizational, and career development in higher education. Our intent here is to place each of these three interrelated dimensions of faculty development in an institutional and organizational context and to argue once again for the vital importance of these issues for growth and survival.

Ten years ago Nevitt Sanford attempted to describe our academic culture and the restrictions it placed on the human and professional development of college and university faculty.[1] That early statement served as one of the rallying points for the emerging faculty development movement. Yet in spite of that movement, the academic culture of 1981 may be even more barren than it was 10 years ago. Faculty earning power has declined, what mobility did exist has vanished, and even the existence of many institutions has been, and is, threatened. Unless college and university administrators and faculty can come to address the incredibly complex personal, organizational, and career

165

issues touched on in the following three chapters, the bleak academic culture that Sanford described 10 years ago may someday come to look like an oasis of health and growth. American higher education is faced right now with perhaps its most severe test of the century; only the most comprehensive of visions will survive the 1980s. Our hope is that these three chapters can be of some assistance in meeting that challenge.

NOTES:

[1]Nevitt Sanford, "Academic Culture and the Teacher's Development," *Soundings* (1971), 1–11.

Chapter Eight

Personal Development in Higher Education

Whether organizational development or personal development has been ignored more widely by most faculty development programs would be difficult to determine. William Nelsen and Michael Siegel found only six examples of attempts at organizational development among the 20 colleges and universities surveyed for the Association of American Colleges;[1] they cite no examples of programs with a primary focus on personal development. Of course, all learning results in personal growth. The increased sense of personal competence that comes from growth in one's discipline, from a growing sense of one's effectiveness as a classroom teacher, or from the mastery of a new approach to teaching and learning is an important part of personal growth. A fuller awareness of one's teaching style and a growing understanding of student needs and expectations can bring about changes in interpersonal awareness and behavior. Such books as Joseph Axelrod's *The University Teacher as Artist* (San Francisco: Jossey-Bass, 1973), Kenneth E. Eble's *The Craft of Teaching* (San Francisco: Jossey-Bass, 1976), or Mervin Freedman's *Academic Culture and Faculty Development* (Berkeley, California: Montaigne, 1979) can lead to increased understanding of one's self and others. And certainly a number of the basic strategies for organizational development discussed in Chapter Nine and in previous volumes of this series are intended to increase the interpersonal effectiveness of both faculty and administrators. In one sense, then, faculty development, whenever successfully practiced, can lead to the increased personal growth of those involved.

If, however, personal development is defined as a direct attempt to increase the self-awareness of faculty as individuals and as people in relationships with others, then it is apparent that most faculty development programs have failed to address the personal growth of their faculty. First, although many faculty may see some professional value in attending a workshop on student advising, they are likely to dismiss one on their own career development, for example, as irrelevant or even self-indulgent. Second, personal growth activities are inherently threatening. At times uncomfortable with their own emotions or with the emotions of others, faculty can defensibly dismiss personal growth as a kind of "touchy-feely" sensitivity training. Third, personal growth programming is not consistent with the cultural norms of American higher education, for it violates both the primacy of cognitive rationality and the insistence on individuality and autonomy. Finally, few programs may have the resources of a skilled facilitator of personal growth activities available to them. Without particular competence in this area, and faced with the natural resistance and even hostility of faculty to this kind of programming, it is not surprising that very few institutions take the risk of offering personal growth resources to their faculty.

In spite of these barriers, however, personal development remains an important component of faculty development—although certainly not for all faculty. Integrated into other programming[2] or offered as an advanced activity for faculty who have experienced other less threatening kinds of workshop learning, personal growth activities often provide important and far-reaching benefits. The remainder of this chapter will touch briefly on two of the most successfully used approaches to personal development—interpersonal skills training and the personal growth laboratory.[3] We will then provide a series of exercises and workshops for personal development.

A. Interpersonal Skills: Training and Theory

None of the approaches to personal development discussed in this chapter is particularly credible to most faculty, and the theory and practice of interpersonal skills is no exception. A workshop on "Improving Interpersonal Relations" is not likely to attract many faculty. However, interpersonal skills training can be successfully integrated into more apparently legitimate activities, such as workshops on "The Advising Process," "Working with Diverse Student Learning Styles," "Improving Class Discussions," or, perhaps, "Interpersonal Relations in the Classroom." Even a seminar on improving lecturing can focus at least partly on interpersonal skills and relationships. Some ingenuity may be required, but it does seem appropriate to seek out as many opportunities as possible to expose faculty to some of the basic but all too frequently ignored practices of interpersonal communication.

Whether interpersonal skills training is incorporated into other activities or offered as a topic in its own right, we have found it useful to offer that training, where possible, in the context of one or more basic models of interpersonal relations. The two that have been found most useful for this purpose are the Relationship Awareness Theory of Elias Porter and the Fundamental Interpersonal Relations Orientations of Will Schutz. Both can be presented with the assistance of a simple questionnaire (Porter's "Strength Deployment Inventory" and Schutz's "FIRO-B"); in each case participants come to understand the theory through an examination of their own scores. As described in Exercises Four and Five, each of these models provides a conceptual framework within which faculty can explore the implications of their own interpersonal behavior.

Training in the theory and practice of interpersonal skills ought to be a far more prominent part of faculty development than it currently is. With some ingenuity and with the expertise available on most campuses through speech communication departments, this training can be integrated successfully and appropriately into a wide range of activities. Faculty are, above all, people relating to other people; when properly and skillfully presented, training in improved interpersonal relationships is almost always received openly and even gratefully.

B. Personal Growth Laboratories

If interpersonal skills training is not highly credible to most faculty, personal growth laboratories and workshops are pure anathema. Perhaps still tainted by some of the excesses of the human potential movement of the 1960s, the direct confrontation with self and others brought about by a successful personal growth workshop could not be further from the intellectual and rational norms of American higher education. The confused terminology of the personal growth field certainly does not help, and even though some attempt has been made to classify certain types of growth groups,[4] it is often difficult to tell the difference between a "T-group," a "sensitivity training group," an "encounter group," or a "Gestalt group," even after participating in one. The "trendiness" of certain sub-movements within the field, such as "EST" and "Rolfing," does little to lend academic credibility to these activities. And finally there is always the fear of a "casualty," the concern that someone will "get hurt" by an intensive personal growth experience, even though research and experience does not seem to support this fear.[5] What Christopher Lasch would dismiss as part of the "Culture of Narcissism"[6] is clearly not the culture of American higher education.

Some of these reservations may be appropriate. The language of the human relations field is certainly confusing, incompetent facilitators do exist, and the kind of learnings promoted by even well run personal growth groups can sometimes be unsettling. Yet with a few basic ground rules the personal growth laboratory can be a valuable resource for any faculty development program. First, participation in personal growth activities must be strictly voluntary; although this is true for almost any faculty development event, it is an absolute necessity for this kind of training. Second, prospective participants should have had previous contact with experienced-based learning activities. A personal growth workshop should not be a faculty member's first exposure to laboratory learning. Third, the workshop should be conducted by experienced and competent facilitators; because of the complexity of this kind of training, personal growth workshops should almost never be led by a single individual. It is appropriate to ask for references, a clear statement of goals and methods, and evidence of having conducted previous successful personal growth workshops in higher education. Finally, personal growth events are best not conducted for people who work together on even an occasional basis, both to insure openness during the group and confidentiality after its completion. Because of this last consideration, directors of faculty development programs, particularly those on smaller campuses, may wish to provide resources for faculty to attend such events off-campus rather than sponsor on-campus personal growth laboratories. The NTL Institute and University Associates,[7] the two national organizations that provide personal growth training on a regular basis, can help keep faculty development programs aware of these resources.

Although it is doubtful that personal growth laboratories would, or should, ever become the central feature of any faculty development program, they can, like interpersonal skills training, be part of the range of resources a college or university can make available to its faculty. If handled with sensitivity and confidentiality, personal growth programming can be of significant value to those faculty ready and willing for the kind of learnings this activity can provide. The workshop designs presented in Planning Document Number One are intended to make available to participants a meaningful first experience with a personal growth laboratory.

NOTES:

[1] William C. Nelsen and Michael E. Siegel, *Effective Approaches to Faculty Development* (Washington, D.C.: Association of American Colleges, 1980), pp. 131–135; in this discussion Nelsen and Siegel give no indication of their sense of the effectiveness of these programs. In an earlier presentation of this research, however, Nelsen estimates that of these six efforts, only two could be considered even partly successful while the other four are judged unsuccessful. Nelsen, "Faculty Development: Key Issues for Effectiveness," *Forum*, 2 (1979), 1–2.

[2] Two organizations, the Academy for Professional Development (P.O. Box 7328, Tacoma, Washington 98407), and the Associated Schools of the Pacific Northwest (1500 N. Warner, Tacoma, Washington 98416), have successfully integrated personal growth programming into the design of week-long faculty development workshops which focus, in addition, on issues of intellectual and instructional development. Other organizations and institutions attempting this integration include the Great Lakes College Association (contact person: Jon Fuller), Azusa Pacific College (James Holsclaw), and St. Andrews Presbyterian College (Ronald Crossley).

[3]Values clarification might well be identified as a third approach, although that is more a process for dealing with values in a variety of areas rather than a methodology for increasing personal and interpersonal understanding and effectiveness. Chapter Eleven of the second volume of this series discusses values clarification as part of faculty development in somewhat more detail.

[4]John E. Jones, "Types of Growth Groups," J. William Pfeiffer and Jones, eds., *The 1972 Annual Handbook for Group Facilitators* (La Jolla: University Associates, 1972), pp. 145–151.

[5]Jack R. Gibb, "The Message from Research," Pfeiffer and Jones, eds., *The 1972 Annual Handbook for Group Facilitators* (La Jolla: University Associates, 1972), pp. 155–177. In conducting personal growth activities with hundreds of participants over the last several years, the authors have not encountered a single "casualty."

[6]Christopher Lasch, *The Culture of Narcissism* (New York: Norton, 1978).

[7]National Training Laboratories, Box 9155, Arlington, Virginia 22209; University Associates, 8517 Production Avenue, Box 26240, San Diego, California 92121.

EXERCISE NUMBER FOUR

TITLE: Personal Strengths and Weaknesses

SOURCE: Gwen Clavadetscher and Steven R. Phillips, based on the *Strength Deployment Inventory,* available from Personal Strengths Assessment Service, 571 Muskingum Avenue, P.O. Drawer 397, Pacific Palisades, California 90272.

GENERAL DESCRIPTION: Personal growth workshops sometimes can be disorienting experiences, especially for those not familiar with such activities. A conceptual framework for personal development often can provide participants with the intellectual base from which they can safely venture into more emotional waters. The *Strength Deployment Inventory* (SDI) is a commercially prepared, copyrighted instrument that helps participants assess both their own characteristic patterns of relating to others and the motivations associated with each pattern. Because the SDI helps participants identify interpersonal strengths as well as weaknesses, it provides a considerable amount of positive reinforcement in addition to a potential agenda for change.

INSTRUCTIONS FOR USE: Prior to taking the SDI, participants might be asked to complete the following sentences:
    "I am at my best in relationships with other people when I can . . ."
    "People I work with best are those who . . ."
    "When I am not getting my way with others, I tend to . . ."
    "The worst thing people can say about me in terms of my relationship to others is that I . . ."
The responses to these questions might be discussed for several minutes in groups of three or four. Following this warm-up, participants should be asked to complete the inventory.
    The SDI produces two scores, the first reflecting the individual's interpersonal orientation when things are going well, the second when faced with conflict or opposition. The first score should be calculated and plotted, followed by a presentation of the basic theory behind the instrument "when things are going well." A "sociogram" might then be made by asking participants to locate themselves spatially in a way that reflects their orientation on the scoring form that accompanies the instrument. People with similar orientations might be asked to form small groups to discuss questions like the following:
    "How do we feel being in the same group with this particular orientation:"
    "What things do we seem to have in common in terms of SDI theory?"
    "What kind of positive feedback from others most pleases us?"
Once these discussions have been completed, the second score should be plotted, again followed by a short presentation of the theory "when faced with conflict and opposition." A new sociogram might then be formed to reflect changes in the two scores. Major shifts in orientation should be noted and discussed. Small groups of people with similar scores again might be formed to

171

discuss the interpersonal strengths and weaknesses identified by the instrument.

The exercise can be ended at this point or, after an appropriate break, the workshop leader can involve participants in one or more of the exercises presented in this series of handbooks as a way of continuing to focus on the dynamics of interpersonal relations according to the theory behind the *Strength Deployment Inventory*. We recommend, of course, that the facilitator be thoroughly familiar with this theory. An interpretative manual, which includes several additional workshop designs, and a three-day "Relationship Awareness Training" workshop are available from the publishers of the inventory.

EXERCISE NUMBER FIVE

Title: Inclusion, Control, and Affection

Source: Marcia Shaw and Steven R. Phillips, based on *FIRO-B,* available from Consulting Psychologists Press, 577 College Avenue, Palo Alto, California 94306.

General description: Like the *Strength Deployment Inventory, FIRO-B* (which stands for Fundamental Interpersonal Relations Orientation—Behavior) provides participants with a conceptual framework for understanding interpersonal relations. *FIRO-B* might be used at the outset of a personal growth workshop in a manner similar to that suggested for the *Strength Deployment Inventory* or, if the workshop is of some length, reserved for use later in the design to heighten personal interaction and insight.

    FIRO-B helps individuals identify the way they typically relate to others in terms of the three fundamental issues of Inclusion, Control, and Affection. Inclusion concerns issues of belongingness and boundaries and tends to address questions concerning membership and entrance into personal relationships. Control concerns issues of responsibility and authority and generally addresses questions concerning the distribution of power and responsibility in relationships. Affection concerns issues of interpersonal closeness and tends to address questions of self-disclosure and intimacy.

Instructions for use: The *FIRO-B* questionnaire should be completed by participants prior to the presentation of the theory behind the instrument. Once this presentation is completed, participants can be asked to share and discuss their scores with one another in small groups.

    As with the *Strength Deployment Inventory,* an opening session on *FIRO-B* can be followed by additional sessions to discuss in greater depth the implication of the theory which allows participants to share their perceptions of each other in terms of the theory, or to engage in further exercises to highlight various aspects of Inclusion, Control, and Affection. *FIRO-B* theory should be well understood before undertaking such a design; in particular, the theoretical presentation should be as non-evaluative as possible and should avoid the often insensitive descriptions of behavior found in Alan Ryan's otherwise useful *Clinical Interpretation of FIRO-B* available from Consulting Psychologists Press. The best sources of information concerning FIRO theory are instead to be found in the writings of its originator, Will Schutz, in *The Interpersonal Underworld* (Palo Alto: Science and Behavior Books, 1966), *Joy* (New York: Ballantine, 1967), *Elements of Encounter* (New York: Bantam, 1975), and *Profound Simplicity* (New York: Bantam, 1979).

Variations:
1. If the group is relatively small and if time permits, the score of each member of the group could be posted and discussed. If this procedure is followed, the facilitator might begin by posting and discussing his own.

2. If even more time is available, individual scores in each category—inclusion, control, and affection—can be posted one at a time, allowing for greater discussion of each dimension.
3. After completing the instrument, but prior to scoring it, participants can be asked to predict their scores on the basis of a presentation of the theory. Similarities and differences between predicted and actual scores can be a rich source of insight and discussion.
4. Before completing and scoring the instrument, a "FIRO Microlab," as described in Exercise Number Six, can be implemented.

EXERCISE NUMBER SIX

TITLE: FIRO Microlab

SOURCE: William H. Bergquist and Steven R. Phillips, based on the writing and workshop designs of William Schutz (see Exercise Number Five).

GENERAL DESCRIPTION: The *FIRO-B* questionnaire described in Exercise Number Five allows participants in a personal growth workshop to assess their orientation on the three fundamental interpersonal dimensions of inclusion, control, and affection. Another way to help participants gain access to this information is to ask them to work through a series of statements which touch on various aspects of each dimension. Although such a procedure does not provide the kind of quantifiable information available from the questionnaire, it does develop some of the same information in a way that allows participants greater control over the amount of self-disclosure they are asked to make to others.

INSTRUCTIONS FOR USE: Participants are asked to form groups of three or four and to complete and discuss their responses to the following statements:
1. "When I enter a new group I feel . . ."
2. "When I entered this group I felt . . ."
3. "When a group starts I . . ."
5. "When I'm in a new group I feel most comfortable when . . ."
6. "When someone does all the talking I feel . . ."
7. "I feel best about myself as a leader when . . ."
8. "I will try to take charge of a group . . ."
9. "I feel most annoyed when the leader . . ."
10. "When I am the leader of a group I usually . . ."
11. "I am most easily hurt in a group when . . ."
12. "I trust others in a group when . . ."
13. "Those who really know me think I am . . ."
14. "I feel closest to others when . . ."
15. "Others feel closest to me when . . ."
16. "People like me when I . . ."
17. "I feel most valued when . . ."

After participants have had at least an hour to work through these statements, the workshop leader should make a brief presentation of FIRO theory. The microlab should conclude with an opportunity for the same groups to review their responses to the statements in light of this theory and to explore the way their small group itself worked through the three dimensions of inclusion, control, and affection.

Variations:
1. Initially, each small group could be asked to address only the first five questions, which involve the issue of inclusion. After about 15 or 20 minutes of conversation, the workshop leader could present the concept of inclusion according to FIRO theory. Next, participants could work on

175

items six through ten, which deal with control, followed by FIRO theory on control. Finally, the remaining questions, which concern affection, could be discussed, followed by FIRO theory on affection.

HANDOUT NUMBER SEVEN

TITLE: Guidelines for Conducting a Personal Growth Workshop

SOURCE: Steven R. Phillips

GENERAL DESCRIPTION: This list of suggestions for personal growth workshops can be useful either to the beginning trainer who would like some direction for the actual conduct of such a workshop or to the more experienced trainer who periodically wants to review several basic principles perhaps once known but all too frequently forgotten.

INSTRUCTIONS FOR USE: These guidelines should be reviewed prior to designing a personal growth workshop and perhaps from time to time during the workshop itself. If the workshop is being conducted by more than one trainer (and, if possible, we recommend that procedure), the guidelines should be discussed jointly.

GUIDELINES FOR CONDUCTING A PERSONAL GROWTH WORKSHOP

1. Provide a clear set of workshop goals and objectives but allow time at the outset for participants to discuss, clarify, and even redefine workshop goals to meet their own learning needs.
2. Develop a learning environment in which people feel free to discuss their needs and expectations by listening sympathetically to their ideas, suggestions, and reservations, by avoiding status distinctions among members and between members and staff, and by making participation as easy as possible for each member.
3. Respect confidentiality by making it clear that although participation is encouraged, the amount and extent of self-disclosure will be the responsibility and under the control of each participant.
4. Assume that the workshop design will need review and revision as participants come to understand and articulate their learning needs more fully.
5. Begin each session by asking participants to share their perceptions of the progress of the workshop up to that point, to clean up any "unfinished business" from previous sessions, and to express any felt need for change or modification of the workshop design.
6. Use the process and development of the workshop itself as a source of information about interpersonal relations and personal growth.
7. Understand the natural resistance of participants to change but do not collude with them to make change more difficult or impossible than it actually is.
8. Provide a combination of theory and skill-training so that participants will have not only a theoretical base for change, but also the skills needed to actually change their behavior.
9. Provide time for planning "back-home" application and change.
10. Provide ample time after each session for staff to meet to discuss the previous sessions and review plans for the next activity.

PLANNING DOCUMENT NUMBER ONE

TITLE: Two Personal Growth Workshops

SOURCE: Steven R. Phillips

GENERAL DESCRIPTION: Personal growth workshops can be of considerable value, even if only one or two days in length. Experienced facilitators are comfortable with providing large amounts of unstructured time for participants to work on their own interpersonal issues in a group setting, hence they often conduct longer workshops. Two rather highly structured designs are presented in the following documents, each lasting one day. The two can be combined easily into a single two-day workshop. With an adequate understanding of the theory behind the *Strength Deployment Inventory* and *FIRO-B,* a sensitive and supportive workshop leader should be able to use one or both of these designs to provide a useful first experience in personal growth for faculty participants.

INSTRUCTIONS FOR USE: Each workshop design can be implemented using material and information provided in the three volumes of this series. Each workshop should begin with a brief overview of the design and a clear statement of workshop objectives. As is always the case with personal growth activities, participants should understand that all activities are strictly voluntary.

PERSONAL GROWTH WORKSHOP
Design Number One

Focus: Assessing Interpersonal Strengths and Weaknesses

Duration: Eight Hours

ACTIVITY NUMBER	GENERAL GOALS	RECOMMENDED EXERCISE	DURATION
1.	Provide a conceptual framework for assessing interpersonal strengths and weaknesses	Personal Strengths and Weaknesses (Volume 3, Exercise Number Four)	Three hours
2.	Help participants explore interpersonal strengths and weaknesses in a simulated setting	Discovery (Volume 1, Exercise Number Six) or Astronaut (Volume 1, Exercise Number Seven)	Two hours
3.	Help participants assess their current situation concerning specific goals and develop specific action plans	Building a Project (Volume 2, Exercise Number Eighteen)	Three hours

PERSONAL GROWTH WORKSHOP
Design Number Two

Focus: Improving Interpersonal Understanding

Duration: Seven Hours

ACTIVITY NUMBER	GENERAL GOALS	RECOMMENDED EXERCISE	DURATION
1.	Introduce participants to the concepts of inclusion, control, and affection	FIRO Microlab (Volume 3, Exercise Number Six)	Two hours
2.	Provide feedback to participants on their interpersonal orientations	Inclusion, Control and Affection (Volume 3, Exercise Number Five)	One hour
3.	Help participants apply their learnings to a current interpersonal problem or issue	Helping Trios (Volume 1, Exercise Number Fourteen)	Two hours

Chapter Nine

Organization Development in Higher Education

Organization development is an important component of the modern theory and practice of faculty development. As originally described by us in *The Journal of Higher Education*, the purpose of organization development (OD) is to improve organizational effectiveness by working with academic and administrative programs, departments, and divisions on such activities as team building, conflict management, decision making, and management training.[1] Subsequent to that presentation, Jerry Gaff proposed a modification of this scheme by suggesting that the purpose of organization development in higher education is simply to create an environment which promotes effective teaching.[2] The distinction here is at least theoretically important. Academic organizations do have other functions than instruction, and the extent to which OD efforts in higher education should be concerned with those functions, particularly in the name of faculty development, has not yet become clear. As we will suggest in the final section of this volume, the future role of faculty development in higher education, if any, may well focus more directly on the organization as a whole. Embedded in both our definition and Gaff's, however, is the fundamental assumption that what faculty can and will do as professionals is a consequence of the nature of the organization within which they find themselves. Organization development is an attempt to help those organizations function more effectively and humanely.

As often happens in the field of faculty development, the gap between theory and practice is of some consequence. Although the theory of faculty development envisions the involvement of the entire college or university, or at least of significant units within the institution, in a search for more effective organizational structures and processes, the practice of faculty development—when concerned with organizational issues—has amounted to little more than a few workshops for faculty and administrators on group decision making and effective meetings. These activities may be intrinsically quite valuable, of course, for faculty do perform a number of administrative functions; yet by themselves they can do little to move academic organizations in the direction of more effective and healthy operations.

Perhaps it would be better to approach faculty development from a different perspective than that upon which these handbooks have been based. Rather than describing faculty development as a three-part undertaking consisting of instructional, personal, and organizational development, it might be better to identify organization development as the broader concern under which would fall such issues as faculty development, administrative development, and staff development.[3] Improved organizational effectiveness, whether defined generally or simply in terms of instructional success, often involves not only changed policies and procedures but also fundamental changes in the culture of the organization; only organization development is broad enough in its scope and methodology to deal with issues of this magnitude.

182

Although a variety of strategies and methods for organizational development have been available to colleges and universities for a number of years, relatively few people in the higher education community are familiar with the basic outlines of this approach to organizational effectiveness. Organization development (OD) may be defined as

(a) A long-range effort to introduce planned change based on diagnosis which is shared by the members of an organization.
(b) An OD program involves an entire organization, or a coherent "system" or part thereof.
(c) Its goal is to increase organizational effectiveness and enhance organizational choice and self-renewal.
(d) The major strategy of OD is to intervene in the on-going activities of the organization to facilitate learning and to make choices about alternate ways to proceed.[4]

The objectives of most organization development programs in higher education usually include

(1) Increased trust and open communication between members of the organization, especially between faculty and administrators and between departments.
(2) The creation of an open, problem-solving environment within the institution.
(3) The location of problem solving and decision making as close as possible to the sources of information.
(4) An increased level of commitment to institutional goals and objectives.
(5) Increased interdependence between individuals and groups in the organization.
(6) An increased awareness of the role of interpersonal relations and interpersonal communication within the institution.[5]

Underlying these objectives is a set of assumptions about the nature of life and change in organizations which include the following:

(1) The attitudes of members of an organization toward their work, each other, and the organization are a function not primarily of individual personalities but rather of the nature of the organization itself. Change efforts consequently should be directed to organizational structures and processes rather than toward individual behavior.
(2) Individuals will work most effectively toward the accomplishment of organizational goals to which they are committed.
(3) Given the opportunity, most members of organizations will seek responsibility and challenge.
(4) The work of organizations is accomplished in groups; consequently, the focus of change must be on groups, not individuals.
(5) Higher education in particular tends to suppress open expression of feelings, which has negative consequences on the emotional quality of work life. Individuals can learn to express appropriate feelings and thus function as more complete human beings.
(6) Choice is the most important organizational value. Given alternatives from which to choose, groups can both make better decisions and increase the commitment of group members to the implementation of those decisions.[6]

Organization development is accomplished most often through the collection and joint diagnosis of information about the organization, community meetings, team building, intergroup consultation, and interpersonal skills training at all levels of the organization.

Organization development is clearly a substantial undertaking, one for which all organizations may not be ready. In recent years, the concept of "OD Readiness" has gained some currency as a way of assessing the potential of an organization for significant development.[7] Before undertaking a major organization development effort, colleges and universities might wish to consider their "readiness for development" in terms of the following variables:

General Considerations

1. Size. A large, complex, multi-purpose university may simply be too big for institution-wide organization development. If the number of faculty and administrators potentially involved in such an effort much exceeds 50, consideration should be given to conducting OD individually with smaller sub-groups within the institution.
2. Institutional Stress. If a college of university is not experiencing some stress, motivation for development is likely to be lacking; on the other hand, situations of intense crisis may not allow for the time and reflection needed for OD. Institutions that are experiencing some stress short of crisis seem most open to organization development.
3. OD History. If an institution has had successful experiences with OD, the likelihood of the success of a new initiative is increased. A history of recent failures with OD may limit severely the potential success of a new program. Consequently, organization development should not be undertaken without some assurance of success, for the failure of a premature effort may well doom OD at that institution for some time to come.

Resources

4. Time Commitment. Are the leaders of the institution willing to devote the time needed to organization development? Because of the complexity of the issues involved, it may well be minimally three years before significant change can be demonstrated.
5. Money. OD should not rely exclusively on external consultants, but considerable long-term external consultation may well be needed. Is the institution willing to commit significant financial resources to OD?
6. Flexibility. Organization development often may require structural reorganization at both the administrative and faculty levels. If organizational structures are essentially immune to change, the potential success of organization development is limited.

People

7. Interpersonal Skills. OD involves interpersonal communication, and the key figures in the institution must possess adequate communication skills, including the ability to listen carefully and openly to negative feedback.
8. Administrative Development. Do administrators, including department chairmen, see themselves as professional managers or are they only holding office for two or three years until it is someone else's turn? Effective administration

requires professional skills. If these skills are seen to violate collegial norms, an organization development program will not have the administrative commitment needed for success.

9. Commitment at the Top. If the leader of an organization is not willing to engage at some point in his own development and change, the prospects for significant change elsewhere in the organization are dim.

10. Internal Consultants. OD is a day-by-day activity, not something that is done only once. Internal consultants must be available to provide the kind of long-term follow-up that cannot be supplied by external consultants. Resources, including training, release time, and institutional recognition, need to be available to these people.

Instrument Number Two, "OD Readiness Inventory," provides a convenient if rough means of estimating the readiness of an organization for development.

If an institution is not ready to undertake organization development (by whatever means the determination is made), two choices short of doing nothing at all remain. First, even though an entire college or university may be unwilling or unable to engage in OD, one or more of its component units may well be. One of the joys and frustrations of higher education is the relative autonomy of departments, divisions, and even programs from the rest of the institution. Although this limits overall organizational effectiveness and cohesion, it also makes those units available for OD. Second, if organization development seems unlikely, training in various organizational and management skills still can be made available to those who are interested. Indeed, this approach may be chosen consciously as a "pre-OD strategy" designed to increase organizational awareness of more effective ways of behaving and to bring the institution to an increased state of OD readiness.

Organization development is a significant intervention in the life of a college or university, one which is likely to have long-range consequences for the institution, its faculty, and students. To change the culture of an organization and the reward systems, policies, and procedures necessary for effective teaching, an in-depth intervention may be needed. Unless an organization genuinely values good teaching, all the faculty development workshops in the world may have little or no positive effect. In spite of the scope of organization development, however, a number of strategies currently exist which have been shown to be effective in improving organizational life. Survey feedback involves the systematic collection of information about the institution on which deliberate decisions about the future can be made. The OD meeting provides a way of reaching relatively rapid agreement on organizational problems and priorities. Both team building and intergroup consultation have helped numerous groups work more humanely and effectively together. Individually and collectively, these strategies, which are described in more detail in the remainder of this chapter, can make significant contributions to increased organizational effectiveness in higher education.

A. Survey Feedback

Organization development almost always begins with the collection of information about one or more aspects of the institution involved. Perhaps the most broadly based process of information collection and analysis for organization development is known

185

as survey feedback. In this process, information is collected from all appropriate members of the organization through written questionnaires or, sometimes, personal interviews. That information is tabulated, summarized, and reported back to various groups within the organization. Each group analyzes that information further, then uses its analysis as a basis for problem solving, proposal recommendation, and decision making as appropriate. If handled properly, the process of survey feedback allows all members of an organization to share in the collection and analysis of information about the organization itself and to participate in the problem solving and decision making occasioned by that information.

The nature of the information collected by the survey feedback process is determined, of course, by the nature of the issues with which the organization is concerned. The two most generally useful instruments available to colleges and universities are the *Institutional Functioning Inventory* (IFI) and the *Institutional Goals Inventory* (IGI), both published by the Educational Testing Service. The IFI allows an institution to describe itself in a number of important dimensions, including the extent to which it values human diversity, supports academic freedom, promotes undergraduate learning, and encourages the advancement of knowledge. This information can be compared to the perceptions of faculty from 37 colleges and universities about their own institutions. The *Institutional Goals Inventory*, on the other hand, provides a college or university with an opportunity to define itself in relationship to a broad range of possible goals, from furthering the academic development of students to providing a vehicle for social activism. Respondents to the IGI are asked to describe their perception of their institutions on both an "is" and "should be" basis, thus allowing for a comparison between the way the college or university is seen currently and the way it should be in the future. Both the IFI and the IGI provide information on the responses of such subgroups as faculty, administrators, undergraduate students, and trustees, which often proves valuable in locating areas of significant agreement and disagreement within the institution.

A number of more specialized instruments for survey feedback are also available. Because the IGI contains a number of items inappropriate to the small college, the Council of Independent Colleges has developed the "Small College Goals Inventory" expressly for those institutions. Student perceptions of their college experience can be assessed by the *College and University Environment Scales*,[8] while the general educational environment of an institution can be assessed by either the *Educational Environment Scale*[9] or the *Institutional Climate Inventory* presented in Instrument Number Three. Faculty attitudes and needs can be surveyed by using either the "Professional Development Questionnaire" or the "Faculty Questionnaire" contained in Volume 2 of this series, while student concerns can be determined by using the "Experience of College Questionnaire."[10] Finally, a number of instruments have been developed for use in non-academic organizations;[11] although these would need to be revised for use in higher education, they can serve as a rich source of ideas and suggestions.[12]

Even though the selection of the instrument or questionnaire to be used in survey feedback is important, the process by which that questionnaire is selected and the use to be made of the information collected is perhaps even more significant. Senior administrators must be involved in the process of instrument selection and development, since it will often fall to them to act on the information collected. If they do not in some sense "own" the questionnaire, it is doubtful they will be committed to acting on its results. Indeed, it is desirable to involve as many members of a college or university in the development and selection of the instrument to be used in survey feedback as possible. Although it may not be feasible to involve everyone who will be completing the questionnaire, the more campus leaders, including department and division heads, who participate in that process, the more likely it will be that the information obtained from the questionnaire will be accepted openly and positively.

Once survey feedback information has been collected, it should be tabulated and summarized in a way that will facilitate analysis and discussion; conclusions should not be drawn at this point. The process of feedback probably should begin with the senior administrative officer involved; once he has understood that information, it then can be taken, first, to senior administrative and trustee groups, then to academic departments and divisions. Throughout this process, it is essential that care be taken not only to disseminate survey information widely in the organization but also to provide a mechanism through which various groups can discuss that information and make appropriate recommendations and even decisions.

During the entire survey feedback process, the role of an internal or external consultant may be crucial. Early in the process that person can provide technical assistance and information as key administrators and faculty leaders develop or select an instrument appropriate to current institutional concerns. That same consultant can help design administration procedures for the instrument selected or developed and can assist in preliminary tabulation and summary of the results. Perhaps most important, however, an internal or external consultant may be of great value in the process of dissemination and discussion, for the open and non-defensive consideration of sometimes disconfirming information is essential to the success of survey feedback. Although a consultant cannot be responsible for the decisions the institution will make on the basis of the information collected, he can help insure that discussion and problem solving proceed in as open and collaborative a manner as possible.

Survey feedback can provide an institution with a rich source of information on which long-range decisions about the future can be made.[13] Most appropriately conducted at the outset of a new administration—early in the planning process of a new general education or CORE curriculum, or during periods of significant institutional reorganization or definition—survey feedback is based on the most central value of organization development, the value of choice. Given adequate information about itself and a viable range of alternatives from which to choose, an institution can manage to take control of its future. Faced with the uncertainties of higher education in the 1980s, this control may be essential to survival.

B. The OD Meeting

Organization development almost always begins with the collection and analysis of information about the organization; the process through which organization development is carried out is meetings. As we will see in the next section, there are a number of ways of working with committee, departments, and divisions to improve the effectiveness of their meetings and of their operation in general. In this section, however, we would like to consider ways in which meetings of representative groups of an organization, and even of the entire organization, can play an important part in the process of organization development.

187

During the process of a survey feedback approach to organization development, tabulated and summarized information about the organization usually is discussed by various formal administrative and faculty groups within the institution. Because that information may be of significant interest to the organization as a whole, however, it might be worth holding one or more community meetings during the survey feedback process, perhaps one shortly after the information has been summarized to report initial impressions and insights, and perhaps one after that information has been discussed by appropriate campus groups to report recommendations and institutional consequences. A community meeting conducted early in the process might involve an overview of the organization development project, followed by a presentation of the preliminary results of the information collection process. Participants in the meeting then might be broken down into groups of five to seven people and asked to address such questions as

1. What are your general responses to the organization development program as described?
2. What are your general responses to the information as presented?
3. What do you perceive as the most important single piece of information presented so far?
4. What do you see as the general consequences of this information for the future of this institution?

After about 20 to 30 minutes of discussion, each group should briefly report its responses to these questions, which might be posted on newsprint. This information can serve as important input into the organization development process, while the conduct of one or more such meetings can help insure continued involvement and investment in these efforts by most of the members of the institution.[14]

A second kind of OD meeting has been developed by Carol Zion and is described in Exercise Number Seven. Although that process is designed to help an institution develop long-range goals, the same structure and sequence of events could be incorporated into a variety of community meetings dealing with a number of other issues.

A third kind of OD meeting is based on a design of Richard Beckhard and involves all faculty and appropriate academic administrators.[15] Designed to identify and give priority to problems currently facing the institution, this type of meeting is of particular value, according to Beckhard, when

a. there is a need felt by the administration and key faculty leaders to examine institutional problems directly and openly;
b. very little time is available;
c. the administration wishes to improve conditions as soon as possible;
d. there is enough administrative cohesion to insure follow-up;
e. real commitment exists on the part of the administration to problem solving; and
f. the institution is experiencing, or has recently experienced, major stress.[16]

The intent of this kind of meeting, described more fully in Exercise Number Eight, is to identify significant institutional problems in a relatively brief period of time, specify those which are most important, and provide a mechanism for problem solving and follow-up reporting. If entered into with an open and collaborative frame of mind, a meeting such as this can do much to bring institutional problems out in the open so that they can be dealt with constructively.

Meetings are a part of organizational life and will be an important part of any organization development effort. Appropriately designed and used, broadly representative OD meetings can help insure the widespread sharing of information and problem solving so essential to organizational health.

C. Team Building

Much of the work of organizations gets done by groups, yet groups are notoriously ineffective and wasteful. This may be particularly true of higher education, with its strong emphasis on the individual teacher and researcher. Yet groups—committees, departments, divisions—play an important role in collegiate life, and an increase in the effectiveness of individual groups within an institution can make a significant contribution to the development of the organization. Team building provides a set of strategies for working with individual groups to help them become more effective in accomplishing the task in front of them. Described by most writers in the field as perhaps the most important group of OD interventions,[17] team building is particularly appropriate for higher education, for the very condition which makes organization development so difficult in colleges and universities—the existence of numerous relatively autonomous sub-groups with their own (and differing) sets of goals, values, and agendas—makes team building so attractive. We have defined organization development as an undertaking involving "an entire organization, or a coherent 'system' or part thereof." A complex, multi-university may indeed be "OD proof," but if significant sub-groups within that institution can be helped to function more effectively, organization development will have in fact taken place.

A variety of approaches to team building are possible, ranging from "process consultation"[18] to long-term training and development.[19] The process described in this section is one that has been found suitable for a variety of academic departments, divisions, and administrative groups in higher education. Almost always conducted by one or more consultants external to the group being worked with, team building should begin with what would be equivalent at the group level to the concept of "OD readiness" at the organizational level. Does the group that is considering team building have a reason for working together? Is there some level of interdependence among members of the group, that is, do they need each other's skills, abilities, and experience to accomplish mutually shared goals? Are the members of the group committed to working together to increase their effectiveness? Do the members of the group and, in particular, does the leader of the group understand the process of team building and are they, and he, committed to it? Is the group accountable for its performance to others in the institution?[20] A number of preliminary meetings and discussions may be necessary to determine the answers to these questions and to prepare the group for the process of team building.

The question often asked is, "Can we do team building without everyone being involved?" The answer varies according to the situation, but if the person or people who will be absent are actually part of the group, that is, if they can be expected to take part in future discussions and decisions, team building should not proceed without them.

Once the group has committed itself to team building and has demonstrated some understanding of what that might involve, the actual process should begin with the collection of information about the current level of operation of the group. This can be done through the kind of interview questions suggested in Instrument Number Four or through a questionnaire like the one presented in Instrument Number Five. Interviews have the advantage of providing the consultant with an opportunity to establish some rapport with each member of the team,[21] while questionnaires have the advantage of being somewhat more quantifiable. With appropriate time and resources, a combination of interviewing and questionnaires can be quite effective. However it is done, sufficient information must be collected prior to the team building meeting to allow for a clear definition of the group's issues and concerns and to insure that the consultant will not be handed any surprises once those meetings have begun.

The actual team building sessions should last a minimum of a day and a half—three and a half days is ideal. The meeting need not be held off-campus, although this is often desirable, but it must be held at a place that will be free of interruptions. The first meeting should begin with what William Dyer calls the "start-up phase," during which the members of the group "come together and begin the process of establishing a climate for work."[22] This may involve a positive opening statement from the leader of the group expressing his hopes for the meeting, a sharing of expectations by the participants, a discussion of the role of the consultants, or even a simple group problem-solving or decision-making simulation. Once the work climate becomes as open and comfortable as can be expected at this point, the consultants should present in a descriptive, summary form the information previously collected from the group. Once that information has been understood, the consultants should work with the group to establish an agenda for the rest of their time together. Those issues and concerns may be clearly self-evident from the information presented, or an agenda-setting process like that described in Exercise Number Nine may need to be used. The agenda might include task issues, interpersonal issues, or both. Once the agenda has been established, the meeting should be turned over to the formal leader of the group, who in essence convenes an extended meeting of the team.

The role of the consultants during the rest of the team building sessions is important but difficult to describe. At a minimum, the consultant should provide feedback from time to time to share his perceptions of the way the group is working on its agenda. The consultant may wish to suggest alternative ways of approaching particular agenda items (small groups, task forces, pairs) or may need to facilitate communication and openness between particular group members. He may wish to help the group examine its own operation and method of working, perhaps using the "Group Expectation Survey" (Instrument Number Eleven) or the "Group Perception Survey" (Instrument Number Twelve) contained in Volume 1 of this series, the "Role Perception Survey" (Instrument Number Fourteen) contained in Volume 2, or the "Work Perception Survey" (Instrument Number Six) and "Leadership in Groups" (Instrument Number Seven) contained in this volume. Finally, the consultant may ask for time to conduct brief workshop sessions on such issues as decision making, problem solving, or meeting effectiveness, perhaps using such methods as those suggested in Exercises Ten, Eleven, and Twelve and elsewhere in this series of handbooks. The issues the consultant chooses to address will depend, of course, on the strengths, weaknesses, and problems facing the group. Consequently, the presence of a consultant to provide appropriate training and direction is an essential aspect of the team building process.

The final team building session should address issues of follow-up. At its best, team building is not a one-time only intervention into the life of a group but rather the beginning of a continuing process of development. Follow-up activities certainly would include the implementation of any decisions made during the meeting but also might involve additional training or workshop sessions and even the continued presence on a regular or occasional basis of one or more consultants to provide additional feedback and perspective on the group's development. Although the responsibilities for follow-up activities must be with the group, the consultant can be of help in encouraging the group to address the consequences of the team building meeting.

Faculty and administrators spend an enormous amount of time in meetings, yet that time is often wasted. For groups that meet together on a regular basis over a significant period of time, team building can provide a powerful means for making committee and departmental life in higher education more productive and even enjoyable.

D. Intergroup Consultation

In spite of the relatively low interdependence among groups in most colleges and universities, sometimes groups that must work together find themselves blocked by misunderstanding and mistrust. A faculty senate may need to improve its relationship with an administrative cabinet, two departments may need to work more closely together to develop an interdepartmental curriculum or major, or several departments in a division may be sharply divided between two academic programs or issues. Reorganization from departments to divisions may be a likelihood or even a fact. In these and similar cases, organization development efforts might well focus on ways of increasing understanding and cooperation between groups.

One approach to improving intergroup relations might involve a modified version of the team building process discussed above. Following separate team building sessions for each group, the members of both groups would be interviewed about their perceptions of the relationship between the two groups, about obstacles they see to more effective cooperation, and about ways of increasing the ability of the two groups to work together successfully. That information can be presented to a joint team building session of both groups. Together, these groups then would explore ways of improving their work together.

A different and perhaps more direct approach to intergroup consultation was developed several years ago to improve relations between union-management groups in industry.[23] Again, after separate team building sessions, the two groups involved are brought together for a two-day intergroup workshop. Following an orientation to the workshop in which the need for cooperation and understanding between the two groups is stressed, each group is given the task of developing on newsprint three lists: (1) a profile or image of how that group sees itself, particularly in relationship to the other group, (2) a description of how it sees the other group, particularly in relationship to itself, and (3) a prediction of how the other group will describe it. Each group should work alone on its three lists for perhaps two or three hours. Each discussion should be facilitated by either an external consultant or an internal consultant from another part of the organization to help the group get past current issues of disagreement between the groups, personality conflicts, and ancient history.

Once each group has developed its individual descriptions, the two groups should meet together to share their perceptions of each other and of themselves. The objective of this session is to help each group understand the other, not to defend or argue the "correctness" of these perceptions. Again, external facilitation may well be essential to help members of both groups listen openly and non-defensively to the other. The sharing of perceptions and the discussions to follow probably will take the remainder of the first day of the workshop.

The second half of the intergroup workshop should begin with each group again working separately for at least two hours to answer the following three questions. First, what is it that our group has done that has contributed to the image the other holds of us? Second, what is it that has led us to describe ourselves as we have? Third, what is there in our relationship with the other group that has caused us to predict as we have their description of us? Coupled with the clarification that one hopes emerged from the initial sharing of perceptions, this self-diagnosis should lead to increased understanding of the nature of the relationship between the two groups. Once each group has answered these three questions, the two groups should be brought together again to share that information. The final part of the workshop should be devoted to clarifying and consolidating key issues that yet stand as barriers to more effective interaction between the two groups. Responsibility for addressing those issues should be assigned clearly to individuals, sub-committees, or *ad hoc* task forces, and a definite time frame should be established for follow-up reporting.

Although it is unlikely that all of the issues facing two groups in conflict can be resolved in two days, a successful intergroup workshop can serve to open communication and increase understanding between groups and to move them from hostility and recrimination to rational problem solving. As with team building, the follow-up phase will be essential to insure that progress made during the workshop will have long-term benefit for the groups and, consequently, for the entire organization.

E. Conclusion

In spite of the availability of a wide range of alternatives, most teaching in American higher education will continue to be done, for better or worse, by a single teacher in a classroom of less than 100 students. What that teacher can and will do in that classroom, however, is not only a function of his instructional skills and disciplinary competence, but also of the organizational climate within which that teaching takes place. In spite of the large degree of autonomy afforded professors in American colleges and universities, organizational behavior remains a consequence of organization culture. Only organization development can provide the means of deliberately changing that climate in ways that will enhance improved performance. Without attention to organizational issues, most faculty development efforts will remain peripheral and even opposed to the dominant value system of the very institutions those efforts are intended to serve.

NOTES:

[1]William H. Bergquist and Steven R. Phillips, "Components of an Effective Faculty Development Program," *The Journal of Higher Education*, 46 (1975), 183.

[2]Jerry G. Gaff, *Toward Faculty Renewal* (San Francisco: Jossey-Bass, 1975), p. 9.

[3]This revision has occured to others, including Walter Sikes, "Organizational Diagnosis: A Key Administrative Skill," John A. Shtogren, ed., *Administrative Development in Higher Education* (Richmond, Virginia: Higher Education Leadership and Management Society, Inc., 1978), pp. 45–46.

[4]John H. Sherwood, "An Introduction to Organization Development," J. William Pfeiffer and John E. Jones, eds., *The 1972 Annual Handbook for Group Facilitators* (La Jolla, California: University Associates, 1972), p. 153.

[5]These objectives are based on similar listings in Sherwood, "An Introduction to Organization Development," pp. 154–155.

[6]Adapted from Sherwood, "An Introduction to Organization Development," pp. 154–155.

[7]J. William Pfeiffer and John E. Jones, "OD Readiness," Pfeiffer and Jones, eds., *The 1978 Annual Handbook for Group Facilitators* (La Jolla, California: University Associates, 1978), pp. 219–225, upon which the following discussion is based.

[8]Contact Robert Pace, UCLA School of Education, Los Angeles, California 90024.

[9]Arthur Chickering and others, *Developing the College Curriculum: A Handbook for Faculty and Administrators* (Washington, D.C.: Council for the Advancement of Small Colleges, 1977), pp. 297–313.

[10]Available from Arthur Chickering, The Center for the Study of Higher Education, Memphis State University, Memphis, Tennessee 38152.

[11]J. William Pfeiffer, Richard Heslin, and John E. Jones, *Instrumentation in Human Relations Training* (La Jolla, California: University Associates, 1973), pp. 237–257.

[12]A detailed bibliography on institutional research for higher education can be found in the PHASE I materials of the *Project Work Manual* for Project QUE of the Council of Independent Colleges.

[13]A discussion of the way survey feedback can become part of a comprehensive institutional development program may be found in William H. Bergquist and William A. Shoemaker, eds., *A Comprehensive Approach to Institutional Development* (San Francisco: Jossey-Bass, 1976).

[14]The community meeting described here is based on a similar meeting discussed in the PHASE I materials of the *Project Work Manual* for Project QUE of the Council of Independent Colleges.

[15]Richard Beckhard, "The Confrontation Meeting," *Harvard Business Review,* March-April (1967), 146–55; a similar design could be developed for student groups or representatives and student affairs administrators.

[16]Adapted from Beckhard's discussion, p. 150.

[17]Anthony J. Reilly and John E. Jones, "Team Building," in J. William Pfeiffer and Jones, *The 1974 Annual Handbook for Group Facilitators* (La Jolla, California: University Associates, 1974), p. 227.

[18]Edgar Schein, *Process Consultation: Its Role in Organization Development* (Reading, Massachusetts: Addison-Wesley, 1969).

[19]Perhaps the range of team building interventions is best represented by Reilly and Jones, "Team Building," which takes a very task-oriented approach to team building, and William Dyer, *Team Building: Issues and Alternatives* (Reading, Massachusetts: Addison-Wesley, 1977), which seems almost to ignore task issues. The model presented in this chapter attempts to combine the two approaches, with some leaning toward Reilly and Jones. For an early discussion of team building in higher education, see Charles K. Bolton and Ronald K. Boyer, "Organization Development for Academic Department," *Journal of Higher Education,* 44 (1973), 352–369.

[20]Several of these questions were suggested by Reilly and Jones, "Team Building," p. 227.

[21]For a provocative discussion of interviewing as part of the process of team building, see John E. Jones, "The Sensing Interview," in John E. Jones and J. William Pfeiffer, eds., *The 1973 Annual Handbook for Group Facilitators* (La Jolla, California: University Associates, 1973), pp. 213–224.

[22]Dyer, "Team Building," p. 53.

[23]Robert R. Blake, Jane S. Mouton, and Richard Sloma, "The Union-Management Intergroup Laboratory: Strategy for Resolving Intergroup Conflict," *The Journal of Applied Behavioral Science,* 1 (1965), 25–57. See also "Intergroup Meeting: An Image Exchange," in J. William Pfeiffer and John E. Jones, *A Handbook of Structured Experiences for Human Relations Training* (San Diego: University Associates, 1971), III, 81–83. The model presented in this section is a combination of these two approaches.

INSTRUMENT NUMBER TWO

TITLE: OD Readiness Inventory

SOURCE: Steven R. Phillips, adapted from a similar checklist in J. William Pfeiffer and John E. Jones, *The 1978 Annual Handbook for Group Facilitators* (La Jolla, California: University Associates, 1978), p. 226.

GENERAL DESCRIPTION: Some assessment of the readiness of an organization or organizational sub-group for organization development is useful for both the organization and prospective consultants. The "OD Readiness Inventory" is not intended to be a statistically validated instrument but, instead, a starting place for discussion of the feasibility of an organization development program.

INSTRUCTIONS FOR USE: Prior to completing the "OD Readiness Inventory," each of the 10 dimensions should be reviewed in light of the discussion of those factors contained in Chapter Nine. The inventory may be completed jointly by the prospective organization development consultant and key figures within the organization or completed separately by them for later discussion. A number of variables may exist, of course, within an organization to temper the results of this assessment, which is best used not as a quantifiable and absolute measure of an institution's readiness for organization development but rather as a focus for discussion and planning. A total score of much below 40, however, should cause serious reconsideration of the value of organization development, while a score above 55 may indicate the possibility of a significant OD effort. A score between 40 and 55 might suggest readiness for a variety of workshop activities perhaps as preparation for organization development.

OD READINESS INVENTORY*

Instructions: Please indicate the extent to which you perceive each of the following dimensions as being of concern to you as you consider the prospect of organization development for this institution.

General Considerations	No Concern	Mild Concern	Moderate Concern	Significant Concern	Critical Concern
1. Size	4	3	2	1	0
2. Institutional Stress	4	3	2	1	0
3. OD History	4	3	2	1	0
Resources					
4. Time Commitment	8	6	4	2	0
5. Money	8	6	4	2	0
6. Flexibility	8	6	4	2	0
People					
7. Interpersonal Skills	12	9	6	3	0
8. Administrative Development	12	9	6	3	0
9. Commitment at the Top	12	9	6	3	0
10. Internal Consultants	12	9	6	3	0

Total Score_____

*Adapted from J. William Pfeiffer and John E. Jones (Eds.), *The 1978 Annual Handbook for Group Facilitators*. San Diego, CA: University Associates, 1978. Used with permission.

INSTRUMENT NUMBER THREE

TITLE: Institutional Climate Inventory

SOURCE: Adapted by Mary Lynn Crow, Mary "Ski" Hunter, Joe C. Ventimiglia, and Paul D. Day from Jerry G. Gaff, "The Faculty Questionnaire," as presented in *A Handbook for Faculty Development,* Volume 2 (Washington, D.C.: Council for the Advancement of Small Colleges, 1977), pp. 44–45.

GENERAL DESCRIPTION: The *Institutional Climate Inventory* consists of seven separate scales which can be used individually or in various combinations. The "Institutional Morale Scale" measures the general positive attitudes toward the college or university in which the respondents are employed and the "Administrative Morale Scale" measures the general positive attitudes toward the administration and administrators of the college or university in which they are employed, while the "Collegial Morale Scale" measures general positive attitudes toward colleagues and colleagueship at the college or university where the respondents ar employed. The "Attitude Toward Faculty Development Scale" measures respondents' perceptions of the adequacy of the faculty development services at their schools. The "Job Satisfaction Scale" measures the degree to which the respondents are satisfied with their academic careers, including interest, success, and teaching. The "Alienation from Standards Scale" measures the felt discrepancy between three selected pairs of actual and ideal criteria for the evaluation of academic personnel. Finally, the "Professional Autonomy Scale" measures the degree to which respondents perceive faculty governance and individual independence as prevailing at the college or university where they are employed.

    The norms for each scale, based in every case on responses from more than 500 university professors in this country and abroad are as follows:

Institutional Morale Scale: mean = 27.05; variance = 79.43; range = 8–40. The reliability is 0.75 (standardized item alpha).

Administrative Morale Scale: mean = 22.95; variance = 48.27; range = 7–35. The reliability is 0.61 (standardized item alpha).

Collegial Morale Scale: mean = 14.28; variance = 33.02; range = 5–25. The reliability is 0.58 (standardized item alpha).

Attitude Toward Faculty Development Scale: mean = 12.97; variance = 28.77; range = 4–20. The reliability is 0.69 (standardized item alpha).

Job Satisfaction Scale: mean = 15.68; variance = 6.31; range = 5–20. The reliability is 0.58 (standardized item alpha).

Alienation from Standards Scale: mean = 5.27; variance = 32.40; range = 0–36 (empirical), 0–48 (theoretical). The reliability is 0.50 (standardized item alpha).

Professional Autonomy Scale: mean = 31.74; variance = 39.55; range = 11–44. The reliability is 0.84 (standardized item alpha).

    For information with regard to the validity of the first six scales, consult the following references: Joe Ventimiglia and Mary "Ski" Hunter, with the assistance of Paul D. Day, "An Inside Look at Academic Life at UTA," *Insight to Teaching Excellence* (published by the Faculty Development Resource Center, University of Texas at Arlington), 6 (1979), 3–7; Joe Ventimiglia and Mary "Ski" Hunter, "The Old Guard and The Young Turks at UTA: Organizational Composition, Values, and Morale," *Insight to Teaching Excellence*, 6 (1979), 3–8; Mary "Ski" Hunter, Joe Ventimiglia, and Mary Lynn Crow, "Faculty Morale in Higher Education," *Journal of Teacher Education*, 31 (1980), 27–30.

For further information about the final scale and the *Institutional Climate Inventory*, contact the Faculty Development Resource Center, Box 19459, University of Texas at Arlington, Arlington, Texas 76019.

INSTRUCTIONS FOR USE: The response categories and scoring for the "Institutional Morale Scale," the "Administrative Morale Scale," the "Collegial Morale Scale," and the "Attitude Toward Faculty Development Scale" are: No = 1; Don't Know = 3; Yes = 5. Total the values for all items.

The response categories and scoring for the "Job Satisfaction Scale" are: Strongly Disagree = 1; Disagree Somewhat = 2; Agree Somewhat = 3; Strongly Agree = 4. Total the values for all five items.

The response categories and scoring for the "Alienation from Standards Scale" are: Not at all = 1; Somewhat = 2; Moderately = 3; Very = 4; Extremely = 5; Computation method: (actual publication − ideal publication)^2 + (actual teaching − ideal teaching)^2 + (actual service − ideal service)^2.

The response categories and scoring for the "Professional Autonomy Scale" are: Disagree = 1; Disagree with reservations = 2; Agree with reservations = 3; Agree = 4. Add all values on 11 items for total score.

The following items on each scale are reverse coded as follows:
"Institutional Morale Scale," items 3, 4, and 5
"Administrative Morale Scale," items 2, 5, and 7
"Collegial Morale Scale," items 4 and 5
"Attitude Toward Faculty Development Scale," items 1 and 2
"Job Satisfaction Scale," items 2, 3, and 4
"Professional Autonomy Scale," items 2, 5, 6, 8, 10, and 11

Variations:
1. In addition to its use as a survey feedback questionnaire, the *Institutional Climate Inventory* can be used as an institutional planning tool for establishing priorities for future development.
2. The information from various scales can be used to focus workshop activities to encourage dialogue between faculty and administrators.
3. The inventory can be used to evaluate an institution periodically for evidence of long-term change.
4. The inventory can be used to collect data for social science research in higher education.

INSTITUTIONAL MORALE SCALE

People perceive their institutions in different ways. Please indicate, from your own perspective, whether you think the following statements describe or do not describe the institution of higher learning where you are employed.

	No	Don't Know	Yes
1. Faculty morale is generally high.	_____	_____	_____
2. Communication between the faculty and the administration is good.	_____	_____	_____
3. This institution does little to help a faculty member develop as a teacher, scholar, or professional.	_____	_____	_____
4. It is very difficult to make any significant change in the quality of teaching or learning here.	_____	_____	_____
5. Rules and regulations are too restrictive.	_____	_____	_____
6. The quality of education a student gets at this school is generally quite high.	_____	_____	_____
7. This institution does a great deal to promote the professional development of the faculty.	_____	_____	_____
8. The atmosphere here is warm and friendly.	_____	_____	_____

ADMINISTRATIVE MORALE SCALE

People perceive their institutions in different ways. Please indicate, from your own perspective, whether you think the following statements describe or do not describe the institution of higher learning where you are employed.

	No	Don't Know	Yes
1. By and large, top-level administrators are providing effective educational leadership.			
2. Teaching is considered to be of little value by the administration.			
3. The institution has a long-range plan that is widely understood and generally accepted.			
4. Department chairmen and central administrators generally encourage faculty members to experiment with new courses or teaching methods.			
5. Rules and regulations are too restrictive.			
6. Relationships between faculty members and administrators tend to be egalitarian rather than hierarchical.			
7. Departmental barriers discourage serious work among faculty members in different fields.			

COLLEGIAL MORALE SCALE

People perceive their institutions in different ways. Please indicate, from your own perspective, whether you think the following statements describe or do not describe the institution of higher learning where you are employed.

	No	Don't Know	Yes
1. There is a strong sense of community, a feeling of shared purposes and interests on this campus.	_____	_____	_____
2. Mutual respect and trust exist among the faculty.	_____	_____	_____
3. Opportunities for interdisciplinary teaching and learning are common.	_____	_____	_____
4. Some faculty members do little more than meet their classes and pick up their checks.	_____	_____	_____
5. For the most part, relationships with colleagues tend to be intellectually sterile.	_____	_____	_____

ATTITUDE TOWARD FACULTY DEVELOPMENT SCALE

People perceive their institutions in different ways. Please indicate, from your own perspective, whether you think the following statements describe or do not describe the institution of higher learning where you are employed.

	No	Don't Know	Yes
1. This institution does little to help a faculty member develop as a teacher, scholar, or professional.	_____	_____	_____
2. It is very difficult to make any significant change in the quality of teaching or learning here.	_____	_____	_____
3. Department chairmen and central administrators generally encourage faculty members to experiment with new courses or teaching methods.	_____	_____	_____
4. This institution does a great deal to promote the professional development of the faculty.	_____	_____	_____

JOB SATISFACTION SCALE

Faculty members express a range of views about their work. At this stage of your career how do you feel about the following matters?

	Strongly Disagree	Disagree Somewhat	Agree Somewhat	Strongly Agree
1. My work generally is exciting and fulfilling.	_____	_____	_____	_____
2. Knowledge in my field is expanding so fast that I have fallen seriously behind.	_____	_____	_____	_____
3. Teaching is not as much fun as it once was.	_____	_____	_____	_____
4. I can't seem to find time to do all the work I want to do.	_____	_____	_____	_____
5. My career to date has been successful.	_____	_____	_____	_____

ALIENATION FROM STANDARDS SCALE

Actual Criteria:

In decisions pertaining to promotion and salary matters at your institution, how important do you think each of the following criteria *IS*?

	Not At All	Somewhat	Moderately	Very	Extremely
1. Publishing professional works	_____	_____	_____	_____	_____
2. Effectiveness as a teacher	_____	_____	_____	_____	_____
3. Departmental and institutional service	_____	_____	_____	_____	_____

Ideal Criteria:

In decisions pertaining to promotion and salary matters, how important do you think each of the following criteria *SHOULD BE*?

	Not At All	Somewhat	Moderately	Very	Extremely
1. Publishing professional works	_____	_____	_____	_____	_____
2. Effectiveness as a teacher	_____	_____	_____	_____	_____
3. Departmental and institutional service	_____	_____	_____	_____	_____

PROFESSIONAL AUTONOMY SCALE

Please indicate whether you agree or disagree with each of the following statements concerning the total administration at your institution.

	Agree	Agree with Reservations	Disagree with Reservations	Disagree
1. The administration acts on faculty recommendations.	_____	_____	_____	_____
2. Very few faculty without an administrative appointment have any input at this institution.	_____	_____	_____	_____
3. Faculty are expected to assume leadership at this institution.	_____	_____	_____	_____
4. Faculty here are encouraged to exercise autonomy.	_____	_____	_____	_____
5. There is little faculty governance at this institution.	_____	_____	_____	_____
6. The administration rarely yields to faculty pressure.	_____	_____	_____	_____
7. Faculty may call administrators by their first names.	_____	_____	_____	_____
8. Antagonistic faculty are pressured to leave the institution.	_____	_____	_____	_____
9. Administrators seldom, if ever, issue direct orders to faculty members.	_____	_____	_____	_____
10. The administration discourages criticism of policies.	_____	_____	_____	_____
11. Faculty who deviate from institutional expectations are made to feel uncomfortable.	_____	_____	_____	_____

EXERCISE NUMBER SEVEN

TITLE: Goal Setting: An Administrative Exercise

SOURCE: Carol Zion

GENERAL DESCRIPTION: This exercise attempts to make goal setting a human endeavor by relating it to real institutional groups. Setting objectives or goals sometimes can be a tedious activity unrelated to the real needs and expectations of those served by the institution; the process described in this exercise makes goal setting somewhat more enjoyable and participatory.

INSTRUCTIONS FOR USE: This exercise is designed for participation by representatives from various campus groups. At the beginning of the exercise, participants should be broken down into their appropriate constituent groups. Each group should represent a major campus constituency. The exercise should be introduced by giving a date five years from the date of the session and announcing that it has been a very good five years. As a result, the following groups wish to commend the administration.

Instructions to:
1. Students
   The administration of the college has done an outstanding job over the past five years and the student newspaper wishes to commend the administrators for their work. *As students,* write an editorial (on newsprint) emphasizing the worthwhile endeavors of the administration.
2. Faculty
   The administration has accomplished much over the past five years and the faculty senate has decided to write a special letter of commendation to them. *As faculty,* write that letter (on newsprint) citing the actions and accomplishments that have benefited the faculty.
3. Board of Trustees
   The administration has pleased the Board of Trustees over the past five years and the Board has decided to write a letter of commendation to them. *As trustees,* write that letter (on newsprint) emphasizing the achievements supported by the Board.
4. Develop similar statements for any group included in the exercise. Post all newsprint and review. The facilitator should underline points which actually are long-range goals and help the participants address such questions as:
   Which goals are identical?
   Which goals are complementary?
   Which goals are in conflict?
   Those goals which are identical or complementary (or both) then can be listed as acceptable long-range goals for the institution. Those goals which appear to be in conflict need to be worked through at that session or a later one.

Variation:
1. Representatives from all campus constituencies need not participate in this exercise. Instead, a planning group or committee that may consist only of administrators or administrators and faculty can be broken down into separate groups and asked to take the point of view of particular campus groups.

EXERCISE NUMBER EIGHT

TITLE: Beckhard's OD Meeting

SOURCE: Adapted from Richard Beckhard, "The Confrontation Meeting," *Harvard Business Review* March-April (1967), 149–55.

GENERAL DESCRIPTION: During periods of significant stress or change, organizational problems can develop or become exacerbated in ways that require direct and rapid action. The problem-solving mechanisms of most colleges and universities, however, are anything but direct and rapid. The OD Meeting, a modification for higher education of Richard Beckhard's Confrontation Meeting, can provide in a brief period of time a vehicle for expeditious problem identification and a starting place for needed problem solving.

INSTRUCTIONS FOR USE: The OD Meeting usually takes place in a single day, although it can be designed to be held the evening of the first day and the morning of the second. As outlined by Beckhard, the meeting has seven steps or phases:

Step One: Climate Setting (30 minutes)
   The OD Meeting should begin with a clear statement from the senior administrator involved concerning the purpose of the meeting, his commitment to act on organizational problems, and his belief in an open and collaborative problem identification process. If important information exists about the institution that is not shared widely, this would be the appropriate point at which to make that information known.
Step Two: Information Collection (one hour)
   Participants are divided into small, heterogeneous sub-groups; efforts should be made to have these groups comprise a variety of people from different academic ranks, disciplines, divisions, and departments. If a senior administrative group meets regularly, it should form a separate group. Each group should be given the following assignment:
      Thinking of yourself as both an individual with your own set of needs and goals and as a member of this institution, what do you see currently existing in this institution as obstacles, poor procedures and/or policies, inappropriate and/or unclear goals, and so forth that inhibit you from being more effective and this school from being more successful? What different conditions might exist that would make this institution better and your work more successful and rewarding?
Step Three: Information Sharing (one and a half to two hours)
   During this step, a reporter from each group reviews the results of the group's discussion, which should be listed on newsprint. Once all groups have reported, the leader of the meeting might wish to categorize various items into more general, related sub-groups. At this point, the meeting should break for lunch (or, if conducted in the evening, for the night). Prior to reconvening, the summary lists should be typed and duplicated for all participants.

Step Four: Priority Setting and Action Planning (one and a half hours)
   The entire group should reconvene for about 15 minutes to review the summary prepared during the break (or the night before). The participants then should be broken into appropriate departmental or divisional groups and given the following questions to discuss:
   1. Which of these problems or issues most directly affect this department? Which of these can we begin to take action on ourselves?
   2. Which issues or problems should be addressed first either by appropriate institutional committees or by the administration?
Step Five: Organization Action Planning (one to two hours)
   The total group reconvenes in a general session during which
   1. Each department reports its plan and commitment to action to the total group.
   2. Each department lists those issues that it feels should be addressed first by institutional committees or by the administration.
   3. The senior administrator reacts to this list, comments on possible actions where appropriate, and solicits responses of appropriate committee chairmen.
Step Six: Immediate Administrative Follow-Up (one to three hours)
   The senior administrative group meets immediately after the general meeting to discuss the results of that meeting and plan for specific administrative action. The results of this meeting should be communicated to all participants in writing as soon as possible.
Step Seven: Progress Review (two hours)
   Four to six weeks later, the entire group should be reconvened to hear reports from departments concerning the progress they have made on their action plans and from the senior administrator and appropriate committee chairmen on their own progress.

INSTRUMENT NUMBER FOUR

TITLE: Team Building Interview

SOURCE: Steven R. Phillips and William H. Bergquist

GENERAL DESCRIPTION: Team building almost always begins with the collection of information about the group from the group itself prior to the first team building session, usually through individual interviews. Personal interviews allow the consultants a chance to establish a relationship with team members individually, explore the personal dynamics at work in the team, and assess potential areas of concern or difficulty. Interviews also can help team members themselves begin thinking in a more reflective or focused way about issues they may be addressing during the team building meetings.

INSTRUCTIONS FOR USE: If possible, the interview questions used prior to team building should focus both on general issues of group effectiveness and on specific issues with which the group already is concerned. One way of identifying those specific concerns is to ask members in a preliminary meeting simply to write down on a piece of paper the issues they think the interviews ought to address. The interview schedule presented here is more general and is intended only as a model on which questions can be developed for particular groups.

　　The interview itself should begin with a review of the team building process to be sure that the team member is clear about what is going to happen and about how his information is to be used. Since the information from the interviews will be summarized and reported back to the group, the interviewer cannot insure confidentiality, but, because the information will be reported anonymously, he can promise anonymity. This distinction should be made clear to the team member at the outset of the interview. Some consultants prefer to establish as a ground rule for the interview that any information discussed may be reported back anonymously to the group; others are willing to hear but not use information identified by the team member as confidential. The choice is an individual one.

　　Once the interviews are completed, the information should be summarized on newsprint for presentation to the group. The nature of the summary will depend on the nature of the information collected but should be organized either as summary responses to individual questions or as general themes or patterns that have emerged from the interviews. In presenting this information, consultants should be as non-evaluative as possible and open to modifications or shadings of their perceptions by the group. Care should be taken, however, not to allow discussion to move at this point into problem solving, which should be reserved for after an agenda has been set.

TEAM BUILDING INTERVIEW

1. What are your professional responsibilities here? Which do you find most gratifying? Most frustrating?
2. What do you see as the role of the group we are going to work with? How does that role relate with your own professional responsibilities?
3. Describe a recent meeting of the group that was particularly effective. Why was it effective?
4. Now describe a recent meeting that was not very effective. What was going on?
5. Tell me about regular meetings of the group. How often are they held? How is the agenda set? What happens during the mettings? How are decisions made? Conflicts resolved? How is leadership handled? How do people seem to feel about the meetings?
6. What are current tasks or issues facing the group? What would you predict your agenda would be for the next several meetings?
7. What are the strengths and weaknesses of the group as it is currently functioning?
8. Is there anything else you would like to tell me about the group or about your concerns for the team building sessions?

INSTRUMENT NUMBER FIVE

TITLE: Team Building Questionnaire

SOURCE: Steven R. Phillips, based on a similar questionnaire discussed in Charles K. Bolton and Ronald K. Boyer, "Organization Development for Academic Departments," *Journal of Higher Education* 44 (1973), 352–369.

GENERAL DESCRIPTION: Collecting information for team building by means of a questionnaire has the advantage of providing anonymous, quantifiable information, as well as the disadvantage of impersonality. When used in combination with the kind of information collected through interviews, however, a careful summary of questionnaire information can be most useful both in focusing on specific areas of concern and in highlighting general patterns of perceptions.

INSTRUCTIONS FOR USE: The following questionnaire is designed for use with an academic department and would need some modification and revision for other groups. The questionnaire should be completed anonymously by all members of the group well in advance of the team building sessions; the average completion time for the "Team Building Questionnaire" is 30 minutes. The information from the questionnaire can be either summarized on a clean copy and returned to participants during the team building meeting or highlighted on newsprint. If both interviews and a questionnaire are being used, the questionnaire might well be completed and summarized first as a means of identifying in a preliminary way concerns that could be followed up in more detail through the interviews.

A TEAM BUILDING QUESTIONNAIRE

Part I
General Information

1. What is your present rank? (Check one.)

   Professor_____   Associate Professor_____   Assistant Professor_____
   Instructor_____   Lecturer_____   Other_____

2. How long have you been in the department? (Check one.)

   0–3 years_____   4–8 years_____   9–15 years_____ Over 15 years_____

3. Within the department, how much emphasis is placed on each of the following? (Mark one on each line.)

	A Very Great Amount	A Great Amount	Some	A Slight Amount	None at All	I Don't Know
a. Instruction of Undergraduate Majors	_____	_____	_____	_____	_____	_____
b. Service to Business and Industry	_____	_____	_____	_____	_____	_____
c. Career Development of Junior Faculty	_____	_____	_____	_____	_____	_____
d. Instruction of Graduate Students	_____	_____	_____	_____	_____	_____
e. Serving on University Committees	_____	_____	_____	_____	_____	_____
f. Instruction of Undergraduate Non-Majors	_____	_____	_____	_____	_____	_____
g. Expressing Departmental Views and Interests in the University	_____	_____	_____	_____	_____	_____
h. Research and Publication	_____	_____	_____	_____	_____	_____
i. Advancing the Discipline and the Professional Nationally	_____	_____	_____	_____	_____	_____
j. Advancing the Reputation of the Department both Locally and Nationally	_____	_____	_____	_____	_____	_____

211

4. From the list in question (3) select the three items you feel *now receive* the greatest amount of emphasis. Indicate the topic or letter for the three items you select.

Greatest amount of emphasis _____

Second most emphasis _____

Third most emphasis _____

5. From the list in question (3) select the three items you feel *should receive* the greatest amount of emphasis. Indicate the topic or letter for the three items you select.

Greatest amount of emphasis _____

Second most emphasis _____

Third most emphasis _____

6. If one your colleagues needed special consideration to solve the following problems, to whom would you recommend he go for assistance? (Mark one on each line.)

	Your Dean	Your Division Chairman	Your Department Chairman	Certain Faculty in the Department	Faculty in Another Department	None	I Don't Know	Other
a. A promotion or tenure action	____	____	____	____	____	____	____	____
b. A larger salary increase	____	____	____	____	____	____	____	____
c. A leave of absence	____	____	____	____	____	____	____	____
d. Travel expenses	____	____	____	____	____	____	____	____
e. A change in teaching assignment	____	____	____	____	____	____	____	____
f. A change in office or research space	____	____	____	____	____	____	____	____
g. Introduction of a new course	____	____	____	____	____	____	____	____
h. Money for research and scholarly pursuits	____	____	____	____	____	____	____	____

7. The following are a number of areas that people usually consider important when thinking about their involvement in a department. Please indicate your thoughts about each of the areas below. (Mark one on each line.)

	Much better than I expect	Somewhat better than I expect	Satisfactory at present	Needs some improvement	Needs a good deal of improvement
a. Relationship among faculty members	_____	_____	_____	_____	_____
b. Salary	_____	_____	_____	_____	_____
c. Academic rank	_____	_____	_____	_____	_____
d. Time available to pursue my own professional interests	_____	_____	_____	_____	_____
e. Size of department	_____	_____	_____	_____	_____
f. Course load	_____	_____	_____	_____	_____
g. Size of university	_____	_____	_____	_____	_____
h. Chances for promotion	_____	_____	_____	_____	_____
i. Office space	_____	_____	_____	_____	_____
j. Library facilities	_____	_____	_____	_____	_____
k. Ratio of secretarial help to instructional staff	_____	_____	_____	_____	_____
l. Relationship between graduate students and faculty	_____	_____	_____	_____	_____
m. Prestige of faculty in the department	_____	_____	_____	_____	_____
n. Ability to influence major decisions which affect me	_____	_____	_____	_____	_____
o. Delegation of authority	_____	_____	_____	_____	_____
p. Relationship between faculty and leadership	_____	_____	_____	_____	_____

8. How would you say this department compares with others you know about or have been a member of?

One of the Best	Better Than Many	About Average	Not quite up to Expectatons	Worse that Most

9. The slopes of the lines below indicate (symbolically) rates of change in a department. Please indicate the rate of change which best describes your department.

Negative Change   No Change   Positive Change

10. The slopes of the lines below indicate the rate of adoption of new ideas in a department. Please indicate the rate of adoption of innovation which best describes your department.

Active Discouragement   Rapid Adoption

Part II

Meetings

The philosopher Martin Buber once said, "All life is meeting." No matter how that statement makes you feel, you will probably agree that university personnel hold a lot of meetings and that much depends on their quality. In this section, I am thinking specifically of meetings in which the entire faculty of the department meets together. Please consider what usually or typically happens in this meeting. Beside each of the items below, put one of the following numbers:

5 This is very typical of this meeting; it happens *repeatedly.*
4 This is fairly typical of this meeting; it happens *quite often.*
3 This is more typical than not, but it *doesn't happen a lot.*
2 This is more untypical than typical, though it *does happen some.*
1 This is quite untypical; it *rarely* happens.
0 This is *not* typical at all; it *never* happens.

1. _____ When problems come up in the meeting, they are explored thoroughly until everyone understands what they are.
2. _____ The first solution proposed often is accepted by the group.
3. _____ People come to the meeting not knowing what is to be presented or discussed.
4. _____ People ask why the problem exists and what the causes are.
5. _____ Many problems people are concerned about never get on the agenda.
6. _____ People tend to propose answers without really having thought the problem and its causes through carefully.
7. _____ The group discusses the pros and cons of several different alternate solutions to a problem.
8. _____ People bring up extraneous or irrelevant matters.
9. _____ The average person in the meeting feels that his ideas have gotten into the discussion.
10. _____ Someone summarizes progress from time to time.
11. _____ Decisions are often left vague—as to what they are and who will carry them out.
12. _____ Either before the meeting or at its beginning, any group member can get items on the agenda easily.
13. _____ People are afraid to be openly critical or make valid objections.
14. _____ The group discusses and evaluates how decisions from previous meetings worked out.
15. _____ People do not take the time to really study or define the problem they are working on.
16. _____ The same few people seem to do most of the talking during the meeting.
17. _____ People hesitate to give their true feelings about problems being discussed.
18. _____ When a decision is made, it is clear who should carry it out, and when.
19. _____ There is a good deal of jumping from topic to topic—it's often unclear where the group is on the agenda.

215

20. _____From time to time in the meeting, people openly discuss the feelings and working relationships in the group.
21. _____The same problems seem to keep coming up over and over again from meeting to meeting.
22. _____People don't seem to care about the meeting or want to get involved in it.
23. _____When the group is thinking about a problem, at least two or three different solutions are suggested.
24. _____When there is a disagreement, it tends to be smoothed over or avoided.
25. _____Some very creative solutions come out of this group.
26. _____Many people remain silent.
27. _____When conflicts over decisions come up, the group does not avoid them, but really stays with the conflict and works it through.
28. _____The results of the group's work are not worth the time they take.
29. _____People give their real feelings about what is happening during the meeting itself.
30. _____People feel very committed to carrying out the solutions arrived at by the group.
31. _____When the group supposedly is working on a problem, it is really working on some other "under the table" issue.
32. _____People feel antagonistic or negative during the meeting.
33. _____There is no follow-up information about how decisions reached at earlier meetings worked out in practice.
34. _____Solutions and decisions are in accord with the leadership's point of view but not necessarily with the members'.
35. _____There are splits or deadlocks among factions or sub-groups.
36. _____The discussion goes on and on without any decision being reached.
37. _____People feel satisfied or positive during the meeting.

38. Suppose Instructor X is present when *two others* get into a hot argument about how the department is run. If instructors you know in your department were in X's place, what would most of them be likely to do?

Would most of the faculty you know in the department probably listen to both arguers and then side with the one they thought was right?

( ) Yes, I thing most would.
( ) Maybe about half would.
( ) No, most would *not* do this.
( ) I don't know.

39. Would they try to help each one in the argument to understand the viewpoint of the other?

( ) Yes, I think most would.
( ) Maybe about half would.
( ) No, most would *not* do this.
( ) I don't know.

40. Suppose Instructor X feels hurt and "put down" by something another faculty member has said to him. In X's place, would most of the instructors you know in the department be likely to . . .

... tell the other instructor that they felt hurt and put down?

( ) Yes, I think most would.
( ) Maybe about half would.
( ) No, most would *not*.
( ) I don't know.

41. . . . tell their friends that the other instructor is hard to get along with?

( ) Yes, I think most would.
( ) Maybe about half would.
( ) No, most would *not*.
( ) I don't know.

42. Suppose Instructor X develops a particularly useful and effective method for teaching something. In X's place, would most of the instructors you know in the department . . .

... describe it briefly at a faculty meeting and offer to meet with others who wanted to hear more about it?

( ) Yes, I think most would.
( ) Maybe about half would.
( ) No, most would *not*.
( ) I don't know.

43. Suppose Instructor X strongly disagrees with something Instructor B says at a faculty meeting. In X's place, would most of the instructors you know in the department . . .

... seek out Instructor B to discuss the disagreement?

( ) Yes, I think most would.
( ) Maybe about half would.
( ) No, most would *not*.
( ) I don't know.

44. . . . keep it to themselves and say nothing about it?

( ) Yes, I think most would.
( ) Maybe about half would.
( ) No, most would *not*.
( ) I don't know.

45. Suppose Instructor X wants to improve his classroom effectiveness. In X's place, would most of the instructors you know in the department . . .

... ask another instructor to observe his teaching and then have a conference afterward?

( ) Yes, I think most would.
( ) Maybe about half would.
( ) No, most would *not*.
( ) I don't know.

46. . . . ask other instructors to let him (X) observe how the other instructors teach, to get ideas about how to improve their own?

    ( ) Yes, I think most would.
    ( ) Maybe about half would.
    ( ) No, most would *not*.
    ( ) I don't know.

47. Suppose Instructor X were present when two others got into a hot argument about how the department is run. Suppose X tried to help each one understand the views of the other. How would you feel about the behavior of X?

    ( ) I would approve strongly.
    ( ) I would approve mildly.
    ( ) I wouldn't care one way or the other.
    ( ) I would disapprove mildly.
    ( ) I would disapprove strongly.

48. Suppose Instructor X were present when two others got into a hot argument about how the department is run. Suppose Instructor X tried to get them to quiet down and stop arguing. How would you feel about the behavior of X?

    ( ) I would approve strongly.
    ( ) I would approve mildly.
    ( ) I wouldn't care one way or the other.
    ( ) I would disapprove mildly.
    ( ) I would disapprove strongly.

49. Suppose Instructor X wants to improve his classroom effectiveness. If X asked another instructor to observe his teaching and then have a conference about it afterward, how would you feel toward X?

    ( ) I would approve strongly.
    ( ) I would approve mildly.
    ( ) I wouldn't care one way or the other.
    ( ) I would disapprove mildly.
    ( ) I would disapprove strongly.

50. Suppose Instructor X wants to improve his classroom effectiveness. If X asked another instructor to let him (X) observe the other instructor teach, how would you feel toward X?

    ( ) I would approve strongly.
    ( ) I would approve mildly.
    ( ) I wouldn't care one way or the other.
    ( ) I would disapprove mildly.
    ( ) I would disapprove strongly.

51. Suppose you are in a committee meeting with Instructor X and the other members begin to describe their personal feelings about what goes on in the department; Instructor X quickly suggests that the committee get back to the topic and keep the discussion objective and impersonal. How would you feel toward X?

    ( ) I would approve strongly.
    ( ) I would approve mildly.
    ( ) I wouldn't care one way or the other.
    ( ) I would disapprove mildly.
    ( ) I would disapprove strongly.

52. Suppose you are in a committee meeting with Instructor X and the other members begin to describe their personal feelings about what goes on in the department; Instructor X listens to them and tells them his own feelings. How would you feel toward X?

    ( ) I would approve strongly.
    ( ) I would approve mildly.
    ( ) I wouldn't care one way or the other.
    ( ) I would disapprove mildly.
    ( ) I would disapprove strongly.

53. Perhaps there are some people in the department with whom you talk rather frequently about matters important to you. Please think of people with whom you talk *seriously about things important to you,* inside or outside formal meetings, *once a week or more* on the average. Write their names below. (If there are fewer than six people with whom you talk once a week about matters important to you, write down only as many as there are; if none, write "none." If there are more than six, list just the six with whom you feel your conversations are the most satisfying.)

  1._____   4._____

  2._____   5._____

  3._____   6._____

54. Now look back at question 53. Each name is numbered. Listed below are all the pairs that can be made among six numbers. Perhaps you know whether some of the six people *talk to each other* about matters important to them. Please look at each pair of numbers below, look back to see what names they represent, and *circle* the pair of numbers if you have good reason to believe that the two people talk to each other *once a week or more* about matters important to them.

1-2
1-3 2-3
1-4 2-4 3-4
1-5 2-5 3-5 4-5
1-6 2-6 3-6 4-6 5-6

HOW LONG DID THIS TAKE YOU? If you can recall within five minutes or so, please write here the time it took you in actual working time to answer this questionnaire:

_____

EXERCISE NUMBER NINE

TITLE: Agenda Setting*

SOURCE: Steven R. Phillips, based on a similar exercise described in J. William Pfeiffer and John E. Jones, *A Handbook of Structured Experiences for Human Relations Training* (La Jolla, California: University Associates, 1975), V, pp. 108–110.

GENERAL DESCRIPTION: Among an almost infinite number of reasons for the failure of groups to be more effective, the lack of a clear agenda for meetings must rank among the most prevalent. The lack of focus and progress often demonstrated by many faculty and administrative groups often can be traced to an unclear or even non-existent agenda. One of the advantages of team building is that it provides an opportunity to demonstrate more effective ways of group functioning. The agenda setting exercise described below is useful not only for developing an agenda for team building but also for setting agendas for regular group meetings.

INSTRUCTIONS FOR USE: After the information from the interviews and/or questionnaires has been presented and understood, participants are asked to divide into pairs and for 10 minutes (five minutes each) interview each other around the following question: "Given this information and our understanding of this group, what are the issues we need to address right now during this team building session?" Once those interviews are complete, the consultant asks each participant to report on the concerns expressed by his partner, which then are listed on newsprint. After the partner has a chance to "correct the record" if desired, he then reports on the issues raised by the other person, who also is given a chance to correct or modify those items. This process is continued until all pairs have had an opportunity to identify their concerns. Similar items should be combined if possible and each item assigned a letter; double letters (e.g., AA, BB, and so forth) should be used if the list exceeds more than 26 items, which is not uncommon.

    The consultant next asks each participant privately to identify by letter what he feels to be the top three items that must be addressed during the team building session. The individual votes are collected verbally and the top ranked items, usually no more than six or eight, are then listed by letter on a separate sheet of newsprint.

    Next, participants are asked again privately to rank order those items in terms of what they see as their priority beginning with 1 as the highest priority. Using a grid like the following,

---

*Adapted from: J. William Pfeiffer and John E. Jones (Eds.), *A Handbook of Structured Experiences from Human Relations Training*, Vol. V. San Diego, CA: University Associates, 1975. Used with permission.

PRIORITY

	1st	2nd	3rd	4th	5th	6th	7th	8th
C								
D								
H								
P								
W								
AA								
FF								
II								

the consultant polls the group by asking (in this example), "How many of you ranked item C first priority?" "Second priority?" and so forth, placing a tally or number in each box as appropriate. A final agenda in order of priority then can be developed from that ranking.

The consultant may then wish to lead the group in a brief discussion of the agenda setting process, perhaps emphasizing the idea that this method can be used by the group itself in setting agendas for its own meetings. If it seems appropriate, the agenda setting process can be concluded by establishing a tentative time limit for the discussion of each item.

INSTRUMENT NUMBER SIX

TITLE: Work Perception Survey

SOURCE: John Wallen, Neotsu, Oregon

GENERAL DESCRIPTION: The "Work Perception Survey" allows members of a task group to describe in a simple and direct manner their perception of the way the group worked together during its most recent session. Particularly for highly task-oriented groups, the survey is useful in providing an opportunity for discussion about the process, rather than the progress, of the group.

INSTRUCTIONS FOR USE: The "Work Perception Survey" should be completed near the end of an actual work session. Once each member has responded to all seven items, a tally should be made of all responses. This can be done privately by the facilitator or, perhaps better, publicly by the group itself. If each member calls out his rating to each question, the other group members can make their own counts on their own copies of the instrument. This kind of public disclosure should stimulate more direct and productive discussions than would a private and anonymous count.

Although the "Work Perception Survey" takes only a few minutes to complete and score, at least a half-hour should be devoted to a discussion of the results.

WORK PERCEPTION SURVEY

Directions: For each question, circle one number from the scale that best represents your opinion of the way this group worked during its most recent session. Disregard how you feel about what the group accomplished and focus instead on how the group worked.

1. What was our usual participation pattern during our most recent session?

    0 - Extremely unbalanced: Not everybody participated. A few did all the talking.

    1 -

    2 - Unbalanced: Everybody talked, but some talked a great deal too little and others talked a great deal too much.

    3 -

    4 - Slightly unbalanced: Some talked somewhat too much; others talked somewhat too little.

    5 -

    6 - Balanced: Although we didn't all talk the same amount, I think each of us talked nearly the right amount.

2. Members who are not talking may be either tuned out or attentively involved. How many were attentively involved when they were not talking?

    6 ——— 5 ——— 4 ——— 3 ——— 2 ——— 1 ——— 0
    All of us   Most of us   Half of us   A few of   None of
                                                  us   us

3. How many occasionally checked to make sure that remarks were understood as they were intended?

    6 ——— 5 ——— 4 ——— 3 ——— 2 ——— 1 ——— 0
    All of us   Most of us   Half of us   A few of   None of
                                                  us   us

4. How many occasionally summarized what we had accomplished, what we agreed on, what we disagreed on?

    6 ——— 5 ——— 4 ——— 3 ——— 2 ——— 1 ——— 0
    All of us   Most of us   Half of us   A few of   None of
                                                  us   us

5. How many helped keep the discussion on the track by orienting us to our task or the goal of our discussion or by bringing back members who digressed?

    6 ——— 5 ——— 4 ——— 3 ——— 2 ——— 1 ——— 0
    All of us   Most of us   Half of us   A few of   None of
                                                  us   us

6. Did we openly state our disagreements and differences and discuss them rather than ignoring them or trying to pretend there were none?

    6 ——— 5 ——— 4 ——— 3 ——— 2 ——— 1 ——— 0
    All of us   Most of us   Half of us   A few of   None of
                                                  us   us

7. When we had trouble making progress did we openly discuss the signs of the difficulty and try to find the reason for it?

6	5	4	3	2	1	0
Almost always	Usually	Slightly more often than not	As often as not	Slightly less often than not	Rarely	Almost never

INSTRUMENT NUMBER SEVEN

TITLE: Leadership in Groups

SOURCE: Donald J. Wolk, University of Bridgeport

GENERAL DESCRIPTION: Although the range of topics to emerge in the process of team building is wide and sometimes unpredictable, the issue of leadership almost always will attract considerable attention. Differing expectations of what a leader is supposed to do frequently exist and usually cause frustration and confusion. "Leadership in Groups" is designed to help group members articulate their assumptions about leadership.

INSTRUCTIONS FOR USE: After members of the group and the leader have completed the instrument and rank ordered those items with which they agree, the top items from each member's list should be posted on newsprint. The ensuing discussion should focus on areas of agreement and disagreement between group members and between the group and the leader.

Variations:
1. Participants also might be asked to rank order those items they disagreed with by assigning a 1 to that item they most disagreed with, a 2 to the one they next most disagreed with, and so forth. Those rankings also could be posted and compared to the rankings of those items group members agreed with.
2. Group members might complete the instrument twice, the first time for themselves, the second time as they think the group leader would complete it. Both listings then could be compared to the leader's actual list.

LEADERSHIP IN GROUPS

A. What is your opinion on the statements listed below? Please give your first reaction by checking the appropriate blank.

	Agree	Disagree	Uncertain	
1.	_____	_____	_____	The primary job of a leader is to bring about change.
2.	_____	_____	_____	The most effective leader is the one who can maintain a pleasant emotional climate at all times.
3.	_____	_____	_____	The effective leader gives his people all the information they need and want.
4.	_____	_____	_____	Leadership is a set of functions that should be distributed within the group.
5.	_____	_____	_____	Very little progress can be made unless every member of the group feels a personal responsibility for constructive change.
6.	_____	_____	_____	Most group assignments could better be discharged by one person with power to act.
7.	_____	_____	_____	If leadership is effective, group members will have no feelings of dependency toward the leader.
8.	_____	_____	_____	Unless group members are pushed by a leader they will make little progress.
9.	_____	_____	_____	In leading, it is more important for the leader to be knowledgeable about a variety of topics than about interpersonal and group relations.
10.	_____	_____	_____	An authoritative leader is better than one who lets the group function without any control.
11.	_____	_____	_____	It is impossible to be absolutely impartial in discussions.
12.	_____	_____	_____	Most democratically-oriented groups in which there is shared decision making make progress if given enough time.
13.	_____	_____	_____	The effective leader should never take a stand in opposition to a majority of group members.

227

14. ———— ———— ————   Initiating ideas is the most important single task of the leader.

15. ———— ———— ————   The ability to influence people and to maintain an authoritative role is necessary for effective leadership.

16. ———— ———— ————   The leader's primary role is to create enthusiasm and to instill purpose in his subordinates.

17. ———— ———— ————   The effective leader is willing to take responsibility for all that occurs within the group.

18. ———— ———— ————   The ability to make unqualified decisions is the primary function of a leader.

B. Rank order those items with which you agree. Place a 1 next to the item which you consider most important; place a 2 next to the item which is second in importance, and so forth.

EXERCISE NUMBER TEN

TITLE: A Quick Decision

SOURCE: Joyce Povlacs, University of Nebraska-Lincoln

GENERAL DESCRIPTION: This simple exercise may be used relatively early in a team building workshop to provide a warm-up activity, a real example of how a group of people perform a task, or an agenda for further discussion.

INSTRUCTIONS FOR USE: The entire group may be assigned the following task or participants may be broken down into smaller groups. In five minutes each group or groups is to agree on a single answer to the question, "What is the single most significant barrier to effective departmental functioning?" When time is called, the answers are posted on newsprint. The discussion that follows might focus on issues such as decision making, communication patterns, and leadership. The barriers identified may provide useful information for helping the group improve its effectiveness, while the discussion that follows the exercise can be an effective way of directing the group's attention to the ways it typically works together.

EXERCISE NUMBER ELEVEN

Title: Decision-Making Roles

Source: Joyce Povlacs, University of Nebraska-Lincoln, in turn based on Robert R. Blake and Jane S. Mouton, *The New Managerial Grid* (Houston, Texas: Gulf Publishing Company, 1979).

General description: Although it is often useful for participants to complete and discuss various questionnaires concerning group behavior, time limitations may make this impractical. In such cases a single set of statements like those presented in this exercise can be used to direct participants' attention to certain aspects of the way they operate in groups.

Instructions for use: Participants first complete "Decision-Making Roles." The consultant then presents the theory behind the decision-making grid (see Volume 1 of this series, pp. 157–160), after which participants should share their rankings with the group, identify which represents a particular orientation on the decision-making grid, and explore the implications of that information for the way the group works together.

DECISION-MAKING ROLES

Determine to what extent each statement is characteristic of your behavior in a departmental meeting by rank ordering each of the following statements from 1 (most characteristic) to 5 (least characteristic).

Many of us would rather play certain roles or functions in groups than others. Which of the following general roles do you tend to play in groups of which you are a member?

_____a. I tend to emphasize group harmony and cooperation, to defuse tension when possible, and to seek out solutions everyone can be happy with.

_____b. I tend to rely on majority opinion by clarifying both sides of an issue and moving toward resolution by voting.

_____c. I tend to move the group in directions I feel are appropriate, to present my ideas forcefully and clearly, and to seek ways of incorporating my conclusions in the group's final decision.

_____d. I tend to look for as many alternative solutions as possible and to keep discussion open until everyone agrees with the group's decision.

_____e. I tend to remain uninvolved in groups, although I am willing to carry out specific tasks and responsibilities under the direction of others.

EXERCISE NUMBER TWELVE

Title: Group Decision Making

Source: Joyce Povlacs, University of Nebraska-Lincoln, in turn based on Robert R. Blake and Jane S. Mouton, *The New Managerial Grid* (Houston, Texas: Gulf Publishing Company, 1979).

General description: Like Exercise Number Eleven, this exercise helps group members focus on decision-making theory without actually having to complete an extensive questionnaire. Unlike the previous exercise, this asks the group as a whole to make a decision about group decision making.

Instructions for use: The group is given 30 minutes to rank order the statements on the "Group Decision Making" sheet. The discussion that follows should address not only the content of the decision reached but also the way that decision was made. The discussion could conclude with a presentation by the consultant of the decision-making grid (see "Instructions for Use," Exercise Number Eleven).

Variations:
1. Instead of asking the group to rank order the statements on the "Group Decision Making" sheet in reference in groups in general, they could complete the ranking in terms of decision making in that actual group.
2. One or more members of the group could serve as process observers and give their observations on the group's decision-making behavior once the task has been completed.

GROUP DECISION MAKING

Rank order from 1 (most common) to 5 (least common) the following reasons, in your experience, groups fail to make good decisions.

_____a. A failure to take the feelings of group members into consideration, coupled with an unnecessarily high level of conflict and disagreement.

_____b. A failure to stay with the task at hand to produce the best possible decision regardless of feelings.

_____c. A failure of leadership to see to it that the decision gets made with as little wasted time and effort as possible.

_____d. A failure to stay with the discussion until the group has reached consensus.

_____e. A failure of groups to compromise when that is the only way a decision will ever be reached.

Chapter Ten

Career Development[1]

Life planning has always been an integral part of a comprehensive approach to faculty development.[2] Often eclectic in its approach and frequently drawing on such diverse areas as values clarification, gestalt therapy, problem solving, and action planning, life planning has been an important component of numerous faculty development workshops over the last several years. Most of this activity, however, has paid little or no direct attention to the career development of participating faculty. Appropriately holistic in its approach, life planning most often assists people in identifying broad life patterns, clarifying basic life values, and setting action plans for the future. Although issues of career development and satisfaction at times arise during such reflections, life planning as a rule does little to help faculty address such fundamental questions as "What pattern, if any, has my career followed so far?" "Where am I right now in my career development?" "What do I want my career to look like over the next several years?"

Much of this, however, has begun to change. Over the last two to three years, a number of institutions and foundations have begun to give more direct attention to the patterns of faculty career development. Frequently drawing on some of the methodologies of life planning, but currently integrating into that process the strategies and techniques of career guidance and vocational counseling, practitioners and programs are now helping faculty to grapple with the often difficult issues of career development. Two forces, one negative and one positive, seem to account for this increased interest in faculty careers.

The negative force is clearly retrenchment. In a recent and, at the time of its publication, definitive review of various projections available on college enrollment for the decade of the 1980s, John Centra points out that "the majority of forecasts reviewed . . . see a decrease in enrollments during the 1980s. Although some predict very large decreases and others even project modest increases, the majority call for annual contractions during the first half of the 1980s that may total 8 or 9 percent. The last half of the 1980s should bring smaller, but continued, decreases according to most of the forecasts."[3] Despite the occasional and continued appearance of more optimistic projections, which usually pin their hopes on the so-called "non-traditional student" as a counter-balance to the decline in the traditional student-age population,[4] it appears almost certain that colleges and universities will need and be able to support fewer and fewer faculty and administrators in the coming years. Higher education is being forced by retrenchment to give serious attention to ways of assisting its members in the process of career transitions.

A second and more positive factor, however, also has accounted for increased interest in patterns of faculty career development. Most widely popularized by Gail Sheehy and Daniel Levinson,[5] the research on adult development has drawn our attention over the last several years to the predictable and age-linked processes of life and career change beyond the end of late adolescence. Much research remains to be done, especially on female adult development, but we are beginning now to understand the broad patterns of adult growth. This understanding has led to a number of speculations about the career development of college faculty and has focused attention not only on ways in which faculty appear to grow and change over their lives, but also on ways in which particular approaches to faculty development can be most appropriate at certain stages of faculty career development. Although extremely tentative and needing much more clarification, these speculations suggest that career planning can be of particular value to faculty at a number of points in their development.

For both good and bad reasons, then, higher education has begun to give more serious attention to the career development of its faculty. In many ways, it is appropriate that colleges and universities show this concern. Certainly, ethical considerations are involved when the forces of retrenchment cause institutions to terminate faculty who were originally hired with the expectation of at least possible lifetime employment. This is particularly true for tenured faculty forced because of declining enrollment to look for alternate positions and even careers. In these situations, colleges and universities have an ethical responsibility to their faculty to provide as many resources as possible to assist in the process of career transitions.

In another sense, however, it is in the best interest of most institutions to help faculty examine the development of their lives and careers. Many colleges and universities can expect significant numbers of their faculty to remain where they are for perhaps the next quarter of a century. Attention simply must be paid to ways in which faculty careers can continue to change and grow within the confines of a single institution. Finally, it is appropriate that faculty themselves begin looking at the predictable patterns of their own career development, if not for themselves then for their students. It now appears that most of our students will go through three, four, or more careers during their lives. There has always been something ironic in the fact that those students have been taught mostly by faculty who themselves have experienced only a single, academic career. To educate students not for their first jobs but for a lifetime, faculty would be well advised to learn something about adult and career development. Career planning, even if not accompanied by a forced or voluntary career transition, can help both faculty and their institutions become more sensitive to the broad patterns of adult development.

A. A Model of Faculty Career Development

If the research on adult development is tentative and incomplete, that on faculty career development is almost speculative. Yet enough is known even at this early point to suggest at least the broad outlines of a career pattern for faculty. Based on information from liberal arts college faculty, and thus generalizing only with care, Roger Baldwin has recently proposed a five-stage model of faculty career development that corresponds with Levinson's stages of adult male development. Baldwin's model (see Table Three) as related to Levinson's stages is as follows:[6]

TABLE THREE

Baldwin's Faculty Stages	Levinson's Developmental Stages	Characteristic Experiences, Tasks
I. Assistant professor in the first three years of full-time college teaching	Entering the Adult World (20–28)	Effort to establish an occupation compatible with interests, values, self-concept. Envision a life dream (establish goals). Locate a mentor who can help young adult get established and pursue dream.
II. Assistant professor with more than three years of college teaching experience	Age Thirty Transition (28–33)	Reexamine initial commitments (e.g., marriage, occupation); question their value. Make desired changes in goals and life style.
	Settling Down (33–40)	Commitment to family usually deepens; life becomes more stable. Adult is concerned with achieving a position of importance in the work setting.
III. Associate professor	Becoming One's Own Person (Late Settling Down Stage, 36–40)	Strong need to achieve objectives set during early 30s (e.g., securing tenure by 38) as validation of self-worth. Desire affirmation by others of success in chosen roles. Wish to become a "senior" member of one's world, to speak with greater authority, to be a truly independent person.
IV. Full professor more than five years from retirement	Mid-Life Transition (40–45)	Question what one has done with one's life. Must deal with disparity between achievements and goals (dream). Urgency of reassessment intensified by growing sense of aging. May eventually revise goals downward or initiate major changes in life.
	Entering Middle Adulthood (46–50)	More stable period where person often establishes more instrinsic goals.
	Ongoing process of transition and restabilization	Sequence of transitional and stable periods continues in later life. Individual development proceeds.
V. Full professor within five years of retirement	Late Adult Transition (60–65)	Experience of bodily decline. Reduction of middle-adulthood responsibilities. Seek new balance of

236

involvement with society and the self. Acceptance of one's failures and successes. Gain a sense of the overall meaning and value of one's life.

Baldwin goes on to describe each of these faculty career stages in more detail.

Assistant professor in the first three years of full-time college teaching:

These individuals are trying to get their careers established. They are seeking professional opportunities in a currently unstable academic employment environment. Thus they experience some pressure and concern about their future. New professors are adjusting to many novel demands, are trying to learn rapidly, and are receptive to help from others with more experience. These educators' careers are oriented primarily to teaching and limited research commitments. They are concerned with improving their performance in both areas. Novice academics are fairly enthusiastic about their young careers in higher education. (After all, they did locate teaching positions.) In some respects their career ambitions may be overly idealistic . . .

Assistant professor with more than three years of college teaching experience:

Experienced assistant professors are more confident about their abilities and performance than are their newer counterparts. They are also more sophisticated about their institution's methods of operation. Professors at this stage are seeking recognition and advancement, both of which are usually signified by the receipt of tenure. At the same time, they may experience discontent with their teaching position, institution, or overall career achievements if these factors do not measure up to original hopes and expectations. Discontent may also surface if these professors fear their upcoming tenure evaluation will be negative. Now professors more seriously question their future in higher education. They sometimes think about alternative careers and may actively seek other employment opportunities. As they await the invitation to permanent membership in the academic community, they must identify options in case their bid for professional confirmation fails.

Associate professors:

Associate professors tend to be enigmatic. They enjoy the peer recognition associated with tenure and promotion. Likewise, they are becoming a more integral part of their college community and are now more actively involved in various college-wide activities, especially important committees. In general, associate professors are satisfied with their career progress to date. Yet occasionally they are nagged by the fear that they have reached a dead end, that their career has plateaued and that they have nowhere to go professionally.

Full professors more than five years from retirement:

Essentially, continuing full professors have reached a watershed in their careers. They know that they have up to 25 years of employment left and are probably locked into higher education by their age, education level, and need for economic security. During this phase professors must decide whether to maintain the same basic career activities or move in a different direction. In a sense, they are faced with a choice between stagnation and diversification. During this period continuing full professors sometimes question the value of their vocation. After many years their enthusiasm for teaching and research has declined somewhat. Their comfort with students may also have decreased. Often full professors seek diversity and new challenges in their career . . . Advanced faculty members who fail to 'branch out' can fall victim to career inertia. Limited opportunities for professional growth may lead to disillusionment or depression, which can very likely affect the performance of these professors.

Full professor within five years of retirement:

Retiring professors are characterized by a high degree of career satisfaction. They are somewhat reflective and generally content with their professional achievements. Senior faculty members are gradually withdrawing from their various responsibilities and thus have very limited goals for the future. They probably will not engage in any novel projects in the time remaining before retirement.

These faculty members also have decreased enthusiasm for teaching but are particularly comfortable with service to their department or college. Although professors near retirement feel little occupational pressure, they do recognize problems. In particular, they may fear that their knowledge is out of date, and yet their comfort with research may have diminished significantly. Yet at a time when efforts to enhance their skills might be beneficial, retiring professors seem isolated . . .[7]

Again, as Baldwin suggests, these stages are based on only a limited sample of faculty from one segment of higher education; further research on career stages for research-oriented faculty, community college faculty, and women in all areas of higher education is clearly needed. Yet what does exist seems to indicate at least some ways career planning can help the course of faculty career development run more smoothly.

Faculty career satisfaction varies with career stage, although in general, satisfaction increases with age.[8] Yet Baldwin did find a number of instances of dissatisfaction and even resignation. This same undercurrent, the shadow side, if you will, of the generally positive pattern of faculty career development, also has been identified with R. Eugene Rice in a study of former Danforth Fellows in mid-career. Perhaps this sense of despair is best articulated by two Fellows, both of whom have been teaching in higher education for the last decade and a half. As the first writes:

It's hard to keep the bitterness out. At this moment in time, we're all victims; we all have something to be bitter about. Yes, I mean the absence of the 'Liberal Dream' (whatever that was) of the Sixties . . . Yes, I mean the prevailing winds of the economy, against which all defenses of ego and ideal are like a paper bag in a hurricane. Yes, I mean all the betrayals, petty and great, willed and unwilled, which leave us the victims of a spiritual landscape from which alien anthropologists might extract samples drier than any moon rock. Handfuls of dust.

This same sense, less dramatically expressed, is echoed by a second Fellow:

Above all I want to avoid the acceptance of my present position as permanent. In short, I am struggling against 'settling down.' Yet at times I feel I am dying a slow professional death in my present position. But given the present situation in academia . . . there may not be a ladder to climb.[9]

238

Life is an interplay between internal and external forces, between nature and nurture. Now and for the foreseeable future, higher education will provide a constrained and limiting environment in which to go through the predictable crises and transitions of adult development.

Yet, career planning can be of genuine value in navigating the difficult and often painful course of a faculty career. In particular, Baldwin suggests, career assessment seems particularly appropriate for faculty approaching a tenure decision and for those who are full professors more than five years from retirement.[10] In Levinson's terms, the "Age Thirty Transition" and the "Mid-Life Transition" are the two times when life and career planning are most needed (regardless of academic rank). Add to these numbers faculty who are facing the transition to retirement, and the potential audience for career reassessment is great, the need pressing.

B. A Model for Career Planning

Like life and work itself, career planning takes many forms. Some approaches focus on values clarification, others on strength assessment, yet others on interpersonal skills and relationships. In one sense, nearly all of the approaches to personal development described in this chapter and in Chapter Ten of the first volume of this series have some relevance to career planning. In another sense, however, career assessment involves a specific set of steps and activities leading to the articulation of an action plan. Although the amount of emphasis given to each step will vary depending on the life and work situation of the people involved, it is nevertheless possible to suggest a comprehensive six-stage model of life and career planning. Each step focuses on a different aspect of the planning process; taken together they represent an integrated approach to a complex and sometimes overwhelming task. Planning Document Number Two provides an example of at least one way these six steps can be incorporated into a workshop design.

1. Life Planning

The reassessment of one's life and career must take place within the broad context of life planning. Although this kind of planning can be approached in a variety of ways, two different strategies have proven particularly powerful. The first is the process of life planning outlined in Chapter Ten of the second volume of this series. The objective at this point, however, is not to move toward the development of a project or plan but rather to allow participating faculty to articulate a comprehensive life picture. Consequently, such activities as "Life Shields," "Life Line," Transitions," and "Images of the Future" described in Volume 2 are most appropriate here, for if faculty can be assisted in gaining a broad perspective on the pattern of their lives as a whole the process of career reassessment will be made that much richer and fuller.

A second approach to life planning is the intensive journal process developed by Ira Progoff.[11] Working in the privacy of a structured journal, participants explore a variety of life dimensions, many of which correspond to the life planning issues addressed in the first approach. The intensive journal workshop has been used successfully by the Center for Faculty Development at California State University, Long Beach. As David and Susanne Whitcomb report, this process has proven useful in helping participants increase self-awareness and knowledge, clarify life issues, and accelerate personal growth.[12] Although more in-depth and retrospective than other approaches to life planning, the intensive journal process can well be included as part of the overall process of life and career assessment.

One final note: as the Whitcombs point out, the intensive journal process

> is essentially private . . . Persons attending [the workshop] 'come together to work alone.' They are listening to short lectures and writing at length in their journals. It is not necessary to read aloud or disclose the journal writings to anyone else.[13]

As a consequence, the journal process is consistent with the norms of both individuality and privacy that tend to dominate many faculty groups. Rather than attempting to change those norms, the intensive journal works within them. This seems entirely appropriate for higher education and for the process of career planning, where the issues being addressed are often intensely personal. Whether or not any particular approach to career assessment uses the intensive journal process, it would be well to consider ways in which private journal work can be incorporated more extensively into career planning activities.

2. Values

Once faculty have had the opportunity to clarify the broad patterns of their lives, attention should be given to the question of values. A number of the values clarification exercises in Chapter Eleven of Volume 2 can prove useful here, as can the exercises on broad life values and occupational values contained in Instruments Number Eight and Nine in this volume. The process of values clarification might well conclude with the completion of the first life inventory list contained in Volume 2.

3. Interests

Values express themselves in our lives as interests. We are interested in those activities we value and not in those we do not value. A third step in career planning, then, would be to explore life and career interests. This perhaps can best be accomplished by using the *Strong Campbell Interest Inventory,* which provides respondents with information about their level of interest in six broad occupational themes, a variety of occupational areas, and numerous specific occupations and vocations.[14] Widely used with students, the SCII has been integrated successfully into a number of faculty workshops. Even though the scoring is computerized and thus requires some advance planning and preparation, the *Strong Campbell Interest Inventory* can provide a powerful means of expanding faculty awareness of their interests and of the way those interests are compatible with a broad range of occupations. Perhaps more than anything else, this expanded occupational awareness is the major positive outcome of the SCII. Most faculty can do more than teach; faced with data from a computerized print-out, it is very difficult to continue to say, "I can't do anything but teach in my discipline."

4. Personal Strengths

The *Strong Campbell Interest Inventory* measures interests, not abilities. To take the next step toward career assessment and planning, therefore, faculty need to be given an opportunity to assess their personal strengths and weaknesses. Strengths may be defined as general, positive personality characteristics, skills as the ability to do certain things. Strengths may be assessed through the kind of reflections involved in various life inventories or through such instrumented approaches as *The Strength Deployment*

Inventory (see Exercise Number Four in this volume) and *The Myers-Briggs Type Indicator*.[15]

A somewhat related and most interesting approach to strength assessment has been suggested recently by Janet Hagberg and Richard Leider in *The Inventurers: Excursions in Life and Career Renewal*. Early in their book, they posit the existence of something they call an "excursion style," the unique pattern of behavior each person shows when he goes about learning and changing.[16] Although the "Excursion-Style Inventory," which they then develop based on David Kolb's work on cognitive learning styles, seems somewhat insubstantial, the concept is excellent. The process of life and career planning is essentially a learning process, and therefore it might be useful for people involved in that process to determine as precisely as possible their own learning (or excursion) styles. To accomplish this, the "Kolb Learning Style Inventory" might well be incorporated in the process of career planning and development.[17] If a person can be assisted in clarifying how he learns, he can plan his most appropriate strategies for encountering new learning experiences.

5. Skills

Skill assessment is perhaps the most difficult, yet one of the most important, aspects of career planning. Especially for those faculty considering the possibility of a career change, skill assessment is essential. Most faculty have a limited and unrealistically modest sense of their abilities, yet teaching, research, and administration have inherent in them a broad range of skills quite appropriate to numerous non-academic careers. Perhaps the most thorough process of skill identification is found in John C. Crystal and Richard Bolles, *Where Do I Go from Here with My Life?*[18] Beginning with an extended and detailed work autobiography, Crystal and Bolles provide a systematic procedure for extracting from that narrative a specific list of occupational skills and skill clusters. Although such a process may be far too detailed for faculty who are not contemplating a career change, some similar assessment may well be appropriate for those considering significant new career directions.

6. Planning and Goal Setting

In general, planning and goal setting are the weakest parts of most life and career planning models. Although it is possible to outline in some detail the steps everyone involved in this kind of reassessment might well wish to take, the process of planning and setting goals often will be so idiosyncratic that general guidelines are most difficult to define. For those faculty who must consider the very real possibility of moving to a non-academic career, perhaps the best guide available is "The Quick Job-Hunting Map" found in Richard N. Bolles, *What Color is Your Parachute?* For those who need considerably less sweeping change, the project planning process outlined in Volume 2 of this series would be more appropriate. Planning strategies are also contained in most career planning manuals and books, including *The Inventurers* and Richard N. Bolles, *The Three Boxes of Life* (Berkeley, California: Ten Speed Press, 1978). Perhaps the best that can be recommended is that the appropriate planning strategy be chosen based on the level of change contemplated; it is essential, however, that some provision be made for translating the insights and understanding gained through life planning and through reflection on values, interests, strengths, and skills into action plans that are as specific and detailed as possible.

C. Implications for Programming

Given the broad and complex variety of issues involved in life and career planning, it would seem only appropriate that programming in support of career assessment take numerous forms. In some institutions these services perhaps can best be supplied by the student counseling office on an individualized referral basis. When an announcement was made to the faculty at one state university in California that such services were available on an anonymous basis, 20 percent of the faculty consulted the counseling center in the first year. In other institutions, one or more workshops focusing on various aspects of the life and career planning process might be more appropriate. Perhaps the best vehicle for these activities, however, is through interinstitutional or consortial arrangements. Although most faculty might well benefit from some kind of life and career planning, at any one time only relatively few people may find themselves in life or work situations that call for this reassessment. In any event, a number of considerations ought to be held in mind regardless of the delivery system chosen to provide these services:

(1) *Focus on work in the context of life.* Work supplied much of the meaning to life, yet major life changes change the value and meaning of work. Even for those people faced with the absolute necessity of developing an alternate career, that choice will be influenced and perhaps even determined by broad life values and goals. One of the most important services life and career planning can provide is the clarification of those issues.

(2) *Focus on the learning process.* As David Kolb points out, the "problem of managing and adapting to change as a central task of adult development in contemporary society is, at its most fundamental level, an issue of the process by which people learn."[19] Whether identified through Kolb's learning styles or Hagberg and Leider's "excursion style," life and career planning is an encounter with new learning opportunities. The strategies and insights gained into a person's learning process may well transfer to other situations or other life transitions.

(3) *Develop alternatives.* Perhaps the most important outcome of the kind of consultation implicit in career planning is the development of alternatives. There is no one right "right answer" to this process but rather a multitude of possibilities. Choices may need to be made, but they should be made only from the broadest range of alternatives.

(4) *Provide follow-up.* The model for career planning suggested in this section and in Planning Document Number Two is in some sense a "core curriculum" generally appropriate for almost anyone in the process of life and career assessment. Yet it is almost certain that individual needs and concerns will emerge from this process. A comprehensive program ought to be prepared to provide such follow-up activities as assistance in establishing support groups, individual and family counseling, financial and retirement planning, and even vocational training. Without this support, the positive expectations often raised by life and career planning may end only in frustration and inaction.

(5) *Respect privacy.* Life and career transitions often call into question some of the most fundamental assumptions we make about ourselves and our worlds. Although some faculty will wish to share these concerns with others, many will not. Particularly in public workshops participants must be provided the privacy to work on these very personal and often difficult issues.

D. Institutional Development and Career Planning

The fields of personal growth and organization development have grown alongside one another over the past two decades, frequently cross-fertilizing each other and sharing common techniques, assumptions, and designs. Yet there has often been a tension between these two fields. The personal growth of employees often has been considered something of a luxury for hard-pressed organizations. Conversely, concerns for organizational issues often have been considered diversions from the more central issue of personal growth and integrity. With limited funds, institutions have been faced with the dilemma of investing dollars in either personal growth programs or organization development.

Several practitioners in both of these fields have recently proposed that an employee's career may serve as a bridge between personal growth and organization development. In the title of a recent book, Edgar Schein has suggested this bridge: *Career Dynamics: Matching Individual and Organizational Needs.* Building on the work of John Van Maanen, Lottle Bailyn, the adult development theorists and researchers, and his fellow organization development practitioners, Schein suggests that "organizations must be concerned with the total problem of human resource development for the sake of not only humanistic values, but organizational survival as well."[20] Schein connects personal and organizational development when he suggests that "organizations are dependent on the performance of their people, and people are dependent on organizations to provide jobs and career opportunities."[21] Career planning and development provides a context within which personal and organization needs can be addressed and matched.

Currently, there are two ways in which American colleges and universities provide career planning and development resources for faculty. The first way is through workshops and individual consultation processes through which faculty are able to explore their own strengths, weaknesses, life patterns, and aspirations, so that they might make more informed and bold career plans. Most of this chapter has been devoted to a description of this process.

A second mode of career planning and development is based in the use and integration of faculty assessment and professional planning procedures. The portfolio assessment procedure described in Chapter Three of Volume 2 of this series enables faculty to assess systematically their own strengths, weaknesses, and emerging responsibilities in collaboration with their immediate supervisor, colleagues, clients (students or representatives of the disciplines or profession). Such a procedure can be used not only for personnel decision making (promotion, tenure, merit salary increase), but also for career planning. A variation on this procedure has been created by the faculty at St. Francis College (Joliet, Illinois). The St. Francis model, which is more detailed than the one presented in Volume 2, is described in Instrument Number Ten.

The professional development (or professional growth) contract first used extensively at Gordon College (Wenham, Massachusetts) also facilitates career planning. A faculty member is able not only to assess current strengths, weaknesses, and emerging responsibilities, but also to prepare a plan and receive funds for professional development activities. The Gordon College model is described extensively in a workbook that can be obtained from the college and is described briefly in *Handbook for College*

Administrators.[22] A shorter and less complex version of the professional development contracting process is contained in Instrument Number Eleven.

When combined, the portfolio and professional development contract procedures provide faculty with a comprehensive career planning and development procedure that makes use of not only the faculty member's own resources and imagination, but also the resources (money, time, educational opportunities, etc.) of the college or university, and the imagination and resources of colleagues. Higher education is today in a state of transition from the affluence of the '60s to the constraints of the '80s. This transition undoubtedly will continue to have profound consequences for the lives and careers of the men and women who make up our teaching faculty. If higher education is at all as value-centered and as human-centered as it claims to be, it will begin to make fuller use of a variety of life and career planning to enrich the lives and work of its members and help both them and itself through the difficult years that lie ahead.

NOTES:

[1] This chapter is based in part on the experience gained during the conduct of a two-year program, "In Support of Career Planning and Development" sponsored by the Council of Independent Colleges and the Associated Schools of the Pacific Northwest and funded by the Northwest Area Foundation, St. Paul, Minnesota.

[2] See, for example, Chapter Ten of Volume 2 of this series.

[3] John A. Centra, "College Enrollment in the 1980s: Projections and Possibilities," *The Journal of Higher Education,* 51 (1980), 35.

[4] The most recent of these is a study by the American Council on Education titled *College Enrollment: Testing the Conventional Wisdom Against the Facts.* According to these facts, college enrollment actually could increase in the 1980s as a result of a number of events, among them an increase in the high school graduation rate from the current rate of 75 percent to 80 percent, a condition over which colleges have no control; the increase of enrollment rates among income groups earning less than $5,000, a change most unlikely given the increasing cost of college attendance, the uncertain economic value of a college education, and a tight national economy; and an increase in graduate students, a development with a number of unlikely and even unethical dimensions, given the state of the current academic job market. (See *The Chronicle of Higher Education,* April 21, 1980, pp. 1, 11.) As Centra suggests from his review, it "appears unlikely that" the enrollment of adults, women, and minorities will exceed "recent trends and affect college enrollments dramatically in the next decade." (Centra, "College Enrollment in the 1980s," 36.) Centra's estimate is supported by an even more recent discussion by Lyman A. Glenny, "Demographic and Related Issues for Higher Education in the 1980s," *The Journal of Higher Education,* 51 (1980), 363–380.

[5] Gail Sheehy, *Passages: Predictable Crises of Adult Life* (New York: Dutton, 1967), Daniel Levinson, *The Seasons of a Man's Life* (New York: Knopf, 1978).

[6] Roger Baldwin, "Adult and Career Development: What Are the Implications for Faculty?" *Faculty Development* Current Issues in Higher Education 1979 (Washington, D.C.: American Association for Higher Education, 1979), pp. 14–15.

[7] Baldwin, 19.

[8] Baldwin, 16.

[9] R. Eugene Rice, "Dreams and Actualities: Danforth Fellows in Mid-Career," *AAHE Bulletin,* 32 (1980), 5.

[10] Baldwin, 17.

[11] Ira Progoff, *At a Journal Workshop* (New York: Dialogue House, 1975). Information concerning journal workshops can be obtained from Dialogue House, National Intensive Journal Program, 80 East 11th Street, New York, New York 10003.

[12] David and Susanne Whitcomb, "The Intensive Journal: A New Faculty Development Process," *Faculty Development and Evaluation in Higher Education,* Winter (1978), 14–16.

[13] David and Susanne Whitcomb, 14.

[14] Information on the *Strong Campbell Interest Inventory* can be obtained from National Computer Systems, P.O. Box 1294, Minneapolis, Minnesota 55440. An excellent theoretical discussion related to the SCII is found in John L. Holland, *Making Vocational Choices: A Theory of Careers* (Englewood Cliffs, New Jersey: Prentice-Hall, 1973).

[15] The *Strength Deployment Inventory* is published by Personal Strengths Assessment Service, Inc., P.O. Box 397, Pacific Palisades, California 90272; The *Myers-Briggs Type Indicator* is available from Consulting Psychologists Press, 577 College Avenue, Palo Alto, California 94306.

[16] Janet Hagberg and Richard Leider, *The Inventurers: Excursions in Life and Career Renewal* (Reading, Massachusetts: Addison-Wesley, 1978), pp. 25–34.

[17] Kolb's "Learning Style Inventory: Self-Scoring Test and Interpretation Booklet" is available from McBer and Company, 137 Newberry Street, Boston, Massachusetts 02116. Also see David A. Kolb and Mark S. Plovnick, "The Experiential Learning Theory

of Career Development," in John Van Maanen, ed., *Organizational Careers: Some New Perspectives* (New York: John Wiley & Sons, 1977), pp. 65–87.

[18]John C. Crystal and Richard N. Bolles, *Where Do I Go from Here with My Life?* (New York: The Seaberg Press, 1974), pp. 3–15, 65–82, 204–221.

[19]Kolb and Plovnick, "The Experiential Learning Theory of Career Development," p. 86; this consideration and the one that follows have been prompted by Kolb and Plovnick's suggestions.

[20]Edgar H. Schein, *Career Dynamics: Matching Individual and Organizational Needs* (Reading, Massachusetts: Addison-Wesley, 1978), p. vii.

[21]Schein, p. 1.

[22]Benjamin E. Sprunger and William H. Bergquist, *Handbook for College Administration* (Washington: Council for the Advancement of Small Colleges, 1978).

EXERCISE NUMBER THIRTEEN

TITLE: Job Exchange

SOURCE: Marcia Shaw, Oregon State University

GENERAL DESCRIPTION: This exercise helps workshop participants begin to articulate the pertinent components of their present job. It also helps them describe what they actually do in their work roles rather than give job titles or formal descriptions. "Job Exchange" is used most effectively early in a career development workshop as a way of helping participants learn more about each other. In addition, this exercise begins the process of clarifying job-related values as participants begin to make choices among options.

INSTRUCTIONS FOR USE: This exercise takes approximately two hours for a workshop of 15 to 20 participants. Each participant should be provided with a large sheet of newsprint and a heavy felt-tip marker. The room in which the exercise is conducted should have ample wall space so that newsprint can be hung and participants can circulate freely around the room.

The exercise is conducted in the following steps:

1. Each participant is given a sheet of newsprint and asked to write a complete description of his current job by providing the following information:
   a. Job title
   b. What do you actually do?
   c. Adequacy of salary: rate from (1) severely underpaid to (5) adequately paid to (10) very well paid
   d. Most positive aspect of the job
   e. Most negative aspect of the job
   f. Organizational climate (participants may comment on one or more of the following);
      1) institutional climate
      2) relationship(s) with supervisor(s)
      3) relationship(s) with colleague(s)
   g. Future prospects for this job
      1) at this institution
      2) at other institutions
   h. Other important aspects of the job

2. When participants have finished their job descriptions, they are asked to post them on the wall and take a seat nearby. When all jobs are posted, each person is given a minute or two to amplify verbally, if they wish, the written job description. Anyone may ask questions for clarification.

3. When all questions have been answered, participants are to take approximately 15 minutes to circulate around the room, reading all of the job descriptions, asking further clarification from their authors if necessary. At the end of this time, each participant is to choose a new

job. Participants may not stay at their current job; they may assume they are competent to fill any job they choose, and more than one person may choose the same job. As each participant chooses a new job, he should sit by that job description.

4. Allow participants a few moments to look around and observe who chose which jobs. Ask participants to form small groups and briefly discuss the following issues:
    a. What is the major difference between this "new" job and their current one?
    b. What were the most important factors in their choices?
    c. Which jobs did they definitely not want? Why not?
    d. Do they have any new perspectives or evaluations of their current positions as a result of this exercise?

As the groups finish their discussions, the leader may ask them to share perceptions that were common to their group or of particular importance or interest.

5. Participants are now instructed to choose a second job, again with the following constraints: it must be a new job (not their original or first choice), participants can assume they are qualified for any job, and each participant may make two changes in this new job to make it more satisfying to them.

6. Each participant should write on their second job choice in contrasting color, if possible, the changes they would make in this job and then sit near that job description. Again, spend a few moments to look around and observe who has chosen what job.

7. Ask participants to return to their original small groups and discuss briefly the important variables in this second choice, perhaps using similar questions to those asked in step four.

8. The leader may use the results of this discussion as the basis for closing comments on such topics as contrasting job values, ways of changing current jobs to make them more satisfying, and anxieties related to possible job changes.

Variations:
1. If time is limited the exercise can move directly from step four to step eight.
2. In one or both of the selections, any given job may be chosen by any one participant. If more than one participant wants the same job, the current holder is to choose between the two candidates.

INSTRUMENT NUMBER EIGHT

TITLE: Broad Life Values

SOURCE: Adapted from George A. Ford and Gordon L. Lippitt, *A Life Planning Workbook* (Fairfax, Virginia: NTL Learning Resources Corporation, 1972).

GENERAL DESCRIPTION: "Broad Life Values" provides a quick and sometimes powerful means of clarifying the relative importance of 13 commonly held values. Since ideally life activities should further the attainment of individual values, this instrument is appropriate early in the process of life and career planning. The results of this instrument might well be compared with the similar results from Instrument Number Nine, "Broad Career Values."

INSTRUCTIONS FOR USE: Participants are asked to rank order as quickly as possible the 13 broad life values defined in the instrument, from 1 (most valued) to 13 (least valued). This rapid ranking then may serve as a departure point for discussion or reflection on life values.

Variations:
1. After completing the initial ranking, and as a way of further clarifying these values, participants may be asked to eliminate from their list as many of the lower ranking items as possible while retaining only those that are most important to them.
2. For at least the higher ranking values, although perhaps for all 13, participants may be given the opportunity to write brief paragraphs or statements for each in which they indicate why they placed that particular value in that particular place.

BROAD LIFE VALUES

( ) AFFECTION   to obtain and share companionship, love, and
             affection

( ) DUTY   to dedicate myself to what I call duty

( ) EXPERTNESS   to become an authority

( ) INDEPENDENCE to have freedom of thought and action

( ) LEADERSHIP   to become influential

( ) PARENTHOOD   to raise happy, healthy, productive children

( ) PLEASURE   to enjoy life; to be happy and content

( ) POWER   to have control and influence over others

( ) PRESTIGE   to become well-known

( ) SECURITY   to have a secure, stable position

( ) SELF-REALIZATION to optimize personal development

( ) SERVICE   to contribute to the welfare of others

( ) WEALTH   to earn a great deal of money

INSTRUMENT NUMBER NINE

TITLE: Broad Career Values

SOURCE: Adapted from Janet Hagbert and Richard Leider, *The Inventurers: Excursions in Life and Career Renewal* (Reading, Massachusetts: Addison-Wesley, 1978), pp. 87–88.

GENERAL DESCRIPTION: Like "Broad Life Values," this exercise focuses on general value issues, now within a more limited career context.

INSTRUCTIONS FOR USE: "Broad Career Values" is to be used in exactly the same manner as the previous instrument. If both instruments are used together, they both should be completed at the same time and before the results from either are analyzed or discussed in any detail.

BROAD CAREER VALUES

( ) CHALLENGE   to meet new and unusual problems

( ) CREATIVITY   to produce new and original ideas or work

( ) INDEPENDENCE   to direct one's own career

( ) LEADERSHIP   to direct and have influence over others

( ) MASTERY   to reach a high level of skill and/or achievement

( ) MONEY   to earn a high income

( ) MORAL VALUE   to have work that is consistent with a moral code

( ) PEOPLE   to work closely and cooperatively with others

( ) RECOGNITION   to have one's work known and acknowledged by others

( ) SECURITY   to establish a secure career

( ) SELF-EXPRESSION   to express one's personality through work

( ) SERVICE   to have a career that benefits others

( ) SOCIAL STATUS   to hold a high prestige job

EXERCISE NUMBER FOURTEEN

TITLE: Career Interests: The *Strong Campbell Interest Inventory*

SOURCE: The *Strong Campbell Interest Inventory* is available from National Computer Systems, Inc., P.O. Box 1242, Minneapolis, Minnesota 55440.

GENERAL DESCRIPTION: The *Strong Campbell Interest Inventory* provides participants with a detailed, computerized comparison of their interests to those of people in a broad variety of occupations and careers. Hence, it is of great value in helping faculty realize that their interests are much wider than just "teaching college." A detailed 19-page, self-paced print-out of the results of the inventory is available from National Computer Systems; we have found this presentation to be much more valuable for working with faculty than earlier and shorter versions.

INSTRUCTIONS FOR USE: The *Strong Campbell* can be introduced with very little comment or preceded by a more detailed presentation of the vocational and personality theory that lies behind the inventory as found in John Holland's *Making Vocational Choices: A Theory of Careers* (Englewood Cliffs, New Jersey: Prentice-Hall, 1973). Because the inventory tends to focus attention on specific careers and occupations rather than on broader life and career concerns, the *Strong Campbell Interest Inventory* generally should be used only toward the end of a career planning workshop. Even then, the workshop leader will need to direct attention away from specific occupations and toward the broader values and interests characteristic of a number of related fields.

EXERCISE NUMBER FIFTEEN

TITLE: Skill Identification

SOURCE: Steven R. Phillips, adapted from a similar process described in John C. Crystal and Richard N. Bolles, *Where Do I Go From Here With My Life?* (Berkeley, California: Ten Speed Press, 1974).

GENERAL DESCRIPTION: Few faculty are aware of the range of specific skills that are required to be a successful college professor. Organizing, writing, designing, planning, administering, and advising are only a few of the transferable skills that make up the life of most college teachers. In addition, all of us possess a wide range of skills from previous jobs and avocations. Skill identification consequently can be a genuinely liberating experience as faculty gradually come to realize that they can do more than "merely" teach.

    Although there is value for anyone in identifying his specific skills, the process becomes imperative for those considering a major career adjustment or change. For faculty actively pursuing the possibility of a non-academic career, the more lengthy and detailed approach to skill identification outlined in *Where Do I Go From Here With My Life?* probably would be more useful than the somewhat abbreviated process outlined below.

INSTRUCTIONS FOR USE: Skill Identification takes place in three separate steps. First, faculty should be asked to complete in outline form a work autobiography, which should contain specific descriptions of what that person actually did in all vocational and avocational experiences to date. Second, that autobiography should be "mined" for a list of specific job skills. An autobiographical outline that takes a half-hour to complete will yield 30 to 50 specific job skills. Third, this list of skills should be reviewed for general skill clusters, that is, for skills which in some way seem related to each other. The most obvious skill clusters should be identified and labeled first. Second and third clusters then should be identified until all skills have been classified in this manner. The same skill may be used in different skill clusters.

    The skill clusters identified in this process can be used as the basis for resume preparation, or may be related to other career planning activities. In particular, skills should be matched with interests as revealed by the *Strong Campbell Interest Inventory* (see Exercise Number Fourteen). Matches between skills and interests provide obvious areas for career development.

PLANNING DOCUMENT NUMBER TWO

TITLE: A Comprehensive Career Planning Workshop

SOURCE: Steven R. Phillips

GENERAL DESCRIPTION: The life and career planning issues and concepts discussed in Chapter Ten of Volume 2 and in this volume can be combined in a wide variety of ways to reflect participants' current life situations and learning needs. The workshop design presented in this planning document is intended to be comprehensive and incorporates all six elements of the career planning model presented in Chapter Ten. As such, it can perhaps best serve as an ideal model from which various more limited and specific designs can be built.

INSTRUCTIONS FOR USE: The following workshop design can and has been implemented in its entirety; however, it can be modified to meet the needs of specific faculty groups.

Variations:

1. Faculty facing almost certain career changes might wish to spend more time on the last four activities at the expense of the first five. Those not facing career change might wish to eliminate activity number eight entirely.

2. Background reading and even discussion time might be used, drawing on a number of the articles and books discussed in Chapter Ten. Again, faculty facing career change will be more interested in such books as *What Color is Your Parachute?*, *Where Do I Go from Here with My Life?*, *The Three Boxes of Life*, and *The Inventurers* than will their colleagues not considering such changes.

A COMPREHENSIVE PLANNING WORKSHOP

Focus: Life and Career Planning
Duration: Three Days (21 hours)

ACTIVITY NUMBER	GENERAL GOALS	RECOMMENDED EXERCISE	DURATION
1.	Create an open environment for the consideration of career planning.	"Job Exchange" (Volume 3, Exercise Number Thirteen)	2 hours
2.	Help participants explore past, present, and future dimensions of their lives.	"Life Line" (Volume 2, Exercise Number Twelve)	2 hours
3.	Acquaint participants with the concept of life transitions.	"Transitions" (Volume 2, Exercise Number Thirteen)	3 hours
4.	Help participants identify assumptions about the future.	"Image of the Future" (Volume 2, Exercise Number Fourteen)	2 hours
5.	Identify, compare, and contrast current career and life values.	"Broad Life Values" and "Broad Career Values" (Volume 3, Instrument Numbers Eight and Nine)	1 hour
6.	Examine a variety of current life issues and values.	"Life Inventory" (Volume 2, Exercise Number Sixteen, Inventory List One)	1 hour
7.	Examine a variety of current life and career interests.	"Career Interests" (Volume 3, Exercise Number Fourteen)	2 hours
8.	Assess interpersonal strengths and weaknesses.	"Strengths and Weaknesses" (Volume 3, Exercise Number Four)	3 hours
9.	Identify current vocational and career skills.	"Skill Identification" (Volume 3, Exercise Number Fifteen)	2 hours
10.	Develop action plans.	"Building a Project" (Volume 2, Exercise Number Eighteen)	3 hours

INSTRUMENT NUMBER TEN

TITLE: Faculty Application for Promotion: A Portfolio Procedure

SOURCE: St. Francis College, Joliet, Illinois

GENERAL DESCRIPTION: In 1978, the faculty and administration at St. Francis College decided to initiate an inexpensive but significant project on faculty evaluation and development. After reviewing pertinent literature, they concluded that:

(1) a system of faculty evaluation must be linked with a faculty development program and must exist within a framework of a reward system;

(2) all parties affected by the system must have an opportunity to provide input into the system;

(3) the system must be unique to the institution and not imported *in toto* from another institution;

(4) the system must be clear (clarity is essential) and must be publicly announced and understood;

(5) the system of evaluation should allow for several types of evaluation since the literature concludes that there is no one, single evaluation process which is foolproof or comprehensive;

(6) the system must be personal as well as systematic;

(7) sufficient time must be allowed for the evaluation process to take place;

(8) the input of student evaluations is unquestioned . . .;

(9) the purposes for the evaluation must be clearly stated and agreed upon by most;

(10) evaluation should occur throughout the college (the institution, faculty, administrators, students and staff);

(11) the procedures for evaluation should be valid, that is, they should do what they're supposed to do . . .;

(12) the system should not be closed, that is, it should be open enough so as to allow feedback to the person being evaluated . . .;

(13) the system shouldn't be overwhelmingly time consuming . . .;

(14) faculty would be evaluated on four primary criteria: teaching, academic advising, professional growth and scholarly effort, and service to the college and community;

(15) the faculty member should be given the opportunity to provide evaluative information from a variety of sources, persons, and offices.*

Two packages of evaluation materials were developed by the St. Francis faculty. One package contained information and materials for a faculty member who was seeking promotion. A second package of materials was given to each appropriate division chairman whenever a faculty member in that division picked up an application. While the system has been set up initially

*Reported in a paper titled "New Dean, Old Problems, and $8,000," by Philip J. Steinkrauss, Vice President for Academic Affairs, College of St. Francis (ERIC Document No. AD 158669, HE010377).

for use in the consideration of faculty promotions, the college hopes eventually to extend the system for use with and by faculty who are being evaluated for the purpose of contract renewal (in lieu of tenure).

INSTRUCTIONS FOR USE: The faculty evaluation procedure at St. Francis is monitored by a Faculty Rank and Promotion Committee. All forms completed by the faculty member, students, and division chairmen are submitted to this committee for review. As noted on the forms, students at St. Francis use the IDEA (Kansas State University) questionnaire to evaluate the instructional performance of faculty. Further information about this questionnaire is contained in Volume 1 (Instrument Number Four) of *A Handbook for Faculty Development.* Other evaluation forms (e.g., Purdue University's "Cafeteria") might be substituted for IDEA.

Any college making use of the St. Francis portfolio system will want to modify it for use with their own unique faculty review and evaluation procedures. The carefully prepared St. Francis materials, however, can serve as an excellent starting point for the preparation of a new portfolio-based procedure. We recommend that the chapter on portfolio evaluation in the second volume of *A Handbook for Faculty Development* also be read. It describes, in general terms, a portfolio procedure that is somewhat more elaborate— though also more flexible—than that being used at St. Francis.

To be maximally effective—as noted above in the St. Francis list of 15 conclusions—faculty evaluation should be closely linked with faculty development. We therefore recommend that a portfolio procedure for evaluation be linked with a procedure for professional growth contracting, such as is described in Instrument Number Eleven. The preliminary assessment of strengths and weaknesses in a professional growth contract can be based on a portfolio assessment such as the one performed at St. Francis College.

APPLICATION for ADVANCEMENT WITHIN RANK
or PROMOTION TO HIGHER RANK

Guidelines and Record of Service

Name: _____   ☐ Advancement within Rank

Division _____   ☐ Promotion to Higher Rank

  and Program: _____   ☐ Other _____
                                                          (Specify)

Present Rank: _____   _____

Years of Service at the institution: _____   _____

  Date of Initial Appointment: _____

Length of Service in Present Rank: _____

  Date of Appointment to this Rank: _____

                    Signature: _____

The categories indicated below by Roman numerals correspond to the criteria for promotion. Some of the numbered items in each category refer to information which will be provided from other sources (e.g., student evaluation, student advising form, evaluation of chairman, support letters, etc.); still other items must be supplied by the applicant on special forms (as indicated). The remaining items are mentioned as examples of possible ways of satisfying each criteria. The Rank and Promotion Committee does not necessarily expect a faculty member to have something to report for each numbered item. Nevertheless, the faculty member is requested to supply the headings and follow the numbering system used in this checklist when submitting this record of activities. Items marked with an asterisk are required.

I. CLASSROOM TEACHING
  *A. *Student Evaluations* (last two semesters)
      IDEA forms or others
  *B. *Self-Evaluation*
      A form is attached.
  *C. *Review of Teaching Materials*—a syllabus for each class must be provided. Other relevant material or commentary could be included at the Instructor's option.
   D. *Anecdotal Reports*—these reports may be filled from time-to-time by the applicant or by others. They may be included in the application or directed to the Chair of Rank and Promotion Committee.
   E. *Classroom Visitation*—a form is attached which is to be completed by the Division Chairman or observer of your choice. An appointment for visitation—arranged by the applicant and Division Chair or observer.

F. *Other*

1. Evaluation reports may be requested from colleagues or students. The person must submit his report directly to the chairman of the Rank and Promotion Committee.
2. New courses or programs developed within the last three years. Specify those approved for inclusion in catalogues of the College.
3. Major revision of established courses or programs. (Explain)
4. Participation in multidisciplinary courses. (Explain)
5. Special teaching assignments, basic skills or remedial work with students, tutoring, placement of students in graduate schools, etc.
6. Special utilization of College Library resources and/or PLATO system.

II. STUDENT ADVISING and PERSONAL COUNSELING (where appropriate)

*A. *Student Appraisal of Advising*—a sample form is attached which you should distribute to your advisees. The student advisee should return the form directly to the Rank and Promotion Chairman.
*B. *Self-Report*—a form is attached.
C. *Other*

III. FACULTY SERVICE TO THE COLLEGE AND COMMUNITY

*A. *Self-Report*—refer to III,D—a form is attached.
*B. *Division Chairman's Report*—a form is attached.
*C. *Administrator's Report* (if faculty member is also responsible to any administrative office for certain management/administrative duties).
D. *Other*

1. Membership on college, governance, or division committees. (Indicate whether chairman or member.)
2. Supervision (last three years).
   a) supervision of independent studies
   b) supervision of internships
   c) supervision of assigned research
   d) supervision of undergraduate assistants (list number and nature of supervision)
   e) adviser or moderator of student groups within the division
3. Non-teaching division duties (indicate whether released time or compensation was granted).
4. Sponsorship, adviser or moderator of campus-wide student groups or activities (List groups).
5. Participation in Divisional affairs. (Explain).
6. Special work requested by the College. (Explain).
7. Student Recruitment (Explain).
8. Cultural activities sponsored (List groups).
9. Assistance to other faculty members (Explain).
10. Assistance to an administrative office, e.g., development, financial aid, admissions, student personnel, campus ministry, etc. (Explain).

11. Membership in or service to community organizations.
12. Speaking engagements to professional and non-professional groups during the past three years. (Include lectures to community organizatons and to intra- and inter-divisional groups).
13. Service to area schools (evaluation committees, school boards, local educational committees, etc.)
14. Active membership in community and civic organizations (List).
15. Participation in college activities (Explain).
16. Amount of time spent in office hours and appointments with students.
17. Involvement in college public relations activities.
18. Involvement in Faculty Assembly meetings.
19. Involvement in the college's Continuing Education program.
20. Work on student orientation or registration sessions.
21. Involvement in Self-Study on accreditation process.
22. Discipline conferences hosted at the college.

IV. EVIDENCE OF PROFESSIONAL GROWTH AND SCHOLARLY EFFORT

*A. *Professional Growth and Scholarly Effort*—See IV,C
   Professional Growth and Scholarly Effort—Self-Report (Form attached).
 B. *Performing and Visual Arts* (where appropriate)—a form is attached.
 C. *Other.*
   1. Activity in professional associations and societies. List current memberships in professional organizations.
   2. Offices in professional associations and societies (Detail).
   3. Papers or other presentations before professional groups (List papers and groups).
   4. Evidence of efforts toward individual professional improvement (elaborate if necessary).
   5. Degrees earned, graduate courses completed, professional institutes, seminars, and conferences.
   6. Current formal study.
   7. Courses audited or correspondence courses completed.
   8. Professional journals subscribed to.
   9. Other professional publications read regularly.
   10. Location and year of professional meetings attended in last five years.
   11. Attendance at special lectures (indicate on or off campus).
   12. Summer enrichment workshops.
   13. Travel and brief statement as to its professional value.
   14. Inter-disciplinary, intra-divisional cooperation.
   15. Research for the past three years (Explain).
   16. Self-Directed Study (current research projects, reading programs, etc.) and research in progress
   17. Other factors you believe should be considered.
   18. Publications (List).
   19. Professional consultation.
   20. Has the research been cited or quoted (Explain).

21. Book reviews, monographs, etc.
22. Grants applied for and received.
23. Institutional research on follow-up studies.

V. SUPPORTING MATERIALS
 *A. Faculty data sheet (attached) and recent Curriculum Vita.
 *B. Division Chairman's overall evaluation and recommendation.
 *C. Vice President for Academic Affairs' overall evaluation and recommendation.
  D. Support letters (optional and pertinent to criteria).
  E. A prospectus describing the faculty member's goals and plans in the criteria areas for the next three years.
  F. Extent of involvement in any formalized faculty support or development program.
  G. List of any professional, academic, civic, religious, or community honors or distinction. Professional recognition in terms of awards and/or honors. (Please explain)

Note:

This *APPLICATION* should be completed and *returned to the appropriate Division Chairman* according to the procedures for Rank and Promotion.

Division Chairman will be evaluated on the same criteria. The Vice President for Academic Affairs will fulfill those responsibilities reserved to the Division Chairmen for their faculty members. Faculty evaluations of Division Chairmen may be requested.

RANK AND PROMOTION CHECKLIST

(For Applicant's use—please submit with application also)

I. Teaching:
    *Student Evaluations, IDEA and others (last 2 semesters) ☐
    *Self-Evaluation ☐
    *Teaching Materials (Syllabi) ☐
    Anecdotal Reports ☐
    Classroom Visitation ☐
    Other: _____

    _____

    _____

II. Advising:
    *Student Appraisal of Advising (To be distributed by applicant but
    returned to R & P Chair by student.) ☐
    *Self-Report
    Other: _____

    _____

    _____

III. Service
    *Self-Report ☐
    *Division Chairman Report ☐
    *Administrative Report ☐
    Other: _____

    _____

    _____

IV. Professional:
    *Self-Report ☐
    Performing or Visual Arts ☐
    Other: _____

    _____

    _____

V. *Faculty Data Sheet ☐
    *Division Chairmen Evaluation ☐
    *Vice President for Academic Affairs Evaluation ☐
    Support Letters ☐
    Prospectus on Goals ☐
    Other: _____

    _____

    _____

* *Required*

SELF-APPRAISAL OF TEACHING

Teacher _____   Date _____

Term _____   Academic Year _____

Thoughtful self-evaluation can help improve teaching effectiveness. This questionnaire is designed for that purpose. You are asked to look at your own performance in teaching.

At your option, questions 11 and 12 may be aded. Use the back of this form for any written comments you might want to express. These might record any unusual circumstances that relate to the courses and to your teaching them.

Directions:
Rate yourself on each item, giving the highest scores for unusually effective performances. Place in the blank space before each statement the number that most nearly expresses your view:

Highest			Average			Low-est	Not Appro-priate	Don't Know
7	6	5	4	3	2	1	X	O

_____ 1. Have major objectives of your courses been made clear?

_____ 2. How do you rate agreement between course objectives and lesson assignments?

_____ 3. Are class presentations well planned and organized?

_____ 4. Are important ideas clearly explained?

_____ 5. How would you judge your mastery of the content of courses?

_____ 6. Is class time well used?

_____ 7. Have you encouraged critical thinking and analysis?

_____ 8. Have you encouraged students to seek your help when necessary?

_____ 9. Have you encouraged relevant student involvement in the classes?

_____ 10. How tolerant are you of student viewpoints that differ from your own?

_____ 11.

_____ 12.

_____   Composite rating.

STUDENT APPRAISAL OF ADVISING

Please fill in the name of your faculty adviser or counselor (whoever signs your class schedule) and also the date.

Name of Adviser _____

Date _____

This survey is given to learn about how you view your adviser. Please DO NOT sign your name. The space on the back of the survey allows you to use your own words, and extra questions may be added. Your assistance is appreciated.

DIRECTIONS: The appraisal instrument is divided into two sections: A. Academic Advising, and B. Personal Counseling. Section B is to be used only if you have had personal counseling from your Academic adviser.

Each statement describes a basic component of advising and/or counseling. Rate your adviser on each item, giving the highest scores for unusually effective performance. Place in the blank space before each statement that most nearly expresses your view.

High			Average			Lowest	Don't Know	Not Appropriate
7	6	5	4	3	2	1	O	X

A. Academic Advising
    _____ 1. Advises in terms of alternatives and encourages you to assume responsibilities for decisions.
    _____ 2. Has personal interest in assisting you through advising.
    _____ 3. Keeps appointments when made in advance.
    _____ 4. Keeps up-to-date with regulations and course offerings.
    _____ 5. Maintains accurate files on your progress.
    _____ 6. Seeks to plan programs consistent with your stated objectives.
    _____ 7.
    _____ 8.

B. Personal Counseling (Answer these questions if personal counseling is an acknowledged aspect of student advising.)
    _____ 1. Able to start working towards a solution to your problems because of this counseling.
    _____ 2. Is helpful to you.
    _____ 3. Is objective and non-punitive.
    _____ 4. Is willing to use college or community resources when your problems seem to be more than he can handle.
    _____ 5. Understands your point of view.
    _____ 6. Would you wish to return to this counselor for help in the future?
    _____ 7.
    _____ 8.

This information is very important to your adviser. Your immediate cooperation is appreciated.

264

STUDENT ADVISING RESUME

(Self-Report of Applicant)

Name _____   For Academic Year _____

Department _____   Date _____

The advising resume provides an opportunity for you to describe your activities in this area. Use additional pages if necessary.

1. What were your advising responsibilities? _____

_____

_____

_____

2. Were there innovative, creative, or special aspects of your advising that you would like to mention?

_____

_____

_____

_____

_____

3. Other comments (any special circumstances or problems that should be considered).

_____

_____

_____

_____

_____

FACULTY SERVICE TO THE COLLEGE AND COMMUNITY

—SELF-REPORT—

Teacher _____ Date _____

Instructions: Using this report form, a faculty member should refer to the Guidelines for Rank and Promotion, III D. Here are mentioned approximately 20 examples of possible ways of satisfying this criterion. It is not necessary for a faculty member to have something to report for each numbered item. Nevertheless, the faculty member is requested to supply the headings as listed in the guidelines and to follow the numbering system used in the guidelines.

Example:

#1. Membership on college, governance, or division committees (indicate whether chairman or member).

_____

_____

_____

_____

_____

#__ _____

_____

_____

_____

_____

#__ _____

_____

_____

_____

(Use reverse side if necessary.)

EVIDENCE of PROFESSIONAL GROWTH and SCHOLARLY EFFORT

—SELF-REPORT—

Teacher _____   Date _____

Instructions: Using this report form, a faculty member should refer to the Guidelines for Rank and Promotion, IV C. Here are mentioned approximately 20 examples of possible ways of satisfying this criterion. It is not necessary for a faculty member to have something to report for each numbered item. Nevertheless, the faculty member is requested to supply the headings as listed in the guidelines and to follow the numbering system used in the guidelines.

Example:

#1.   Activity in professional associations and societies (list).

_____

_____

_____

_____

_____

#__   _____

_____

_____

_____

_____

#__   _____

_____

_____

_____

(Use reverse side if necessary.)

PERFORMING AND VISUAL ARTS

Self-Evaluation

Teacher _____ Date _____

Title of presentation _____

Place or occasion of presentation _____

Time spent on this project _____

_____ 1. Describe the presentation, including a statement of your intention or purpose. _____

_____

_____ 2. Discuss briefly any special difficulties that you encountered in producing the work or in making arrangements for its presentation or exhibition. _____

_____

_____ 3. Were other faculty members or students included in this production, performance, or exhibition project? If so, who and to what extent?

_____

_____

_____ 4. How was the work received by the audience or spectators? _____

_____

_____

_____ 5. How was the work received by the critics? _____

_____

_____

_____ 6. Do you think the reaction of the audience or spectators and the reaction of the critics were justifiable in terms of your stated intentions for the project?

_____

_____

_____ 7. How did you feel about this production or exhibition? _____

_____

_____

Other Comments: _____

_____

_____

FACULTY DATA SHEET

Name: _____ Date: _____

I. *Academic Qualifications* (list chronologically starting with bachelor's degree):

Degree	Subject Area	Institution	Date Awarded

If you do not have a doctorate, how many *years* (i.e., equivalent of full grad. load, nine months) of graduate study have you had? _____. Years credited here and above may not be counted in the *Professional Experience* category.

When and where were the years accumulated?

Subject Area	Institution	Dates

II. *Professional Experience:*

A. College Teaching Experience: Total years, including current year: _____ .

Dates	Institution

B. Other Professional Experience (i.e., experience that you would see as the equivalent of college teaching, such as the ministry, administrative work, etc.) Total Years: _____ .

Dates	Institution	Position	Total Years

Explain the nature of the work if it is not self-evident: _____

_____

III. Publications: (list chronologically on the reverse side)

ANECDOTAL REPORT

Regarding _____

Appraiser _____   Date _____

Title _____

Description of incident:

_____

_____

_____

_____

_____

_____

_____

_____

_____

_____

_____

DIVISION CHAIRMAN'S
RANK AND PROMOTION MATERIALS

_____ has picked up and is completing his/her *Application for Promotion*. These forms are part of the application process and are to be completed by the appropriate Division Chairman.

The Vice President for Academic Affairs will coordinate the IDEA Student Evaluation. The Student Appraisals of Academic Advising were distributed by the applicant and have been returned to my office. They are available for your review.

Date Application picked up:

_____

_____
Chairman, Rank and Promotion

TEACHING MATERIALS APPRAISAL

Teacher _____   Course _____

Term _____   Academic Year _____

Appraiser(s) _____   Title of Appraiser(s) _____
              (Division Chairmen)

_____

The following appraisal form contains questions which should be helpful in judging this category. Additional questions may be added. Also, you may want to add a summary statement in your own words. Materials must include the syllabus; other materials could include pass-outs, bibliography, examinations, slides, tapes, etc.

Directions: Rate each item, giving the highest scores to unusually effective teaching materials and procedures.

Highest			Average			Lowest	Not Appropriate	Don't Know
7	6	5	4	3	2	1	0	X

____ 1. How would you rate the overall quality of the course outline, if one is used?

____ 2. From what the instructor distributes, or from what is said, do you believe that the students gain a coherent picture of the course?

____ 3. Do the grading procedures seem reasonable and fair?

____ 4. Do the materials reflect the most acceptable authority sources as well as new views and evidence in the field?

____ 5. From what can be gleaned from the course materials and procedures, do you believe that the students have a challenging and meaningful experience in the classroom?

____ 6. Based upon an examination of course materials and procedures, how would you rate the course preparation and teaching concern of this individual as compared with other teachers in the department?

____ 7. As compared with others in the institution as a whole?

____ 8.

____ 9.

_____ Composite rating.

CLASSROOM VISITATION APPRAISAL

Teacher _____   Course _____

Visitor(s) _____   Academic Year _____

Title _____

The following appraisal form contains 12 questions, many of which are found on the student appraisal of teaching form. In addition, you may want to develop a narrative description of your visitation.

Directions: Rate teaching on each item, giving the highest scores for unusually effective performances.

Highest			Average			Lowest	Don't Know	Not Appropriate
7	6	5	4	3	2	1	O	X

_____ 1. Were the objectives of the class session made clear to you?

_____ 2. How well was the class presentation planned and organized?

_____ 3. Were important ideas clearly explained?

_____ 4. How would you judge the professor's mastery of the course content?

_____ 5. Was class time well used?

_____ 6. Did the professor encourage critical thinking and analysis?

_____ 7. Do you believe the professor encouraged relevant student involvement in the class?

_____ 8. How did the professor react to student viewpoints different from his own?

_____ 9. How would you describe the attitude of students in the class toward the professor?

_____ 10. Do you believe your visitation was at a time when you were able to fairly judge the nature and tenor of the teaching-learning process?

_____ 11. Considering the previous 10 items, how would you rate this teacher in comparison to others in the department?

_____ 12. As compared with others in the institution?

_____ 13.

_____ 14.

_____ Composite rating.

Yes _____ No _____ Did you make prior arrangements with the teacher for the visitation?

Yes _____ No _____ Did you have a follow-up conference?

Comments after class visitation: _____

_____

_____

Comments after follow-up conference: _____

_____

_____

FACULTY SERVICE APPRAISAL

Name of teacher _____   Year _____

Appraiser _____   Title _____
      (Division Chairman)

Directions:

Please write in the blank space the number that describes your judgment of that factor as it relates to an individual's faculty service and relations. Rate the individual on each item, giving the highest scores for unusually effective performances. Additional questions may be added.

Highest			Average			Lowest	Don't Know	Not Appropriate
7	6	5	4	3	2	1	O	X

____ 1. Acceptance of college assignments. Does he/she accept college assignments willingly? Does he/she volunteer occasionally?

____ 2. Attitude. Does he/she act in the best interest of the division and the college? Does he/she take a professional attitude toward human relations and personnel problems? Does he/she have a positive cooperative attitude?

____ 3. Cooperation. To what extent does the faculty member assist colleagues and others with their problems? Is he/she a good team member?

____ 4. Performance on college assignments. What is his/her performance level? How do colleagues perceive his performance?

____ 5. Professional behavior as it relates to his/her professional activities and the goals and nature of the institution. Does he/she act responsibly?

____ 6.

____ 7.

_____ Composite rating.

Description of specific assignments and services:

_____

_____

_____

_____

Comments:

_____

_____

_____

RECOMMENDATION FORM

Applicant's Name:

☐ Advancement Within Rank
☐ Promotion to Highest Rank
☐ Other _____

_____

_____

_____

_____

I.   I recommend _____ for

_____ .

(type of action)

Statement: _____

_____

_____

_____

_____

_____

_____

_____

_____

Signature: _____

Division Chairman

Date: _____

(To the Division Chairman:
Submit this form, along with the faculty member's Application and your
Classroom Visitation Appraisal, Chairman's Report on Faculty Service to the
Chairman of the Rank and Promotion Committee.)

II. We recommend _____ for

_____ .

(type of action)

(continued on next page.)

Special and unique contributions which have been made by this candidate to the institution.

_____

_____

_____

_____

_____

Does the candidate meet the established criteria for advancement or promotion? Yes ( ) No ( ). If no, upon what basis is it recommended that an exception be made?

_____

_____

_____

_____

_____

_____

_____

Signature: _____

Chairman, Rank and Promotion
Committee

Date: _____

III.   I recommend _____ for

_____ .

(type of action)

Signature: _____

Vice President for Academic Affairs

Date: _____

Statement attached.

INSTRUMENT NUMBER ELEVEN

TITLE: Professional Growth Contract

SOURCE: William H. Bergquist, derived in part from the procedures used at Gordon College (Wenham, Massachusetts) and the California State University at Dominguez Hills

GENERAL DESCRIPTION: During the past seven years, one of the most successful methods for planning and implementing faculty development activities has been the professional growth (or professional development) contract. Beginning with the extensive work on professional growth contracts at Gordon College, a growing number of institutions are making use of some procedure for the assessment of a faculty member's: (1) strengths and weaknesses, (2) current areas of responsibility, (3) professional growth goals (overcoming weaknesses to meet current or newly-emerging areas of responsibility), (4) proposed activities to achieve these goals, and (5) proposed modes of evaluating the achievement of these goals.

Typically, a professional growth contract is completed by a faculty member in conjunction with a general faculty development committee or a committee specifically convened for this faculty member's contract. The faculty member and the institution (as represented by the committee, the dean of the college, or a division or department chairman) both make a commitment of the needed time, money, effort, and resources to accomplish the proposed professional development goals—these goals presumably being of value to both the faculty member and the institution. The growth contract is often used in conjunction with plans for sabbaticals, career retraining, or a shift in disciplines. Less dramatically, the growth contract can be coupled with planning for participation in a summer institute, a course design or instructional improvement consultation, or a national conference.

In developing a professional development contract procedure, a college or university also might wish to consider establishing a professional fund—which enables a faculty member to participate in long-term professional development planning. Developed at Fresno Pacific College (Fresno, California), the professional fund requires a commitment of the college to set aside (on paper or in fact) an equivalent of 8 to 10 percent of the faculty member's salary each year. This fund is not taken from the faculty member's salary, but rather from the college's travel, sabbatical, and other professional development budgets. Each faculty member may submit a proposal for the use of all or part of the funds accumulated for him at any time. The funds might be used to cover travel costs to a disciplinary workshop, secretarial services for preparation of a manuscript for publication, freight costs for the shipment of several paintings to an exhibit, and so forth. The funds can also be used by the faculty member after six or seven years to buy up a portion of time (one-half time for a year, full-time for one term, etc.). Thus, the fund can substitute for both a travel budget and a sabbatical policy.

The professional fund holds several advantages over more traditional professional development programs. By combining all professional development activities or resources under one professional fund, there can be greater equity in the distribution of funds, greater sensitivity to the different styles of professional growth among faculty, and greater opportunity for a faculty member to plan ahead. Rather than asking a faculty member to apply to one place for travel funds and to another for a sabbatical, he applies to one place for all faculty development resources. Thus, if one faculty member will benefit most from frequent attendance at conferences, while another faculty member would benefit most from an occasional, concentrated sabbatical, then both can plan for their own type of professional development activity. When travel costs and sabbatical leaves are considered separately, the latter of these two faculty members is often at a disadvantage, for the non-use of travel funds is not taken into consideration when applying for sabbatical leave.

A professional fund need not be financed solely by institutional revenues. This fund can be an excellent vehicle for solicitation of grants and donations from alumni, philanthropists, or other sources. These donations would help to ensure continuing support for faculty growth and development, even when the college is experiencing financial difficulties—the time when the professional growth of faculty is particularly important.

A professional fund can be effectively coupled with a professional development contract plan, for a faculty member is not assured of receiving money (or release time) through a professional fund. He is only assured that this money is available if a worthy proposal is submitted that meets both professional and institutional development needs. In submitting a proposal to receive part or all of the funds that have been set aside, a faculty member might formulate a professional growth contract such as the one described in this document.

INSTRUCTIONS FOR USE: The "Professional Growth Contract" consists of 10 sets of questions that a faculty member should answer in preparing for a professional development project. This contract either might be filled out by the faculty member individually and then submitted to the contract committee for further discussion and possible modification, or it can be worked out during the committee meeting itself, as members of the committee ask questions of the faculty member and jointly explore each of the 10 sets of questions. This contract form might be modified to reflect different institutional policies or might be shortened—especially when being used by a college that has had no previous experience with professional growth contracts. Questions that might be eliminated include: new roles (question 4) and professional competencies (question 5—assuming that question 6 is modified to incorporate question 5). The question regarding dissemination and use of outcomes from the professional development project (question 9) should not be eliminated, nor should the question on the evaluation of the project (question 10).

An individual professional growth contract committee should be constituted of the faculty member, the faculty member's immediate supervisor, a colleague of the faculty member (chosen by the faculty member), a consumer of the faculty member's work (student, alumnus, or member of the faculty member's profession or discipline), and a facilitator of the professional development planning process (often the head of a faculty development program or instructional development center). This committee composition is comparable to that recommended for the review of faculty portfolios (see Chapter Three of the second volume in this series)—another reason for coupling faculty portfolios and professional development contracts. When a third element is added—the professional fund—a college has established the base for effective, long-term professional development planning, implementation, and evaluation.

PROFESSIONAL GROWTH CONTRACT

Name: _____

Department/Division: _____

Date: _____

Members of the Committee:

_____

_____

_____

_____

_____

1. What are your primary roles and areas of responsibility in this institution?

2. What unique or particularly outstanding strengths do you bring to these roles and/or responsibilities? How do these strengths contribute to the overall welfare of this institution?

3. What are your primary limitations or weaknesses in performing these roles and/or meeting these responsibilities?

4. What new roles and/or responsibilities are you about to assume or do you anticipate assuming in the near future? What are the implications of these roles/responsibilities for your current strengths and weaknesses? How might these roles/responsibilities contribute to the overall welfare of this institution?

5. How might you expand and extend your own professional competencies so that you can:
   (a) perform current roles and meet current responsibilities more effectively;
   (b) effectively assume new roles and responsibilities;
   (c) overcome present deficiencies/limitations that affect current or future roles and responsibilities; and/or
   (d) build on present strengths as these strengths relate to present roles and responsibilities?

6. Please restate your responses to question five in terms of specific professional development goals. Each goal should be stated in explicit terms, so that you (and others) will know by a certain time whether this goal has been achieved.

7. In what specific activities would you like to engage to achieve these goals?

8. What resources (e.g., release time; money for travel, conference fees, transportation of paintings, etc.; secretarial services; consultative assistance; and so forth) do you need to complete these activities? Who will provide these resources—you or the institution? A successful professional growth contract usually is based on a reciprocal agreement between a faculty member and institution in which both make an extraordinary effort to assist in the accomplishment of specific professional development goals.

	Resource (Brief Description)	I Should Provide	Institution Should Provide
1.			
2.			
3.			
4.			
5.			
6.			
7.			
8.			
9.			
10.			

9. How will the institution benefit from the achievement of your professional development goals? What are your plans for dissemination and use of learnings from or products of this professional development project among students and colleagues (faculty, administrators) at your institution and elsewhere?

10. How will this professional development project be evaluated? How will you and others know the extent to which your professional development goals have been met? You may wish to identify specific benchmarks (products, events, outcomes, recognition) that will indicate the accomplishment of your goals.

COMMENTS BY PROFESSIONAL DEVELOPMENT COMMITTEE

1. Current Roles/Responsibilities

2. Strengths

3. Limitations

4. New Roles/Responsibilities

5. Professional Competencies

6. Specific Professional Development Goals

7. Professional Development Activities

8. Resources Needed

9. Plans for Dissemination and Use

10. Evaluation

Section IV

Present and Future

Chapter Eleven

The Present and Future of Faculty Development: An Overview

In bringing this third and final volume on faculty development to a close, we felt it would be appropriate to address what we see as three of the major questions facing these efforts in the 1980s. First, where is funding likely to come from for current and future faculty development activities? Most of the major private foundations, whose support was crucial in establishing the modern theory and practice of faculty development, have terminated that support, at least for activities similar to those that have been conducted over the last several years. In Chapter Twelve we attempt to identify methods for obtaining continued funding for professional development in the face of such circumstances.

Second, perhaps the major challenge facing faculty development in the 1980s is to bring its activities into closer alignment with the direction individual institutions are taking as those directions are increasingly defined by institutional research. In Chapter Thirteen we suggest ways in which information about faculty can be integrated more fully into institutional planning and thinking. And finally, in Chapter Fourteen, we address the very uncertain issue of the future of faculty development in the 1980s. In the face of increasing financial restraints, how can faculty development continue to promote the vitality of the men and women who form the heart of the enterprise? We hope the last chapter in this our final volume suggests some viable alternatives and answers.

Chapter Twelve

Seeking Funds for Faculty Development Programs[1]

The professional development of faculty and administrators in higher education has been supported generously by both public and private philanthropy during the past decade. The total amount of money granted for professional development activities during the past 10 years amounts to perhaps well over a half-billion dollars. Much of this money has gone to undergraduate colleges and universities and major research universities, with a proportionately smaller amount of money going to professional schools. Within the past five years, however, government and private support for this area has significantly declined. Such major foundations as the Lilly Endowment and the W. K. Kellogg Foundation have announced that they no longer are going to be deeply involved in the funding of professional (or at least faculty) development programs in the near future. This decline in funding comes precisely at a time when a large number of programs are seeking support for establishment or continuation. The competition for dollars therefore is intense and most grant seekers in the area of professional development can expect to be turned down.

This pessimistic picture can be tempered by observing that foundations are still interested in specific aspects of professional development and are providing substantial grants in several related areas. Many foundations, for instance, recently have expressed interest in professional development programs for college administrators and trustees, and in such areas as curriculum development and institutional planning significant funds are available. Thus, even though a professional development program that specifically aims at faculty will probably receive limited attention, one that involves college presidents, deans, business managers, or other administrators or that makes use of faculty development as a means to some other end, such as the development of a new interdisciplinary program or a program for a specific disadvantaged population, may still be given careful consideration by many foundations.

To obtain funds for a professional development program, an institution must not only write a compelling proposal but also plan and implement an effective "courtship" of the foundation(s) from which funds are being sought. In this chapter consideration will be given both to the preparation of a proposal and to personal contact with foundation executives. These observations and suggestions certainly are not definitive and several may soon be dated, as foundations change their interests, stylistic preferences, and procedures. Furthermore, many of the recommendations are appropriate only for certain kinds of foundations. Before turning to suggestions about the courtship of foundations and proposal writing, therefore, we should draw several distinctions among types of foundations.

A. Types of Foundations

Important differences exist among several different kinds of foundations. First, significant differences exist between government and private foundations. Because governmental funding organizations are giving away money that "belongs" to the taxpayer, a great deal of the review of funding applications generally is associated with strict bureaucratic control and attention to accountability. Conversely, the executives of private foundations usually are representing the concerns and interests of a smaller number of individuals or stockholders. They therefore usually have much greater flexibility and autonomy in considering proposals. Consequently, a private foundation executive can be courted much more easily than an executive of a government foundation.

Second, governmental foundations are themselves quite diverse, particularly in the degree to which each agency expects to be involved in the planning and execution of a project. Some governmental agencies, such as the Title III Developing Institutions office, have set up rather strict guidelines concerning the ways in which professional development funds can be requested and spent. These agencies also tend to monitor extensively the projects they fund; hence, the project staff's relationship with the foundation does not end when funding is received. In general, these more "interventionistic" foundations provide rather large grants ($100,000-$1,000,000). Other government agencies, which usually offer smaller grants ($1,000-$200,000), are much more flexible about proposals and will rarely be involved with a college or project staff after the grant is awarded. Usually a yearly progress report and end-of-project evaluation report will suffice for communication with the staff of this latter type of government foundation.

Third, several different kinds of private foundations exist and have been categorized by the Council on Foundations according to the source of funds:

> *Independent foundations* receive their funds from a single person, a few individuals, or a family. Many of these, especially those that are small, function under the voluntary direction of family members, and such foundations are commonly known as "family foundations." However, others which may bear a family name—e.g., the Rockefeller Foundation—have independent boards of trustees and are managed by a professional staff.
>
> *Corporate foundations* have been created by profit-making businesses to set more money aside in good years to continue to support charities in lean years.
>
> *Community foundations* build their endowments from bequests and gifts from a number of donors, who primarily want their gifts to serve the charities of a city or region. Generally their boards are representative of varied interests in that city or region. For these reasons, community foundations were exempted from some of the more stringent provisions of the 1969 Tax Reform Act that apply to private (i.e., independent and corporate) foundations.

When considering the solicitation of funds for professional development activities, one usually looks to such independent foundations as the Lilly Endowment, the W. K. Kellogg Foundation, and the Exxon Education Foundation. Unless otherwise noted, we will be refering to independent foundations throughout this chapter when speaking of private foundations.

Fourth, a distinction also can be made between grants and contracts in soliciting government (primarily federal) funds. A grant usually is considered a gift that is being awarded for past preformance or the merit of an idea. The recipient of a grant has relatively little responsibility to the awarding foundation, other than accounting for how the money has been spent. A contract, on the other hand, is awarded for the provision of specific services; hence the foundation is much more of a partner in the enterprise and may expect frequent communication and cooperative planning with the contract recipient. Most on-campus professional development projects are supported by government agencies through grants rather than contracts.

In this chapter, we will focus on the solicitation of funds from government agencies that do not provide strict guidelines, and on grants rather than contracts. Government agencies that do provide strict guidelines usually offer extensive guidance to the potential grant writer about how to prepare proposals; these agencies also tend to control rather strictly the nature of any "courtship" of the foundation staff. These interventionistic agencies tend to be unique. A novice grantsman who is approaching one of these governmental agencies should, in addition to reading the published guidelines carefully, consult with others who have already had extensive experience with that particular agency. We also would recommend that the government agency be visited early in the proposal preparation phase.

Fifth, it is important to distinguish between regional and national foundations. Many of the private foundations and most government agencies at the state or municipal level limit their range of support to a specific geographic area. Most of the private, regional foundations belong in either the independent (family) or community foundation categories described above. The regional foundations generally follow rather than establish the general funding trends in American postsecondary education established by the more visible and cosmopolitan national foundations. Thus, in the case of professional development, many of the regional foundations are only now beginning to move into the field. Frequently, these regional foundations are ignored in favor of the better-known nationals. Admittedly, in many cases the regional agencies must be educated about current trends in postsecondary education and must be convinced that professional development is a viable, established procedure for institutional advancement. The odds of getting support from these regional foundations, however, may be greater than is the case with the nationals, especially if the project being proposed is not particularly distinctive but instead is based on already accepted practices and concepts.

B. Preparing a Proposal

Ten principles seem to account repeatedly for the success of proposals that have been written in the field of professional development. These ten principles can be summarized as follows:

1. The proposal is written to promote a good idea rather than to demonstrate the scholarly competence of the writer.
2. The proposal is based on and reflects significant past accomplishments in related areas by the institution that is seeking funds.
3. The proposal demonstrates significant institutional commitment to the project in terms of both resources (dollars, release time, facilities) and knowledgeable support from key institutional leaders.

4. The proposal conveys a clear sense of the direct involvement in the preparation of the proposal of those people in the institution (faculty, administrators, staff, trustees) who will benefit from the project.

5. The proposed project incorporates thoughtful and creatively conceived mechanisms for the identification and use of existing campus resources, the delivery of services to all potential consumers, and the continuation of services after external funding has ended.

6. The proposed project either makes efficient and effective use of external resources and demonstrates the need for such resources or relies exclusively on internal resources.

7. The proposal includes a thoughtfully and creatively conceived plan for project evaluation that is both quantitative and qualitative in nature, that provides a definitive answer to the question, "How do you know if you have been successful?," and that incorporates plans for the dissemination of learnings from the project to other on-campus and off-campus personnel.

8. The proposal presents a clear and graphic description of the use of resources and scheduling of events and an appropriate and clearly presented budget.

9. The proposal contains a plan for professional development that is unique, responsive to the specific needs of the campus, coordinated with other ongoing campus activities, and either comprehensive in nature or sensitive to spin-off effects if successful.

10. The proposal is written with a specific foundation in mind and is responsive to the specific concerns and stylistic preferences of that funding organization.

Following is a more detailed consideration of each principle.

The first principle is given primacy because it is perhaps the most frequent source of difficulty for the novice grant writer. In developing their first programmatic proposal, many faculty and administrators have in mind the traditional proposal for funding of a research project, which almost always must demonstrate the scholarly competence of the proposal writer. Mastery of the subject area must be shown through an extensive review of the literature, careful documentation and footnoting, and command of the disciplinary language (jargon) of the field. By contrast, a proposal that is being written to fund a new professional development program should be free of jargon, sparsely footnoted, light on literature review, and heavy on persuasive argumentation, conceptualization, and imagery. The basic idea of the program must be sold, not the competence of the proposal writer. In general, a programmatic proposal is shorter than a research proposal. It also is less bound by convention. The writer of a professional development proposal can take more liberty with the form and structure of his work and be more innovative in the sequencing of components. The grant writer should first of all, therefore, eliminate many of his preconceptions about proposal writing that emerge from a research background.

The second and third principles are based on a "Catch 22" that often is frustrating to the proposal writer. In a very real sense, most foundations will fund a project if the proposer can demonstrate that the funds aren't really needed but will not fund a project if it cannot operate without external funds—"the rich get richer and the poor get poorer." The proposal, consequently, should reflect the institution's impressive track record in the broad area in which funding is sought. Preferably, the project for which funding is being sought should already have been in existence for a year or more and have been supported by hard, institutional dollars before external funding is requested. The longer a college can wait before requesting external funds for a project, the more likely it is to receive these funds—provided the foundation hasn't lost interest in this area in the meantime. Foundations want to fund winners so that their own track records look good. This desire is quite understandable and requires a detailed description of past accomplishments at the college including, if possible, the demonstration of wise and prudent use of funds granted to the institution in the past. Even if the project itself isn't already in operation, related projects should be described and linked to the one being proposed.

As the third principle suggests, the college must be able to offer a firm commitment to the project in terms of such tangible resources as dollars, release time, equipment, space and support services. Ideally, a college ought to provide as much financial support (direct and indirect) as is being requested from the foundation. This matching support might comprise in part equivalent dollars for release time or for the purchase of new equipment that is being donated by the college for use in the project. The grant writer, however, should not be too loose or imaginative in deriving figures regarding financial support, because foundation executives are very skillful at seeing through a financial smokescreen. There must be substantial, clear-cut financial support for the project from internal, hard money sources. Furthermore, this support should not be offered for just one year on a declining basis. Rather, it must be offered throughout the funding period and even after external funding is withdrawn. In most cases, no steps should be taken in drafting a proposal until this commitment is ensured. The time-consuming process of proposal preparation becomes a time-wasting enterprise if this commitment is not forthcoming.

Several funding strategies can be used to reduce the adverse impact of this desire to provide institutional support for the proposed project. First, in many instances, foundations will look favorably on a funding pattern that enables the college to absorb an increasingly large proportion of the total budget from year to year during the funding period. The foundations support thus will decline over several years, resulting eventually in the elimination of all financial support from an external source. Second, some of the "hard money" support can come from revenue that is generated by the project: for example, conference registration fees (from off-campus participants), book sales, or off-campus consulting fees. Third, a college with an excellent record in receiving and making effective use of grants sometimes can convince a foundation that support from another foundation will be obtained and used to support not only the current project, but also future extensions of the project. Thus, in this instance, a grant writer is demonstrating not so much the commitment of the institution to the project as the competence of the staff at the institution to obtain other outside grants which would ensure continuation of the project.

Ultimately, the best strategy in obtaining hard money support for a project is to link the project with the mission and goals of the college. Not only is more hard money likely to be available, but the chance of obtaining foundation support also is increased, for the executives of these agencies increasingly are impressed by a project that has been designed, not in a vacuum, but rather in the context of institutional decision-making processes. Institutional commitment is expressed, in other words, not just through the commitment of dollars and time, but also through a carefully-conceived correlation between the goals and strategies of a single project and the long-term goals and plans of the college. If a foundation executive believes that a project is being proposed only to generate income for the college and not to advance the institution toward a consensus-based mission or set of institutional goals, the chances of obtaining a grant are remote.

Institutional commitment also should be reflected in the knowledgeable support of key campus leaders for the project. Letters of support from the president, dean, or chairman of a major campus committee should contain enough detail to indicate that the letter writer knows what commitment is being made, why it is being made, and how he will be actively involved in the project. If possible, the letter should indicate why the campus leader is personally interested in the project—why he is willing to take time out of a very busy schedule to give this project significant attention during the next few years. This commitment is particularly important if a portion of the leader's time is being released for the project.

The fourth principle also builds on the past history of the college, reflecting both commitment and ownership. The proposal should be the product of considerable on-campus input from those people who will be its beneficiaries. If a project is for faculty development, it is essential that the proposal be faculty-produced. The proposal might even be a bit rough, editorially and stylistically, reflecting the involvement of many people at various stages in its development. An appendix might contain a brief history of proposal preparation, indicating the type and number of people who were involved in the preparation of the proposal at each stage.

The proposal also should demonstrate ownership by the potential beneficiaries through letters of endorsement from representatives of this group. Governance mechanisms should be built into the project to ensure continued ownership. A faculty development proposal, for instance, might contain a letter from the head of a major faculty personnel committee and a description of the ways in which members of this committee will oversee, act as advisors to, or even manage, the proposed project. In the area of professional development, foundation executives are becoming increasingly convinced that those being served must have significant control over a program.

A grant writer who wishes to work alone in the development of a proposal or who feels most comfortable in assigning the drafting of proposals to a single person is best advised not to bother with the project in the first place. Unless a proposal is tossed around a bit, it usually will lack conviction. Furthermore, if funded, it is less likely to be successful than is a proposal that has been developed at least in part by those people who will be intimately involved in its daily operation.

The fifth principle leads us directly into the heart of the proposal. The document should demonstrate that effective and efficient use will be made of current on-campus resources. Within the past few years, some foundations have become increasingly interested in providing financial support for "natural helping networks." Rather than funding new people and projects that must establish themselves and gain credibility, the foundation executive looks for people and projects that already are serving the campus community. A grant writer might survey existing campus resources in relevant areas, then establish an information and referral clearinghouse through which those on campus who need specific types of expertise or resources can be linked with those who can be most helpful. A proposal is then submitted after this clearinghouse is established.

Funds are requested to provide more training, release time, or visibility for the "natural helpers." This programmatic model has been employed very effectively in the field of community development and seems to be equally applicable in postsecondary educational institutions.

Innovative mechanisms for the delivery of project services also should be identified. Many successful proposals contain some mechanisms for the "training of trainers" through which key staff are involved at least part of the time not in the direct delivery of services but rather in preparing other members of the college community to provide those services. In this way, there will be a greater spread of impact and greater chance for low cost continuation of these services after external funds are used up.

The sixth principle concerns the effective and efficient use of external resources. Too frequently, a proposal writer will envision rather extensive use of external consultants in the project. While a consultant can add credibility as well as expertise, and in this way increase chances of funding, consulting fees (and associated travel, room, and board expenses) can consume large sums of money rapidly in a project budget.

Consultants can be used efficiently in several ways. First, cooperative arrangements can be made to share the costs of consultation. Several colleges might join together to host a consultant, or two departments within a single college might combine financial resources. Second, a consultant can be used primarily as a designer rather than as an implementer. For instance, instead of asking a consultant to conduct a workshop, one could ask him to spend a shorter period of time, perhaps even by mail or phone, to design a workshop which, in turn, could be run by someone at the college. Or, if the consultation involves on-campus collection of information, the consultant need not do all of the time-consuming interviewing or questionnaire analysis, but rather could assist in the design of the interview schedule or questionnaire. The information is then collected and analyzed by on-campus personnel.

Third, consulting expenses can be reduced by using different consultants for different tasks. An expensive, nationally known consultant, for instance, might be brought in briefly for his special expertise or to lend credibility and visibility to a project. Longer-term consultation (training, data-collection, mediation) often can be done by lower priced, less well-known, or more locally-based consultants.

Perhaps most important in planning for a project and writing a proposal, serious question should be given to whether external resource people really are needed at all. The prospect of receiving a grant should not dissuade one from being frugal. Furthermore, one of the negative impacts of many funded projects is the neglect of local resources in favor of an outsider. The problem of a prophet being without honor in his own land is compounded when money is available to bring in a prophet from another land. Natural helping networks can be identified and used in lieu of an external consultant, or an external consultant can be brought in briefly to bring visibility and legitimacy to internal resource persons. If extensive use is to be made of external consultants in a proposed project, thoughtful justification must be given. If internal resources have been systematically surveyed and found to be wanting, then the use of external resources can perhaps be more justified.

The need for project evaluation has been identified as the seventh principle. This issue deserves a great deal of attention, yet, since so much has already been written in this area we will not dwell for long on the topic. Most foundations are becoming increasingly interested in program evaluation, and will accept and even encourage the allocation of at least 10 percent of the total budget to this area. The increased interest of foundations in program evalaution seems to be related to an increasing concern with both accountability and dissemination. Thus, the plan for evaluation not only should enable a project director both to improve the project while it is in operation and to determine the extent to which it has been successful, but also enable him to convey effectively learnings from the project to others within and outside the institution.

Our eighth principle concerns project implementation. This aspect of a proposal often is ignored in the rush to convey the excitement of an idea. Some of the most successful grant writers have developed strategies for showing the reviewer that this project can, in fact, be implemented. Often these writers will use a graphic or visual presentation to convey a convincing, pragmatic impression. At the very least, the proposal writer should provide a time schedule which indicates when certain critical events will take place and when major assignments will be completed.

Through the use of scheduling and planning procedures, a grant writer can demonstrate feasibility—the most important criterion for many skeptical foundation executives and proposal readers. Feasibility is usually displayed even more directly in the budget that is submitted along with the proposal. This budget must, first of all, be appropriate to the size of the project. If too little money is requested, the reader may assume that the proposal writer is naive and that the project, as a result, is likely to be unsuccessful. If the budget is too large, a foundation executive may assume that the grant writer is simply trying to squeeze out some extra dollars and will reject the proposal outright. Consequently, while an initial budget might be a bit "fat," it should always be appropriate, and each expense item should be justifiable.

The ninth principle concerns the difficult issue of professional development. Foundation executives are somewhat jaded at this point about professional development programs in higher education. They tend to be particularly suspicious of professional development projects for faculty that make extensive use of sabbaticals, leaves, or other release time mechanisms—particularly if the events that are to take place during these periods are not carefully planned and are not linked directly to institutional priorities. Foundation executives also tend to be suspicious of professional development projects that lead only to "consciousness raising" about teaching and learning issues, without providing the faculty member with resources needed to act on this heightened interest.

Foundation executives would like professional development projects to be directly related to institution-wide concerns. A faculty development project, for instance, might be linked to curriculum development, to the recruitment of a new clientele, to problems of attrition, or to attempts at increasing productivity. For the sake of both funding and project effectiveness, the proposal should reflect an understanding of the need for comprehensive services. If one attempts to affect the role of a faculty member as a teacher, one also must be prepared to deal with both the personal and organizational consequences of this role change.

The last principle to be considered leads us directly into the final section of this chapter. The proposal should be tailor-made for the foundation to which it is being submitted. While it is appropriate that a grant writer submit a proposal to more than one foundation, it also is worth taking time to rework the proposal so that it is particularly responsive to each foundation.

At least two ways can be suggested of tailoring a proposal to a specific foundation. First, a foundation often will have published some kind of request for proposals; in some cases this may be nothing more than a few pages of general guidelines, in others elaborate and extensive directions for proposal preparation. In any event, the grant writer should pay careful attention to that material and should make as much effort as possible to show that the proposal being presented is responsive to the problems or issues outlined in the request or guidelines. Second, under the Freedom of Information Act, federal agencies must make copies of all funded proposals available to the general public; unfunded proposals need not be made public and usually are not. One should read some of the proposals funded by a particular agency before preparing a new proposal for that agency. Look for general themes among the proposals rather than for exceptional projects. If possible, read the comments of proposal reviewers as well as the proposals themselves. Brief, informal conversations with foundation staff of a preliminary, exploratory nature also might be considered, as should discussions with successful grant writers.

Elaborate and elegant courtship of most foundations is rarely possible; even when it is, success is unlikely if there is no substance to the proposal. The proposal writing phase is important and should not be short-circuited in favor of the less arduous and more glamorous task of courting foundation executives. The ten principles we have discussed should prove useful to the reader in preparing a persuasive proposal.

C. Contacting the Foundation

Each grant writer will contact and work with a foundation in a distinctive way. The means by which successful writers have established close working relationships with foundation executives are varied and often difficult to describe. In some instances, apparent favoritism is shown. The foundation executive perhaps knows the person submitting the proposal from an earlier time when they both worked together or is a close friend of the president of the college. At other times, a foundation will fund a proposal primarily because it has been submitted by a prestigious person or institution. To be able to fund a "Harvard" program supposedly makes a foundation more prestigious. There is not much that can be done to counteract this type of preferential treatment. The "old boy" network thrives in the foundation and grantsmanship world as elsewhere.

Nevertheless, there are several important principles that can help increase the probability of gaining support for a project. First, it is imperative that the foundation to be courted is selected carefully. Information about the foundation should be reviewed thoroughly and the funding initiative fully understood. It also is highly advisable to look at the funding record of the foundation. As a rule, the information about foundations that can be obtained from public documents is already out of date— especially for private foundations. Only the type of projects funded during a previous round of proposal reviews can be identified, and a foundation may change its funding patterns radically in a short period of time. The best strategy is to contact the foundation directly about current funding priorities. This is not always possible or politic, however, so the second best approach is to look at trends.

In what direction does a particular foundation seem to be moving? If you were to look ahead several years, in what areas do you think this foundation will be funding?

For example, several years ago it was relatively easy to predict that several of the key national foundations would move from an interest in faculty development to an interest in other types of professional development—particularly administrative and trustee development. Having predicted the direction of a foundation during the next year or two, one is in a good position to prepare and submit a proposal. There is nothing more impressive or exciting to a foundation executive than receiving a thoughtfully prepared proposal at the very moment when the foundation has made a commitment to move into that very area.

Consideration also might be given to a plan for joint funding by several foundations. One component of a project can be financed by one foundation and a second component by another funding agency. Or a basic project format might be established, followed by proposals for certain foundations related to a special theme within this format. In the area of professional development, for instance, a basic clearinghouse for information about instructional innovations on campus might be established. One proposal then might be drawn up that relates to the collection of information about innovations that are specifically effective when used with certain minority populations, while a second proposal might be drafted to generate funds for a clearinghouse initative that focuses on competency-based instructional innovations.

Foundations are sometimes quite supportive of joint funding projects, for if designed properly, these projects can provide "more bang for the buck" than single, isolated projects. The foundation can take not only direct credit for the component of the project that it funded but also indirect credit for the component another foundation funded. It is still imperative, however, that the college itself put up a substantial proportion of the funds. Foundations are skeptical about a college using funds from another foundation to demonstrate solid institutional support, unless the college has established and can document a solid track record of consistently receiving external funds and of using these funds very effectively.

Two general principles apply to the courtship of a foundation that has been selected for fund solicitation. First, involve the foundation staff early in the formulation of the proposal, but do not expect them to generate project ideas or write the proposal and, second, get to know and work with the foundation staff in contexts other than just the submission and review of proposals. The first of these principles is perhaps the most widely accepted piece of advice for the courtship of foundation executives—particularly from private foundations. To the extent that a foundation executive (like any other person) feels involved in the formulation of a project, he is likely to feel some ownership for it. This advice is certainly warranted, yet can be taken to too great an extreme. Very few foundation executives enjoy writing a proposal for someone else or helping a writer clarify his purposes in preparing and submitting a proposal. An effective writer will present several well-formulated ideas to a foundation executive. Each idea will be directly related to the major theme, problem, or need on which the institution has decided to focus. The foundation executive should be presented with these alternatives, asked to comment on each, and given an opportunity to suggest entirely different approaches.

A writer should not hesitate to question or even challenge the foundation executive's observations and suggestions. Most of these people are tired of "yes men" and appreciate vigorous and articulate interaction with people who expand and clarify their own perspectives. A grant writer, on the other hand, should not use this preliminary meeting as an occasion to argue for a specific alternative. Each option that is presented should be viable. If only one idea is really being considered, then the foundation executive is likely to feel "hustled" and may view the meeting as a waste of time.

In a government foundation, a staff member is usually not allowed to comment on the desirability of a proposal before it is formally submitted. Comment can be made, however, on the appropriateness of the proposal in light of funding guidelines, priorities, and sometimes, the review process. Private foundation executives usually do not operate under these restrictions, and even a second review of a proposal before submission is often acceptable and even appreciated. The foundation executive usually will be able to indicate whether the draft proposal is worth submitting formally and may make general suggestions concerning its improvement. The final proposal, however, usually should not include a formal recognition of the contribution made by the executive. Informal recognition, however, is possible through the incorporation of specific terms or concepts that have been suggested by the executive. Even if no one else is aware of that contribution, he will be appreciative of this informal recognition.

The second principle of courtship is more informal than the first but no less important. Especially in the case of governmental foundation executives who cannot get actively involved in the proposal preparation process, it is often highly desirable to get to know and work with foundation executives in a context other than the preparation and submission of a proposal. This second form of courtship requires a much longer perspective, for the benefit of this activity may not accrue for several years. Furthermore, this second form of courtship must be supplemented—and even superseded—by a genuine interest in the foundation executive as a person and professional rather than as just a source of money.

There are at least three different ways in which this more indirect mode of courtship can take place. First, one can invite a foundation executive to participate on an on-campus activity as a resource person. Many foundation executives are excellent speakers, consultants, trainers, or evaluators. Their breadth of knowledge in a variety of areas is often exceptional, yet they rarely are called on to share this expertise outside the foundation. Foundation executives can even be brought in to conduct workshops on grant writing—provided the participants in the workshop agree not to submit proposals to this specific foundation for a specified period of time, usually a year or two.

Second, a foundation executive can be indirectly courted by asking his advice about other foundations and about proposals that will be mailed elsewhere. While the executive should not be expected to spend a great deal of time on such activities, most of these people are very knowledgeable about other foundations and are complimented by a request for this knowledge. Once again, one is relating to the foundation executive not just as a person with money, but as a person with knowledge and expertise. Rarely will a foundation executive be offended by the acknowledgement and use of these resources.

Third, indirect courtship can be made more successful by simply spending some time talking to foundation executives about concerns other than those involved in the submission and review of proposals. Become aware of a foundation executive's academic background and interests, and read articles and major reports written by the executive. Let him know about the exceptional value of a proposal that has been submitted to another agency or of some major (but as yet unannounced) development in an area of foundation concern. In these conversations, one also should be sympathetic to and supportive of the complex and often frustrating job that is performed by the foundation executive. Since these people are rarely treated as individuals by those seeking funds and rarely given a straightforward or honest response in a working relationship, they are inclined to feel isolated and undervalued. Productive relationships between foundation executives and grant writers often begin with a mutual understanding of personal and professional perspectives and needs.

We hope that this chapter has provided the reader with several observations and suggestions that will improve the quality of proposals that are being prepared and the relationships with foundation executives that are being estasblished. The planning of a project does not end with submission of a proposal, nor does contact with a foundation end with the granting of funds. The quality of a proposal and of relationships with foundation executives determines not only the acquisition of funds for a project but also, if funded, its ultimate success.

NOTES:

[1]This chapter is based on a report prepared for the American Association of Osteopathic Medicine, Washington, D.C. (1978) by William H. Bergquist, with the assistance of Daniel H. Pilon, former Vice President for Campus Services of the Council of Independent Colleges.

Chapter Thirteen

Collecting and Using Information about Faculty

In recent years, two of the major areas of change in the basic concepts of administration and management of the higher education enterprise have been faculty development and institutional research. Programs have flourished in both areas. New committees, directors, and centers of faculty (or instructional or professional) development have sprung up in many colleges and universities, while at the same time new offices of institutional research have opened, often in the same institutions. In both fields, much has been learned during the past decade. We are now able to plan faculty development programs that can affect the personal, professional, and organizational lives of faculty. We also have available a number of tools, techniques, and other resources to assess a variety of institutional dimensions with sensitivity and accuracy.

Unfortunately, in most instances, these two areas have grown up independently of one another. This independence has been costly to practitioners of both faculty development and institutional research. The faculty development practitioners often must plan for activities without adequate information about faculty needs and interests, the nature and dynamics of the culture in which the program is to be conducted, and needs and challenges of the institution itself. The field of faculty development may have created a robot, one that is strong and powerful, but is without vision. The faculty development robot sometimes does not seem to know where to go, and hence may wander aimlessly. People ask, "What are faculty being developed for?" We often do not have adequate answers to this question.

Similarly, in the field of institutional research, a robot is also being built. This robot has extraordinary vision. It can see through the walls of the college or university and clearly perceive the complex inner workings of the institution. Yet this robot cannot move. It has no capacity to change what it sees. Much of the information being collected by institutional research officers collects dust on a shelf. Only in the case of budgetary information do they feel they have much impact; hence, budgetary information tends to dominate institutional research. Furthermore, these officers tend to prepare information primarily for the president of the college or university and other key administrative leaders. Rarely does this information percolate down to the mid-level managers or faculty—let alone to students.

The time has come for a closer relationship between faculty development and institutional research. The powerful, mobile robot of the faculty development practitioner needs the vision of the immobile institutional robt and vice versa. A first step in bringing together faculty development and institutional research is the systematic collection of information about faculty that can be used in planning for programs and institutional development and faculty resource linkage and faculty reassignment, as well as faculty development.

In this chapter we will review these four uses of faculty information and identify ten different types of information about faculty that can be employed for these purposes. We conclude the chapter with brief consideration of several issues involved in the ways in which this information is made useful to faculty in their planning activities.

A. Ways in Which Faculty Information Is Used

Information about faculty can be used effectively in the following four ways: (1) for program and institutional planning, (2) as a clearinghouse for faculty resources, (3) for faculty reassignment, and (4) for faculty development and training. We will review each of these four areas briefly.

1. Program and Institutional Planning

Information about faculty can be used effectively for planning in several different ways. First, it can be employed to assess the current strengths, resources, and attitudes of the faculty so that new goals can be formulated in a realistic manner; critical points of support, resistance and intervention can be identified; and criteria can be established by which changes in strength, resources, and/or attitude can be measured and evaluated. Without information about faculty, effective planning is most difficult.

Second, information about faculty is of value in the selection of faculty for participation in specific projects. Typically, when we recruit faculty for a new program, committee, or other assignment, one of two procedures is adopted: (1) the faculty member is selected because someone knows and is supportive of his work, or (2) because a request for proposals has been sent out and this particular faculty member's proposal was found to be of merit. The first of these two procedures usually involves an "old boy" network, and, as a result, is exclusive, reactive, and often results in the neglect of valuable—but unacknowledged—faculty resources. The proposal route is often inadequate as well, for the conceptual and proposal writing skills of a faculty member are being judged rather than the ability of that person to perform a specific task or implement a specific type of project. If information about faculty has been collected systematically, then more reasonable and equitable selection decisions can be made.

Third, faculty information can serve as an impetus for change. Information can be influential when its introduction into a system is planned carefully. For instance, if the information about faculty is collected and used by faculty, rather than exclusively by administrators, faculty ownership of important information about themselves may itself create momentum toward change. Similarly, information about discrepancies in student and faculty attitudes or perceptions can provide an impetus for a new project to improve faculty-student communication. Information about the extent and quality of faculty resources on campus can create a felt need for the kind of clearinghouse activities discussed below.

If information is to have effect, then those who are to change as a consequence of that information should become aware of and feel some ownership for the data collection procedures. Furthermore, these same people should be actively involved in analyzing and exploring the implications of that information. The data not only must translate into emergent concerns or altered perspectives, but it must also ultimately translate into action. One therefore should develop plans for implementation of recommendations that emerge from the data collection and analysis even before the information is collected. Who is responsible for developing, presenting, reviewing, evaluating, and implementing recommendations? Do all of these people know what their responsibilities are? At what point should the potential opposition to emergent recommendations be brought into the process? Action research that does not incorporate satisfactory answers to these qestions rarely will be successful.

2. A Faculty Clearinghouse

A clearinghouse can be used by faculty to find one or more people on campus or at another campus who can be of assistance in helping improve current activities or explore new areas. The success of a clearinghouse depends not only on the collection of valid and useful information about faculty, but also on the skill of the clearinghouse staff in helping the person contacting them clarify the need for a faculty resource person and in setting up the conditions for this resource person to be of maximum assistance. The resource person who is selected must be able to deliver the services being sought. For this to occur, there should be cross-validation of the resource person's skills and clarification of the client's expectations and constraints. A clearinghouse staff is best advised to begin with a few contacts that have been planned and carried through carefully, and to evaluate these contacts extensively.

In establishing a clearinghouse, several different problems are immediately encountered. First, one confronts a chicken-and-egg problem. Do your first collect information about faculty resources without knowing what resources will be requested, or do you wait for requests, then seek out resource people? The first approach often creates problems for the resource people. They spend time identifying and describing their skills, yet they may never be contacted for assistance. These unmet expectations often lead to disillusionment or anger, making it more difficult to collect information in the future. Furthermore, these faculty will not be inclined to use the clearinghouse for their own purposes if they have not been contacted.

Alternatively, if the clearinghouse does not initiate the resource identification process until a specific request is received, the client may be dissatisfied. The search usually will take some time and often will be inadequate, given the limited amount of attention that can be devoted to any one request. Furthermore, faculty may soon become intolerant of multiple requests for information about their skills.

There is no simple answer to this dilemma. One should employ both strategies from the start. Collect some information about faculty that is likely to be of value to potential clients, but wait for faculty requests before developing detailed analyses of faculty skills. One can conduct "strength" interviews which ask faculty to assess their unique talents and experiences, and conclude by asking faculty to indicate what type of faculty resources they might be able to use in the near future. The strength interview provides data about available faculty resources, while at the same time assessing the potential need for these resources.

3. Faculty Reassignment

Many colleges and universities are now confronted with an oversupply of faculty in disciplines where student enrollments have declined (frequently in such areas as physics, philosophy, or history), and an undersupply of faculty in disciplines which have experienced growth (for example, business, English composition, or biology). This problem could be resolved readily by releasing faculty from the declining disciplines and hiring faculty in the growing ones. Ethical reasons, coupled with tenure and unionization, however, prevent the implementation of this solution. Some colleges and universities instead are looking toward the part-time or full-time reassignment of faculty from declining to growth departments. For this to occur, information about faculty background and expertise is required, as is information about needs and requirements in the receiving department.

Information needed for reassignment will vary somewhat, depending on the extent of reassignment. If a faculty member is to teach one course in another department, the receiving department need only know if this faculty member is specifically qualified to teach in the area being covered by the course. If the faculty member is being reassigned full-time to another department, members of this department undoubtedly will want to know more about that person's general background, educational philosophy, approach to solving intellectual and interpersonal problems, interpersonal style, and competence in working with students and colleagues.

4. Faculty Development and Training

In planning for faculty development and training, information about faculty is essential. There is an obvious connection between an assessment of faculty development needs and planning for faculty development. In addition, an assessment of faculty perceptions, attitudes, skills, and styles is valuable to the formulation of successful strategies for introducing faculty development concepts and implementing faculty development services.

The information which is collected about faculty will be used in quite different ways depending on the nature and extent of faculty development that is initiated. In Table Four we have outlined briefly five different levels of change or development that faculty members might undertake. At the first and second levels, faculty often will make extensive use of information about other faculty on-campus who have had some experience in using a particular instructional method, strategy, or design. For these levels of change, a campus-based clearinghouse of information about faculty is invaluable.

At Levels Three and Four, different kinds of information are needed. A faculty member is not attempting to do better what he is already doing, but instead is being asked to do something new in his own discipline or in another discipline. In most instances, information about the faculty member's skills, attitudes, and style, as well as information about the needs and prevalent attitudes and styles of another department, will allow for smooth transitions, as noted above in our discussion of faculty reassignments. In some instances, when reassignment is not possible or acceptable, retraining programs may have to be initiated (see Table Five).

Over the long run, the use of information about faculty to plan and implement faculty development and training programs may prove to be of major importance. It almost certainly will be the area of greatest controversy in the use of faculty information. Some faculty will be threatened by the collection of information for the purposes of reassignment or development. In some instances this perceived threat will be quite justified. It is imperative, therefore, that information collected for these purposes be treated in a careful and sensitive manner. Data collection procedures should be described explicitly and publicly and subject to revision by those faculty members who might be affected by the outcomes of these procedures.

309

TABLE FOUR*

FIVE LEVELS OF CHANGE FOR FACULTY

Level of Change	Nature of Change	Consequence of Change	Resources for Change	
			Institutional	Faculty Development
One	• Change in one segment of a new course *or* • Use of new instructional method	• Faculty member experiences new challenge: renewed, interest, excitement, performance anxiety • Faculty member must learn some new content and skills • Faculty member is likely to temporarily experience some failures, student dissatisfaction, and confusion	• Mini-Grants ($50-500) • Mini-Sabbaticals (1-2 weeks) • One-time "experimental" courses • "Error-embracing" environment and reward system: tolerance of temporary increase in error rate of faculty member	• Short-term design consultation • Instructional design and methods workshops • Teaching laboratories • Instructional innovators support group • Classroom diagnosis • Peer consultation
Two	• Change in the design of an entire course *or* • Use of new instructional strategy	• Faculty member often changes image of self (role): becomes instructional designer or manager rather than information-giver. Temporary feeling of no longer being valuable to students • Faculty member is temporarily more busy, than less busy • Faculty member is likely to temporarily experience some failures, student dissatisfaction and confusion	• Release time (one month or one course) • Equipment • Content-Consultation • "Error-embracing" environment and reward system	• Long-term design consultation • Instructional innovators support group • Peer consultation • Organization development (department)

Three	• Faculty member changes primary teaching responsibility to new area within same discipline *or* • Faculty changes to new interdisciplinary program (making use of knowledge in current discipline)	• Faculty member must redefine role in discipline • Faculty member must learn new content • Faculty member must learn new instructional methods and designs • Faculty member is temporarily very busy • Faculty member is likely to feel temporary rejection from some colleagues in his or her discipline • Faculty member is likely to temporarily experience some failures, student dissatisfaction, and confusion	• Sabbatical (at least one year) • Books, content, consultation, instructional materials • Money for conferences, travel, visits to other programs, etc.	• Long-term course design consultation • Instructional diagnosis • Instructional design/methods • Instructional innovators support group • Life and career planning • Organizational development (department)
Four	• Faculty member changes discipline: begins to teach in a new field	• Faculty member must redefine self and life purpose • Faculty member must learn new field (and hopefully integrate with previous field) • Faculty member must learn new instructional and research methods, designs, and language • Faculty member is likely to feel overwhelmed for extended period of time	• One or two-year sabbatical • Financial support for new agencies and institutes for retraining and renewing faculty • Safe environment for faculty member to try out new discipline on campus • Support of faculty in new discipline from new colleagues	• Help faculty acquire knowledge in new field quickly and effectively • Help faculty integrate new knowledge and instructional methods • Organizational development (Inter-department) • Supportive counseling to faculty member and family
Five	• Faculty member changes to profession outside higher education	• First major institutional shift for many faculty • Variable consequences depending on nature of shift	• Development of skills and attitude matrix • Collection of information about manpower needs outside of higher education • Match up faculty matrix with high demand fields	• Career planning • Supportive counseling to faculty member and family

*Taken from an evaluation report prepared for the Center for Professional Development, Chancellor's Office, California State University System, July 1, 1977. A variation on this table is contained in William Bergquist, "The Liberal Arts College," in Jack Lindquist, *Designing Teaching Improvement Programs* (Washington, D.C.: Council for the Advancement of Small Colleges, 1978), pp. 49–51.

311

TABLE FIVE

Steps in Faculty Reassignment and Development

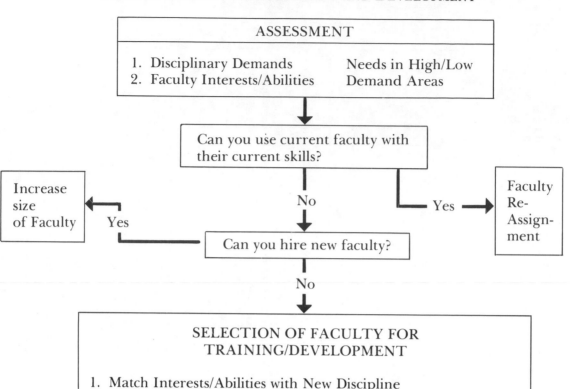

ASSESSMENT

1. Disciplinary Demands
2. Faculty Interests/Abilities

Needs in High/Low Demand Areas

↓

Can you use current faculty with their current skills?

No ↓

Can you hire new faculty?

Yes → Increase size of Faculty

Yes → Faculty Re-Assignment

No ↓

SELECTION OF FACULTY FOR TRAINING/DEVELOPMENT

1. Match Interests/Abilities with New Discipline
2. Low Enrollment in Old Discipline—Low Demand Area in Old Discipline
3. Characteristics of Faculty Member: Flexible, Intelligent (general), Status

↓

TRAINING

1. Disciplinary Development:	a. Basic Knowledge and Skills	b. Advanced Study in 2-3 Areas
	c. Creative/ Original Work	
2. Interdisciplinary Development:	a. Integration of Old/New Disciplines	b. Paradigm Awareness
3. Personal Development:	a. Career Transitions	b. Life Planning
	c. Family Support	
4. Organizational Development	a. Old Department	b. New Department
	c. Institution	
5. Instructional Development:	a. New Methods	b. New Strategies

↓

REENTRY

Faculty must be respected for their individuality. Their unique skills, experiences, and perspectives should be identified and valued. Virtually any faculty member can become a valuable campus resource if time is taken to discover his strengths. The ultimate purpose of any procedure for the collection and use of information about faculty should be to make more effective use of and enhance the current resources of the campus, while preparing for inevitable renewal and change in these resources. The people, programs, and procedures that have been described and discussed in this section can contribute to this end.

B. Areas of Information About Faculty

Though information about faculty is not now being widely collected, our discussion above indicates the clear need for it. At least ten different kinds of information might prove to be useful: (1) daily activities of faculty, (2) areas of primary teaching experience and curricular expertise, (3) areas of specialized and exceptional expertise, (4) role assignments or expectations, (5) instructional effectiveness, (6) demographic characteristics and educational background, (7) general attitudes, (8) perceptions of the campus environment, (9) teaching styles and philosophies, and (10) professional development needs and interests. Following is a brief description of the ways in which each type of information is or might be collected.

1. Faculty Activity Analysis

As part of their fiscal and institutional planning efforts, many colleges and universities assess the type and extent of activities in which faculty engage. These faculty activity analyses usually involve an estimate by faculty of the amount of time spent preparing for and conducting courses, advising students, meeting committee responsibilities, providing community services, doing research and scholarship, and so forth. An activity analysis usually is based on an estimate of the number of hours per week a faculty member spends performing each type of activity. This approach may be unsatisfactory, however, for a faculty member will frequently overestimate the number of hours per week he spends performing each type of activity. One university recently implemented a faculty activity analysis of this type and found that faculty estimated their average work week at approximately 65 hours—almost certainly an overestimation.

This problem can be partially avoided by keeping the survey instruments anonymous or by translating hours per week into percentages. The faculty member estimates the percentage of time per week that he spends in each activity category. These percentages are usually based on a ratio between hours per week in each category and total number of hours of work per week. Alternatively, the data analyst can translate the hours per week into percentages.

Currently, the most widely used and perhaps best faculty activity analysis tool has been developed by the National Center for Higher Education Management Systems (NCHEMS). This tool ("Faculty Activity Analysis") and a technical report titled "Faculty Activity Analysis: Interpretation and Uses of Data" (Technical Report 54) are available from NCHEMS (P.O. Drawer P, Boulder, Colorado 80302). The NCHEMS form is particularly valuable in that data can be compared with that collected on other campuses. Instrument Number Twelve provides a model that can be used to collect this kind of information for individual institutions.

313

2. Teaching/Curricular Responsibilities

At least two consortia of colleges and universities, the College Center of the Finger Lakes (Corning, New York) and the New Hampshire College and University Council (Manchester, New Hampshire), have collected information about teaching and curricular responsibilities from faculty at each participating institution. This data was published by each consortium and used primarily to promote inter-institutional exchange of faculty and cooperative course of curricular planning.

A single institution might adopt a similar procedure to make information available to all faculty about what their colleagues are doing. A university catalogue or bulletin rarely provides the kind of detailed information that would be of value to faculty. Several universities publish descriptions of particularly innovative projects that have been conducted and/or designed in consultation with a campus instructional development service. Michigan State University publishes a small book each year containing this type of information.

3. Specialized/Exceptional Expertise

During the past five years, several national organizations and regional consortia have become increasingly concerned about the isolation of many faculty and collegiate administrators. In starting new projects, many faculty and administrators are unaware of comparable projects on other campuses, or of relevant and available people and publications. As a result, there often is wasteful duplication of efforts and painful duplication of mistakes. Several national and regional clearinghouses have been established to promote low cost, inter-institutional exchange of information and expertise. During the 1970s, the American Association for Higher Education established a national clearinghouse of information about innovative projects and resource people called NEXUS. The ERIC Clearinghouse on Higher Education, offers comparable clearinghouse services for printed documents. ERIC is located at several universities and other educational agencies throughout the country. Each location specializes in certain areas of information. One should contact the central office in Washington, D.C. (George Washington University), or a campus librarian, to identify the appropriate location for certain types of information. ERIC is particularly valuable for the identification of unpublished documents such as speeches, reports, and proposals.

The Council of Independent Colleges (CIC), has sponsored a National Consulting Network and has produced a taxonomy that may be of even more direct use in the establishment of an on-campus clearinghouse. A copy of this taxonomy is included in Pilon and Bergquist's *Consultation in Higher Education*.[1] The procedures, policies, and forms that have been developed by the CIC staff and consultants should be examined by those planning a campus clearinghouse. One should also investigate the resource clearinghouses developed by the Great Lakes College Association and the Resources for Planned Change Program of the American Association of State Colleges and Universities (Washington, D.C.).

4. Role Assignments and Responsibilities

In addition to information about a faculty member's activities, teaching responsibilities, and areas of specialized expertise, one may wish to determine the roles which this faculty member plays at his institution. James Bess of the higher education department at Columbia University has recently completed a major project concerning the assessment and description of faculty roles. A final report on this project is available from the Fund for the Improvement of Postsecondary Education (Washington, D.C.). Carol Zion of Miami-Dade Community College (Miami, Florida) similarly has been involved in the assessment and description of roles, though she has concentrated on administrators. Her role analysis is coupled with various organizational development and staff training functions. Robert Blackburn of the Center for the Study of Higher Education at the University of Michigan has been involved for several years in a similar examination of faculty roles.

In many instances, the assessment of roles may provide a more useful portrait of a faculty member's expertise and background than will an assessment of activities or of teaching and curricular responsibilities. The roles of a faculty member often reveal a pattern of activity that is lost in the more differentiated and fragmented analysis of individual activities. In addition, an assessment of roles often will be more revealing of informal responsibilities and expectations than an exclusive assessment of teaching and curricular responsibilities will be.

5. Instructional Effectiveness

Over the past decade, one of the most common and controversial sources of information about faculty is student evaluation of instructional effectiveness. Information about instructional effectiveness also may be collected from peers and the individual faculty member. This information has been used primarily for personnel decisions (retention, promotion, tenure) rather than for developmental or planning purposes, yet, these latter purposes are certainly appropriate and important. A carefully designed evaluation instrument, such as the Teaching Analysis by Students (TABS) questionnaire described in Volume 2 of this series, can be used as a diagnostic device with which faculty members identify primary areas for instructional improvement. An evaluation tool can be of developmental use to faculty if they also are given a choice of evaluation items to be included in the instrument (as is the case with the questionnaire developed at Purdue University), if faculty are the sole recipients of the evaluation, or if faculty are asked to rate themselves using the same instrument and to predict—before seeing the results—how they think their students will rate them (a technique used with the TABS instrument and with the Instructional Assessment System presented in the first volume of this series.

A student evaluation form can be valuable as a planning tool. Students are asked to evaluate not only the characteristics of a faculty member or course, but also the extent to which certain instructional outcomes have been achieved (for example, acquisition of new skills). The Instructional Development and Effectiveness Assessment (IDEA) instrument, which is distributed by the Center for Faculty Evaluation and Development at Kansas State University, provides an assessment of outcomes, as does the Instructional Assessment System. The staff of an on-campus clearinghouse might collect evaluative data about faculty, using the IDEA instrument, to identify faculty members who are particularly successful at achieving certain kinds of instructional outcomes. If a faculty member wanted to improve his ability to help students acquire an increased appreciation of a specific discipline, he would be put in touch with a faculty member in a simliar discipline who had received particularly high ratings in this outcome area. More traditional evaluation instruments could be used in a similar manner. A faculty member who obtains low ratings in the area of student rapport might be linked through a clearinghouse with a faculty member who has obtained consistently high ratings in this area.

6. Demographic Characteristics of Faculty

Virtually all campuses possess basic demographic information (age, sex, birth place, and so forth) about faculty, as well as information about their educational background (degrees and so forth). Although this information is rarely used by individual institutions for planning or developmental purposes, it is used quite effectively by regional and national organizations. Through the American Council on Education (ACE), Alan Boyer conducted a study in the early 1970s on the demographic characteristics, educational backgrounds, and work histories of faculty throughout the United States.[2] Basic demographic information can be useful to an individual institution that is engaged in long-term planning. For example, the mean age and period of time since a faculty member's last formal educational experience can yield important conclusions concerning the need for professional development resources over the next 10 to 15 years.

7. General Faculty Attitudes

Boyer not only studied faculty demographics in American Council on Education studies, he also made an assessment of faculty attitudes about educational policy, collective bargaining, religious and political preferences, and so forth. A more extensive survey of faculty attitudes was completed in the mid-1970s by Ladd and Lipsett, as a follow-up to the ACE studies. Their findings were reported in a series of articles appearing in *The Chronicle of Higher Education* during the late 1970s. Comparable intra-institutional data on faculty attitudes (particularly educational policy) could be valuable for long-term institutional planning—especially the introduction of new, innovative programs or policies at the college or university.

8. Campus Environmental Perceptions

While the general assessment of faculty attitudes may be of some value in understanding faculty, it is rarely of direct use to a college or university. The attitudes and perceptions of faculty members concerning the campus environment are usually of more direct relevance for program planning or implementation. Several questionnaires have been developed to assess a faculty member's opinions about what is or should be happening on campus. In most cases, these questionnaires also are distributed to administrators and/or students at the institution to record their environmental perceptions. A number of these instruments are discussed in Chapter Nine of this volume.

9. Teaching Styles and Philosophies

More specific information about faculty attitudes can be derived from an assessment of their teaching styles and educational philosophies. While no widely used teaching style questionnaire is now available, such a questionnaire could be derived readily from the items contained in a card-exchange exercise that is described in the first volume of this series. The categories developed by Richard Mann and his colleagues and by Joseph Axelrod as discussed in Chapter Two of the first volume of this series are also directly relevant for this type of information collection.

Extensive information about teaching styles and philosophies of education can be obtained readily through in-depth interviews with faculty. Perhaps the most useful information to be obtained in planning for professional and curricular development derives from such an initiative. Questionnaires or environmental scales rarely tap the rich insights, telling biases, and deep-felt convictions that often surface during an intensive interview.

10. Professional Development Needs and Interests

In recent years, numerous colleges and universities have collected information about faculty for the explicit purpose of planning for professional development programs. The three most widely-used questionnaires designed for this purpose are: (a) the Professional Development Questionnaire, written by Jack Lindquist for the colleges participating in the Strategies for Change and Knowledge Utilization project; (b) the Faculty Questionnaire, developed by Jerry Gaff of the Project for Institutional Renewal through the Improvement of Teaching for colleges and universities participating in this project, and (c) the Faculty Questionnaire created by Clare Rose for use in the California State University and Colleges system. Copies of the first two questionnaires are included in the second volume of this handbook series; the third questionnaire is presented in the first volume of this series, as is a fourth questionnaire, the "Faculty Development Outcome Questionnaire." All four have been valuable in planning for professional development programs and activities—particularly if modified for local use. The first two questionnaires also yield general information about faculty that may be of value in planning for other institutional programs.

Our review of these ten different types of faculty information touches on several pervasive issues. First, it is difficult to determine an appropriate level of specificity for the information to be collected. One might, for instance, identify the key roles played by faculty—a rather high level of generality—or ask faculty to identify the unique skills that they possess or activities in which they frequently engage—a high level of specificity. Highly general information is easily collected and verified but often is of only limited value. Highly specific information often is of more tangible use yet usually is difficult to collect and analyze or validate. The assessment of skills or frequency of specific daily activities, for example, often is hard to confirm without an impractical expenditure of time and money. One must frequently make a difficult choice between general and specific information.

A second pervasive issue involves the use of the information that is collected. Some of the information seems to be used primarily for the purpose of better understanding faculty. Often this type of information is rather diffuse and imprecise, for it tends to touch on faculty attitudes and perceptions. Yet these dimensions of a faculty member are very important to assess when planning a program with or for faculty. Other types of information tend to be more concrete (background, skills, roles) and are particularly useful in setting up clearinghouse programs. A broad-based data-gathering initiative should include both types of information.

Finally, the issue of data processing and analysis emerges from our identification of various types of information. In some instances, the information that is collected can be analyzed in only one way: this particular faculty member possesses this specific attribute. In other instances, a second step can be taken: a certain number of faculty at this institution possess this attribute. At a third level of analysis, information about faculty can be considered in interaction: this particular attribute seems to be associated with a second attribute. In general, the third level of analysis is possible only if the information is specific and concrete.

C. Ways to Process Information About Faculty

Whether being used for clearinghouse, planning, or developmental purposes, the information being collected from faculty must be analyzed and interpreted if it is to be of use to other people. Two principal aspects of data analysis will be briefly reviewed: validation and codification.

1. Validation

If nothing else, the data that is collected should be subjected to some form of validation. How do we know that the information obtained is accurate? In some instances, one or more internal validating procedures can be used. Is one unit of information consistent with another? If a faculty member claims to have expertise in a specific area, does his background seem to justify this claim? When using psychometric instruments (for example, an environmental rating scale), one can determine if the responses to one randomly-selected subset of items correlates highly with another randomly-selected subset.

It is usually preferable to validate the information from an outside source. Any self-selection device for the identification of expertise or knowledge should be used in conjunction with a peer-nomination. If a faculty member indicates that he possesses a certain skill, several colleagues should be asked if they have observed this faculty member using this skill.

Alternatively, faculty members may first be asked to identify skills in certain areas among their colleagues. If a faculty member is identified by two or more colleagues as having a specific skill, then he can be contacted to determine if this is in fact the case. Peer-nomination is often preferable to self-selection as a first step, because some faculty are hesitant to nominate themselves, or may not realize that they are particularly skillful in a specific area. Self-selection procedures should not be ignored, however, for often unique skills or expertise are unknown to colleagues. Self-selection and peer-nominations are often initiated at the same time, and a single questionnaire or interview is used to collect both types of information.

Cross-validation of information also can take place through longitudinal collection and analysis of information. If the data is collected systematically and periodically over an extended period of time, then not only can trends be noted, but, if the data is invalid on one particular occasion, this invalidity will usually be obvious and can be corrected. Cross-validation often is achieved through the use of several data-collection devices. Both can be checked against direct observation or client follow-up evaluations once the first contacts in a clearinghouse program have been made.

2. Codification

A second important aspect in the analysis of faculty information is the codification of data. In the case of psychometric (questionnaire) and demographic data, this is quite simple and direct, for the data usually are received in quantifiable form. Data of a "softer" variety (interviews, descriptions, and so forth) are much harder to codify. How does one quantify the intricate set of skills a superior teacher possesses? One can leave the description quite general and diffuse; however, as noted above, this often means that the information is of less value to the user.

Two solutions to this problem can be suggested. First, two forms of information can be provided: one form is quantitative, the other is qualitative. The first form allows

318

for cross-person comparisons and portrays the resources generally available to the institution. The second allows for in-depth single-person analysis, and portrays the individual faculty member's unique skills or perceptions. Using this two-form system, a faculty skills-analysis would contain both a listing of faculty who have expertise of background in each set of skill areas, and a narrative description of each faculty member's areas of expertise (including the ways in which these areas interact).

A second solution to the problem of codification resides in the use of faculty profiles—a blending of the quantitative and qualitative. A set of five to 20 categories are established, based on the type of information that has been collected (skills, attitudes, characteristics, roles and so forth). In the case of a role-analysis, the following categories might be established: (a) lower division instruction, (b) upper division instruction, (c) formal advisement to students, (d) departmental governance, (e) research, (f) scholarship, (g) campus governance, (h) departmental management, (i) colleague assistance, (j) informal advisement to students, and so forth. Based on the quantitative and qualitative data that have been collected about each faculty member, a profile is drawn up, indicating the relative strength (commitment, expertise, activity) in each category. Thus, in the case of a role analysis, the extent of a faculty member's activity as a lower division instructor, departmental manager and so forth is assessed.

The profile can be based on either interpersonal or intrapersonal comparisons. In the first case, the extent of a faculty member's strength in each category is based on a comparison with other faculty (in the department, division, or entire institution). A faculty member could receive a high score in all of the categories. Intrapersonal comparisons require that a faculty member's strength in each profile category be assessed against his strength in other categories. Usually some form of percentile score is used, and the total score for each faculty members always adds up to 100. Interpersonal comparisons are preferable if the profile is being used to identify specific campus resources. Intrapersonal comparisons are of greater value if one is planning for the use of these resources. A profile analysis is quite compatible with the use of portfolios to evaluate the performance of faculty (see Chapter Three in the second volume of this series).

NOTES:

[1]Daniel H. Pilon and William H. Bergquist, *Consultation in Higher Education: A Handbook for Practitioners and Clients* (Washington, D.C.: Council for the Advancement of Small Colleges, 1979), pp. 120–130.

[2]Alan E. Boyer, *Teaching Faculty in Academe: 1972–73* (Washington, D.C.: American Council on Education, 1974).

INSTRUMENT NUMBER TWELVE

TITLE: Faculty Activity Survey

SOURCE: William H. Bergquist

GENERAL DESCRIPTION: In meeting a variety of institutional planning needs a college or university may wish to collect information about how faculty currently spend their time on the job and how they would like to spend their time. Ideally, faculty should be observed doing their job. Since this is usually not possible, faculty can be asked to estimate their own distribution of time. They also can be asked to indicate how they would like to spend their time in the future. Discrepencies between current and desired time spent can provide a basis for reassignment of job-related responsibilities, for departmental reorganization, and so forth.

INSTRUCTIONS FOR USE: The Faculty Activity Survey should be distributed to all faculty (or a sample of at least 50 faculty in a large institution). A small sample is not particularly useful, for any one faculty member can only provide a rough estimate of time spent doing specific activities. A large sample will reveal general conditions and trends—though data from this survey should always be viewed in a tentative manner and, it is hoped, supplemented by other data, such as interviews with some faculty about how they spend their time.

The Faculty Activity Survey should be filled out anonymously. Results from the survey should be transformed from hours per week to percentage of total amount of time per week devoted to this activity (hours per week assigned to specific activity divided by the total number of hours per week estimated by the respondent). An overall average percentage of time spent by faculty performing each activity then can be calculated by combining percentage scores from all of the survey questionnaires that have been filled out for each of the activities in the questionnaire. An average figure may not be the most useful statistic, however, and may be invalid by some statistical standards. The range of percentages for each activity may be of greater value to a planning group, as might a frequency tabulation (the number of faculty who are engaged in or would like to be engaged in each activity from 0 to 0.5 percent of the time, 0.5 to 1.0 percent, 1.0 to 5.0 percent, 5.0 to 10.0 percent, 10.0 to 15.0 percent, 15.0 to 25.0 percent, and over 25.0 percent.

FACULTY ACTIVITY SURVEY

General Instructions:

This survey asks you to estimate the average number of hours per week you have spent during this year engaged in different types of activities and the number of hours per week that you optimally would like to devote to each of these activities. Please be as honest as possible in filling out this form. You have nothing to lose and we all have a great deal to gain from your candid appraisal of time spent, and the time you would like to spend, doing various activities.

As you complete this form, you may find it difficult to arrive at an average figure regarding current levels of activities, since your work varies widely from week to week. If you find it difficult to arrive at an average figure, you might wish to estimate the total number of hours per activity for three or four random weeks during the past two months, then calculate a weekly average for each activity from these weekly estimates.

Please read over the entire survey before beginning to fill it out, so that you can get a sense of the full range of activities that you are being asked to assess.

FACULTY ACTIVITY SURVEY

Activity	Estimated Actual Hours Per Week	Preferred Hours Per Week
I. Teaching		
A. Primary Teaching Activities		
1. Meeting scheduled classes (in-class time)	_____	_____
2. Reading student assignments	_____	_____
3. Evaluating students	_____	_____
4. Contacting/hosting guest speakers	_____	_____
5. Preparing individual class presentations (lectures, demonstrations, simulations, etc.)	_____	_____
6. Preparing instructional materials (graphics, video-tapes, etc.)	_____	_____
7. Supervising student projects on campus	_____	_____
8. Supervising field trips or off-campus student projects	_____	_____
9. Supervising independent studies or tutoring students	_____	_____
10. Meeting informally with students in a course	_____	_____
B. Secondary Teaching Activities		
11. Discussions with colleagues about teaching	_____	_____

Activity	Estimated Actual Hours Per Week	Preferred Hours Per Week
12. Assisting another faculty member with preparation of his/her course presentation	_____	_____
13. Giving general presentations at this institution	_____	_____
14. Assisting students in gaining academic credit based on work outside this institution	_____	_____
C. Academic Advising		
15. Giving advice to students concerning course selection	_____	_____
16. Giving advice to students concerning selection of a major or minor area of academic specialization	_____	_____
17. Assisting students with academic grievances against other faculty or students	_____	_____
D. Course and Curriculum Development		
18. Preparing course outlines	_____	_____
19. Developing book lists for a course	_____	_____
20. Evaluating one's own teaching effectiveness	_____	_____
21. Designing new instructional materials or techniques	_____	_____
22. Revising existing course materials or techniques	_____	_____
23. Developing objectives for a new curriculum	_____	_____
24. Assisting in the design of a new curriculum	_____	_____
25. Planning for curricular changes	_____	_____
II. *Scholarship, Research and Creative Work Activity*		
A. Specific Projects		
26. Departmental/group/institutional research	_____	_____
27. Sponsored research	_____	_____
28. Individual research (independent)	_____	_____
29. Reviewing a colleague's research work	_____	_____
30. Writing or developing research proposals	_____	_____
31. Administering research grants	_____	_____
32. Writing articles	_____	_____

Activity	Estimated Actual Hours Per Week	Preferred Hours Per Week
33. Writing books		
34. Writing reviews or commentaries		
35. Giving speeches or public presentations		
36. Inventing new procedures, tools, etc. related to your profession or discipline		

B. General Scholarship and Professional Development

Activity	Estimated Actual Hours Per Week	Preferred Hours Per Week
37. Reading articles and books related to your area of expertise		
38. Reading articles and books related to curriculum areas in which you are not an expert		
39. Officer in a professional society or editor of a professional journal		
40. Attending professional meetings		
41. Attending off-campus seminars or other off-campus professional development activities		
42. Attending on-campus seminars or other on-campus professional development activities		

III. *Service Activities*

A. Student-Oriented Services

Activity	Estimated Actual Hours Per Week	Preferred Hours Per Week
43. Personal or career counseling		
44. Preparing recommendations for students		
45. Participation in social/athletic interaction with students		
46. Attending student activities (as observer) outside the classroom (athletics, formal presentations, etc.)		

B. Administrative Duties

Activity	Estimated Actual Hours Per Week	Preferred Hours Per Week
47. Performing the duties of a department chairman		
48. Managing clerical/secretarial personnel		
49. Record-keeping		
50. Preparing minutes/other recording activities		
51. Writing and answering memoranda		
52. Preparing budgets or institutional reports		

Activity	Estimated Actual Hours Per Week	Preferred Hours Per Week
53. Interviewing or recruiting candidates for faculty positions		
54. Escorting visitors to this institution		
55. Advising on library or other instructional purchases		
C. Committee Participation		
56. Departmental/group meetings		
57. Faculty personnel/policy meetings		
58. Budget meetings		
59. Overall institutional policy meetings		
60. Other meetings concerning this institution		
D. External Service Activities		
61. Teaching at another institution		
62. Consulting/advising at no charge (other than expenses)		
63. Consulting/advising for a fee		
64. General community service (youth activities, community governance, etc.)		
TOTAL NUMBER OF HOURS PER WEEK		

Thank you for your help

Chapter Fourteen

The Future of Faculty Development

In the preface to the first volume of *A Handbook for Faculty Development,* we referred to Joseph Axelrod's comparison of

> the state of college and university faculty to that of Daedalus and his son Icarus trapped in the Labyrinth of King Minos of Crete centuries ago. Just as Daedalus and his son could not escape the labyrinth by following its winding ways, neither can today's faculty member find the freedom he needs to teach effectively by following the ways of his own academic labyrinth. To escape, Daedalus had to craft wings to carry him out of his captivity. The faculty member of today must do the same; to be free he must turn his attention to the art and craft of teaching.[1]

In the eight years since Axelrod's *The University Teacher as Artist,* faculty development has become part of the personal and professional lives of thousands of faculty and administrators. Millions of dollars in funding and institutional support have been invested in creating and implementing a variety of methodologies for faculty development. Now, as higher education enters a decade which is certain to bring about profound changes in the nature and scope of the entire enterprise, faculty development must face the question of its own effectiveness. What has faculty development accomplished during the past decade? What role, if any, might faculty development play in higher education as we face the uncertainty of the 1980s? This chapter will attempt to provide some tentative answers to these two questions.

A. Professor Stephen Abbot

A central though generally unacknowledged figure in the faculty development movement is Professor Stephen Abbot, whose career is followed from its beginnings "before Berkeley" to the early 1970s by Joseph Axelrod in *The University Teacher as Artist.* Although as far as we can tell, Professor Abbot has never been to a faculty development workshop, his career in many important ways provides a touchstone both for the changes that have taken place in higher education over the last 20 years and, perhaps, for faculty development itself.

At the beginning of his career, Professor Abbot quickly established himself at his institution as a successful teacher conforming to what Axelrod describes as the "principles-and-facts" prototype of the university teacher as artist. According to Axelrod, this instructor "focuses on principles, concepts, and other kinds of subject matter; he is concerned with the systematic coverage of his subject. He believes the primary functions of a university teacher are to inform the student directly about certain topics and, above all, to provoke the student into additional learning through the process of inquiry and discovery."[2] Appropriately enough, Abbot lectured and, more frequently, served as discussion leader. During discussions, Abbot believed it was his job "to keep the discussion moving without long and embarrassing breaks, and it was his responsibility to introduce new topics and to make statements to summarize the topics already discussed. He prepared the topics or discussion carefully, so that tangential issues could be avoided and so that he could maintain control. He never for a moment considered that the class as a whole, or any student in it, might wish—or should be asked—to undertake any of the responsibilities he had assigned to himself."³ It was not until 1964 that Professor Abbot began to question seriously this approach to teaching and learning.

A number of changes shook American higher education in the early 1960s, perhaps most fully symbolized by the student revolution at Berkeley in 1964. Just as the educational establishment was forced by these and similar outbursts to re-examine a number of fundamental assumptions it had operated under during the 1950s, so too did the student demand for relevance cause many faculty to reconsider seriously what and how they were teaching. "Stephen Abbot was one of those professors. In the aftermath of the Berkeley revolt, he began to develop a new attitude toward his students and toward his own educational methods."⁴ He was on his way to becoming what Axelrod describes as the "student-as-mind" prototype characteristic of the instructor who organizes "course content so that material is suitable for helping students learn to perform complex intellectual operations. His goal is to encourage his students to develop ease in a variety of intellectual skills . . . moving from the formulation of problems, to the analysis of data, to solutions."⁵ Consistent with this prototype, Abbot had come to believe at this time that "the most important thing students could acquire was a specific set of complex skills for reading literature. With these skills, he said, students would be able to continue their study and appreciation of literature long after they had left their formal study with him. . . . He believed, in short, that the most significant aspects of the interpretation of a work of art could be discussed in a rational way following the usual tenets of logic."⁶

The later 1960s and early 1970s saw another period of crisis for higher education and for the people who taught in its institutions, for the revolution at Columbia University, the Cambodian invasion, Kent State, and Jackson State all forced a reassessment of the role and mission of this country's colleges and universities at least as profound as that of the early 1960s. It was this period that saw a shift in Professor Abbot's teaching from the student-as-mind prototype to what Axelrod identifies as the "student-as-person" prototype descriptive of the instructor who "emphasizes the personal development of the whole student—his entire personality and not just his mind. . . . Such a teacher organizes his class sections around his desire to help students develop as individuals, along all the dimensions—particularly the nonintellectual dimensions—where growth appears necessary or desirable."⁷ Professor Abbot, known for the first time to his students as "Steve," had now come to see the young men and women in his classes as whole people. Less certain of his own views, no longer a source of absolute truth, Professor Abbot, in the words of one of his students, "joined the human race."⁸

Stephen Abbot's career thus parallels and reflects many of the changes that have swept American higher education since 1960. Berkeley and Columbia, Cambodia and Kent State, all had profound effects both on Professor Abbot and on this country's colleges and universities. In another sense, Abbot's career also reflects the changes that have taken place in the way higher education has conceived of and promoted the growth and development of its teaching faculty. Prior to about 1970 Professor Abbot taught, first, his discipline and, second, the critical and logical habit of mind. In the same way, faculty development until about that time was largely concerned with helping

326

faculty keep current in their discipline, providing resources for research and publication, and stimulating continued intellectual growth and excitement. In essence, faculty were expected to develop in exactly the same ways Professor Abbot was asking his students to learn.

As we have seen, Professor Abbot's view of teaching and students began to change during the early 1970s until he came to view students as whole people and teaching as a holistic activity. At that same time, prompted in part by Axelrod's book, in part by *Change* magazine's "Faculty Development in a Time of Retrenchment," a number of administrators, writers, and consultants began calling for an approach to faculty development that dealt with the faculty member as a whole person, as an individual with personal and organizational, as well as instructional and intellectual, dimensions to his life. Just as Professor Abbot began to teach the whole student, faculty development began to be concerned with faculty as whole people.

Axelrod leaves Stephen Abbot in the early 1970s deeply immersed in learning the skills needed to teach the whole student, at about the same time that faculty development was learning the methodology of its approach to the faculty member as a whole person. We will return to Professor Abbot later in this chapter to learn of his experiences during the 1970s; in the meantime, let us turn our attention to faculty development during that same period of time. As Professor Abbot struggles with his new approach to teaching and learning, we must examine the comparable efforts of faculty development during the last decade.

B. Faculty Development, 1970–1980

The question of the effectiveness of various approaches to faculty development has always been of concern to faculty, administrators, and practitioners from the very outset of the movement. End of workshop evaluations, formal end of program evaluations, informal testimony, and follow-up observation all seemed to indicate that these efforts were having positive consequences, but, until recently, little or no formal evaluation of faculty development across programs and institutions was available. Within the last two years, however, that situation has changed significantly with the publication of three important new books. Jerry G. Gaff's *Institutional Renewal Through the Improvement of Teaching* (San Francisco: Jossey-Bass, 1978) is a review of Gaff's Project on Institutional Renewal Through the Improvement of Teaching, which addresses a number of broad questions concerning the effectiveness of faculty development; Kenneth E. Eble's *Improving Teaching Styles* (San Francisco: Jossey-Bass, 1980) provides a number of case studies of various approaches to instructional change; and William C. Nelsen and Michael E. Siegel's *Effective Approaches to Faculty Development* (Washington, D.C.: Association of American Colleges, 1980), reviews 20 externally-funded faculty development programs and concludes with two important chapters on the effectiveness and future of faculty development.[9] Although we probably never will have the kind of rigorous pre- and post-data on faculty development inappropriately demanded by a few evaluators, these three books taken together provide a nearly exhaustive account of faculty development in the 1970s. From this wealth of information, three conclusions about faculty development are inescapable.

Conclusion Number One: A coherent set of theories, models, strategies, and methodologies exist for faculty development. Over the last several years, a wide variety of resources for faculty development have come into existence, "including questionnaires and interview forms, summaries of research on teaching and learning, guidelines for designing workshops, video and audio teaching cassettes, simulations, and games."[10] The conceptual, intellectual, and practical tools for faculty development are at hand.

Conclusion Number Two: A variety of approaches to faculty development have been field-tested thoroughly in a wide range of institutional settings. The three books identified above cover almost every existing approach to faculty development from faculty exchange to growth contracting in institutions ranging from a few hundred to several thousand students. Although undoubtedly every approach has not been tested in every kind of institution, faculty development has faced the practical, political, social, and economic challenges of program implementation.

Conclusion Number Three: Given adequate support and competent program implementation, faculty development works. Although criteria of success will vary from program to program and institution to institution, evidence of the effectiveness of faculty development is clear. As Nelsen and Siegel summarize their interviews of more than 500 faculty and administrators,

> In general, the faculty development programs reported in the essays . . . have facilitated significant improvements on the campuses where they have been implemented. Many of the faculty we interviewed . . . expressed feelings of revitalization, indicating that their lives had actually changed as a result of faculty development activities. Instead of settling for the despair which seems so ubiquitous today, these faculty seek to breathe new life into the academy and to pass it on, renewed and revivified, to the next generation of teacher-scholars. . . . Faculty have discovered new areas of academic inquiry, developed new teaching interests, designed new courses, utilized new modes of teaching, worked with colleagues from other disciplines, and written long-term growth plans. Administrators have seen improvements in scholarly output on their campuses, the design of new interdisciplinary courses which attract students and the increase of collegial interaction among the faculties. Campuses as a whole have been improved also, even in these difficult times. Committee systems have been streamlined and reward structures more clearly formulated as a result of faculty development.[11]

Although Nelsen and Siegel identify some approaches to faculty development as more difficult and less likely to succeed than others and rightfully criticize the failure of most programs to address such fundamental issues as faculty evaluation, rewards systems, and student advising,[12] all available evidence points to the significant contribution faculty development has made to the lives of numerous people and institutions in the last ten years.

The 1970s have consequently seen the development of a methodology for faculty development, the practical testing of that methodology in a variety of situations, and an accumulation of evidence attesting to the success of these efforts. The future of faculty development, however, is far less clear than its past. The pressures of declining enrollment and accelerating inflation that caused so much stress in American higher education during the 1970s can only increase during the next ten years. In what ways, if at all, can the experience and expertise of faculty development gained during the 1970s be of value during the 1980s? To answer that question, we must return to the career of Professor Stephen Abbot.

328

C. Professor Stephen Abbot: 1980

Although *The University Teacher as Artist* only follows Professor Abbot up to the early 1970s, Axelrod recently returned to him to trace his development through the end of that decade. Once again, the career of Professor Stephen Abbot provides some important signposts for both higher education and faculty development.

During the several years that Professor Abbot was learning to teach the whole student, he was, Axelrod reports, very happy with his career.

> But around 1975, he began to feel that something was not quite right. For one thing, the curricular reforms of the 1960s that he had so vigorously supported were beginning to crumble, not only on his own campus but all over the country. Moreover, a new kind of student was beginning to appear in the universities, and this new student, it was evident, felt no responsibility and no sense of commitment to academic pursuits or to society. . . .
>
> Once again, but more slowly this time, Abbot's teaching style underwent a change. The shift was inevitable because a new kind of relationship was required for dealing with this new kind of student. It was true, of course, that in each of his classes, Abbot found a few students who displayed a commitment to their studies, and he continued to care about them personally. But for most of his students he no longer had any personal feeling. They began, in fact, to lose their individual identity. He could no longer fix his attention on them while he was teaching. More and more, his attention reverted to his own concerns as a scholar, and these concerns now became the focal point of his own teaching.[13]

Once again, the changes that Axelrod traces in Professor Abbot's teaching reflect in a very direct way Abbot's perception of and response to the changes he saw going on around him, both in higher education and in society at large.

> At the end of the 1970s, Abbot saw all around him an academic society that behaved as though the 1960s had never happened. The reforms in teaching and learning that had taken place on his campus during the preceding decade had been eradicated quietly and without notice. Certain overt changes had been made democratically, of course, because his campus was noted for democratic governance. But the development was so pervasive, and the elimination of the reforms of the 1960s had been accomplished so smoothly, that Abbot was convinced there could be only one explanation: conspiracy and counterrevolution.
>
> The academic revolution of the 1960s had been noisy and bloody, but the counterrevolution of the 1970s had taken place so quietly that no one knew about it until it had been accomplished. The conspiracy, Abbot felt, had started with the conservative faculty (which is to say, the majority of the faculty) and their administrative officers. Joining with them were powerful outside forces: the accrediting agencies, the disciplinary organizations and learned societies, and above all the controllers of the sources of funds—boards, government agencies, and state legislatures. Strengthened and encouraged by the business world and the professions—and by the new breed of students who would be seeking success in those areas—this powerful alliance of reactionary forces, Abbot believed, had launched a counterrevolution which, at the time of Nixon's resignation from the presidency, had reversed the direction of teaching and learning in the American university.[14]

Axelrod concludes his revisitation of Professor Stephen Abbot with the following brief paragraph, one that is even more sobering than those that have gone before:

> When the year 1984 arrives, Abbot will have completed his twenty-fifth year of college teaching. How will things go between now and then? When that question is put to him, Abbot quietly sighs and shakes his head. He says only that he is not optimistic.[15]

D. Faculty Development: 1980–1990

Faculty development, as it has emerged during the 1970s, has been neither a fad nor an isolated event. It has, instead, been part of a larger movement in this society that has sought relevance, wholeness, and integration. That whole movement may well be doomed. Just as Stephen Abbot's teaching now resembles more closely the way he taught in the 1950s, higher education itself is giving every indication of returning to the quiet and passivity of 20 years ago. If this happens, faculty development at most institutions will appear as if the 1970s had never happened. As external funding becomes less and less available and as program after program fails to make the transition to substantial internal support, the prospects look dim.

And yet, in spite of the emergence of "new" core curricula and general education requirements that bear more than a faint resemblance to the distribution requirements of 20 years ago, one significant difference exists between what higher education was in the 1950s and what it will be in the 1980s. Quite simply, the enrollment declines and inflationary pressures of the next ten years will be unlike anything higher education has ever experienced in the recent past. Colleges and universities may respond to these pressures by settling merely for survival. If this is the case, faculty development as it has emerged during the past ten years will play little or no role in American higher education during the next ten years. If, however, institutions have the courage and creativity to demand more than survival, faculty development can continue to make significant contributions to the health of the entire enterprise. These contributions will center on three levels.

At the individual level, faculty will experience a continued shrinking of intellectual and geographic horizons. Many faculty, hired during the affluence of the 1950s and '60s, today face the prospect of as much as a quarter-century of teaching the same courses at the same institution. Currency in one's discipline will be more and more difficult to maintain; the excitement of teaching increasingly faceless students more and more to difficult to generate. In addition to continued emphasis on traditional approaches to faculty development, the methodologies for creative, innovative teaching that have been created in the last ten years may be essential in helping faculty stay in touch not only with their disciplines, but also with the genuine joy and excitement that can come from effective teaching. Faculty will remain whole people during the 1980s in spite of efforts to fragment them into a variety of separate and unrelated roles. Practitioners of faculty development now know how to work with those people in their wholeness, in their concern for their own personal and professional growth, career development, and teaching effectiveness.

At the group level, departments and divisions, committees, and even administrative councils will continue to feel increased pressures for accountability and productivity. Individual group members no longer will be able to operate in relative isolation from their colleagues; groups will need to recognize their interdependence with other groups. An English department at a private west coast university was once described by the school's academic vice president as containing 14 faculty and 13 factions. Such a condition can be tolerated no longer. Even with a self-serving reinstitution of the most traditional of distribution requirements, academic departments, programs, and majors will stand or fall on the ability of faculty to work together. The strategies for team building and curriculum development described in these handbooks and elsewhere may be essential to faculty development in the 1980s.

It will be at the institutional level, however, that faculty development will face its greatest challenge in the coming years. Never before have colleges and universities faced such intense pressure for survival with quality as they will in the coming decade. As Jerry Gaff suggests, this will demand

> a role for faculty development that is rather different from what it is today. Begun in a time when faculty were in need of help, faculty development programs will have to adjust to a period when institutions are in need of help. The success of these programs in the next decade will depend on their capacity to translate the technologies developed in response to faculty concerns, particularly in regard to their teaching, and apply them in an institutional context. They will have to help mold the personal and professional concerns of faculty members to fit the altered roles of their institutions. Faculty development programs will be asked not only to help faculty members improve the quality of their teaching, but also to give them a better understanding of and capacity to participate actively in the management of a larger learning community. Faculty will need to recognize the constraints as well as the opportunities that confront both their institutions and postsecondary education as a whole.[16]

This is consistent with the emphasis we have placed in this volume on the potential role of organization and career development in higher education. As Edgar Schein has suggested, "if an organization development program is to involve any real change in organizational culture, it probably must be combined with an explicit career development program which considers how such cultural change can be initiated and sustained over longer periods of time."[17] Although these methodologies have been tested less fully in colleges and universities than other approaches to faculty development, it nevertheless does exist. The willingness and ability of higher education to make use of institution-wide approaches to renewal may simply spell the difference for many institutions between survival and extinction in the next ten years.

E. Second Wave or Third?

In his most recent book, Alvin Toffler posits the existence of three major waves of civilization progressively rolling across this planet since the human race first began moving away from survival "by foraging, fishing, hunting, or herding. At some point, roughly ten millenia ago, the agricultural revolution began, and it crept slowly across the planet spreading villages, settlements, cultivated land, and a new way of life." This First Wave of civilization "had not yet exhausted itself by the end of the seventeenth century, when the industrial revolution broke over Europe and unleashed the second great wave of planetary change."[18] This Second Wave, industrial civilization, has dominated life in every developed country in the world for the last 300 years.

The Second Wave brought with it not just a change in the way the human race made a living, but also fundamental changes in the family, in society, in politics, in our very conception of time and space, changes necessary to support the factory model on which industrial civilization is based. In many ways resembling a factory, "mass education taught basic reading, writing and arithmetic, a bit of history and other subjects. This was the 'overt curriculum.' But beneath it lay an invisible or 'covert curricullm' that was far more basic. It consisted—and still does in most industrial nations—of three courses: one in punctuality, one in obedience, and one in rote, repetitive work. Factory labor demanded workers who showed up on time. . . . It demanded workers who would take orders from a management hierarchy without questioning. And it demanded men and women prepared to slave away at machines or in offices, performing brutally repetitious operations."[19]

It is possible to argue, although Toffler does so only by implication, that higher education in this country and elsewhere is simply an extension of mass public education. Based on standardization, specialization, concentration, and centralization, four of the basic building blocks of Second Wave civilization,[20] the primary task of higher education has been to train the technicians, managers, and executives of the hierarchical organizations characteristic of an industrial society.

The central thesis of Toffler's book, however, is that for the last quarter of a century the Second Wave of industrial society has come under increasing attack by the Third Wave of a new civilization. "A powerful tide is surging across much of the world today, creating a new, often bizarre, environment in which to work, play, marry, raise children, or retire. In this bewildering context, businessmen swim against highly erratic economic currents; politicians see their ratings bob wildly up and down; universities, hospitals, and other institutions battle desperately against inflation. Value systems splinter and crash, while the lifeboats of family, church, and state are hurled madly about."[21] The signs of this conflict are all around us. "The price of gold—that sensitive barometer of fear—breaks all records. Banks tremble. Inflation rages out of control. And the governments of the world are reduced to paralysis or imbecility."[22] To this list we might add Berkeley and Columbia, Kent State and Cambodia.

The outlines of this new civilization are beginning to become clear. "The Third Wave brings with it a genuinely new way of life based on diversified, renewable energy resources; on methods of production that make most factory assembly lines obsolete; on new, non-nuclear families; . . . and on radically changed schools and corporations of the future."[23] Central to this change is a "move from a Second Wave culture that emphasized the study of things in isolation from one another to a Third Wave culture that emphasizes contexts, relationships, and wholes."[24] From a systems approach to organizations, the "holistic health" movement, an awareness of ecological interrelationships, and an emphasis on interdisciplinary thinking to Professor Abbot's concern with the whole student to faculty development's attention to the whole person, interrelationship and interdependence have become the hallmark of the Third Wave.

American higher education, like all the other organizations and institutions that have developed over the last 300 years, is a Second Wave phenomenon. The challenges colleges and universities have been facing over the last 25 years, including the challenges proposed by the modern theory and practice of faculty development, have emerged from the Third Wave. As higher education enters the 1980s, it stands at a crossroads. Faced with the pressures of inflation and declining enrollment, it can choose to emphasize the past. In so doing, American colleges and universities will become more and more isolated and irrelevant, and the approach to faculty development that has emerged in the past decade will have little to offer institutions seeking to maintain or return to the status quo of their Second Wave heritage. On the other hand, higher education may choose the future. If this happens, the methodologies of a holistic approach to faculty development, particularly as they become deployed at an organizational level, can be central to that development. Faculty development can play an important role in helping American colleges and universities join the Third Wave. The future of faculty development then becomes the future of higher education. The next ten years will make that decision.

NOTES:

[1] William H. Bergquist and Steven R. Phillips, *A Handbook for Faculty Development,* Volume 1 (Washington, D.C.: Council for the Advancement of Small Colleges, 1975), p. vii.

[2] Joseph Axelrod, *The University Teacher as Artist* (San Francisco: Jossey-Bass, 1973), p. 42.

[3] Axelrod, p. 60.

[4] Axelrod, p. 85.

[5] Axelrod, p. 43.

[6] Axelrod, p. 86.

[7] Axelrod, p. 14.

[8] Axelrod, p. 115.

[9] The basis of these evaluations is largely testimonial, as is perhaps appropriate for something as difficult to measure as professional and personal growth. For a more empirically-based study of faculty development, see John A. Centra, "Faculty Development Practices," in Centra, ed., *Renewing and Evaluating Teaching* (San Francisco: Jossey-Bass, 1977), pp. 49–55. "Hard" data on the effectiveness of various faculty development practices also is beginning to emerge. See, for example, the research studies developed at Syracuse University's Center for Instructional Development and Glenn R. Erickson and Bette L. Erickson, "Improving College Teaching: An Evaluation of a Teaching Consultation Procedure," *Journal of Higher Education,* 50 (1979), 670–683.

[10] Jerry G. Gaff and David O. Justice, "Faculty Development Yesterday, Today, and Tomorrow," in Gaff, ed., *Institutional Renewal Through the Improvement of Teaching* (San Francisco: Jossey-Bass, 1978), p. 87. Kenneth Eble provides an annotated list of many of these in *Improving Teaching Styles* (San Francisco: Jossey-Bass, 1980), pp. 99–104.

[11] William C. Nelsen and Michael E. Siegel, *Effective Approaches to Faculty Development* (Washington, D.C.: Association of American Colleges, 1980), p. 3.

[12] Nelsen and Siegel, *Effective Approaches to Faculty Development,* pp. 131–135.

[13] Joseph Axelrod, "From Counterculture to Counterrevolution: A Teaching Career," in Kenneth E. Eble, *Improving Teaching Styles,* p. 10.

[14] Axelrod, "From Counterculture to Counterrevolution," p. 19.

[15] Axelrod, "From Counterculture . . . ," p. 20.

[16] Jerry G. Gaff and David O. Justice, "Faculty Development Yesterday, Today, and Tomorrow," in Gaff, *Institutional Renewal Through the Improvement of Teaching,* p. 96.

[17] Edgar H. Schein, *Career Dynamics: Matching Individual and Organizational Needs* (Reading, Massachusetts: Addison-Wesley, 1978), p. 9.

[18] Alvin Toffler, *The Third Wave* (New York: Morrow, 1980), p. 29.

[19] Toffler, p. 45.

[20] Toffler, pp. 62–76.

[21] Toffler, pp. 17–18.

[22] Toffler, p. 17.

[23] Toffler, p. 26.

[24] Toffler, p. 318.

HANDOUT NUMBER EIGHT

Title: A Plea for Faculty Development

Source: Adapted from the *Report of the Presidential Task Force on Faculty Development*, California State University, Fresno, March 12, 1975.

General description: "Faculty development" can encompass a wide variety of activities, programs, and procedures—at times it almost seems as if the term can mean anything anyone says it means. More than once in this confusion of definition, the individual faculty member has been lost sight of. Yet it is that man or woman who properly ought to stand at the center of the movement. It is consequently fitting that we end this final volume of *A Handbook for Faculty Development* with a plea for the importance of that individual. Although written before much else was available on faculty development, the following document nevertheless provides a remarkably eloquent statement on what must always remain the central focus of all our efforts, the individual faculty member.

Iinstructions for use: This statement can be distributed without comment or used to stimulate discussion in a faculty seminar or workshop. Although such an eloquent statement is perhaps best left unanalyzed, it might be useful to explore the image of the ideal faculty member implicit in this document in light of Joseph Axelrod's taxonomy of teaching styles discussed in this chapter and in Chapter Two of the first volume of this series. Once again, we seem to have come full circle.

A PLEA FOR FACULTY DEVELOPMENT

As Kingfishers catch fire, dragonflies draw flame;
As tumbled over rim in roundy wells
Stones ring; like each tucked string tells, each hung bell's
Bow swung finds tongue to fling out broad its name . . .

Gerard Manley Hopkins

Faculty development is not a matter of technological devices, nor of organizational structures. It has little to do with the latest fad or gimmickry. "Faculty Development," rightly seen, is the proper development of the individual faculty member, and that is primarily a function of his integrity—professional, societal, personal. That which encourages such development is, finally, what we are seeking; that which impedes it is what must be eliminated from our institutional environment.

The professor must be first of all one who "professes," who has a commitment. That commitment may be expressed in terms of subject matter—but somehow that is not enough. The great teacher (and the only proper goal of "faculty development" is the creation of great teachers) is not one who is a mere conduit for information with which he is uninvolved. If the subject matter, the "information," is the print upon the slide, the teacher is the light shining through it, giving it the power to project upon the screen. Does the student learn from the print on the slide or from the light shining through it? Such is the intricate relationship of the teacher to his materials and students.

Or, to change the image, the conventionally correct professor approaches a student to speak in favor of his subject matter, only to be told, "Speak for yourself." The student is, at heart, too wise to be deluded by the formality of things. He wants to know first what is the nature of this voice that speaks so grandly. For if the speaker be facile and false, how can the message be replete with truth and wisdom?

All of us have had the experience of being, at some time, in the presence of great teaching. And always what remains in our minds and feelings are not the structure of the subject, nor its myriad facts, but the force and integrity with which the great teacher approaches the subject. Whether speaking from elaborate notes or a scratched outline, the speaker is always making one point: this matters, by God. We may at times be playful and witty, but this is damned serious business—too serious for any authority to censor, to inhibit, to control. It is even too serious to allow vanity and self-righteousness to corrupt it, which means that one must listen to adversary forces, evaluating them rightly, yet never being intimidated by them if they are judged inadequate—whatever the source. A teacher who speaks with such a voice, one that rings out loudly and clearly its own integrity, can have his subject matter taken seriously, for the wholeness of the person demands that it be taken seriously.

Where do we go wrong? To the young person, fresh from graduate school, heavy with enthusiasm for his subject and confident in his ability to convey it as a matter of serious consequence to the world, the road ahead is as clear and unmistakable as Thoreau's highway running westward from the small frontier towns, which starts out so broad and grand, yet soon disintegrates to a rutted lane, and ends as a squirrel track running up a tree. And for many a dedicated young teacher the route is the same: starting on a broad highway of intensity and conscience, he soon finds diverging forks with no clear sign of direction. And yet there are pressures all too willing to bend and divert: cynical colleagues, disappointed in their own lost ways; administrators concerned with avoiding the friction of criticism by keeping all bearing surfaces smooth, however the rough edges of truth must be ground down in the process; a community and society which would like him as a private in the ranks, or at most an obliging lieutenant, deferential and grateful for a place at the officers' mess. Sallying forth to blow a clear blast of prophecy in the wilderness, the new faculty member is soon lost in a thicket of institutional procedures and academic ambition, engaged in minor skirmishes of spite.

And yet we would be mistaken to put all the blame on institutional and societal pressures. There has been something else amiss. For the young man or woman going forth almost certainly carries something else inside besides the hard clear light of intensity. Within there has been implanted, during professional preparation, a gnawing worm, however minute, which will eat away through the years, finding ready food in the disappointments and complexities ahead. That worm was birthed by the very process which gave the young person the hard clear light of confidence and seems inextricably related to it. To the idealistic young Ph.D., there is a separation between himself and the members of his profession on the one hand, and society at large on the other. He feels that separation is based upon the knowledge of what is truly significant in the subject, and society's ignorance of that significance. And that is partly the truth. His mission is to approach that society, to somehow make it see the force of argument, though he often does not realize that the real strength of the argument will lie in his own integrity.

But, usually unknown at the start, there is another basis for that separation. From teachers he has absorbed another trait, and carries it unaware. It is a sense of elitism—and unchecked, it gnaws away through the years, fed by the fact that prophecy is ignored by the society he feels destined to lead. And, ironically, it is here that a society fearful of disruption of its creeds of fear and greed can seduce the new faculty from the path it both hopes and dreads he will choose. Take these robes of rank, these prerogatives of power, they tell the new teacher. The men of power have them—security, complacency, a certain luxury (compared with those who have to scratch for a living)—you deserve them too. Prophetic bugles blowing in the wilderness are all well and good, in their time, but how about a bigger house—or a third car? And so, if unchecked, the little worm of elitism will have grown until it is feeding on the prerogatives of power, unconcerned that the prerogatives have been offered only as a substitute for the substance of power. And this abandonment of real leadership in the society has come from within the individual. The choice has been made; like the narrator in Emerson's "Days," he has watched the "hypocritic Days" parade by with their gifts, has chosen "hastily . . . a few herbs and apples" and "too late, under her solemn fillet saw the scorn."

Faculty development, then, is a matter of restoration—of restoring an individual to a right relationship with himself, with students, and with the society of which he is a part. It should be obvious that, if we accept this truth, such a restoration can come only from the inner desire of the faculty member. No external conditions or structures can force it to appear. Indeed, most systems imposed from the oustide have almost the opposite effect, as they concern themselves only with what is superficial in the matter, ignoring the dynamic inner relation between the individual teacher's integrity and his work, and resulting in further alienation and resentment.

This is not, however, to say that nothing can be done, that a college or university must sit in dismay hoping that salvation may strike some few of the many treading the escalator downward. But it is to say that an institution must be sensitive concerning what it can do and what it cannot do.

What it can do is to create conditions which will assist the individual faculty member to further the process of restoration once it has started. It can make clear, by its structures and its systems, that it places the highest value on great teaching, that it recognizes such teaching must proceed from that hard clear light which it can encourage but never create itself. And it can provide the teacher with such support as is possible as he attempts to find a vital and creative means of dealing with that separation from society which can never be eliminated, if the faculty member is to live true to his vocation.

Finally, the college or university can recognize that, if it aspires to greatness itself, its only means to attain it is in a faculty made up of individual teachers, each striving in his teaching (like Gerard Manley Hopkins' kingfishers, dragonflies, and bell tongues) to "fling out broad its name."

Index

This is an index to all three volumes of *A Handbook for Faculty Development*. After each entry, the first number indicates which volume that entry will be found in; the second number (or numbers) indicates which page (or pages) the entry will be found on. For example, Abrahamson, Stephen, 1:290, will be found in *Volume 1* on page 290.

342

characteristics of, 3:316; on diagnostic team, 1:87; as ego ideal, 1:11, 1:12, 1:22; environmental perceptions of, 3:316; expertise of, 3:314; as experts, 1:10, 1:12, 1:16, 1:22; as facilitators, 1:11, 1:12, 1:22; as formal authority, 1:10–11, 1:12, 1:16, 1:22; freedom for, 1:vii; growth contacts for, 2:64; information about, 3:306–324; instructional effectiveness of, 3:315–316; interview of, on teaching, 1:203–205; learning contract role of, 3:100–101; leaving family stage of, 2:19; levels of change for, 3:309–311; means for growth for, 1:vii; mentor role of, 2:19; mid-career transition stage of, 2:20, 2:21, 3:236; motivation of, 2:16–29; as mystic healers, 1:10, 1:12; needs and interests of, 3:317; new, and innovation, 1:4–5; in 1970s, 3:325–327; in 1980, 3:329–330; peer evaluation of, 2:64; as persons, 1:11, 1:12, 1:22; as priests, 1:10, 1:12; restabilization stage of, 2:20, 3:236; role assignments of, 3:314–315; settling down stage of, 2:19–20, 3:236; as shaman, 1:9–10, 1:12; skills needed by, in seminar discussions, 3:111–112; as socializing agents, 1:11, 1:12, 1:22; student evaluation of, 2:64; teaching/curricular responsibilities of, 3:314; teaching styles of, 1:9–13; 1:20–27, 3:316–317; transition to retirement stage of, 2:20, 3:236–237

Faculty development: administration united with, 3:11–12; approaches to, 3:328; assumptions for, exercise in, 2:13–15; attitude, process, and structure in, 1:5–6; breadth of, 1:vii–viii; by career transitions, 1:265; centers and programs for, 1:287–299; and changes in higher education, 2:3; components of, 1:258–259; comprehensive approach to, 1:3–6; conceptual tools for, 3:327–328; by consultation, 1:261; by discussion, 1:263–264; effectiveness of, 3:328; by equipment, 1:263; by evaluation, 1:264; evaluation of, 2:286–313; factors in, 1:9; and foundation support, 3:294–305; funding for, 3:294–305; future of, 3:325–333; goals and rationales for, 2:309–313; handout for, 3:334–337; implementation of, 1:235–285; implications of, 2:3–12; and information about faculty, 3:306–324; institutional context of, 2:11; by institutional development, 1:265–266; by institutional research, 3:306–324; by

instructional materials, 1:262–263; and instructional technology, 1:4; introduction to, 1:1–6, 2:1–64; maturation of, 3:3; by method-promotion, 1:262; models for, 2:6–11; and motivation, 2:16–55; and new faculty, 1:4–5; newsletters on, 1:301–303; in 1970s, 3:327–328; in 1980s, 3:330–331; paradigms and assumptions in, 2:3–5; past approaches to, 1:3–5; past support for, 3:294; by personal and organizational development, 1:261–262; plea for, 3:334–337; portfolios for, 2:56–64; present and future of, 3:291–337; prominence of, increased, 1:3; propositions basic to, 1:3; by reward system, 1:264–265; strategies for, 1:260–266; and student/faculty ratio, 1:3–4; tacit dimensions of, 3:3–67; by training, 1:260–261

Faculty Questionnaire, 3:317

Fantasy/suggestopedia methods, content-based, 3:72, 3:85–86

Faris, K. Gene, 1:292

Farquhar, Barbara B., 3:88

Feedback: constructive, 1:223–225; descriptive, 1:213, 1:215–218, 1:223–225; for observation and diagnosis, 1:89–90

Feeling description: as interpersonal skill, 2:212–217; for understanding, 1:217–218. *See also* Emotions

Festinger, Leon, 2:224

Fiedler, Fred E., 2:162, 2:193

Field placement: journals for, 3:107–109; student based, 3:72, 3:94

Filep, Robert T., 1:290

FIRO Microlab, 3:175–176

Fisch, Richard, 2:141

Fish bowl, as discussion variation, 3:143

Fisher, Charles, 3:51, 3:118, 3:130

Fisher, Kathleen M., 1:289

Flachman, Kim, 1:288, 1:303

Flair, Merrel D., 1:296

Flanders Interaction Analysis System, 1:89, 1:101–103

Flanders, Ned A., 1:101, 1:102, 1:104

Florida, University of: Office of Dental Education at, 1:290; Office of Instructional Resources at, 1:290, 1:302; Office of Medical Education at, 1:290

Florida State Department of Education, Program for Staff and Program Development of, 1:290

Florida State University, Division of Instructional Research and Service at, 1:290

Ford, George A., 3:248

344

Harding, Gene, 1:294

Harmin, Merrill, 1:209, 1:210, 1:212, 2:266, 2:267, 2:268, 2:272–273, 2:276

Harris, John, 1:290

Harrison, Patrick, 1:289

Harrison, Roger, 1:44, 1:137

Hartley, Eugene L., 1:299, 1:302

Hartley, James, 1:111

Hartnett, Rodney, 2:44

Harvard University: Bureau of Study Counsel at, 1:293; Business School's Intercollegiate Case Clearinghouse of, 3:51, 3:118; Center of Teaching and Learning at, 2:293

Hassett, Matthew J., 3:89

Hastings, J. Thomas, 2:288, 2:302

Hatala, Robert, 1:290

Havelock, Ronald G., 1:141, 1:143

Hawley, Robert C., 2:276, 3:144

Hefferlin, JB, 2:193

Helping relationship: defined, 1:213; factors in, 1:213

Helping skills: constructive feedback as, 1:223–225; development of, 1:213–233; exercises for, 1:226–232; handouts for, 1:215–225; of paraphrasing, 1:219–222; of responses for freeing and binding, 1:226–228; trios for, 1:229–232; of understanding, 1:215–218

Helping trios, in helping relationship, 1:229–232

Henry, Mark, 3:88

Herrick, Merlyn C., 1:294

Herzberg, Frederick, 2:23–24, 2:30

Heslin, Richard, 3:193

Hess, Joseph W., Jr., 1:294

Higher education: clearinghouses for, 2:285; constraints in, 3:165–166; problems in, 2:157–158; as second or third wave, 3:331–333

Hildebrand, Milton, 2:64

Hill, Joe E., 2:126, 2:141

History, role playing in, 3:130

Hodgkinson, Harold, 2:19, 2:20, 2:21, 2:30, 2:265

Hoffer, Eric, 2:224

Hofstetter, Fred T., 3:88

Holcomb, David, 1:298

Holland, John L., 3:244, 3:252

Hollinger, David A., 2:11

Holloway, Lewis D., 1:292

Holloway, Ralph, 1:298

Holmes, Thomas H., 2:237, 2:239n

Holsclaw, James, 1:288, 3:169

Hook, Harold, 2:241

Hopkins, Gerard Manley, 3:335, 3:337

Horn, Robert E., 1:111, 3:126–127, 3:130

Hough, John B., 1:104

Howard Community College, Learning Resources at, 1:293

Howe, Leland W., 1:212, 2:229, 2:276

Hoyt, Donald P., 1:78n

Huber, Curt, 2:141

Hudspeth, Delayne R., 1:297

Huffman, Stanley A., Jr., 1:299

Hughes, L. J., 3:89

Humble, John W., 1:143

Hungar, Julie, 3:51–67

Hunter, Elizabeth, 1:ix, 1:232n, 2:viii, 2:142

Hunter, Mary "Ski," 3:196–203

Hunter, Walter E., 1:294

Hurlbut, Howard, 1:289

Huxley, Laura Archera, 2:265

Huxley, Thomas, 2:286, 2:302

I

Idaho, University of, 1:50, 1:87; Center for Organization and Human Development at, 1:viii, 1:291

Idea domain, in instructional consultation, 3:157

Idea inventory. See Brainstorming

Ignatovich, Frederick, 2:141, 2:150

Illinois, University of, 3:77; Center for Educational Development at, 1:291; Curriculum and Evaluation, College of Medicine at, 1:291; Office of Instructional Resources at, 1:291

Illinois State University, Instructional Development at, 1:291

Implementation: guide to, 1:235–285; and program design, 1:258–285; and workshop design, 1:237–257

Inclusion, concept of, 3:173

Independent study, student based, 3:72, 3:90

Independent style, and participation, 1:116

Indiana University System, Learning Resources at, 1:292

Information about faculty: analysis of, 3:306–324; areas of, 3:313–317; for clearinghouse, 3:308; for development and training, 3:309–313; instrument for, 3:320–324; and planning, 3:307–308; processing, 3:318–319; and reassignment, 3:308–309; uses of, 3:307–313

Informational domain, in instructional consultation, 3:155–156

Ingersoll, Ralph, 1:299

Ludlow, Spencer, 3:12
Luft, Joseph, 1:233
Luskin, Bernard, J., 1:289, 1:302
Luszter, Margaret Barron, 1:90, 1:104
Lyon, Douglas, 1:295

M

Maas, James B., 1:295
Macalester College, Faculty Renewal Program at, 1:294, 1:301
Madaus, George, 2:288, 2:302
Mager, R.F., 1:111
Maher, Thomas, 1:292
Maine, University of: Improving Teaching Effectiveness Project at, 1:292; Instructional Systems Center at, 1:292
Malkoff, Karen I., 1:302
Managerial Grid, 1:142
Managerial training, and organization development, 1:142
Mann, Richard, 1:10–11, 1:12, 1:13–14, 1:15, 1:19, 1:20, 1:23, 2:44, 3:12, 3:316
March, James, 2:193
Markely, Susan, 3:85, 3:88–89
Marrow, Alfred J., 1:266
Mars Hill College, 1:296
Maryland, University of, 1:293
Martens, Mary, 1:293
Martorana, S. V., 2:193
Maslow, Abraham H., 2:17, 2:22, 2:30
Massachusetts, University of, at Amherst, 1:87, 1:107; Center for Instructional Resources and Improvement at, 1:141, 1:293, 2:78; Clinic to Improve University Teaching at, 1:79–84, 1:293, 2:64, 2:69–78, 2:80–97, 2:103–107, 2:110–123, 3:12, 3:73, 3:155, 3:156
Mastery learning, 3:80
Mathematics, PSI in, 3:89
Mathis, B. Claude, 1:291
May, Rollo, 2:265, 2:276
Mayo, Douglas, 1:297
McBay, Shirley, 1:291
McBeath, Ron J., 1:49, 1:289
McCallum, Neil, 1:289
McGill University: Centre for Learning and Development at, 1:303; Instructional Development Service Project at, 2:98–102
McGrath, Earl, 2:193
McGregor, Douglas, 2:22–23, 2:30, 2:193, 2:302
McGuire, Christine, 1:291
McIntyre, Charles J., 1:291
McKeachie, Wilbert J., 1:6, 1:19, 1:126, 1:127, 1:128, 1:129, 1:137, 3:73

McKean, Joseph D., Jr., 2:239n
Mackenzie, Clara, 1:302
McKnight, Philip C., 1:292
McLuhan, T. C., 1:19
Meadows, Dennis L., 1:6
Meadows, Donella H., 1:6
Medical College of Georgia, 1:291
Medicine, computer-assisted instruction in, 3:88
Meeth, L. Richard, 1:143
Melnick, Michael A., 1:104, 1:108, 1:293, 2:69, 2:78
Memphis State University, Center for Learning Research and Service at, 1:297
Menges, Robert J., 2:64
Meramac Community College, 1:294
Messick, Samuel, 2:141
Methods, educational: exercise for, 1:113-121; handouts for, 1:122-136
Miami-Dade Community College, Office of Staff and Organizational Development at, 1:141, 1:290
Miami University of Ohio, Audio Visual Service at, 1:296
Michael, Donald, 2:30, 3:5, 3:12
Michigan, University of: Center for Research and Utilization of Scientific Knowledge at, 1:141; Center for Research on Learning and Teaching at, 1:294, 1:301; Center for the Study of Higher Education at, 3:315; Educational Resources Department, School of Dentistry at, 1:294; Office of Educational Research and Resources, School of Medicine at, 1:294
Michigan State University, 3:73, 3:155, 3:314; Educational Development Program at, 1:293; Learning Services at, 1:293; Office of Medical Education Research and Development at, 1:293
Micro-macro dichotomy, in course design, 2:146-147
Microteaching: analysis of, 1:105-108; assumptions in, 1:105-106; as component skills approach, 1:106; and cosmetic effect, 1:109; higher education modifications of, 1:107-108; strengths and limits of, 1:106-107
Middle Tennessee State University, 1:298
Mignault, Louis B., 3:89
Miles, Matthew B., 1:104, 1:142-143
Milivojevic, Dragon, 3:89
Miller, Edith, 1:90
Miller, Richard I., 1:49, 2:64
Milton, Ohmer, 1:6, 1:137, 1:298, 3:85, 3:88, 3:97

Mink, Walter D., 1:294
Minnesota, University of: Center for Educational Development at, 1:294, 1:302; Consulting Group on Instructional Design at, 1:294; Medical School Curriculum Evaluation at, 1:294
Missouri, University of, at Columbia, Educational Resources Group at, 1:294
Missouri, University of, Kansas City, 1:294
Mizell, Al P., 1:293
Moakley, Frank X., 1:289
Modular instruction, described, 1:124
Mooney, Ross, 2:193
Morgenstern, Oskar, 2:25, 2:30
Morphological analysis, and course design, 2:150
Morris, John, 2:24, 2:30
Morris, W. H., 1:6
Morrow, Richard, 2:64
Morse, Kenneth, 1:291
Morstain, Barry R., 2:44
Motivation, faculty: analysis of, 2:16-29; and developmental tasks, 2:19-21; extrinsic-state theories of, 2:21-27; faculty questionnaire for, 2:44-55; and grid management, 2:23; instruments for, 2:31-55; intrinsic-state theories of, 2:19-21; intrinsic-trait theories of, 2:16-18; model of, 2:27-29; needs related to, 2:16-17, 2:23-24; organizational factors in, 2:22-24; and prisoner's dilemma, 2:25-26; professional development questionnaire for, 2:31-43; systemic factors in, 2:24-27
Moury, Daniel N., 1:295
Mouton, Jane S., 1:90, 1:143, 1:162, 1:163, 1:195, 2:23, 2:30, 2:159, 2:162, 2:193, 2:302, 3:193, 3:230, 3:332
Mullally, Lee J., 1:296
Mundelein College, Faculty Development Program at, 1:291
Murphy, Richard, 2:287-288, 2:302
Murray, Henry, 2:16, 2:17, 2:30
Music, computer-assisted instruction in, 3:88
Myers-Briggs Type Indicator, 3:241

N

Nader, Ralph, 2:283
National Center for Higher Education Management Systems (NCHEMS), 1:142, 2:61, 3:313
National Education Association, 1:111
National Laboratory for Higher Education, 1:296
National Society for Performance and Instruction, 3:88

National Training Laboratory, 1:23, 1:142, 1:200, 1:237, 1:243, 2:265, 3:169, 3:170; Institute for Applied Behavioral Science of, 1:183, 1:195
Nebraska, University of, Teaching and Learning Center at, 1:294
Neff, Charles, 1:295
Nekritz, Leah, 1:293
Nelsen, William, 3:51, 3:167, 3:169, 3:327, 3:328, 3:333
Nelson, Donald, 1:290
Netherton, Jean C., 1:299
Nevada, University of, at Reno, 1:295
New Hampshire, University of, Teaching/Learning Council at, 1:295
New Hampshire College and University Council, 3:314; Faculty Development Program of, 1:295
New Mexico, University of, 1:295
New York Friends Group, Center for War/Peace Studies of, 3:130
Newport, Donald L., 1:290
NEXUS, 2:285, 3:314
Nicholson, Stanley, 1:289
Niemi, Richard, 1:302
Non-verbal behavior, in active listening, 2:207
Noonan, John F., 1:viii, 1:20-22, 1:28, 1:104, 1:141, 1:205n, 1:299, 2:viii, 2:287, 2:288, 2:291, 2:302, 3:vii
North Carolina, University of, 1:296
North Carolina, University of, System, Institute for Undergraduate Curriculum Reform of, 1:296, 1:301
North Carolina Central University, Learning Resources at, 1:296, 1:302
Northeastern University, Office of Educational Resources at, 1:293
Northern Virginia Community College, Faculty and Staff Development Program at, 1:299
Northwest Area Foundation, 3:244
Northwestern University, Center for the Teaching Professions at, 1:291, 1:302
Nuffield Foundation, 2:297
Nunney, Derek N., 1:293

O

Oakland Community College, Personalized Educational Programs at, 1:293
Ober, Richard L., 1:90
Objectives, instructional, 2:133
Observation: of decision-making, 1:163-165; of leadership functions, 2:163-167; for teaching improvement, 2:71, 2:87-89

Suchman, Edward, 2:291, 2:302
Suggestopedia, content based, 3:86
Sullivan, Harry Stack, 1:49, 1:233, 2:297
Summarizing, in active listening, 2:207
Survey feedback, in organization development, 3:185-187
Swenson, Karen, 2:141
Symposium: interaction based, 3:72, 3:114-116; technique of, 3:149
Synectics: in course design, 2:138-139; and seminar discussions, 3:111
Syracuse University, 1:263; Center for Instructional Development at, 1:295, 2:131-134, 2:141, 2:289, 3:155, 3:333

T

Tacit dimensions: analysis of, 3:3-12; exercises for, 3:13-67; of faculty development, 3:10-12; of institutional domain, 3:8-10; of instructional domain, 3:4-8; simulation/role play on, 3:13-50
Tarkio College, Teaching-Learning Center at, 1:294
Taylor, D. Dax, 1:291
Teachers. See Faculty
Teaching: content-based, 1:12, 1:15, 1:16, 1:18, 3:5, 3:6-8, 3:72, 3:73-89; didactic modes of, 1:11, 1:12, 1:16; evocative modes of, 1:11-12, 1:16; interaction-based, 1:17-19, 3:6, 3:7-8, 3:72, 3:110-154; interrelationships in, 3:4-5; modes of, 3:5-7, 3:72; philosophy of, 3:7; psychological perspectives on, 3:7-8; student-based, 1:12, 1:18, 3:5, 3:7-8, 3:72, 3:90-109; styles of, 1:9-13, 1:20-27, 2:126-127; 3:316-317; teacher-centered, 1:12, 1:15, 1:18
Teaching, discussions of: analysis of, 1:202; exercises for, 1:206-211; faculty interview for, 1:203-205; instrument for, 1:203-205; questions for, 1:206-207; self-analysis for, 1:208; values testing for, 1:209-211
Teaching Analysis by Students (TABS), 1:79-84, 2:64, 2:71, 2:72-73, 2:90-107, 2:110-114, 3:315
Teaching improvement: analysis of, 2:69-78; consultation process for, 2:69-123; and course information, 2:83-84; data collection for, 2:70-72; data review and analysis for, 2:72-76; evaluation of, 2:77-78, 2:115-123; handouts for, 2:80-82, 2:108-109; information review in, 2:108-109; instruments for, 2:83-107, 2:110-123; observation for, 2:71, 2:87-89; and

predictions of student responses, 2:96-97; process of, 2:80-82; and self-assessment, 2:85-86; strategies for, 2:76-77; TABS for, 2:71, 2:72-73, 2:90-107, 2:109, 2:110-114; video-taping for, 2:71, 2:87-89, 2:109
Teaching laboratory, analysis of, 1:108-109
Team-building: analysis of, 1:144-146; and group expectations, 1:151-152; and group perceptions, 1:153-155; group process in, 1:147-150; handout for, 1:147-150; instruments for, 1:151-155; interview for, 3:208-209; and organization development, 1:144-156, 3:189-191; questionnaire for, 3:210-220; stages in, 1:144-146; as temporary society, 1:144
Team teaching: interaction based, 3:72, 3:116-118; inventory for, 3:134-141; and role playing, 3:117, 3:128
Technology, sources for, 1:110-112
Teleometrics International, 1:142, 1:179, 1:195, 2:193
Temple University, Instructional Development at, 1:297
Tennessee, University of, Educational Resources, College of Medicine at, 1:298; Learning Research Center at, 1:298, 1:301
Terezini, Patrick, 2:302
Texas, University of, Arlington, 1:298; Faculty Development Resource Center at, 1:298, 1:303
Texas, University of, Austin, Center for Teaching Effectiveness at, 1:298
Texas, University of, Health Science Center, 1:298
Texas, University of, Medical Branch at Galveston, 1:298
Texas, University of, Southwestern Medical School at Dallas, Instructional Communications at, 1:298
Texas State Technical Institute, Curriculum Development at, 1:298
Thompson, George, 1:302
Thompson, Richard B., 3:89
Thorne, Gaylord L., 1:297, 2:64
Toffler, Alvin, 2:265, 3:331-332, 3:333
Trow, Martin, 2:44
Trust, in helping relationship, 1:213, 1:226-228
Trzebiatowski, Gregory L., 1:297
Tuckman, Bruce W., 1:144, 1:146
Tufts University, 1:293
Turner, Joy, 1:301
Tutorial teaching: described, 1:125; student based, 3:72, 3:90
Twelker, Paul A., 1:111

U

Understanding: developing, 1:215-218; in helping relationship, 1:213, 1:219-222; as interpersonal skill, 208-211

United Kingdom, educational technology in, 1:110-111

United States International University, Office of Instructional Development at, 1:297

University Associates, 3:169, 3:170

Utah, University of, 1:298

Utah State University, Learning Resource Center at, 1:298, 1:303

V

Value domain, in instructional consultation, 3:156-157

Values: assessment of, in life planning, 2:252-255; in career development, 3:240, 3:248-251; inculcation, clarification, and expansion of, 3:156-157; testing of, for discussion on teaching, 1:209-211

Values clarification: analysis of, 2:266-267; continuum for, 2:272; criteria for, 2:266-267; exercises for, 2:268-275; grid for, 2:273; metaphors in, 2:271; and objectives, 2:274-275; values sheet for, 2:268-270

Van Maanen, John, 3:243

Vattano, Frank J., 1:290

Ventimiglia, Joe C., 3:196-203

Video-taping, for teaching improvement, 2:71, 2:87-89, 2:109

Virginia, University of, 1:299

Virginia Commonwealth University: Center for Improving Teaching Effectiveness at, 1:141, 1:299; Medical College of Virginia of, 1:299

Virginia Polytechnic Institute and State University, Learning Resource Center at, 1:299

VOCOM (Vocal Communication), 1:166, 1:170, 2:175

Von Neumann, John, 2:25, 2:30

Votaw, Robert G., 3:88

W

Wallen, John L., 1:viii, 1:147-155, 1:160, 1:179, 1:181, 1:186, 1:195, 1:215-222, 1:226-228, 1:233, 2:168-170, 2:195-205, 2:208-217, 2:219, 3:223-225

Warren Wilson College, Faculty Development Program at, 1:296

Washington, University of, 1:299, 1:302

Watson, Goodwin, 1:6, 2:6, 2:12

Watson, J., 1:49, 1:90

Watzlawick, Paul, 2:141, 2:265

Wayne State University, 1:294

Weakland, John, 2:141

Weatherman, Richard, 2:141

Webb, Eugene J., 1:104, 2:292, 2:302

Webb, Jeaninne, 1:290

Weiner, Bernard, 2:30

Weingartner, Charles, 1:137

Weir, John, 1:200, 2:222

Weir, Joyce, 1:200, 2:222

Wellesley College, Faculty Development Program at, 1:293

Werntz, James H., 1:294

West, Theodore C., 1:289

Westbury, Ian, 1:104

Western Illinois University, Illowa Higher Education Consortium at, 1:291

Western Michigan University, Office of Instructional Development at, 1:294, 1:301

Westley, B., 1:49, 1:90

Wheelis, Allen, 2:265

Whitcomb, David, 1:239, 3:239-240, 3:244

Whitcomb, Susanne, 3:239-240, 3:244

White, R. K., 2:162

White, Robert, 2:265

Whitla, Dean K., 1:293

Whitlow, S. Scott, 3:130

Wight, Warland D., 1;291

William and Mary, College of, and Indian education, 1:16-17

William Rainey Harper College, Learning Resources Center at, 1:291

Williams, Hayden, 1:289

Williams, Martha, 1:162, 2:159, 2:162

Williams, W. Loren, Jr., 1:299

Williamson, Joe, 1:293

Wilson, Robert C., 1:289, 2:44, 2:64, 2:279

Winsor, Donald L., 1:291

Wisconsin, University of, Green Bay, Office for Educational Development at, 1:299, 1:302

Wisconsin, University of, Madison, 1:299

Wolk, Donald J., 3:226-228

Wood, Evelyn, 1:141

Wood, Lynn, 2:44

Wooster, College of, 3:96-97

Work perception survey, in organization development, 3:223-225

Workshop design: analysis of, 1:237-242; and assumptions about learning, 1:243-244; evaluation form for, 1:245-248; handouts for, 1:243-244, 1:255-257; instrument for, 1:245-248; micro-college topics for, 1:255-257; planning document for,

1:249–254; principles of, 1:240–242; samples of, 1:249–254

Workshops: brief on-campus, 1:238–239, 1:240; for career development, 3:254–255; extended on-campus, 1:238, 1:240; as learning community, 1:237; for life planning, 2:225–228; long-term residential, 1:237–238, 1:239; short-term residential, 1:238, 1:239–240; types of, 1:237–240

Wright, Al, 1:223

Wright Institute, 1:290, 2:20–21, 2:297

Y

Yellow Pages on Innovation in Undergraduate Education, 2:285

Yelon, Stephen, 2:141

Youmans, Hubert L., 3:88

Young, Jon I., 1:292

Z

Zero-sum game: concept of, 1:189; and faculty motivation, 2:25–26

Zimny, George, 1:294

Zion, Carol, 1:141, 1:290, 2:viii, 2:142, 3:188, 3:204–205, 3:315

Zoecklein, Walter, 1:288

Zuckerman, David W., 1:111